The Sense of Adharma

The Sense of Adharma

ARIEL GLUCKLICH

New York Oxford
OXFORD UNIVERSITY PRESS
1994

Oxford University Press

Oxford New York Toronto
Delhi Bombay Calcutta Madras Karachi
Kuala Lumpur Singapore Hong Kong Tokyo
Nairobi Dar es Salaam Cape Town
Melbourne Auckland Madrid

and associate companies in
Berlin Ibadan

Published by Oxford University Press, Inc.
200 Madison Avenue, New York, New York 10016

Library of Congress Cataloging-in-Publication Data

Glucklich, Ariel.
The sense of adharma / Ariel Glucklich.
p. cm.
Includes bibliographical references and index.
ISBN 0-19-508341-5
1. Dharma. 2. Adharma (Hinduism)
3. Hindu symbolism.
I. Title
B132.D5G58 1994
181'.4—dc20 92-45768

2 4 6 8 9 7 5 3 1
Printed in the United States of America
on acid-free paper

For Leslie Anne Levy

Acknowledgments

Although it took me four years to write this book, its title is only half complete. It is missing the punchline: "And the Nonsense of Dharma." The full paradox intended was thereby lost when that bulky—and politically touchy—ballast was jettisoned. The structure of chaos and the chaos of structure was roughly the intended meaning of the phrase, and along with it the *double entendre* in reference to sense as a somatic property. Maybe I was reaching for too much. I mention all this now to alert the reader to my first acknowledgement, owed to Merleau-Ponty (author of *Sense and Nonsense*) and to the existential phenomenologists who were interested in perception. Intellectual fashions come and go, some failing to outlast a mediocre presidency, or an unrushed publication pace. The manuscript for this book was completed when Bush was riding high, and James Gleick's *Chaos* had not yet brought the new science to the woods of Oregon. But my reliance on a theoretical framework that some would regard as having expired in the fifties—existential and perceptual phenomenology—makes me immune to the breathless anxieties of the methodologically correct. Still, I feel that there is a great deal to be said for perception, and always will be.

I owe a tremendous, and ever-increasing debt of gratitude to Wendy Doniger who wrote chapter 7 and contributed insight and moral support to the rest. Other scholars have generously offered criticism and suggestions to earlier drafts of individual chapters. I am grateful to Kenneth Zysk, Hanns-Peter Schmidt, Frank Reynolds (and the other editors of *History of Religions*), Carl Ernst, Scott Warren, Mary Douglas (with my apologies for remaining a hopeless "intellectualist"), and Oxford's anonymous reader.

This book was written on a 20,000 mile shuttle from southern Oregon to Berkeley and UCLA. The closest thing to an institutional support which I can claim is due to the folks at GMC for the fantastic conversion van that doubled as motel room and moving office. Similar credit goes to Albert Gitlow, Linda Hess, Padmanabh Jaini, and Steven Poulos. I also wish to acknowledge the help of Rony Oren, Avner Glucklich, Leonard Levy, Brian MacDonald for his patient editorial work, Cindy Vangroff, and Natalie and Elon who just want to be mentioned.

Ashland, Oregon A. G.
June, 1993

Contents

Abbreviations, xiii

Introduction: On Understanding Culture Through the Body, 3

Dharma, 7

Adharma, 9

1. Images and Symbols of Dharma, 11

Smṛti as Remembrance, 11

The Symbol and the Image, 14

Mahāvrata Images, 23

The Structure of Images, 25

Indian Images, 27

2. The Duration of Images in Time, 38

Conceptions of Time in India, 39

Temporal Images—Method, 41

Time in the Rāmāyaṇa, *44*

Time in the Mahāvrata *Ritual, 51*

Musical Time, 55

Conclusion, 59

3. Why Rivers Purify (And Only Bad Witches Are Ugly), 66

Conceptual Approaches to Pollution and Sin, 67

Bathing (Snāna), *71*

The Phenomenology of Bathing—A Gestalt Approach, 76

Isomorphism, 77

Good Forms in Perception, 78

The Phenomenal Ego, 79

Perception and Proprioception, 80

The Meaning of Bathing, 82

Concluding Remarks, 85

4. Dermatology and Cosmology, 89
Apālā and Indra, 91
The Symbolism of the Apālā Sūkta, *93*
Skin Therapy, 96
Dermatology, 97
Interpretation, 100
Kṣetriya *and Jaundice, 102*
Nonsymbolic Analysis of Disease, 105
Animal Skins (Carman), *108*

5. Boundaries in Space and Time, 115
Dharma Metaphors, 115
Perception and Forms in Space, 116
Being and Becoming—Time and Space Reversed, 118
The Picture Frames of Tribal India, 120
House Walls, 124
Temple Walls, 127
Fences, 128
Doors, 130
Crossing Boundaries, 134

6. Passage to Marriage—The Dharma Agent, 143
The Marriage Ritual, 144
The Marriage as a Rite de Passage, *147*
Sociological and Cosmological Meaning of Passage, 150
The Wedding in Verbal Formulas, 151
The "Person" in Passage, 153
The Perception of Passage, 156
The Dharma Agent: Intention by Extension, 161

7. Playing The Field: Adultery as Claim Jumping, by Wendy Doniger, 169
The Appeal of the Human Lover: The Kāmasūtra, *170*
The Wife's Reasons for Committing Adultery, 171
The Wife's Reasons for Not Committing Adultery, 172
The Lover's Reasons for Committing Adultery, 173
The Lover's Reasons for Not Committing Adultery, 175
The Appeal of the Divine Lover: Bhakti *Texts, 176*
The Appeal of Theft: The Romance of Adultery, 179
Breaching the Boundary: The Husband's Nightmare, 181
Conclusion, 186

8. Thieves and Dharma in the Story Literature, 189
Thieves and Kings, 192
The Theft of Identity, 195

Achievements of the Best in the Trade, *196*
Idiot Thieves, *198*
Brahmin Thieves—A Digression on Dharma Itself, *199*
Divine Thieves: The Theft of Soma, Vedas, Amṛta, *205*

9. The Adharmic Force of Punishment (*Daṇḍa*), 213
Vertical Space, *213*
Daṇḍa *in Nature,* *216*
Daṇḍa *in Society,* *220*
Daṇḍa *in the Sacrifice,* *223*
Daṇḍa *in Mythology,* *225*
Daṇḍa *and the Goddess,* *232*
Conclusion, *234*

Conclusion: Back to the Body, 239

Bibliography, 243

Index, 261

Abbreviations

AB	*Aitareya Brāhmaṇa*
Āp	*Āpastamba Dharmasūtra*
Āp. G.S.	*Āpastamba Gṛhyasūtra*
Āp. Ś.S.	*Āpastamba Śrautasūtra*
Āśv.	*Āśvalāyana Gṛhyasūtra*
AV	*Atharvaveda*
Baudh. D.S.	*Baudhāyana Dharmasūtra*
Brah. Pur.	*Brahmāṇḍa Purāṇa*
BŚS	*Baudhāyana Śrautasūtra*
DKC	*Daśakumāracarita*
DV	*Daṇḍaviveka*
Gaut.	*Gautama Dharmasūtra*
Gobhila G.S.	*Gobhila Gṛhyasūtra*
Hiraṇyakeśin G.S.	*Hiraṇyakeśin Gṛhyasūtra*
Hit.	*Hitopadeśa*
JB	*Jaiminīya Brāhmaṇa*
Kāt.	*Kātyāyana Śrautasūtra*
Kath.	*Kathāsaritsāgara*
Kāṭhaka G.S.	*Kāṭhaka Gṛhyasūtra*
Kauś.	*Kauśikasūtra*
KK	*Kṛtyakalpataru*
KP	*Kūrma Purāṇa*
Mānav.	*Mānava Gṛhyasūtra*
Mbh.	*Mahābhārata*

MS	*Manu Smṛti* (=Manu)
MP	*Mantra Patha*
Nār.	*Nārada Smṛti*
PB	*Pañcaviṃsa Brāhmaṇa*
Rām.	*Rāmāyaṇa*
Ṛgvidh.	*Ṛgvidhana*
RV	*Ṛgveda*
Śāṅkh.	*Śāṅkhāyana Gṛhyasūtra*
Śāṅkh. Ś.S.	*Śāṅkhāyana Śrautasūtra*
ŚB	*Śatapatha Brāhmaṇa*
SR	*Saṅgītaratnākara*
Su. S.	*Suśruta Saṃhitā*
TA	*Taittirīya Āraṇyaka*
TB	*Taittirīya Brāhmaṇa*
TS	*Taittirīya Saṃhitā*
Vāj. Sam.	*Vājasaneyi Saṃhitā*
VP	*Viṣṇu Purāṇa*
VS	*Viṣṇu Smṛti*
Yāj.	*Yājñavalkya Smṛti*

The Sense of Adharma

Introduction

On Understanding Culture Through the Body

The title of this book is not as paradoxical as it first seems. After all, it is perfectly reasonable to try and make sense of chaos (*adharma*) and perhaps discover the lurking irrationality of order (dharma). Still, there is something subversive about suggesting that *adharma* might somehow make more sense than dharma. And at the same time, the tip of the hat to Merleau-Ponty shows a deference to a prominent tradition that cannot be accused of a deconstructive agenda. The following brief introduction will explain both our mild subversion of common sense in the study of Hinduism, and the choice of existential phenomenology for a job it has not yet been assigned.

No task in the humanities may be more daunting than trying to understand other cultures. It is not always clear what we are trying to understand: persons, symbolic systems, kinship groups. Nor is it entirely clear what understanding means. Is it the formulation of dualistic explanations, scientific theories that reduce cultural phenomena to causal principles? Or is it the empathetic but nonsystematic intuition of the hermeneutical *verstehen*? I think most historians of religion opt for versions of the latter.[1] Ultimately we are all trying to understand the other because we acknowledge its otherness. We aspire to allow the other to speak through us. In mythical terms, to borrow from Wendy Doniger, this has required that we understand fish because we love them in the way only ex-fish can.[2] Our work oscillates between becoming other and returning to ourselves in order to communicate with our currently land-bound colleagues. This then is the new monism that dominates the study of other cultures in our universities today: Study the language of fish(!), learn to hold your breath, and swim with them. But avoid at all costs mere fishiness, an amphibious fence-straddling indecisiveness.

A massive paradox, however, lurks in the swampy waters of this new monism: the more fishlike the observer, the greater the chance of becoming a participant, and starting to alter the context situation.[3] Therefore, in order to understand the other, which has become increasingly complex and amorphous, we must now devote greater systematic reflection to the observer-turned-participant. Still, it is not enough, or much of a beginning, to acknowledge that we are "Standard Average Europeans" (in Benjamin Whorf's wry designation) and university professors. Here is the heart of the paradox: even as we cultivate sophisticated *monistic* intuitions about the other, we are firmly locked within *dualistic* assumptions about ourselves. I do not just mean to say that we are intellectually committed to a dualistic world view but, more profoundly, that we are trapped by a certain static givenness, or estrangement, concerning our very identity. Writing on the specular nature of our self-image and the resulting alienation, Merleau-Ponty reflected: "I am no longer what I felt myself, immediately, to be; I am that image of myself that is offered by the mirror. To use Dr Lacan's terms, I am captured, caught up by my spatial image."[4] Intuitively our sense of self owes too much to Plato and Descartes. Scientifically it still owes everything to Newton and Freud. This does not necessarily imply that we are condemned to apply dualistic theories to other cultures. But we are being ripped apart on the horns of a dilemma without even knowing it. The wonderfully attuned intellectual apparatus we bring on our trips east must either become permanently "disembodied" through cultural schizophrenia, or else we are still traveling in the first-class carriage that Plato built and Freud oiled. So how do we avoid a state of fishiness?

The first step is to become even more conscious of our unchallenged operative axioms and be prepared to act subversively. The most fundamental axioms, greatly oversimplified of course, are the following three:

1. We possess a self, which is enclosed somewhere in our body, but which is essentially separate from the body and the world, while it directs the body to act in the world.
2. The body moves in a world that may be perceived in different levels of subjectivity, but which is ultimately objective. Above and beyond all our individual perceptions there exists a "god's-eye view of the world" and that is the real world.
3. The world gradually unfolds its meaning to the observing self by the increasingly complex semiotic perception of the self. At the most basic level, meaning is attained when relations between simple

> natural signs "out" in the real world are discovered. In short, meaning and knowledge are, by definition, conceptual.[5]

These axioms, presented somewhat crudely here, are not esoteric at all. We can call them, following Whorf, Standard Average Epistemology. They are the very stuff of our common sense and they accompany the most empathetic studies. Even a scholar like Marriott, who has spent years looking for the emic terms of Hindu thinking, is still interested in Hindu thinking rather than, say, perception.[6] The assumption is still that the most valuable data to be found in any culture are conceptual and that the body, essentially, is silent.

The study of religion as a whole is profoundly committed to the belief that the world communicates meaning through the operation of symbols. The symbols need not be read theologically or metaphysically, of course. Depth psychology provides another key for reading symbols, and so do the various schools of sociology and anthropology. The common denominator of two centuries of sustained thinking is semiotics, broadly understood: the symbol (or sign) is the keenest instrument for reading the meaning of the world. Symbols encapsulate the three axioms of the self (reader), the world (signs and referents), and semiotics (the signifying operation).

But is it possible to study any cultural fact without these assumptions? Can we, for instance, understand purification in Hinduism without reference to symbolic boundaries or conceptual order? The answer to each question is yes and no. The basic assumptions have to be severely curtailed but not altogether abandoned. Our book is not remotely deconstructive; at best it is somewhat subversive. And even this subversion is rooted in a prominent Western tradition—phenomenology. Rigorous phenomenology subjects the observer to the same degree of scrutiny that the object receives. The observing self, as the subject of intellectual activity, as the "knower" of the other, is bracketed and becomes another "other." If the new monism mentioned earlier is like shooting a moving target, the phenomenological project entails shooting a moving target off the back of a bucking horse. When the complacency of self is abandoned, because both sides keep shifting, temporality and, to some extent, irrationality possess the act of observation. The other can only emerge when the self is thoroughly temporalized, which, of course, means deabsolutized. With the loss of the sovereign subject, the logical relations among objects in the world cease to be indexical and become contextual. We can recognize then that the body simultaneously registers meaning and creates a world by means of perception. The body is no longer a mere metaphor for conceptual notions, it claims attention as a noetic force, a creator of truths. Perhaps an example will illuminate my thoughts, but since gods and animals are far too intimidating as others, let us look at something simpler and sturdier, say a bridge.

Bridges never span rivers silently; we force them to tell stories. Richard Parmentier relates the tale of Latmikaik in Belau.[7] This is a story of an upright bridge, which leads from the depth of the sea to the heavens. It was built by mythical ancestors of the people of Belau who sought to escape the crowded life of fish in the ocean. However, the bridge became too high and tilted, and so they kicked it down to a prostrate position and journied to land. For the people of Belau the bridge may be a trace of their life as fish, I do not know. We insist on the "sturdier" semiotic construction: a vertical cosmological axis replaced by a horizontal one and indicating that "the aspiration to climb to the heavens becomes a quest for land-based cultural existence as distinct from the amorphous precultural life beneath the sea."

Symbolic discourse, in its various permutations, can make a bridge say almost anything, inasmuch as any two things that enter a relationship become bridged. But what about the bridge itself, the *thing*? Heidegger reminds us that even that thing has begun an elementary discourse, because it is intrinsically ambiguous: "The bridge, if it is a true bridge, is never first of all a mere bridge and then afterward a symbol. And just as little is the bridge in the first place exclusively a symbol, in the sense that it expresses something that strictly speaking does not belong to it."[8] The bridge, according to Heidegger, takes its meaning by virtue of existing as some thing that expresses man's dwelling (presencing) in the world. It gathers what Heidegger calls the fourfold, that is, the absolute spatial and temporal context in which man finds his being: earth, heaven, divinities, and mortals. More than bridging two banks the bridge creates them. It sets one side of the river against the other and brings two landscapes together at the water's edge. The bridge as thing does not exist by virtue of its function as transportation, but it also leads men from city to city and finally from life to death. In sum, Heidegger's bridge spans space and time and so it actually contains our own being.

But even Heidegger has said too much about the bridge, because it is still thoroughly mythical. Although Heidegger's human beholders are temporal, they still force the thing into their own context. The bridge loses its otherness in the safety of human dwelling in the world. In contrast, the deconstructed bridge, like Frank Gehry's fish building, can be the perfect other in architecture.[9] To the mind it will always be different and may seem like an absurd non sequitur. But whereas deconstructive architecture is self-consciously absurd (it replaces the shock of the new with the shock of the fish), the bridge comes truly alive when we explode the myth of the static omniscient observer and replace her with the observer who always arrives too late and always out of breath. Or, to switch metaphors, if you overexpose the bridge on film of a hand-held camera, if you temporalize the viewer's vantage point, it will become transparent. The duration of the viewer alters the very substance of the perceived object.

The phenomenology of religion must expose all cultural data to the operation of time, and it must abandon the myth of the disembodied observer who stands outside time. The only way of doing this consistently is to study symbols by means of images.

The first chapter will explain how this is done, in general and in relation to Indian symbols. The basic idea is to observe the function of images and the body along with symbols and the mind. It is clear that every conscious experience has a physical-perceptual component that plays a key role in the way the world and the self are fashioned. The Hindu bather who goes into the river at daybreak does not leave his body in bed. We are obligated to examine more than the *mantras* he mumbles in the water. What happens to the body in the water, and in what sense is the body purified? Similarly, the bride who undergoes passage by means of an elaborate ritual is not just being intellectually indoctrinated into a new status. The new identity she acquires is contingent on the conscious perceptual and physical manipulations that take place during the rite.

It is a well-known fact that the existential phenomenologists recognized the body's priority in the consciousness of images. The methodological foundation for this supposition is the phenomenology of perception and especially the school of Gestalt psychology. The work of Köhler and Koffka, so influential on the thinking of Merleau-Ponty and even Cassirer, has largely evaded the scrutiny of religion scholars, who are more interested in the explicit symbolism of depth psychology. Consequently I discuss at length Gestalt and perception in general, which is likely to displease historians of religion. If theories of perception and the phenomenal self were a staple of our common sense view of the world, these long methodological passages would not be necessary. For those who wish to avoid theory, the following are the offensive sections: chapter 2, the section on temporal images; chapter 3, the sections on the phenomenology of bathing, isomorphism, good forms in perception, the phenomenal ego, and perception and proprioception; chapter 6, the section on marriage as a *rite de passage*; and, of course, the introduction. I must emphasize, however, that it is the theory of images and perception that holds this book together as a work about the somatic imagination and its world. Finally, the phenomenology of perception need not defend itself against the charge of ethnocentrism when "simple" common sense is also a matter of culture; it is neither common nor sensual. The historical purists simply have no ground left to stand on.

Dharma

The subject of dharma eludes almost every attempt to develop a system of conceptualization. This may be due to the fact that dharma is not a "subject" at all. Dharma is not a *what*, it is a *how*: there is the dharma of conduct, of course, and this we usually understand as law and morality. But there is also the dharma of stealing and robbing, the dharma of painting and making music, the dharma of laying cornerstones, plowing, and everything else. Tradition tells us that this has something to do with following the Veda, but the speciousness of this claim will be exposed in the first chapter. The subject of this book, as the introduction thus far has probably made clear, is not a conceptual analysis of dharma and its apparent opposite, *adharma*. Nor will the paradoxes identified by Louis Dumont and others, then resolved, encompassed, or abandoned, be explicitly addressed. We are more interested in the structure of the imagination that insists on seeing and doing things in a particular manner, and just so. At a basic level dharma is related to the way the world is perceived and fashioned, but also to the manner in which the world behaves in time. This is the level at which dharma means something to Hindus before it has acquired its extremely diverse lexical meanings and social functions.

The subject of this book, then, is neither law nor morality. We shall look at dharma as a basic orientation toward order, meaning, and chaos. How, in short, is a normative "world view"—a view of the world in fact—constructed and what are its parameters. The theory of images claims that it is built from the ground up, from the body and the senses to the mind, so to speak. At the root of dharma perception, when its metaphorical language is stripped down to basics, is the sense of boundaries in space and in time. Chapter 1 will examine the theory of images, chapter 2 the temporality of images. The data of perception in space and time furnish the imagination with the basic tools for constructing a world, so this is where we too must begin. Dharma is prefashioned perceptually by the actual encounter with boundaries in the landscape. Chapter 5 will look at several types of boundary, and will find that even solid borders are surprisingly transitive, perhaps even transparent.

However, by demonstrating that the essential transitivity and temporality of dharma is prefigured in the spatial orientation toward simple objects that constitute the metaphors of dharma, we have not gone far enough. It would still seem to imply that we are looking for a dharmic agent who passes through life by means of laws (and landmarks) and is variously affected by such laws. Chapter 6 will show that it may be misleading to focus on an agent or subject who possesses an interiority and who seeks external symbols to articulate internal processes. The individual exists as a nexus of relationships and there is no either/or logic operative between her internal and external world. The boundaries in space discussed in chapter 5 are, therefore, not symbolic or metaphorical expressions of such processes as growth, initiation, and so forth. The landscape of India, as depicted by means of humanly constructed boundaries and natural landmarks in space, is the actual source of meaning. Crossing into the forest does not represent symbolic death; it registers a powerful transformation that can only be grasped on its own terms. The power of what we call external conditions to effect so-called internal changes is consequently made possible through the body's sensitivity to meaningful external events. The body must become an instrument for spatialization and temporalization and for coordinating its own orientation in the empirical world with a rich symbolic world. This is achieved by means of purification in water (chapter 3) and is articulated by means of the unique properties that the skin possesses (chapter 4).

All this will lead to a strictly phenomenological and sense-based analysis of dharma. It will show that dharma is more than a norm that governs action: it is a self-conscious effort to articulate and structure a notion of personhood against a powerful stream of raw, flowing existence. But the effort is never meant to transcend the profound ambiguities that a life lived with the body demands. Like molten lava that had never completely solidified, dharma still flows with images.

Adharma

The world gradually unfolds as the body moves and acts in its own contextual space. But even as it is created in space, the world loses its solidity in time. We shall see that the same act that establishes dharma as the structure of the world also fashions a consciousness of chaos. The sense of dharma only emerges in relationship to nondharma. However, *adharma* is not the binary opposite of dharma because this would imply the absence of a temporal relation. Instead, *adharma* is the temporal ranging of consciousness across boundaries, and over the world felt by the body. The discussion of marriage in chapter 6 will show that creating a dharmic person requires that borders be crossed: passage creates an awareness of self because it allows the body to register basic perceptual contrasts. Only the mind fixes the contrasting impressions with labels such as order and chaos. Consequently *adharma* is only conceptually chaotic or unlawful. The sensory experiences on which such a conception rests are as essential to structure as are boundaries.

Of course, the Brahmin writers on dharma prefer to characterize *adharma* in absolute and ethically negative terms. However, other Brahmin writers, equally well versed in dharma, often give vent to other sentiments. As you leave the Dharmaśāstra literature and explore the story (*kātha*) literature, a far more complex picture emerges. The ambivalence of Brahminical attitude toward adharmic behavior will be examined in chapter 7, on adultery, and chapter 8, on theft. The central point, I believe, is not that mischief sometimes serves a useful purpose in a functional sense. Rather, the very nature of dharma as a world view built by means of the body, and the conception of the Indian person as an embodied and relational self, make complex attitudes toward boundary crossers such as thieves and lovers more sensible. As a result, the punishment that awaits such boundary crossers is not a simple restoration of dharma, but an affirmation of its temporality and somewhat irrational ambiguity (chapter 9). Like the bather who marks a sacred space in the river before entering the water, dharma only has the appearance of permanence: the flow of the river—*adharma* if you will—instantly sweeps the boundaries around the unperturbed bather. In the final analysis, while dharma texts may fool us into thinking that dharma is fixed and homogeneous, a vast array of texts, which the Hindus never repressed, proves that entropy has always had its say.

Notes

1. In the final analysis, the popular toolbox approach is no more than empathetic intuition, for how else do you know which tool to use when?

2. Wendy Doniger O'Flaherty, *Other People's Myths* (New York: Macmillan, 1988).

3. For a full discussion on the terminology of monism and dualism, see Murray J. Leaf, *Man, Mind and Science* (New York: Columbia University Press, 1979); see also R. K. Narayan, *Storytellers, Saints and Scoundrels* (Philadelphia: University of Pennsylvania Press, 1989), p. 9; Ronald L. Grimes, *Beginnings in Ritual Studies* (Lanham, M.: University Press of America, 1982); Stephen Toulmin, *Return to Cosmology* (Berkeley: University of California Press, 1981), in the case of science.

4. M. Merleau-Ponty, "The Child's Relations with Others," in James M. Edie, ed., *The Primacy of Perception* (Evanston, Ill.: Northwestern University Press, 1964), p. 136.

5. See E. H. Gombrich, *Art and Illusion: A Study in the Psychology and Pictorial Representation* (New York: Pantheon Books, 1960), p. 23, and K. Popper's ridicule of the "bucket theory of the mind," which he contrasts with a "searth-beam" metaphor of the interactive perceptual mind. Or as T. S. Eliot put it: "And the unseen eyebeam crossed, for the roses had the look of flowers that are looked at." Cited and Quoted in Rudolf Arnhiem, *Art and Visual Perception: A Psychology of the Creative Eye* (Berkeley: University of California Press, 1974), p. 28.

6. See most recently, McKim Marriott, ed., *India through Hindu Categories* (New Delhi: Sage, 1990); discussions about the body in India are confined to *conceptions of* the body, rather than *perceptions by* the body—a world of difference. See, for instance, David Smith, "Aspects of the Interrelationship of Divine and Human Bodies in Hinduism," *Religion* 19 (1989): 211–20.

7. Richard Parmentier, *The Sacred Remains* (Chicago: University of Chicago Press, 1987).

8. Martin Heidegger, *Poetry, Language, Thought* (New York: Harper & Row, 1971), p. 153.

9. Andreas Papadakis, Catherine Cooke, and Andrew Benjamin, eds., *Deconstruction* (New York: Rizzoli, 1989), p. 120.

1

Images and Symbols of Dharma

Smṛti as Remembrance

A most revealing fact about the Indian religious imagination is that the literature that tells Hindus how to live in the world calls itself a literature of remembrance—Smṛti. For what has been forgotten—or intentionally blotted out—are the facts and the insights to make such a life meaningful. When Manu Prajāpati first composed a dharma book that encompassed all topics ranging from creation to penances, it contained one hundred thousand *ślokas*. But Nārada then abridged this compendium to twelve thousand *ślokas*, and again to four thousand due to the shortening of human life and attention span in the later aeons (*yugas*).[1]

Smṛti thus opens with an acknowledgment that what it teaches is a mere trace of a vast store of knowledge. The original reservoir of ultimate, lasting, but humanly forgettable *gnosis* is Veda itself. Veda is imagined in general as that which makes the true nature of the world necessarily (innately) known by means of words.[2]

According to the *Manu Smṛti* (*Mānava Dharmaśāstra*; or Manu), whatever is taught now as dharma by Manu, "has been fully declared in the Veda: for that (sage was) omniscient" (MS 2.7). The speciousness of such a pious declaration is beside the point as long as we do not

This Chapter was previously published as the following article: "Images and Symbols in the Phenomenology of Dharma," *History of Religions*, 29, no. 3 (1990).

mistake Manu's omniscience for mere encyclopedic erudition. *Jñāna* (knowledge) here applies to the intuition that is necessary to fathom the authoritative (*prāmāṇya*) relation of contemporary assertions about the world with the Vedic revelation (*śruti*) about such a relation. In Heesterman's words, "the catchword is vision—the supranormal vision of the *ṛṣi*, *vipra*, or *kavi*, who attains his vision through his own efforts, especially through tapas."[3] Such insight, encapsulated in the words of the Veda and lost to our memory, cannot be recovered by mere knowledge. The original insight was both pure and ecstatic and these experiences must somehow be recaptured not merely cognized.[4] Although, obviously, Smṛti is neither ecstatic nor particularly poetic, it promises the "pramanic" recapitulation of Veda *śabda* (word).

A related idea is elaborated in Indian poetics and philosophy of language. It is found, for instance, in Bhartṛhari's *Vākyapadiya* (1.5) which states that the Veda , though one, was handed down in a variety of forms of expression (*dhvani*). The commentary on this *kārikā* explains that the seers "saw" (experienced) the unity of Veda (or dharma) as an ultimate transcendental Reality.[5] The words (*śabda*) with which they communicated their experience to those who did not share such insight can potentially convey the fullness of Veda, but have in fact been the source of variations and omissions. Forgetting the Veda implies then a distancing in and through language between the unity of the Absolute and the fragments of contingent experience. But language also remains a necessary lens for perceiving the Real by means of phenomenal experiences and expressions.

Since collective as well as individual memory, as Bergsonian psychology emphasizes, is not simply an intellectual repetition of an original event but contains its experiential rebirth through an intensive and internalized reinterpretation, the symbolic imagination becomes a necessary element of true recollection. Hence, according to Cassirer, poetic recollection, religious memory, and even simple retrospection are thoroughly imbued with the symbolic matrix of one's personal and cultural millieu.[6] This connection is dialectical, of course, and operates equally from individual experience to cultural symbolism, and vice versa. Since our present goal requires an investigation of symbolic consciousness and discourse ("the classic Hindu themes of dharma") in their relation to nondiscursive experience ("naïve images") on the one hand, and to the noumenal (Veda) on the other, a brief digression may be justified here. The issue, which is of great interest to philosophers, psychologists, and poets, is the relation between memory as a symbolic structure and the naïve images of experience.

Chaim Nahmam Bialik once observed that one truly sees and experiences the world only once—in childhood. The first sights, still in their pristine purity, as in their moment of creation, are then identical to the essence of the world's objects. Those sights that follow are lesser reproductions, defective images and mere hints of the original.[7] But while our most vivid experiences are attained in childhood, intensely original ("naïve") images can be met throughout life, and often feed the roots of poetic appreciation. Paul Valéry and Gaston Bachelard were both fascinated by naïveté, both writing on sea shells, when they mused over our ability to produce or recapture a pure image.[8] For Valéry the naïve question about the sea shell in our hands is the question asked "before we remember that we are not newborn, but already know something."[9] For Bachelard, who is slightly more tentative but also more attuned to the child's eye, if we could naïvely glimpse a sea shell again, "we should give fresh impetus to the complex of our fear and curiousity that accompanies all initial action on the world."[10] We shall return to the image of the shell shortly. Here we are reminded by French poetics that a naïve childlike experience of the world is not only possible. It is a necessary condition for all poetic imagination and stands as one side of the dialectic between discursive thought, even symbolic apperception, and pure experience, which enables us to live creatively in the world.[11]

At work in the poetic or sometimes even prosaic word is not systematic recollection but remembrance as reexperience. The naïve image is empty if it cannot be smelled and tasted again. Here precisely is Proust's grandest insight. When Marcel soaked the innocuous—now famous—"petites madeleines" in lukewarm tea, what became triggered was more than remembrance of things past. It was a complete return to original experience. The moment of "recall," condensed and recoiled in one morsel of dipped cake, exploded in his consciousness with all the vividness and force of life, or what Bergson would call the *élan vital.*[12] This, as we shall see, can be the power of the word, the power of *śabda*, which had been lost to the present age.

This anecdotal digression forces us now to return to the Smṛti. That literature, which claims to include, besides Dharmaśāstra and Dharmasūtra, also Purāṇas, Itihāsās (including the Epics), and others, contains a large number of elements designed to evoke "Vedic" memories.[13] As in *kāvya* and the other arts, Smṛti places its symbolic themes in the dynamic middle ground between experience and metaphysics. But this is a point we shall return to later.

The Dharmaśāstra, *Manu Smṛti*, for instance, does more than set rules of conduct. It places its norms within the context of a highly symbolic world view consisting of milk-bleeding trees that mark boundaries, wives who are identified with fields and hunted deer, water tanks that must be purified like persons, rivers that menstruate, and others.[14] Consider, for instance, the following rule in *Kātyayana Smṛti* about river bathing: "In two months, beginning with Śravaṇa, all the rivers get their menstrual courses. (No one) shall bathe in them, excluding the rivers which go to an ocean."[15] And this is how the *Manu Smṛti* establishes the rules for setting boundaries: "Let him mark the boundaries (by) trees, (e.g.) Nyagrodhas, Aśvatthas, Kiṁśukas . . . by clustering shrubs . . . creepers . . . reeds, thickets of Kubjākas" (MS 8.246–47). According to J. D. M. Derrett, this text, and other similar lists throughout the Dharmaśāstras, reflect an inability to abstract the general qualities of diverse objects for the purpose of systematic classification.[16] However, this is not an accidental collection of discrete objects and qualities but rather distinct phenomena, which are thematically interrelated on the symbolic level. It is hardly surprising that the Smṛti participates in the symbolic world view of classical Hinduism. What I wish to demonstrate in this chapter is that the vibrancy of these symbols, as well as more clearly "religious" ones, derives not strictly from the symbols themselves but from the dialectic they posit between "naïve images" and the metaphysical referents of symbols. I must begin then, with the thorny task of defining both symbols and images particularly those I have called "naïve images."

The Symbol and the Image

Because the symbol has probably been the most extensively discussed subject in the theory of the history of religions, we need only recall the following: the symbol is generally understood as an indirect mode of signification, which is intuitive and sense-based, and the signified object of which, since it is indirect, cannot be reduced to a single cognitive idea.[17] In contrast, it is virtually impossible to formulate a straightforward definition of image in the context of its philosophical or theoretical uses in the West. Harder yet is determining the precise relation of image and symbol.

To say that in common usage image means likeness or sensory representation begs the question for it is the divergent epistemological interpretations of perception that give rise to difficulties. Images can be taken as a "mental pictures" (Aristotle), which may be based either on previous sense perception (e.g., Hume) and are thus sort of "pictures" of the world, or are symbolic creations of the imagination whose relation to the "real world" is problematic at best (e.g., H. H. Price).[18]

At the extremes are two irreconcilable positions, which, in the context of art history, Todorov calls the "romantic" and the "classic."[19] The romantic aesthetic distinguishes and separates the symbol from the image because the latter, as representation, remains firmly rooted in the concrete, whereas the symbol proceeds to the nonrepresentational. In the words of Schelling,

> We are not content, it is true, with the purely non-signifying being, the one rendered, for example, by the pure image, nor is pure signification any better; we want what must be the object of an absolute artistic representation to be so concrete that it is equal to itself like the image, and at the same time as general and charged with meaning as the concept; that is why the German language renders the word "symbol" by Sinnbild, meaningful image.[20]

The romantic aesthetic regards the image, then, as a nonsignifying concrete sensory representation and aesthetics become freed from the relation of representation to undertake the agenda of pure expression.

The classic position, by contrast, delineates an imitative aesthetic that is based on the search for an absolute essence within phenomenal manifestations. This position, taken to an extreme, regards the image as a natural sign, a signifying medium that can be used artistically by means of the allegory. The image in the classic conception is not merely the intuitive sensory instrument that is left behind; even as sensory representation of the world it communicates meaning, it signifies a transcendental *eidos.*

These extreme or ideal positions often become blurred in fact. For example, where Saussure's semiology rejects the symbolic status of the linguistic sign, that is, its "natural" relation to an image, it also rejects natural images (as signs) altogether and emphasizes the absolute arbitrariness (conventionality) of signs.[21]

It may be possible to generalize that symbols are always somehow related to images, if by the latter we mean sensory or intuitive representations. But what happens to the image in its relation with the symbol is a matter of some difficulty. Is the image itself "silent" as the extreme romantic position would have it, or does the image somehow signify as in the transsubjectivity of French existential phenomenology?[22] A brief look at Eliade's *Images and Symbols* reveals one influential interpretation that favors a transcendental phenomenology of symbols. Numerous passages make it clear that Eliade identifies image with the symbol, or uses the terms interchangeably: "It is therefore the image as such, as a whole bundle of meanings, that is true, and not any one of its meanings, nor one alone of its many frames of reference. To translate an image into a concrete terminology by restricting it to any one of its frames of reference is to do worse than mutilate it—it is to annihilate, to annul it as an instrument of cognition."[23] Not only is the image here more than sensory or mental representation, it is even more than the sensory dimension of the symbol. The passage quoted previously is easily interchangeable with Eliade's theoretical discussion of the symbol in *The Two and the One.* However, whereas Eliade's symbolism is "romantic", his symbolic images are classic: "To 'have imagination' is to enjoy a richness of the interior life, an uninterrupted and spontaneous flow of images . . . Etymologically, 'imagination' is related to both imago—a representation or imitation—and imitor—to imitate or reproduce. And for once, etymology is in accord with both psychological realities and spiritiual truth. The imagination imitates the exemplary models—the images—reproduces, reactualizes and repeats them without end."[24] The problem here is not necessarily the inconsistency of two theoretical positions staked out by a historian (Todorov). More important, as the preceding sentence quoted indicates, Eliade's images lack any phenomenological rigor.

If images "imitate" paradigms then the starting point for a phenomenology of religion is precisely the place where we wish to end up. The problem is encountered again in Eliade's call for a return to the archaic, which is echoed with greater refinement and intensity by Charles Long: "This archaism or return to beginnings is predicated on the priority of something already there, something given . . . In our case, this priority and otherness is the history of those primary religious intuitions—religious symbols and their intentionality."[25] The critique of the phenomenological reduction is familiar and bears no repetition here. My concern is the total abandonment of the image, or rather, its complete subjugation to the realm of the symbolic, especially in the case of religious symbolism. If the archetype is present in consciousness—a problematic point—then it is always couched within a concrete image or images. To say, then, that the images of experience are given meaning only through an interaction (instantiation?) with the images of the religious archetype is tautological. For it is unclear where the latter obtain their own meaning. Such a phenomenology suffers from severe transcendental reductionism. I believe that Ricoeur expressed such a view when he stated that "man first reads the sacred on the world, on some element or aspect of the world, on the heavens, on the sun and moon, on the waters and vegetation . . . (The cosmos) in return, loses its concrete limits, gets charged with innumerable meanings, integrates and unifies the greatest possible number of the sectors of anthropocosmic experience."[26] The world does not lose its concreteness, only one specific configuration of its images, which is imposed by the structures of rationality, in favor of another—symbolic—rationality.

Paradoxically, Eliade's position is also anticlassic because that which has been defined as image (e.g., sensory perception) is entirely lacking in referential meaning. For Eliade, symbols derive little of their meaning from the expressivity of the specific images but rather from the paradigmatic models that become manifest as hierophanies (for instance) through them. Such observations are perfectly consistent for Eliade. Religion is ultimately suprasensuous and yet ever familiar. The fears of history and of the radically new are accompanied by the cyclical repetitions of paradigmatic events and the automatic absorption of new phenomena into a polyvalent but static symbolic world view.[27] It is easy to see how such an interpretation could emerge out of Husserl's transcendental phenomenology, or Cassirer's neo-Kantian philosophy of symbolic forms. But this position must be revised because the phenomenal image is as important as the symbol, and the repetition or reenactment of the paradigmatic is vacuous, that is, lifeless and meaningless, without the excitement and awe of the new—the naïve. Moreover, the existence of a paradigm, the truth value of a hierophany, must be examined on the basis of the images that are the "elementary" units of intentional acts of consciousness.

Another major problem with such a strong commitment to the referential dimension of the symbol is the frequent blurring of distinction between symbol and concept (or category). Though symbols are said to be concrete whereas concepts are abstract, symbols, or symbolic interpretations, often take on a concept like abstraction. In India this is most frequently seen in philosophical discussions but is highly pervasive in general. For instance, even a cursory reading of Gonda's *Vedic Ritual* or Meyer's *Trilogie* reveals a great number of so-called fertility symbols gleaned from Vedic and Brahmanical sources.[28] A short list would have to include beans, garlands, fish, moles, bees, honey, corn, barley, bulls, Soma, the Udumbara fruit, sea shells, women, and the Lotus plant. If "fertility," *phaladatā* in a lexical sense, has any general categorical meaning, all of these objects would have to be essentially related, which of course, they are not. Garlands, for instance, contain the power of the living tree or plant of which they are made.[29] Moles live under the earth and churn out its interior substance. Shells, we often hear, resemble the vagina and thus embody, symbolize, or imitate the latter's fecundity.[30] Thus each of these objects participates in specific, concrete, and often unique acts of fertility. Yet we group them together in a category ("fertility"), which is assumed to be organized by a logic of relations determined by their similar or shared characteristics—their fertileness.

This isolation and categorization of fertility symbols, for instance, is thus based on the classical theory of categories, which makes the following fundamental assumptions: meaning concerns an objective relationship between symbols and a real world; and there is a single correct, "god's-eye view of the world" to which symbols point.[31] Categories, or symbols in this case, are abstract "containers" in which certain objects reside because they represent—through shared characteristics—a certain (abstract) aspect of the objective world. Recent research in cognitive psychology and philosophy has shown that categorization is in fact based on experiential aspects of human psychology: "gestalt perception, mental imagery, motor activity, social function, and memory."[32] Understanding the meaning of symbolic objects does not require a categorization of abstract symbolic references in an existential vacuum but an equal examination of the flexible experiential processes that lend concrete images an efficacious meaning in specific contexts. Symbols can then become universal, that is, transcending the limits of the concrete in Ricoeur's sense, if and only if they are accepted first of all as grounded in the concrete.[33]

Once the conceptual function of relations among classic categories has been set in motion, its logic overrides the specificity of the individual symbol and yields always predictable results. Thus, if shells are taken to belong to the series of fertility symbols, their presence in graves, ex post facto, signifies the belief in a second birth and attendant postmortem ideas.[34] One problem stands out here: most, if not all, of these objects display more than one "power," for instance growth and destructiveness at the same time. Fish and bees, for example, and deer as well, which have been taken as fertility symbols, have also served in other contexts as symbols for rashness and danger. The *Śukranīti Sārah* (1.209–210) states: "The fish though it dives into unfathomed depths and lives in distinct abodes, tastes the angle with meat for death." The text cautions against an exaggerated reliance on the five senses, in this case *rasa*. The deer succumbs to *śabda* (sound), the bee to *gandha* (smell). Similarly, in a far older example, when Uddālaka teaches Śvetaketu the nature of Self, he utilizes what a classical aesthete would call an allegory of the bee and its honey. The honey produced by the bee contains no identifiable traces of the "juice" derived from specific flowers.[35] Similarly the seed of the Banyan tree is split up not for the purpose of demonstrating the generative powers of the seed (*bija*) but the powers of nothing at all, the invisible potency of Brahman at work in the entire universe. Or, if bees are taken only as symbols of fertility how are we to interpret *Ṛgveda* 1.114.8 in which penances are described for members of a house in which bees have produced honey? It is too easy to forget that the "polyvalence" of symbols is contingent on the physical qualities of their constituting images in space and time. To put it more precisely, the so-called polyvalence of symbols reflects the fluidity of existential image structures ("schemata") by means of which physical characteristics (images) are organized into coherent and meaningful entities. If our experience of shells (inhabited stone) relates them to domesticity, would their presence in graves not equally suggest a notion of optimistic finality about death?

We are thus led to the conclusion that the symbolic efficacy of phenomena lies not only in the supra-"imagistic" symbolic intuition, but in the unique way that the image "resonates" in our symbolic consciousness.[36] Or, more accurately, the symbolic intentionality of religious consciousness manifests itself—becomes prefashioned, so to speak—at the image level.[37] This topic will be taken up shortly. At this point I wish to compare the results of the phenomenology of one symbol with that of a corresponding image. The results should demonstrate the need to clarify the symbol/image distinction.

The phenomenology of any concept or symbol requires that we trace it back to a naïve experience or the experience of a naïve image. This is what Ricoeur attempted with the symbolism of the evil of fault, which he traced back (by "reenactment") to the symbolism of sin, then to the experience of defilement. At the root of the experience are a fear and repulsion toward a "quasi-material something that infects as a sort of filth, that harms by invisible properties."[38] However, phenomenological rigor is abandoned for historical speculation when the dread of pollution is linked to moral trepidation in a (historical) stage "in which evil and misfortune have not been dissociated, in which the ethical order of doing ill has not been distinguished from the cosmobiological order of faring ill: suffering, sickness, death, failure."[39] It is precisely such a link that we need to demonstrate phenomenologically rather than historically or psychologically.

But moral guilt aside, even the physical experience of defilement is difficult enough to "reenact." Researchers agree that it is not matter itself, but matter out of place, "dirt" or chaos, that defiles. Thus, as Douglas tells us, the root of the experience of pollution is the conception of boundaries, fashioned after the human body and homologous with social boundaries.[40] Dirt is matter or substance transposed across boundaries, from within the body outside and vice versa, from the yard into the house, from one caste to another. Although this may be a satisfying conceptual and sociological analysis, I think it fails to meet Ricoeur's criteria for tracing the phenomenon back to its very roots in consciousness. For we do not experience our bodies categorically or conceptually, nor is our most fundamental bodily experience one of interiority versus exteriority, important as that may be. Before we experience transitions across the edges of our bodies, so to speak, we must experience the skin-enclosed body as whole and as "ours."

Oliver Sacks' fascinating work demonstrates what can happen when proprioception, the internal sense of one's body, is either absent or destroyed. One of his patients was an athletic young woman who had lost all sense of her body. Her five senses, including touch, functioned at near normal levels but proprioceptive perception was lost in a medical accident. She could not feel her muscles, joints, tendons: as she put it, her body went blind.[41] As a result she felt disembodied and could not assert her will over her body and command it to perform the simplest tasks such as sitting up in bed. Interestingly, Christine felt whole or "connected" when she rode in convertible cars and allowed the wind to rush over her body, the way, say, the current of a river rushes a bather.[42] In the following chapter, Sacks discusses the similar case of a man who lost the proprioceptive sense of his own leg. Discovering a cold hairy limb in bed with him, the man was so repulsed that he threw it off the bed. The hospital staff would repeatedly find the patient lying on the floor, for, though he failed to realize this, the rest of his body was attached to the repulsive leg.

This digression illustrates a point that is so obvious, it is easy to overlook. The experience of bodily pollution cannot emerge before the body is self-appropriated, a necessary condition according to Freud, for the emergence of ego. A proper phenomenology of pollution would have to take into consideration the emergence of a body-self Gestalt (or self-objectification) as a condition of perception and cognition. This state entails a variety of skills that enable the child to recognize spatial relations, permanence, movement, wholeness, continuity, constancy, connectedness, and others. Moral cognition, or simple external standards of "propriety" at their infancy here, are cogeneric with, not derivative from a fundamental experience of defilement. The latter is not fundamental at all.

Thus, the return to the basic experience of either sin or pollution requires that we look at the existential conditions of perception and basic cognition. Cognitive psychology, for instance, allows us to retreat from the propositional level of awareness through (prelinguistic) concepts to images—for instance, "a consciously elaborated representation created from the schema" —and finally to schemas, which are the structure of what I have termed naïve images: "a representation of experience that bears a relation to an original event," or which makes awareness of an event possible.[43]

One alternative approach, the intuitive contemplation of the image as a condition for the emergence of the symbol (then concept), can yield unpredictable results precisely because the newness or naïveté of such a contemplation is not overwhelmed by symbolic paradigms. The shell, to return to our favorite example, strikes both Valéry and Bachelard as the very conquest of perception over mind. If the French critics are on target, then long before the shell symbolizes anything, it is simply domesticity—an inhabited rock, a perfectly shaped natural home. Before its spiraling line becomes symbolic, it merely traces the achievements of imperceptible growth, and a life that accomplishes not by reaching upward, as it were, but by turning in upon itself.

Could the ancient Aryan, the pre-Columbus American, or the New Guinean, who even today transports sea shells inland, have shared such day dreams with the French philosophers about what their eyes saw and their hands felt? Could the shells, which abundantly adorn the image of Kāmadeva, represent the domesticity and constancy of love, rather than its passionately erotic dimension?[44] We cannot answer such questions as long as we are locked out of the lives—images, associations, memories, reveries—of the people who lived by these symbols. But we know that all symbols are already prefigured by the intense awareness of new images. We must, as far as possible, devote more attention to the images that constitute the so called nonreferential dimension of symbols and to the manner in which the physical qualities of the image complement its symbolic values.

I shall return to the image-symbol dialectic shortly and should now like to summarize, in outline form, the main features of the two poles of all religious consciousness: the symbolic and the imagistic.

Symbolic	*Imagistic*
general-universal	concrete-particular
suprasensory	perceptual
holistic	divisible
polyvalent	univocal
monadic	relational

I should emphasize that what is being compared are not the qualities of objects but the twin poles of human symbolic consciousness in its encounter with the world. Consequently, these are complementary, not mutually exclusive properties. For instance, a symbol can be particular, of course, but symbolic consciousness always passes through the specificity of the sign to its universal voice. Enough has been said about the first two poles; I shall now address the indivisibility of the symbolic consciousness.

Symbols, though based on the visible qualities of a phenomenon, cannot be divided into the elements of that phenomenon. When a cow, for instance, is taken as a symbol for the earth, our symbolic intuition operates through the intentional consciousness of "cowness" as a whole. The ears, eyes, and tail of a particular cow are not, properly speaking, elements of the symbol—they disappear entirely in the referential reality of the cow symbol. Imagistic consciousness, on the other hand, attends to the particular and moves over its objects with an eye for the detail of phenomena. Two examples should illustrate this distinction. Consider the Aurignacian cave drawing of a charging bison at Pech-Merle (see fig. 1). An utterly sophisticated attention to the power of pure motion is manifest in the contraction of the animal's head and front quarters into a swift single line that thrusts forward from the steep, heavy mass of its enormous humped shoulders. Now, some have speculated that the "absence" of head indicates a rite of multiplication or fertility. However, the drawing is not a symbolic abstraction pointing at a general quality of bisons as sacrificial animals. It is a true image of the animal's awesome power in motion, recaptured artistically by an emphasis on the curved line. No symbolic or other referential analysis can take place without first realizing that the raked line is an image, not a concept.[45]

Or, to return to India, consider Mayūra's eight poems in the *Mayūrāṣṭaka*.[46] Here is an exercise in an erotic (*śṛṅgāra*) poem in eight variations. The indicated referent, sometimes depicted through tropes (symbols, metaphors, metonyms), sometimes directly, is always the same: a young woman (*bālā*), shortly before or after a secretive bout of lovemaking. Many of the themes and embellishments (*alaṁkāra*) are standard and repetitive: the woman is described as *mṛgī* (deer), *haṃsagamanā* (whose gait is like a goose), *tāmbūlaṁ vāmahaste* (betel in her left hand), and other formulas associated with erotic poetry. These thematic formulas are vaguely symbolic, purely referential, and not truly evocative. However, an occasional well-placed word or compound gives rise to a genuine sensation of joy and appreciation through the use of varying techniques of resonance (*dhvani*).[47] A compound like *priyāṅgagahanaṁ*, for instance, refers on the surface to the adornment (*gahanā*) of the elephant's temple to which the lover in the song is compared. But as a *tatpuruṣa* compound with *priya* (lover) and *aṅga* (limb), it can also refer to the lover's secret parts—a strong erotic

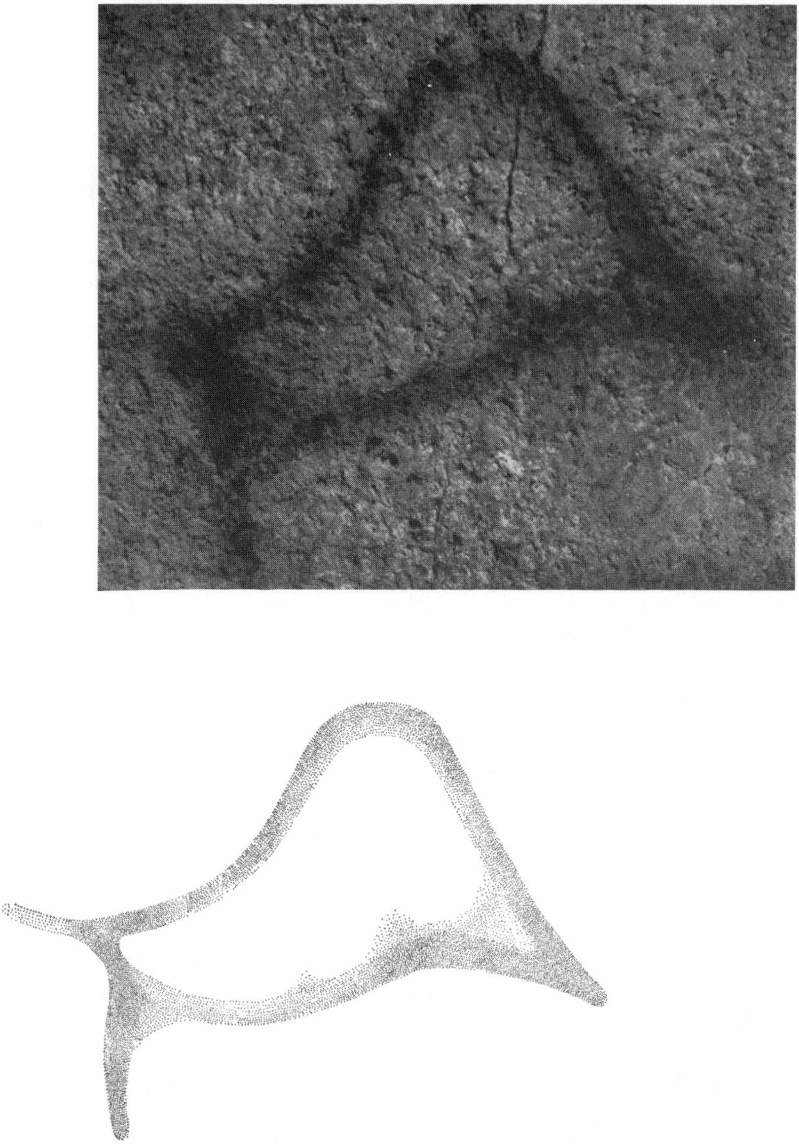

Figure 1 Pech-Merle: Detail of the attacking bison. Head and forelegs are merged into a single line. From S. Giedion, *The Eternal Present*, p. 27; by permission of the National Gallery of Art.

allusion that affects the poem as a whole. The surprise of the pun produces the aesthetic pleasure (*rasa*) and the insight of a "true" (imagistic) reality (*sphoṭa*), which the poet can so skillfully evoke.

Unlike symbols, images are essentially divisible. An image is neither simply "tree" nor "cow" but any element in the sensory field that attracts an intentional act of consciousness at its most elementary level. This can be illustrated most dramatically in A.R. Luria's recorded case of Zasetzky's brain injuries leading to visual impairment, sense of body loss (right half), and traumatic aphasia. When his field of vision is cut to its left half, for instance, the loss is sustained regardless of the width of the image, in a telescoping effect. A broad landscape, a face, a whole sentence, or just one word is equally affected by the loss of the right side.[48] The image, whether neurologically or phenomenologically speaking, is constituted as a single act that unifies by means of preconscious schemata a variety of elements into a coherent representation. Tracing such an act to its origins in consciousness leads back to experience through these schemata and, as some existentialists and cognitivists tell us, back to the body.[49]

The distinction between the divisiblity of images and indivisibility of symbols is important in the manner we approach a phenomenology of cultural ideas, in India for instance. The present work takes dharma as such an idea. If dharma is constituted only by complete symbols and symbolic narratives, not to mention theological and philosophical ones, then phenomenology has no scope in its study. But if the symbols of dharma—or, I should say, its images—can be studied individually as discrete but interacting elements of the imagination, then our study is both more interesting (unpredictable) and fruitful.

Because symbols are suprasensory, the relations among them are not experienced and are purely intuitive. One symbolic referent can never, properly speaking, "evoke" the experience of another symbolic referent. When woman and moon are said to be related in a symbolic intuition, this relation neither is grounded in experience nor entails an experiential (affective) vitality. According to historians of religion the relationship, if it exists, is transcendental and pertains to the roots of our being as "homoreligiosus," a problematic realm indeed. Not so images: these are related concretely and experientially. The shell is related to the house because it has an inside and an outside and it is inhabited. The experience of habitation in a body or house is the trans-subjective ground for relating distinct images in specific configurations. More generally, the phenomenological emphasis on *Lebenswelt* places our perceptions in a relational world, not an atomistic realm of radical empiricism or abstract rationalism. Objects in the world are related because they are related in our experience. The great Aśvattha tree connects the heavens and earth because it touches both. It is divine because it grows, as far as the eye can tell, upside down, that is, from the heavens to the earth.[50]

Mahāvrata Images

In a myth or ritual in which symbolic relations form an essential part of the narrative and its syntax, it is the imagistic dimension that makes such relationships possible. Images are the mortar, so to speak, that binds symbolic relations and animates them. I shall demonstrate this with a brief example from the Mahāvrata ritual. The Mahāvrata is the next to last day of the year long Sattra sacrifice. It represents either of the two solstitial points of the year and is designed as a feeding of Prajāpati and as a wedding ceremony of sun and earth as well as the reenacted victory of the Devas over the Asuras in their primordial battle for the sun. This ancient ritual contains a variety of fascinating and intriguing elements. There is a Hotṛ priest sitting on a swing, a Brahmin and a Śūdra sitting at opposite ends of the *sadas* and alternating praise and abuse respectively of the proceedings. There is a contest for a white circular skin, sexual copulation in a separate shed, a warrior who shoots arrows at a hide, aiming to hit but not pierce the skin, the beating of an earth drum half inside half outside the *vedi.* These among other details have drawn a considerable amount of scholarly attention and a surprising degree of agreement on their interpretation.[51] The consensus on the general meaning of the ritual is dominated by what the ancient texts themselves describe as its meaning, for instance, fertility (feeding Prajāpati), or the battle of the Devas and Asuras over the sun.[52] But the ritual contains much more than the ancient Brahmins can reduce it to. Staal has warned us, if nothing else, that ritual syntax needs to receive much more attention in interpreting meaning than the semantics of symbolic elements.[53]

As we separate the ritual from its presumably cohesive totality into the syntactical units, we must abandon symbols and take up images.[54] There are two reasons for this. First, symbols cannot be dissected or taken apart without losing their referential orientation. For instance, the circular piece of white hide, said by all interpreters to symbolize the sun, requires a totality of characteristics to act as a symbol of the sun. If we disregard its color and shape, in favor of texture, for example, it loses the general symbolic value and could be identical with other skins used in this or other rituals. Second, symbols cannot interact empirically. The objects that interact in the ritual do not mirror the actions of the metaphysical (or mythological) realities, which they are said to symbolize, in a direct corresponding fashion. The ritual assumes its own life and logic of relations, which are greatly determined by the nature of the actors and objects utilized.[55] To say that the mythical narrative, which the ritual enacts, determines the relation of a given object with other ritual elements merely begs the question. We need to look at the images (concrete representational structures in consciousness) active in the ritual first, then what they point to as symbols. It becomes clear that the Mahāvrata is dominated by the use of various skins in a variety of applications. As symbols these skins share very little, but as images they are strongly related, for instance, as the outer layers of animal bodies. What are skins? What are the specific and general powers and qualities they embody having come off the bodies of specific animals? These types of questions and their answers will then determine how we address the symbolic level of representation and the dialectic of the two can help us solve issues such as an arrow that clings to the skin but does not penetrate it.[56]

Once we begin by asking questions about the sign and its context—not what it points to—we enter the experiential relationship between the participant and his immediate environment. For instance, the swing may be said to point symbolically at the copulation (or mediation) of heaven and earth or to the course of the sun.[57] However, we shall not have said much if we do not examine the substance and shape of the rope and seat, the wooden structure to which the swing is fixed, the sitting position, the placement of feet during the swinging, and so forth. We may also, if possible, contemplate the subjective phenomenon. A child or adult who swings widely becomes attentive to the vacillating horizon and feels a part of the sky at one instant and the earth at the next. Whatever metaphysical idea stands behind the symbolic act, it is only the feeling of a lived action, with its memories and associations, as well as the specific qualities of the objects used, that animates the ritual.[58] Ricoeur has observed that the symbol is "donative" as it is the "movement of the primary meaning which makes us participate in the latent meaning and thus assimilates us to that which is symbolized without our being able to master the similitude intellectually."[59] This movement, I wish to claim, is based on the way in which existential images resonate in our consciousness and enable the imagination to leap into symbolic realms and live in worlds we have never actually experienced.

But how do we speak of meaningful images that are, at the same time, presymbolic even prediscursive? As the earlier definition indicated, image is understood as a function of one's epistemological commitment. For the phenomenologist image may be the object of perception, which is meaningful, because it is constituted by the intentional act of consciousness.[60] This meaning (*Sinn*) is not symbolic; it is perceptual, that is, immanent in the act of Gestalt perception and distinct from recollection, cognition, and so forth.[61] The image, then, straddles the boundary between objectivity and subjectivity.[62] Frege compares it to the projection of the moon ("object") on the lens of a telescope and on the retina of an observer. The first he calls "real image," which is likened to the sensory stimulation. The second he calls "retinal image" and likens to the "idea" or experience.[63]

The Structure of Images

The object as image assumes a meaning (constitution or structure) through an apparatus that is general, perhaps universal. Only then it is synthesized into more personal and symbolic intentionalities. There is a paradox here: the phenomenon at its more concrete level (naïve image) is also most universal. A similar paradox operates in *kāvya* where universal meaning is revealed—by suggestion—through the most concrete and immediate image.[64] The question arises, then, how images are constituted perceptually, or what shapes their Gestalt forms. Positions again vary from the idealist and rationalist to the existentialist. Contemporary cognitivists in a variety of fields seem to favor existentialist (Merleau-Ponty, Heidegger, Sartre) interpretations of the body as a form-giving basis of perceptual intentionality.[65] This stands in contrast to a rationalist position, shared by philosophers, psychologists, and scientists who claim that concepts originate in a purely mental correspondence of ideas to an "objective" (even idealistic) world. Prominent among recent existential critiques of the "objectivist" position are Mark Johnson's *The Body in the Mind* and George Lakoff's monumental *Women, Fire, and Dangerous Things.* According to these works embodiment provides "basic experiential structures" that act preconceptually to shape our experiences of the world.[66] The structures, which have been termed "kinesthetic image schemas" provide both semantic and logical correlates to our experienced images, rendering them both meaningful and communicable in (metaphorical) language. For instance, our experience of the body as container shapes our perception of the spatial relations among phenomena. Everything has an "inside" and an "outside" and all objects stand in relation to others by being inside them or outside of them. Such an experience carries on metaphorically to social concepts where we are situated "in" relationships, "in" a marriage, "out" of work, or "in" debt.

Other schemata include part-whole, link, center-periphery, and source-path-goal schemata. The fundamental principle is the same: images, or the phenomena of our consciousness, are structured by schemata that are not cognitive in Piaget's sense, nor strictly experiential either.[67] That such image schemata are susceptible to empirical verification through a number of disciplines is not our concern here. Two issues stand out among others for consideration: what is the relationship between structurally "meaningful" images and symbols; and, while symbols are particularly well suited for religious insights and expression, do images possess any religious intentionality?

As noted previously, symbols or other forms of figurative speech are often taken as signs that, though grounded in perception, are immediately and entirely sense transcending. In the case of religious symbols these qualities are intensified because symbols "must express an object that by its very nature transcends everything in the world."[68] If we thus examine the religious efficacy of images on the basis of their referential transpicuity, we remain locked within the same transcendental fallacy I have been criticizing. The transcendental ontology of the "religious" object must (here) be set aside in favor of the religious experience as a mode of being in the world. In other words, the images of the religious life are not regarded as standing in a causal relation with archaic or metaphysical archetypes. They do not explain the existence of archetypes nor do they owe their own nature to transcendent or subconscious causes. The lived ritual, for instance, "reverberates" (*retentir*) on the threshhold of the participant's consciousness and reaches as echo the depths of his awareness.[69] The phenomenologist who traces the movement of such reverberations can never go fully beyond consciousness.[70] Religious symbols, like containers of transcendental worlds, or like the leaves in Minkowski's metaphor, only come to life through the "sonorous waves" of these living images. The container itself cannot burst open without the loss of the echoing waves that animate such worlds with existential passion. The waves, to continue the metaphor, are generated in the active consciousness of the ritual actor. The meaning of an image consists of the experiences that brought it into being, and the dynamism of its conscious movement between experience and religious symbols. In this sense, a cosmogonic ritual, for instance, lacks "meaning" if the participant has never stood in awe at the sight of a new dawn and felt the excitement of its new possibilities.

Phenomenology of religion cannot study only religious symbols and ideas. It needs to focus on the act of consciousness that brings such symbols to life. In so doing phenomenology raises images, with their structures and relations, to an equal footing with the structure of metaphysical realities. Only thus is the absolutely Real seen within the imagination of those whose lives and works are dedicated to its expression and realization.

Indian Images

India presents formidable problems that seem to confound the phenomenolgy being proposed here. Its religions and arts seem to place an exclusive emphasis on the symbolic and formal. Religious norms and standards of dharma, in their classical formulation, stand rather starkly against the intensity of the lived religious life. Aesthtic categories seem to reduce—or elevate —the chaos of the sensory world to precise abstract standards applied with exacting rigor. Even the Sanskrit of Indian poetry (*kāvya*) appears to be entirely detached from the Prakrit of daily life, in which Indians fashioned their living sensory and emotional images. In short, the near absolute separation of symbol from the naïve image seems to justify an exaggerated preoccupation with the metaphysics or structuralism of symbolic discourse. But would a rigorous phenomenology of imagistic consciouness founder at the threshhold of the written text, the temple icon, or the wall painting? Can the classical themes of Hinduism truly tell us anything about the feelings, experiences, and reveries of ancient Indians?

In order to answer these questions properly I must digress to Indian arts and aesthetic thought. Although my observations must remain very general, even banal to specialists, the purpose is not just a summary of the principles of *kāvya* and the other arts. I intend to show the manner in which the gap between symbol and image is formed, then bridged, despite the classic emphasis on symbolic formulas. The import of these observations for the Smṛti literature will subsequently be clarified.

Where the daydreams and discoveries of the young Bialik, Rilke, or Blake and their readers furnish their adult Hebrew, German, and English with a subtle power of evocation, a Kālidasa wields his Sanskrit in pursuit of another end. Ingalls observed that since Sanskrit was not an everyday language, it "furnished no subconscious symbols for the impressions which we receive in childhood nor for the emotions which form our character in early adolescence."[71] However, the issue predates systematic poetics and extends far beyond poetics in scope. It may have started with the earliest speculations about the nature of language and its concomitant removal from phenomena. This will have been due to the Aryans' need to find substitutes for materials used in ritual injunctions.[72] Subsequently, in Mīmāṁsā theories and in Patañjali's psychology, language began to universalize phenomena into classes of individuals in injunctions like "A Brahmana should not be killed."[73] The noun clearly could not refer to one individual or all other Brahmins would be excluded . The result is practically useful in ritual and legal contexts, but it devitalizes language because words are raised to the level of an abstract symbolic container. Following this phenomenal "break," the history of India's philosophy of language, grammar, and poetics is dominated by a concern for determining the relation of noumenal to phenomenal in verbal expressions, and bridging the gap in art.

Possibly the pivotal figure in this history was Bhartṛhari, whose metaphysics of language—primarily the theory of *sphoṭa*—made Ānandavardhana's and Abhinavagupta's theories of resonance religiously significant. Bhartṛhari's *sphoṭa* closely resembles his understanding of Veda, which, as we have seen earlier (VP 1.5) is a unitary, transcendental reality expressed in a variety of manners (*dhvani*). The word, according to the *Vākyapadiya* (VP 1.49), contains a phenomenal-empirical element (*naḍa*) as well as an unmanifest intrinsic meaning—equivalent to the Mīmāṁsā's *śabda* (word). There is some disagreement as to whether *sphoṭa*—this intrinsic meaning of the word —is metaphysical or merely grammatical.[74] At the very least, however, the intrinsic meaning (*sphoṭa*) of the word or empirical expression in general, is the ultimate cause and intent of verbalization. As meaning, it is paradoxically both universal and particular. That is, *sphoṭa* emerges through language because of the word's (and sentence's) power to systematically unify individuals and universals in the consciousness of the speaker and listener alike.[75]

According to Bhartṛhari, language makes the metaphysical meaning manifest through the extreme characteristics or powers of reference of words. These include denotation (*abhidhā*), indication (*lakṣaṇā*), and evocation (*dhvani*)—the latter understood here as the external aspects of language.[76] Subsequent speculation on the nature and function of language in poetry internalized the characteristics of evocation and raised it to a sui generis method for producing artistic appreciation (*rasa*). *Rasa* is understood as an artistically inspired psychomental state equivalent to Patanjali's *prajña* (insight) in which the ultimate meaning of an expression is intuited and appreciated. For Ānandavardhana evocation is the heart of poetry (*kāvya*) and distinguishes poetry from other forms of literature as the most efficacious manner of bridging the gap between the phenomenal and the noumenal.[77]

Abhinavagupta's aesthetic evocation (*rasadhvani*) transcends the phenomenal altogether: it is beyond individual words and even cognitions. *Rasa* becomes equivalent to a religious experience though it is produced and sustained in aesthetic contexts.[78] Progress in evocation (*vyañjanā*) from outer to inner resonance (*dhvani*) can be illustrated by means of the classic example usually cited, the "house on the Ganges."

The denotative (*abhidhā*) import of the phrase cannot be sufficient for a full artistic appreciation because it would simply refer to a house in the middle of the river. The indicative (*lakṣaṇā*) sense refers to a house on the bank of the river. However, the poetic resonance of the phrase (*vyañjanā*, *dhvani*) produces in the imagination of the qualified reader an image of a cool, pure, serene, and holy house.[79] Or, consider the word Ganga in the three phrases: "we drink the water of Ganga," "Vārāṇasī is on the Ganga," and "While boating on the river, the Ganga has washed away my fatigue." The same word, used in three functions, relates distinct and separate images, depending on how it is read.[80]

Or in another example, Ānandavardhana quotes the following line from Yaśovarman's *Rāmābhyudaya* to illustrate the resonance of one word—Rāma.[81] "Rāma, whose wife is dear to him, has not done what is appropriate for love, my beloved." In the case of the hero who mistakingly mourns Sītā, the literal meaning of the name is transferred to an implied (*dhvanya*) moral self-reproach. "Rāma" implies an inclination to use force and the abandonment of love, according to Ānandavardhana.

Though *rasa* is a purified, almost transcendental mood, it is evoked most effectively through the resonance of words in poetry, not through the utter abandonment of words in mystical introspection. Such *dhvanya kāvya* is poetry in which both the conventional meaning and the conventional words are subordinate to a transcendent reality but, paradoxically, through a surprising, and therefore living, image.[82] Despite the emphasis on a transcendental mood, the ultimate aesthetic criterion must finally succumb to the newness of life:

Though he had often seen the mountain, Kṛṣṇa
was filled with surprise as if it was for the first time;
That it becomes new at every moment
is just the nature of the beautiful.[83]

The psychology of evocation or resonance (*vyañjanā*) is particularly noteworthy here. Impressions or situations one encounters in life are complex events involving causes and effects that trigger transitory and lasting psychological responses of varied types. The poem, play, or icon, employs this process in formulas that set up an artistic set of determinants (*vibhāva*), consequents (*anubhāva*), and transitory states (*vyabhicāribhāva*). These are the aesthetic equivalents of common psychological responses to contingent events. What all this means, more simply, is that the psychology of our everyday experiences is duplicated in artistic contexts to produce that sublime artistic mood called *rasa*.[84] However, whereas in daily life even the most sublime experience is based on the contingency of our psychological responses to empirical events, and can also be triggered by memory or inference, the aesthetic experience (*rasa*) is unique. It rests entirely on the perfect configuration of determinants, consequents, and transitory feelings.[85] In short, *rasa* is evoked by the images of our own consciousness, an artistic consciousness cultivated with great and prolonged effort. Here then is an artistic, elitist "secondary" phenomenology, in which the world plays an indirect role by becoming distilled and transposed not as symbol but as refined image in the consciousness of the poet and his appreciative reader.[86] *Dhvani*, the word's ability to hint, excites the reader by suddenly removing the obstacles of everyday perceptions on the one hand, verbal formulas on the other, from the poetic imagination and allows a revelation of the world's intrinsic possibilities.

The same general observations made in reference to poetics apply also to the dramatic and visual arts (*citra*) in which the doctrine of *rasa* prevails. The same nine artistic moods listed in Bhārata's *Nāṭya-śāstra* are prescribed by the *Visṇudharmottara* for painting, image making, clay filling, and the other arts.[87] Although paintings are again subclassified into genres according to their *rasa*-producing qualities, it is reasonable to expect that classifications be based on the aesthetic content rather than the media of art.[88] Just as ordinary experience is refined into poetic consciousness, which is then reanimated through the word's ability to go beyond itself, the sculptor may borrow material and forms from the world in order to proceed beyond. The language of the sculptor is both the physical medium of his art: stone, iron, or wood, as well as the language of *nāṭya* (drama, dance), and thus indirectly, *kāvya*.[89] Similarly, the tension between empirical reality (*dṛṣṭa*) and idealized absolute reality (*adṛṣṭa*) is articulated by means of an ambiguity toward mimesis on the one hand and symbolic representation on the other: "The chief aim of painting is to produce an exact likeness," but then, "Rivers should be represented in human form, with their conveyances [*vahanas*]."[90]

Of course, philosophers of art and poetry insist on a distinction between "dhvanya" (aesthetic) modes of expression such as poetry and drama, and apodictic texts such as Smṛti. The point of the foregoing discussion is not to develop a "*vyañjanā* (evocative) hermeneutic" of Smṛti, but to show that despite the formulaic and impersonal nature of its language, there is a vivid imagination behind the words used in standard formulas. The formulas of dharma contain the same tension between phenomenal experiences and absolute Being that runs throughout Sanskrit literature. And Bhartṛhari does in fact extend his system over Smṛti when he claims (VP 1.7) that indication (*lakṣaṇā*) links an act executed according to Smṛti, with a Vedic act.[91] Reasoning alone could never point to dharma and a reliance on tradition is as necessary as the connection between Smṛti and Veda. Our concern here is not how dharma is grasped for legal purposes but how it is imagined to begin with.

For instance, when Manu prescribes trees that bleed a milky sap (*kṣiriṇa*) for marking boundaries (8.246), the words used are evocative because the text could simply have listed Akra, Udumbara, or other fig trees. Put in these terms, "milky tree" acts as a symbol that combines a mythological reference with a vivid living image, neither of which suffices in conveying the phenomenon of boundary or dharma. The myth is Pṛthu and Pṛthivī, the primordial civilizing king and Earth in the shape of a milking cow. Pṛthu cut the forests, leveled the ground, and marked the boundaries where Pṛthivī's milk could flow and irrigate the fields. Like the trees, which the poet describes as rivers flowing to the sky, these milky trees are the rivers of milk running between fields. However, the *śāstra-kāra* and his reader, not to mention farmers who may have lived by such a rule, will have had something more vivid in their mind's eye than a myth. The myth of Pṛthu means little to those who do not dread exuded bodily fluids and do not, at the same time, delight in the fecundity and nurturance of milk. In addition the trees that mark boundaries are "legal" (the Udumbara is royal, the boundary is public domain) but are also a source of the fields' fertility—a royal domain of authority and fecundity at once.[92]

One could still argue that, even granting the thesis that Smṛti religious formulas once evoked living images, we could never identify these images given the literary data available today. Consider even royal inscriptions that recorded grants of land, tanks, and other donations to temples. Even such historic documents are so formulaic and thematic that they render the concrete events they "record" utterly one-dimensional. The king is always depicted as the embodiment of the *dharmarāja* (righteous king), his sons are always worshiping his water-lily feet, he is the clearer of forests, founder of civilization, and so forth[93]. So how is it possible to reconstruct a proper phenomenology of dharma if there are no descriptions of the living images associated with the concept in its variety of uses? This objection is perfectly valid for classical studies where, unlike ethnographic investigations, thick descriptions have very little to go on.

However, an alternative path can be explored. If dharma is an existentially grounded—metaphorically transformed ("homologized" as Eliade would put it)—conception, then the images of which it consists can be recaptured through the spatial and temporal elements of its symbols. For instance, Smṛti texts are more deeply concered with the boundaries of spaces (as well as social realities) than with their "interior" or content. The phenomena of boundaries, then, are critical to an understaning of dharma. Consequently, a proper phenomenology of dharma would include, along with the all-too familiar boundaries of castes, professions, and so forth, the more mundane, but equally instructive boundaries of the human skin, animal hides, house walls, picture frames, field boundaries, and others. The same (embodied) imagination that conceptualizes the human skin along medico cosmological lines is at work in the formulation of the bounds of proper conduct and social propriety. Of course, even skins and walls are depicted with symbolic formulas rather than images, but the collection of spatial evidence from such disparate contexts enables us to reconstruct the spatial imagination of ancient Indians. We can thus discover more than structural homologies in the process that conceived of a world after the human body. We may not be able to imagine dharma as Bachelard imagines a sea shell, but we can reconstruct it from the ground up, that is, from simpler and more concrete symbolic thought to metaphysical or legalistic conceptions. The reconstruction of the structure of dharma can then be followed by a hermeneutic of its dynamic aspects, that is, the crossing over of boundaries, the transformations within adjacent bounded areas, and the enforcement of rules against transgression. In order to do this we must examine the temporality of images, which, unlike symbols, are subject to experience in duration. Only then can we proceed to the somatic conditions, and conditioning, for experiencing images, namely purification in rivers. These are the subjects of the next two chapters.

Notes

1. *Nārada Smṛti*, introduction; On another chain of transmission, see *Manu Smṛti* (MS) 1.58-59; *Mahābhārata* (Mbh). 12.59.87.

2. See for instance Ramanuja's *Vedārthasaṁgraha*, para. 21 (p. 83), quoted in J. Lipner, *The Face of Truth*, (Albany: SUNY Press, 1986), p. 20.

3. "Veda and Dharma," in Wendy D. O'Flaherty and J. D. M. Derrett, eds., *The Concept of Duty in South Asia* (s.l.: South Asia Books, 1978), p. 82.

4. Harold G. Coward, *Sphoṭa Theory of Language* (Delhi: Motilal Banarsidass, 1986) p. 5.

5. *Vākyapadīya of Bhartṛhari*, trans. K. A. Subramania Iyer (Poona: Deccan College, 1965) chap. 1, pp. 7–8.

6. *An Essay on Man*, (New Haven: Yale University Press, 1944), pp. 51–52; cf. John Ashbery, *As We Know* (New York: Penguin, 1979) p. 74.

7. *Kol Kitvei Ch. N. Bialik*, 7th ed. (Tel Aviv: Dvir, 1970), pp. 145–46.

8. G. Bachelard, *The Poetics of Space* (Boston: Beacon Press, 1969), chap. 5; Paul Valéry, *Aesthetics*, 45, 13 (New York: Bollingen, Bollingen Series, 1964), pp. 3–30.

9. P. Valéry, *Aesthetics*, p. 11.

10. G. Bachelard, *The Poetics of Space*, p. 110.

11. The special case of Sanskrit poetry (*kāvya*) will be discussed later.

12. *Swann's Way* (New York: Modern Library, 1928), p. 62

13. For a broad definition of the tradition, see *Yājñavalkya Smṛti* (Yāj). 1.3; see also P. V. Kane, *History of Sanskrit Poetics* (Delhi: Motilal Banarsidass, 1971), p. 332.

14. For instance, MS 8.44, 5.108; Yāj 1.159; on the sensuous Iravati river/ woman, see *Matsya Purāṇa*, esp. 114–17.

15. Kāt. 10.5.

16. "Dharmaśāstra: The Origin and Purpose of the Smṛti," in *Contributions to the Study of India Law and Society*, South Asia Seminar 1966–67, (Philadelphia: University of Pennsylvania Press, 1967), pp. 9–10; cf. Manu's amusing list of excluded persons from the Śraddhas (3.150), which includes animal trainers, ill and handicapped people, a man who constantly asks for favors, a man who seduces his sister-in-law. On the symbolic value of classification and categorization, see subsequent discussion. See also M. Foucault, *The Order of Things* (New York: Vintage Books, 1973), p. xv and chapter 6.

17. See for instance, Charles S. Peirce, *Collected Papers of Charles Sanders Peirce*, ed. Hartshorne and Weiss, vol. 2 (Cambridge, Mass.: Harvard University Press, 1931–35); Ernst Cassirer, *The Philosophy of Symbolic Forms*, vol. 3 (New Haven: Yale University Press, 1985), chap. 5. The latter has been particularly influential on the notion that symbols are transparent.

18. For a summary discussion of these issues, see A. R. Manser, "Image," in the *Encyclopedia of Philosophy* (New York: Collier Macmillan, 1976), 4:133–36.

19. The distinction is familiar from a variety of other contexts. See, for instance, Murray J. Leaf, *Man, Mind, and Science* (New York: Columbia University Press, 1979), and Mark Johnson, *The Body in the Mind* (Chicago: University of Chicago Press, 1986).

20. *Philosophie der Kunst*, 5:411–12 quoted in Tzvetan Todorov *Theories of the Symbol* (Ithaca: Cornell University Press, 1982), pp. 209–10.

21. *Course in General Linguistics* (New York: McGraw-Hill, 1959), p. 68

22. Existential cognitivists would criticize the romantic position on the "objectivist" or arbitrary method by means of which a given image is linked to symbolic representation. See, for instance, Roy Wagner, *Symbols That Stand for Themselves* (Chicago: University of Chicago Press, 1976), p. x; M. Johnson, *The Body*, pp. xxx–xxxi.

23. M. Eliade, *Images and Symbols*, (New York: Search Book, 1969), p. 15; see also A. K. Coomaraswamy: "To have lost the art of thinking in images is precisely to have lost the proper linguistic of metaphysics and to have

descended to the verbal logic of 'philosophy.'" *Figures of Speech* (New Delhi: Munshiram Manoharlal, 1981), p 223.

24. Eliade, *Images and Symbols*, pp. 201–8.

25. *Significations: Signs, Symbols and Images in the Interpretation of Religion*, (Philadelphia: Fortress Press, 1986), p. 47.

26. *The Symbolism of Evil*, (Boston: Beacon Press, 1969), pp. 10–11

27. See his *Myth of the Eternal Return*, Bollingen Series 46 (Princeton: Princeton University Press, 1974), chap. 4.

28. In fairness, Gonda seems uneasy with the verb "symbolize" with which objects are said to be related to abstract ideas such as fertility.

29. Jan Gonda, *Vedic Ritual* (Leiden: E. J. Brill, 1980), p. 123.

30. J. J. Meyer, *Trilogie altindischer Machte und Feste der Vegetation* (Zurich: Max Niehaus, 1937), 1:233.

31. George Lakoff, *Women, Fire, and Dangerous Things* (Chicago: University of Chicago Press, 1987), p. 9.

32. Ibid., p. 37; see also W. Faulkner on Wallace Steven's "Thirteen Ways of Looking at a Blackbird," in Frederick L. Gwynn and Joseph Blotner, eds., *Faulkner in the University* (Charlottesville: University of Virginia Press, 1959), pp. 273–74

33. For another critique of rational religious categories, see John Krois, *Cassirer, Symbolic Forms and History* (New Haven: Yale University Press, 1987), pp. 45–50; for an alternative system of classification, see subsequent discussion.

34. Eliade, *Images and Symbols*, p. 135.

35. *Chāndogya Upaniṣad* 6.9.1–2.

36. I have intentionally avoided *imaginary* and *phenomenal* due to complicating connotations associated with each. The imagistic is roughly equivalent to *bildlich* and *pratyakṣa*.

37. See, for instance, Wagner, *Symbols.*

38. *Symbolism of Evil*, p. 25; see also R. Pettazzoni, *La Confessione dei Peccati*, vol. 1 (Bologna: Nicola Zanichelli, 1935).

39. Ricoeur, *Symbolism of Evil*, p. 27; cf. Wendy D. O' Flaherty, *Origins of Evil in Hindu Mythology* (Berkeley: University of California Press, 1976), p. 7

40. *Purity and Danger* (London: Routledge & Kegan Paul, 1979), esp. chap. 7.

41. O. Sacks, *The Man Who Mistook His Wife for a Hat*, (London: Picador, 1985), p. 46.

42. This is reminiscient of the purification of the subtle body (*sukṣma śarīra*) in Manu 5.108 and Yāj. 3.32. Vāyu, the wind god, is a great purifier, of course.

43. Jerome Kagan, *The Nature of the Child* (New York: Basic Books, 1984), pp. 206, 35; Kagan and the other cognitivists owe their "schemata" to Piaget. Cf. Rudolf Arnheim, *Visual Thinking* (Berkeley: University of California Press, 1969), and Jacqueline Goodnow, *Children Drawing* (Cambridge, Mass.: Harvard University Press, 1977). A more existential analysis of image schemata within contemporary cognitive sciences will be taken up shortly.

44. Meyer, *Trilogie*, 1:29.

45. See Siegfried Giedion's splendid analysis in *The Eternal Present*, Bollingen Series 35 (New York: Bollingen, 1962), 1:25

46. Edited and translated by George Payn Quackenbos (*Eight Sanskrit Poems of Mayura* [New York: AMS Press, 1965], pp. 72–79).

47. See subsequent discussion.

48. A. R. Luria, *The Man with a Shattered World* (New York: Basic Books, 1972), pp. 37–45; cf. J. Gerstmann, "Reine Taktile Agnosie," *Monatsschrift für Psychiatrie und Neurologie*, 44 (1918):329–42

49. But see R. Jackendoff for a critique of this position in *Consciousness and the Computational Mind* (Cambridge, Mass.: MIT Press, 1987).

50. *Bhagavadgītā* 15.1; on indexical logic, see chapter 6.

51. A. B. Keith, *Religion and Philosophy of the Vedas and Upanisads* (Cambridge, Mass.: Harvard University Press, 1925), pp. 351–52; H. Oldenberg, *Die Religion des Veda* (Berlin: Verlag von Wilhelm Hertz, 1894), p. 444; P. V. Kane, *History of Dharmaśāstra*, (Pune: BORI, 1974), 2.2:1244; S. A. Dange, *Vedic Concept of Field*, (Bombay: University of Bombay Press, 1971), pp. 37–39.

52. See for instance, *Pañcaviṁśa Brāhmaṇa* (PB), V.5.15, The ritual is described in numerous texts including *Taittirīya Saṃhitā* (TS) 7.5.9, *Śāṅkhāyana Śrautasūtra* (Śāṅkh. Ś.S.) 17, *Āpastamba Śrautasūtra* 24.2.18, and others.

53. Staal goes considerably farther afield. On the "Science of Religion" (*Religionswissenschaft*) he says: "Instead of developing a systematic method of analysis appropriate to its object, it fell prey to phenomenology, existentialism, hermeneutics and other warring factions." See "The Sound of Religion," *Numen* 33, no. 1 (1987):40.

54. If I read Victor Turner correctly, this cannot be done because objects can only act ritually when they connect the "known world" to an unknown and invisible realm. *The Ritual Process*, (Ithaca: Cornell University Press, 1969) p. 15. The temporal or narratival dimension, critical to understanding myths and ritual, is discussed in the next chapter.

55. The semiological term for the analysis of this level is *syntagmatic*. It is an appropriate contextual complement to the symbolic and paradigmatic (homological) modes of analysis. See, for instance, Roland Barthes, *Critical Essays* (Evanston, Ill.: Northwestern University Press, 1972) pp. 205–211.

56. Sexual interpretations prevail in this specific case, obviously (Dange, *Vedic Concept*, p. 38). The imagistic approach—not meant to replace the symbolic—looks for considerably more detailed and concrete explications however.

57. Keith, *Religion and Philosophy*, p. 351.

58. Ethnography pays closer attention to physical detail but its reductionism tends to be functional rather than metaphysical.

59. *Symbolism of Evil*, p. 16.

60. Husserl, *Ideas—General Introduction to Pure Phenomenology* (New York: Macmillan, 1931), p. 238.

61. Incidentally, according to Husserl, the ontological consciousness, that is, the judgment as to the existence or nonexistince of objects, pertains to higher levels of intentionalities than the perceptual—to syntheses of reason, which is a necessary structural form belonging to the transcendental ego. *Cartesian Meditations* (The Hague: M. Nijhoff, 1960), pp. 56–57.

62. For Merleau-Ponty, subjectivity and objectivity are only two moments of the same phenomenon. *Phenomenology of Perception* (London: Routledge & Kegan Paul, 1962), p. 304.

63. Quoted in Hubert Dreyfus, "Sinn and Intentional Object," in Robert C. Solomon, ed., *Phenomenology and Existentialism* (Lanham, M.: University Press of America, 1980), p. 203.

64. See Daniel, H. H. Ingalls, *Sanskrit Poetry* (Cambridge, Mass.: Harvard University Press, 1979)), pp. 28–31, and my subsequent discussion.

65. "Consciousness is being towards the thing through the intermediary of the body." Merleau-Ponty, *Phenomenology of Perception*, pp. 138–39; on Merleau-Ponty's dialectical *Lebenswelt*, see Scott Warren, *The Emergence of Dialectical Theory* (Chicago: University of Chicago Press, 1984), chap. 4.

66. See for instance Lakoff, Women, Fire, chap. 17.

67. See Jackendoff's critique of both embodiment and objectivism and his mid-level theory of consciousness in *Consciousness.*

68. P. Tillich, "The Religious Symbol," p. 77; in Eliade's language, the sacred "bursts open" the profane so it may reveal itself.

69. E. Minkowski, *Vers une cosmologie* (Paris: Fernand Aubier, 1936), pp. 101–3.

70. To echo René Daumal's learned Totochabo who states defiantly: "As for the unconscious, I might not speak *of* it, granted, but I speak *to* it. Let the unconscious answer me, if it can do so without expiring in the process." *A Night of Serious Drinking*, p. 15.

71. *Sanskrit Poetry*, p. 6.

72. R. Hertzberger, *Bhartṛhari and the Buddhists* (Dordrecht, Holland: D. Reidel, 1986), p. 19.

73. Ibid., pp. 16–17.

74. See *Sphoṭanirṇaya of Kaundabhaṭṭa*, ed. S. D. Joshi, introd. H. G. Coward (Poona: University of Poona Press, 1967), p. 67.

75. Harold Coward, *Sphoṭa Theory*, p. 86.

76. VP I.47.

77. A. Sankaran, *Some Aspects of Literary Criticism in Sanskrit* (Madras: University of Madras Press, 1929) p. 79.

78. Donna Wulff, "Religion in a New Mode," *Journal of the American Academy of Religion* 54, no. 4 (1986):675–81.

79. See Coward, *Sphoṭa Theory*, pp. 68–69; according to the Dhvani school, but not Bhartṛhari, this suggested level distinguishes poetry from ordinary language. For another splendid example, see ibid. p. 69.

80. S. N. Ghoshal Sastri, *Elements of Indian Aesthetics* (Varanasi: Chaukambha Orientalia, 1978), 1: chap. 1

81. The play has not survived but fragments, quoted by numerous critics, were collected in Raghavan, *Some Old Lost Rama Plays*, pp. 1–25.

82. *Dhvanyāloka*, 1.7–13.

83. Abhinavagupta (Locana) quoting Raivataka, translated by A. K. Warder, *Indian Kāvya Literature* (Delhi: Motilal Banarsidass, 1983), 4:138, from Ānandavardhana's version.

84. *Nāṭyaśāstra*, trans. Ghosh (Calcutta: Granthalaya Private, 1966–67), xvi.

85. The precise relationship is described by Abhinavagupta as combination

(*saṁyoga*), relation (*saṁbandha*), and concurrence (*aikāgrya*). See *Abhinavabharatī* I.10.

86. In the context of dance, see Frederique Marglin, "Refining the Body, Transformative Emotion in Ritual Dance," in Owen Lynch, ed., *Divine Passions: The Social Construction of Emotion in India* (Berkeley: University of California Press, 1990), pp. 220–23.

87. Part III, chap. 43, 1–39 (Kramrisch trans., pp. 59–62).

88. Doris Clark Chatham, "Rasa and Sculpture," in J. E. Van Lohuizen-De Leeuw, ed., *Studies in South Asian Culture* (Leiden: E. J. Brill, 1981), p. 22.

89. See Hieinrich R. Zimmer, *Artistic Form and Yoga in the Sacred Images of India* (Princeton: Princeton University Press, 1984) p. 11.

90. Ibid., p. 20.

91. In fact, he maintains that tradition itself (*āgama*) contains the seeds of insight that link it to the "own-being" (*svabhāva*) of things, that is, to Veda. VP 1.30–31.

92. On the androgynous qualities of milky trees, see Edith Turner, *The Spirit and the Drum* (Tuscon: University of Arizona Press, 1987), pp. 58–81.

93. See, for instance, Vasudev Vishnu Mirashi, ed., *Inscriptions of the Kalachuri-Chedi Era*, Corpus Inscriptorum Indicarum Vol. 4 (Ootacamund: Government Epigraphist, 1955), passim.

2

The Duration of Images in Time

If religion is anything at all, it is something that links the present moment to eternity. (W. C. Smith)

Professor Smith's observation may sound persuasively in our ears, but it is also deceptively simple. The weight of its considered judgment rests squarely on the relation between two levels of temporality—as though time itself were something we fully understood.

In the previous chapter we distinguished symbols and images without any reference to their temporal nature. It is appropriate now to observe that whereas symbols can be *about* time, only images exist *in* time. Symbols are nontemporal, systematic, and spatial representations of various aspects of reality. When symbols become subject to temporal contingencies, ongoing scrutiny and contemplation, or physical manipulation, they cease to be mere symbols and begin to function as images. Put differently, the subjective experience of time flow—duration—can only be articulated by means of images of various types. Symbolic expression can tell us a great deal about conceptions of time, but very little about the experience of duration. Consequently, if we take Smith's observation as a starting point for an inquiry on religion, we need to grasp the "present moment," in a nonsymbolic fashion. This is precisely what I have set out to do in this chapter. I shall begin by reviewing some of the problems that arise from the symbolic analysis of time in India, then proceed to explore a method for studying duration as temporal experience. The remainder of the chapter examines three levels of temporality in three separate contexts in India, and evaluates the practical methods for mediating among them.

Conceptions of Time in India

Indian conceptions of time, so it seems, are split by a profound ambiguity between the phenomenal and the Absolute. The imagination and conceptualization of temporality are taken as one key aspect of Hindu ontologies in which, one way or another, absolute unity stands over and against contingent plurality. These observations have been easy to ground in traditional sources: "There are, assuredly, two forms of Brahmā: Time and the Timeless. That which is prior to the sun is the Timeless [a-*kāla*], without parts [*a-kāla*]. But that which begins with the sun is Time, which has parts."[1] The ontological priority for Hindus, according to Western researchers, rests on the Absolute to such a degree that it has ostensibly resulted in "a kind of paralysis of the individual's sensitivity to time."[2] If time, within this context, is understood as an awareness of the passage and flow of specific events, or as the duration of emotional and mental states, Nakamura's observation is both dramatic and surprising. Less surprising is the often-repeated truism that Hindus have lacked a sense of history, that even so-called historical texts, including such texts as Kalhana's *Rājataraṅgiṇī*, are more poetic formulas than empirical records of unique events in time.[3]

And indeed, mythical chronologies seem to share nothing with our historical time. The Purāṇas, Smṛtis, and Vedas paint the history of the world with strokes of vast time spans, *yugas* or aeons, following one another in eternal cycles of creation and destruction.[4] The point, however, is not the immensity and power of time, which everyone recognizes, but the fact that such conceptions seem to fail in articulating the experience of contingent temporality over and against absolute timelessness (or eternity). The problem may be formulated in a variety of ways but it always stems from the failure of mythical time to bridge the apparent irreconcilability of time perception with the unity and atemporality of absolute Being. Pocock may have formulated the issue most precisely as the need to reconcile "an experience of change and duration set against a system of values that appears to deny it."[5] One obvious example for this paradox can be taken from a social system that rests on the eternal dharma, but which is undeniably subject to shifts in the status of castes. The manifest conflict between experienced contingency and systematic immutability inspires a variety of solutions. Again Pocock has set his parameters with precision: "The changes which duration inevitably brings about are recognized, but they are recognized only to be subordinated in a wider and changeless scheme."[6] Such a scheme may include the theory of the *kalivarjya*, a built-in safety valve in the *yuga* dharma conception, which places the changes of the degenerate Kali age within the context of a broader, more flexible, but still ultimately static conception of absolute norm (dharma).

The paradox remains unsolved, however, because while the problem is essentially experiential, the "solution" is thoroughly ideological. A far simpler —even radical—solution describes time and change as a delusion.[7] This is a lofty philosophical approach, which requires a drastic epistemological shift, and it results in the denial of the original existential problem.[8] More efficacious existentially are the mythical and ritual solutions to the problem of contingent temporality, which contain practical, though complex means for "arresting" the flow of time. These are implicit and hypothetical solutions detected by methodological approaches that often rest on Eliade's enormous influence. Consider the following two brief points concerning myth and ritual: "Par le simple fait qu'il écoute un mythe, l'homme oublie sa condition profane, sa 'situation historique.'"[9] But participation in the ritual event also combines the mythical element by taking place at the same time always ("in principio"); the ritual abolition of time takes place through the "imitation of archetypes and the repetition of paradigmatic gestures" taken from the mythical beginning.[10] This solution to the problem of history (contingent temporality) is not a complete denial of time but its incorporation into the apparent timelessness of myth. The irrationality and inexplicability of contingent duration are thus surpassed in favor of "sacred time."

The result of a theory that claims that time can be transcended in favor of a nontemporal structure is that even Kālī, the mythological embodiment of time as problem, loses much of her irrationality in our will to assimilate time into reason. It may be that we simply lack the means (deconstructive no doubt) to discuss the meaninglessness of a temporal force like Kālī. As a result we incorporate Kālī into a broader rationality in which "meaninglessness" is reduced to the other side of all positive values: "And as life must be affirmed, the most complete philosophies . . . must find some ultimate way of affirming that which has been rejected."[11]

The problems generated by the effort to reconcile temporality with the Absolute are not alleviated by focusing exclusively on experienced temporality and projecting it onto the cosmos. Within the empirical world too, the relation between systematic, chronological time and pure duration is highly problematic. Consider, for instance, the theories that analyze time as a phenomenon that is homologous with natural processes: "Within the living organism time moves rhythmically. Breathing, pulsating, alternating like day and night, the vital breath is the microcosmic homology to cosmic time."[12] Everywhere one sees evidence for this "homology" in the processes of nature, including sunrises, seasons, and so forth.[13] However, the homologies, paradigms, and symbolic relations by which cosmic processes are said to be related to natural human rhythms only confuse the issue.[14] For conscious awareness the cycles of breathing and the movements of the sun are both objective conditions of a physical world; they differ only in degree of subjectivity. One needs instead to look at the duration of conscious states, as Bergson or even Augustine conceives them, which underlie all aspects of reality passing before our eyes. Moreover, it is unclear, to say the least, how the objective and subjective conditions of their lives affect Indians' sense of time. No evidence has been marshaled anywhere to show that Hindus actually experience time cyclically.[15] We need only recall that the Hindus also spoke about the arrowlike quality of time, which is explicated so well in Kramrisch's interpretation of the Śiva myth.[16] The arrow of time is the linear, unidirectional progression of yesterday-today-tomorrow given to consciousness in daily experience. Does the daily march of time give any evidence of the vast cosmic cycles that Hindu cosmology describes? The hermeneutic assumption that the two levels of experience are homologically related places an enormous burden on a function of the imagination that we scarcely understand.

In the space of this limited review two problems emerged, one substantive, the other stealthily methodological. The first problem concerns the precise relation of the experience of time and the great chronological theories in India. This relation remains unclear and problematic, perhaps because scholarly interpretations have tended to focus on the great temporal conceptions and ignored the more subjective images of time in India. But the problem runs deeper because the chronological orientation of scholarship points to a profound need for operating on the basis of a systematic—that is, spatial—understanding of time. This has produced a rationality that suffers from a huge blind spot to the fact that every traditional solution to the problem of time also exists in time. As we shall see, every ritual in which time is said to be abolished possesses an irreducible existential duration to which both implements and participants are subject, and which can never be transcended. When Augustine made his famous observation about time ("when I wish to explain time, I do not know it"), his point was not the ineffability of time but the atemporal nature of reflection and the failure of rationality to seize the passage of time.

Our agenda, then, contains an interrelated focus on substance and method: what are the images of time in India and how can we explicate these without reducing them to nontemporal spatialized systems? We must begin, as usual, with an exposition of method.

Temporal Images—Method

The irrationality and nonsystematic nature of time is minimized by the Aristotelian view of time as "the measure of motion according to the before and after."[17] Such a view implies an ontological reduction of temporality to the circular motion of heavenly bodies or, in other words, the reduction of time to space.[18] This "clock maker's time" is said to be experienced as a succession or flow of "identifiable nows which follow one after the other. The future and past are viewed strictly as the coming to be or passing away of nows for action."[19] Time, accordingly, is regarded as an objective measure of motion in space, a "background" or context in which life evolves. This type of spatialization lies behind the absolute detemporalization of Being, and its contrast with becoming. According to Heidegger, underlying Kant's entire opus was a colossal ignorance of the truly temporal nature of Being itself.[20] However, the problem is more general and more thoroughly epistemological; it involves the externality and nonintentionality of all objectivist analyses of time.

Existentialist analyses of time have recognized the fact that temporality cannot be rationalized. Time simply escapes every system that tries to assimilate it. In Kierkegaard's words, "time cannot find a place in pure thought."[21] Time, in fact, disrupts every effort to establish a system, because conceptual systems, as defined by Saussure, are essentially "synchronic." But if thought is incapable of siezing the temporality of becoming, then the latter must seem (to thought) as irrational. In its pure temporality, becoming appears absolutely dynamic, primitive, and almost mystical: "With its waves it covers over all that we might be tempted to set over against it. It knows neither subjects nor objects. It has neither distinct parts, nor direction, nor beginning, nor end. It is neither reversible nor irreversible . . . It becomes chaotic, And yet, it is quite close to us, so close that it constitutes the very basis of our life."[22] A philosophy of time is thus no longer possible, nor is it necessary in order to "see" images in time. Once we recognize that human expression, in India as elsewhere, is not only about time (when it is) but always *in* time, then it becomes imperative to develop a hermeneutic that focuses not only on conceptions and measurements of time (e.g., chronologies), but on the essential temporality of expressivity itself.

Despite this irrationality, temporal existence possesses a coherent structure, and a forward projecting—rather than haphazard—direction. This is the dynamic structure on which philosophers such as Heidegger and Bergson focused phenomenologically. For instance, the essential temporal unity of Heidegger's Dasein is equivalent to Bergson's duration (*durée*) in which we experience the passage of time as the overlapping, or interpenetration, of mental states: duration is "the form which the succession of our conscious states assumes when our ego lets itself live, when it refrains from separating its present state from its former states."[23]

If becoming contains a consciousness of unilinear time as well, this is due to the essential futuricity of human existence. As noted, this futuricity is implied in the structure of Heidegger's Dasein, which projects forward in the "horizon-opening act of existence."[24] Bergson and Minkowski call this the *élan vital*, which "creates the future before us."[25] Even pure duration, then, has a "fixed point" or a point of reference that gives the waves in Minkowski's metaphor (for instance) a given direction—a spatial element.

Rhythms in Space and Time

It is significant, clearly, that the existentialist and phenomenological interpretations of temporality or becoming recognize the dialectical relation of space and time, even in the very origin of consciousness and the emerging sense of time.[26] They seem fully cognizant of the physicist's dictum that space and time can no longer be discussed separately.[27] Pure time and pure space alike can never be objects of experience: "The phenomena of the spatiotemporal order are staggered in our life between becoming and being, between time and space."[28] According to J. T. Fraser, our experience of time includes both being and becoming, permanence and change.[29] Temporality, more specifically, is the conflict generated in our awareness between the lawlike, orological spatialized time and the generative time of the existentialists. And indeed, research indicates that temporality takes its origins in rhythmicity or the consciousness of rhythms.[30]

Absolute temporality, or pure change is meaningless and in fact nonexistent to our consciousness: "Schism is meaningless without reference to some prior condition: the absolutely new is simply unintelligible even as novelty." This is due to the fact that "novelty of itself implies the existence of what is not novel, a past."[31] The relation between the old, or permanent, and the new, or changing, is resonant. The experience of duration consists of rhythms, which, at the most elementary level, are the reflexivity at the root of consciousness itself. It is the Hegelian self-consciousness that finds its source in the dialectic of the consciousness of other.[32] Piaget would certainly agree with the basic observation that the temporal horizon develops in relation to the development of the child's conception of self and the child's increasing ability to objectify its dialectical relation with a surrounding world.[33]

The experience of time (duration) is thus neither pure change nor absolute permanence. It is an ongoing rhythmic oscillation—a "conflict"—between the two. This rhythmicity or periodicity is so basic that it is known even to animals. Interestingly, if time is the experience of conflict between permanence and change, timelessness need not be the elimination of change, it can also be the elimination of permanence. Dance, for instance, produces the "experience of timelessness, a radical decrease in existential tension that accompanies the increased emphasis on becoming (through continuous rhythmic change) and decreased emphasis on permanence."[34]

All this indicates that we should not look for the Indian's experience of time in his theoretical (even mythological) statements *about* time. Instead we need to look at fundamental rhythms that are expressed *in* time, rhythms between change and permanence, or even between experience and ideas.

If the discussion, up to this point, has created the impression that temporal rhythms are universal, it is critical to emphasize that they contain a strong cultural component: "A person moves in the rhythms and timing of his or her culture, and this rhythm is in the whole body."[35] The relation of basic rhythms and culture works in both directions: perception, conceptualization, and communication within a given cultural context depend no less on synchronized natural rhythms than they do on verbal exchange.[36] This is a radical point, one that is not easy to accept, but is strongly suggested by recent research. It is a critical point for us because it demonstrates that nonsymbolic behavior is a major cultural force. The explicit consequences are significant: "Once we recognize that participants regularly, continually and generally act in synchrony, we could no longer entertain an action-reaction mode or any simpler Aristotelianism."[37]

In the other direction, the fixed, spatial poles of temporal rhythms is culturally conditioned: they may be a particular symbol, concrete spaces, or even the definition of "person" in relation to which change is measured. If fundamental rhythms are somehow culturally conditioned, and are also determinative with respect to the consciousness of time, two questions remain. What precisely are the two poles of the temporal dialectic (change and permanence) in India? What did the Indians experience (not conceptualized!) as fixed and what as fluctuating? The search for these poles occupies the remainder of this chapter and will take place in three distinct contexts: a section of the *Rāmāyaṇa*, a Vedic ritual, and music. Each of these contexts expresses Indian images in time and helps us articulate, more or less systematically, the manner in which ancient Indians may have experienced the passage of time.

Time in the Rāmāyaṇa

In the following section I shall describe the conception and experience of temporality in the *Rāmāyaṇa*. Due to the enormity of the context I have isolated the narrative of Sītā's abduction in the Āraṇyakāṇḍa, *sargas* 40–49, and, to a lesser extent, 52, 56–58. Unquestionably, this is one of the central moments in the entire epic, the second or third most dramatic turning point in the narrative. The passage selected may reveal some of the methods by means of which time is described, felt, manipulated, and pushed forward along with the plot.

The events of these chapters unfold as Rāvaṇa lays out his plans to a reluctant Mārīca. Mārīca eventually obeys Rāvaṇa's instructions and uses his unique skills to turn himself into a beautiful golden deer, which is spotted by Sītā. Ignoring Lakṣmaṇa's warnings, Sītā persuades Rāma to go after the deer, while Lakṣmaṇa stays behind to protect her. Mārīca is then killed by Rāma, but with his dying breath he calls out to Lakṣmaṇa, imitating Rāma's voice. Again Sītā ignores Lakṣmaṇa's warning and bullies the young brother into seeking out Rāma. Left in Rāma's hermitage with no protection, Sītā becomes easy game for Rāvaṇa, who comes and takes her away.

The story reveals at least three levels of temporality, which may typify all literature that originates in an oral, bardic tradition.[38] These may be termed theoretical (chronological) time, plot or narrative time, and performative time. The first consists of explicit chronological statements, which are the author's reference to an "objective" time in which the heroic events were supposed to have taken place. The second refers to a complex manipulation of narrative techniques in order to move the plot forward, and fashion a literary duration. The third (performative time) is related to the oral character of the epic and describes the duration in which the audience experiences the text. I shall discuss these three levels in order and conclude with some reflections on their mutual effects.

Theoretical Time

According to tradition, the events told in the *Rāmāyaṇa* took place in the Tretayuga. The frame story of the Bālākāṇḍa reports that the epic was "once" told by Nārada to Vālmīki. However, the events of Rāma's life are told in a more explicit and detailed chronological context.[39] Rāma, along with his brothers, was born on the month of Caitra (in the spring), on the waxing fortnight (*śuklapakṣa*), on the ninth day after the new moon. Even astrological facts are detailed: five planets were auspicious, *lagna* was Kaskataka, and the planet Guru was rising with the moon.

Our selected passage in the Āraṇyakāṇḍa also contains a multitude of chronological facts. Sītā, for instance (47.4–15), reveals to Rāvaṇa that she had lived with Rāma for twelve years after their marriage. The crisis leading to their exile took place on the thirteenth year. Rāma was then twenty-five years old, while she was eighteen. According to Kaikeyī's demands, the exile was to last fourteen years. Several chapters earlier, the narrator informed us that ten years had gone by between the time Rāma had entered the Daṇḍaka forest until he met the *ṛṣi* Agastya. As the narrative in the Daṇḍaka forest progresses, several narrative indications provide information about the passage of chronological time. For instance, the events of the abduction took place shortly after the month of Hemanta, at which time (winter) the rivers were very cold for bathing.

As Brockington notes, numerous expressions, often formulaic, are used in the epic to convey chronology in an explicit and straightforward fashion.[40] These refer to days, fortnights, months, seasons, and years. Some are more general and just indicate a "long time" (e.g., *atha dīrghasya kālasya*). However, these expressions have little to do with the narrative itself. In the abduction story, if the chronology were not explicitly stated, it would not be known, let alone felt, even by the heroes. In sum, chronological time does not play any role in the progression of human events within the epic. It is passive time, a mere background to life.

Narrative Time

At the outset of this section, it is important to illucidate two points: since I shall claim that the three levels of temporality are distinct and autonomous, I must distinguish the chronologcial time described in the narrative (but depicted as background to the events) from the time of the narrative. Having done this, it becomes necessary to explain the meaning and structure of narrative time.

The distinction within a text between chronological time and narrative time is equivalent to the distinction, discussed earlier, between clock time (spatialized time) and duration. The story presents itself as being about some reality, an ancient affair that took place "once upon a time" (e.g., Tretayuga) and lasted for many years. This time flows in a fixed progressive manner "behind" the narrative, so to speak. In contrast, the events depicted take place within a distinct temporality. The fourteen years of exile may seem like two years or one hundred years. They may flow forward or backward. They may take place in a succession of present moments (as told by the narrator) or as a subjective, temporally distorted recollection of events already passed. Narrative time has little to do with chronological time because it can be as subjective, irrational, and changing as our own nonspatial experience of time, all depending on the author's intentions and skills.[41] Narrative time, in other words, can never be separated from the flow of narrated events: it is the rhythmic movement—external or internal—of characters from one state to another. A splendid analysis of narrative time techniques in *kāvya* can be found in a work by A. V. Rajwade on the *Uttara-Rāmacarita*.[42] The *Rāmāyaṇa* is not as sophisticated as the much later work, but it needs to come to grips with the temporal issue of change and novelty. Narrative time, that is, progression of time through the movements of events, depends on the interplay of fixed or known events with novel ones. A new situation must always follow the stasis of an earlier condition if the plot is to take place in a recognizable temporal context. But novelty is a highly problematic issue for the epic.

The *Rāmāyaṇa* is a story of foretold eventualities. The entire epic is previewed by Nārada in the Bālākāṇḍa (a later interpolation). The audience knows precisely not only how the tale will end but how it must end. Even the characters are aware of the inexorable predictability of their actions on the stage, so to speak. The plot, the nonrandom progression of events, must take place despite the static force of absolute prescience. Consequently, the temporal movement of events is made possible by the conflicting play of truth and illusion. If all the characters recognized the truth, as the narrator presents it, nothing would happen. Illusion (*māyā*) acts as the predominant narrative force in the story of Sītā's abduction. Here are a few examples.

As Mārīca paraded in front of Rāma's hermitage in order to lure Rāma away, Lakṣmaṇa observed: "I believe that the deer is the Rākṣasa Mārca, who is knowledgeable in the art of illusion [*māyāvidya*] and took on the form of a deer [*mṛgarūpa*]" (43.5–8). Sītā was entirely fooled by this deception (*chadman*) and insisted that Rāma capture or at least kill the deer. At a major turning point in the plot, an element of novelty and surprise (essential for temporality) must be injected into the narrative. At the sight of the deer, Sītā rejoiced: "I have never seen another deer to match this one (in beauty)" (43.13a). It is inconceivable that she would have been motivated to act in any manner had she known what Lakṣmaṇa knew. Meanwhile, Rāma suffered from the same allurement [*lobha*] and was thoroughly surprised by the novelty or uniqueness of the deer "*mano vismaya āgatam*" (43.23, 29), despite his brother's prescience.

Similarly, as Mārīca lay dying he cried for help, imitating Rāma's voice (45.1). Once again, Lakṣmaṇa recognized the deception and assured Sītā that the voice was no more real than a Gandharva city (45.17). Sītā ignored Lakṣmaṇa's advice, forced him to leave the hermitage, and pushed the plot to another climax.[43] The creation of visual and auditory deception, by means of disguise and magical transformations, takes the part of a narrative device such as character flaw in Western tragedies. This is not to say that character plays no role. As R. Goldman has noted, the plot is complicated and furthered by "a series of closely associated but clearly differentiated composite character sets."[44] In other words what one character cannot achieve by inner ambivalence, a composite set can achieve by external conflict. As we saw, recognition of the truth by one character (Lakṣmaṇa) neutralizes the very effect of novelty. Surprise and deception are then replaced by a reluctance to acknowledge the truth, which introduces the effect of another device—the interplay of dharma and *adharma*.

When Sītā heard Mārīca call with Rāma's voice, she entered into a verbal contest with Lakṣmaṇa, not only on the identity of the voice but on dharma itself. The narrator, and the audience, identify Lakṣmaṇa's position with dharma: he remains kind, patient, loyal, and truthful throughout the argument. Meanwhile Sītā's petulant attacks on his integrity are characterized as verbally abusive (*paruṣaṁ vākyaṁ*), a term used in the Dharmaśāstras for verbal abuse. Sītā's offensiveness is sharpened by drawing attention to her feminine nature, which is almost intrinsically adharmic (*vimukta dharma*) (45.30). But finally, when Lakṣmaṇa abandoned Sītā under the pressure of her relentless attack, he too failed to perform his own dharma, as Rāma correctly pointed out to him later (45.59).[45] *Adharma* introduces uncertainty into the stasis of events but moves the characters forward haltingly, even lurchingly, because dharma is never completely abandoned or forgotten. Dharma serves as a proximate backdrop, a contrast, to the dynamic force of *adharma*. As it is "dragged along" with *adharma*, dharma acts again and again as a counternovelty structural element that operates through the machinery of karma. Whenever dharma is violated in the story, the results are always predictable, and never fail to materialize (e.g., 41.2, 41.16, 42.2, 45.32, 48, 49). The time of the narrative is structured as a rhythmic progression between the fixity of dharma and the consequences of *adharma*. The duration that characters experience is measured by the interplay of the act and its consequence.

A number of less significant devices are used in the temporal construction of the narrative. The future, for instance, is repeatedly foretold, either by the narrator or by one of the characters. In 40.1 Mārīca predicts Rāvaṇa's downfall. Several *ślokas* later (19–22) Rāvaṇa accurately predicts the details of his plans to distract Rāma and the immediate results. The plan is not just Rāvaṇa's personal fantasy, but the story's way of getting ahead of itself. Rāma himself later describes with precision the slaying of the deer (43.49–50). In another example the narrator predicts that Rāvaṇa, by kidnapping Sītā, will bring about his own destruction (46.37). When the future is not explicitly foretold, it is hinted at (with equal accuracy) by omens. Omens, it is well known, are an extremely common theme in Indian literature and *kāvya* (it virtually runs rampant in the *Bhaṭṭikāvyam*).[46] In the present example at least two omens are given (57.1–3): the voices of jackals and the throbbing of Rāma's left eye. These draw Rāma's attention after he kills Mārīca and senses that something is somehow very wrong. The narrative effect of predicting or suggesting the future is static, not dynamic. It presents a fixed point toward which events are now inexorably pointed, but it provides no reason why the characters should hurtle themselves forward in the direction of known eventualities.[47] Foretelling the future thus surprisingly serves to counteract the uncertainty of a present act (or motive) and provides the static pole of the temporal dialectic.

Recounting past events (personal and paradigmatic) serves a similar and complementary purpose. Three examples for the use of this device stand out. The first two are related. When Rāvaṇa promised Mārīca that he would destroy Rāma (40.5), he emphasized the fact—by now all too well-known—that the fool left his kingdom at the instigation of a woman (*strīvākya*). This past event has become a predicate of Rāma and thus takes on an ominous predictive power, because it is Rāma's vulnerability to *strīvākya* that will send him after Mārīca. Further on (47.3) Sītā recounts to Rāvaṇa, now disguised as a mendicant (Rāma and Lakṣmaṇa are away), the essential facts of her life. The emphasis in her brief recollection is on Kaikeyī's entire plot to drive Rāma to the forest. Sītā placed the onus squarely on Daśaratha's subjugation to passion, which was induced by a woman. The reader or listener cannot fail to recall that just a short time earlier Sītā had accused Lakṣmaṇa of desiring her, and of abandoning his own brother in order to fulfill his desires. While I doubt that the author intended to produce explicit irony, the ironic effect is inescapable. Sītā's recollection places her within a clear sequence in which women are regarded as a major motivating force, in a negative (*adharmic*) sense. The (unintentional) irony is generated by Sītā's absolute blindness to her own role in that chain of events.

The third recollection of past is not personal. Before setting out to hunt the deer (43.41–44), while acknowledging that it might be Mārīca, Rāma tells the story of Agastya, who ate and digested Vātāpi. Rāma recalls the story as a paradigm for his own action, but again, the effect is ironic because his motive differs completely from that of Agastya, and he remains oblivious to the consequences of his contemplated act. The episode explains, at the very least, Rāma's false expectations regarding the result of the hunt. Meanwhile, the narrator has already informed his audience that Rāvaṇa's plan merely calls for luring Rāma away from Sītā. Once Rāma has gone on the hunt, he has already lost, regardless of whether he kills the deer.

The final two temporal devices sit squarely on the boundary between narrative time and performative time. They can serve as a transition to that final topic. I am referring to techniques for compressing and stretching narrative time. While usually the narrative proceeds at a leisurely pace, occasionally an action is greatly speeded up as on the occasion of Rāvaṇa's trip with Mārīca from Laṅkā to the Daṇḍaka forest (42.10–11). The effect of speed is achieved by stringing plural accusatives describing the towns, forests, and countries that the two behold from Rāvaṇa's flying chariot (*paśyantau pattanāni vanāni ca, girim ca . . . rāṣṭrāni nagarāni ca*). The trip is a unilinear movement in space and covers half a continent in one simple sentence. An opposite effect—the stretching of time—is attained when the movement is not linear but haphazard, and a tremendous amount of activity (described in numerous redundant verses) is compressed into a given amount of time. This happens during Rāma's hunt of Mārīca (44.1–17), who at one moment appears in one place only to disappear and then reappear in another place, and so on. It is not clear how long the hunt lasts in clock time, but the narrative effect stretches its duration to a maximum, thereby increasing the sense of uneasy restiveness Sītā must have felt while waiting for Rāma.

The straightforward *śloka* of 42.10–11 and the busy *ślokas* of 44.1–17 with their repetitions, redundancies, and pedantic details, are both related to the manner by which the text is performed. As narrative devices, they effect the pace of events; as performative devices, they effect the tempo of the telling, which directly relates to the listeners' time.

Performative Time

It is a well-established fact that the *Rāmāyaṇa*, as an oral epic, was meant to display the musical qualities of its performed recitation, no less—perhaps more—than its dramatic narrative.[48] As we sit and read a fixed text in the privacy of our studies, we lose the adventure of a uniquely created perfomance in favor of a leisurely and meandering narrative.[49] The musicality of oral performance, its tone, pitch, intonation, tempo, rhythm, repetitions, omissions, embellishments, and other qualities, produced a profound effect on the temporal dimension of the performed epic. For instance, an accelerating speed of recitation, with a crescending pitch, not only increases dramatic effect and mood but speeds up the sense of time's passage. This point is so important that the last part of this chapter will be devoted to musical time in India. For the present moment I am only drawing attention to the fact that the passage under discussion retains several elements of oral poetry that have a direct bearing on the "pace" or temporality of the performed epic. I shall cite two examples of the use of repetition and of formulaic expressions, designed for metrical convenience and to facilitate the singer's memory. Both are taken from sarga 42 in which Rāma hunts down Mārīca. The first example is the repetition of the word *roamed about* describing Mārīca's predominant activity as a deer. The verb *vicāra* occurs in 42.14, 22, 24, 25, and 35. Similarly, the expression "he (Mārīca) assumed the form of a deer" is repeated with extreme redundancy in a number of variations in 42.14, 15, 19, 20, 22, and 27 (*mṛga bhūtvā*; *rūpam . . . samāsthāya*; *rūpam kṛtva*; *mṛgatam gata*, etc.). These two examples (there are far too many to list) merely reinforce the need to add an entirely distinct mode of analysis to the temporality of the *Rāmāyaṇa* "text."[50] Like every myth or epic that is told or sung, the *Rāmāyaṇa* possesses an irreducible nonliterary duration that does not derive from the text's theoretical chronology or from its narrative. The text can be experienced as part of an empirical temporality of the listener and, like a song, it can only be heard in actual time.

In sum, the brief portion of the *Rāmāyaṇa* I have discussed displays three distinct and autonomous levels of temporality: theoretical, narrative, and performative. Although it is intuitively clear that at least the latter two can resonate together (for instance, a heroic subject is accompanied by a specified meter and rhythm), we must defer any discussion of this point until we have studied musical time. I may state now, as preview, that since musical time contains a high degree of "freedom" (through improvisation, for instance), the experienced duration of the epic is also surprisingly free, and narrative temporality is hypothetically flexible and independent of the text's chronological rigidity.

Time in the Mahāvrata Ritual

The *Rāmāyaṇa*, as we have seen, and other performed texts, contain three distinct levels of temporality. Rituals, in contrast, possess only two levels: the separation between narrative and performative time does not apply here. The "narrative" of a ritual is contained in its performance and its performative duration. On the other hand, the temporal manipulations and the general characteristics of the ritual performative time are far more complex than the recitative time of a performed text. The Mahāvrata ritual within the year-long (Gavāmayana) Sattra sacrifice demonstrates the distinction between the two levels of time (theoretical and performative) very clearly because the ritual is itself about time. The "narrative" (action-oriented) features of the ritual, in sequence, and beginning about midway through the day's activities, are as follows.[51]

a. A wooden lute (*vīṇā*) is strung with one hundred strings of Muñjā or Darbha grass, in order to be played by the Udgātṛ. The instrument's resonance box is covered with the skin of a red ox (hair outside) and has ten holes, each with ten strings stretched above it (PB 5.6.12–13, JB 2.45.418; TS 7.5.9.2).

b. As the *stotra* chanting proceeds with the accompaniment of the lute, the Udgātṛ mounts a throne made of Udumbara. The mounting and dismounting are timed precisely to coincide with the *stotriyas*—he gets off at the precise ending of the last verse (PB 5.5).

c. The Hotṛ priest climbs aboard a swing, which had been carefully crafted for this occasion out of a fig tree and Muñjā grass (for the ropes)(Śāṅkh. S. S. 18.1–3; PB 5.5).

d. The Adhvaryu stands on a board of Udumbara wood (according to Śāṅkh. S. S. on drums) covered by a bundle of Muñjā or Kuśa grass. There he makes the responses (*pratigṛṇāti*) to the chants.

e. Meanwhile, a Brahmin praiser (*abhigara*) and a Śūdra reviler (*apagara*) alternate praise and abuse toward the participants (PB 5.5.13)

f. An Ārya and a Śūdra fight a staged battle, west of the Agnidhra, for the possession of a white circular hide, and the Ārya wins it (PB 5.5.14–17; ŚB 16.7.28–32).

g. At this point sexual intercourse between a man and a woman, who are not part of the sacrifice, takes place in a private shed south of the Mārjālīya (Kāt. 13.3.9).

h. The king, or someone representing him, mounts a horse-drawn chariot armed with a bow and three arrows. North of the Agnidhra shed two posts are erected with a hide stretched between them. As he rides around the posts, the charioteer must shoot the arrows to pierce the hide but not fly through it: The arrows must remain clinging to the hide. (Śāṅkh. 18.5.1–7; *Drāhyāyaṇa Śrautasūtra* [Drāhy.] 10.2.13).

i. Numerous wooden drums are beaten all around the Mahāvedi. At the same time an earth drum is prepared behind the Agnidhra shed: it is made of a large hole in the ground, which is half inside half outside the Mahāvedi. The hole is covered with oxhide, hairy side facing up, and is beaten along with the wooden drums (PB 5.5.18–19; TS 7.5.9.3; AP. S. S. 21.18.2–3). The drumming is accompanied by numerous voices making noise (*sarva vaco vadanti*, TS 7.5.9.3).

j. Meanwhile, several servants of the king dressed in military gear march around the sacrificial ground, apparently in a clockwise direction beginning in the east (PB V.5.21; Kāt. 34.5: 39.15).

k. The priests then begin to chant the primary verses of the ritual—the Mahāvrata laud, by means of which the body (head, wings, tail, and trunk) of the sacrifice is constructed (PB 5.6.7).

l. As the priests chant, their wives provide musical accompaniment with flutes and guitars (*kāndavīṇa* and *piccharā*). (Drāhy. 11.2.6–8).

m. The food for the sacrificers is cooked in each of the participants' houses.

n. As the Udgātṛ grates on the *vīṇā* with a reed or piece of bamboo, several female slaves bearing water jars on their heads dance around the Mārjālīya seat, stomping with their right foot, and singing songs praising cows or chanting, "here is honey"(PB 5.6.15; AP.S.S. 21.19.17–20).

Despite the relative wealth of detail, the origin and meaning of this ritual are extremely vague. In fact, none of the texts actually describes such elements as (f). How long does the "battle" last? How detailed are the stage directions that are given to the combatants? Is the battle timed and paced by means of the chants? The numerous existing versions give evidence of significant variations even in the most explicit details of the ritual. No shortage of interpretations has been offered either, but P. V. Kane has voiced his deep exasperation with the numerous agricultural and naturalistic theories advanced by Western scholars.[52] As one follows the played out narrative of the ritual, it becomes clear that even if various agricultural or ecological elements were incorporated into Brahminical versions of the rite, the whole is structured toward a broader and more distinct goal. On the other hand, the indigenous Brahminical interpretations that explicitly accompany specific phases of the ritual are not very helpful or even mutually consistent. Nonetheless, it is safe to conclude that ideologically, the ritual is about Prajāpati's creation of Devas and Asuras, about the enthronement and feeding of Prajāpati, the conflict between the two groups of Prajāpati's children over the sun and the world, and the victory of the Devas.[53] Inasmuch as the present issue under consideration encompasses the two levels of time in the ritual, the ideological hermeneutic proposed by the Brahmins to explain the ritual object provides a sufficient contrast with the performative (concrete) temporality of the Mahāvrata.

The Mahāvrata, in the sequence described, parallels the Brahmanically fabricated narrative of Prajāpati's creation of the Devas and Asuras. According to the *Taittirīya Brāhmaṇa* (TB) (1.2.6.1, 7.5.9), Prajāpati became emptied by his act of creation. The gods decided to restore Prajāpati by offering him "mighty food" (hence "Mahāvrata"), so they brought him food that ripens during a full year.[54] For this reason the Mahāvrata is to be offered on the last day, save one, of the year long Sattra sacrifice: In the course of the year all food ripens and everything can be offered.[55] In a number of mythical versions the two types of creatures, which were equal but different, inherited and then fought over time. In one version they inherited the month (two half-moons), with the Devas winning the waxing moon.[56] In another version they received and contended for the sacrifice, which is Prajāpati himself in the form of the year.[57] The familiar battle between them over the sun is a battle over light and darkness, or the two parts of the day.[58] Victory in the battle for the sun meant conquest of time itself, in a cosmological (chronological) sense. When the Asuras were at first winning the battle over the entire earth, they divided the world into sections with oxhides.[59] The gods, however, tricked them by asking for a share that Viṣṇu, in the shape of a dwarf, could cover lying down. As he lay down (east to west), Viṣṇu covered the entire world and became identical with the cosmic altar or the sacrifice.[60]

In very broad terms this, then, is the theoretical story of the Mahāvrata. The Brahmins tirelessly supplied explicit connections between the stages of the ritual (stages a–n and others) and the cosmological narrative. For instance, in stage (b), the Udgātṛ "plays" the role of Prajāpati on his celestial throne as he chants the Rājana chant ("May I gain the kingship over them—my creatures") with which Prajāpati created his offsprings.[61] In (c) and (d) the Hotṛ and Adhvaryu are said to express the attainment of heaven (and earth?) and the sun. Stage (f) describes the exchange of merit that takes place between the Asuras and Devas in the myth. The demons take away the gods' bad merit and transfer their own good merit.[62] The battle over the circular skin in stage (g) is the battle for the sun.[63] This fabrication of ritual and mythical analogies, goes on throughout the remainder of the ritual. Some acts are particularly difficult, regardless of the Brahmins' ingenious simplifications. The earth drum corresponds to the "voice in the world," which the Devas won, but this is an imagist, not a symbolic, Brahminical interpretation (the drum does indeed produce that voice), and it hardly explains why the drum must be half inside and half outside the Mahāvedi.

Until I have discussed the spatialization of time in myth and ritual (in the following chapter), my focus here must remain limited to delineating the two distinct temporal narratives of the ritual. It is important to emphasize that the empirical (performative) time and the theoretical time are prima facia irreducible to one another: the whole point of the ritual is to mediate between the two. However, it is very difficult to see what "sacred time" means in a ritual context, when the ritual (performative) duration shares more with the contingency and subjectivity of daily time than with the mythical chronologies being depicted symbolically. The simple fact of the ritual participation does not explain the mediation that must take place between the two temporalities.[64] At the very least this is a question that deserves a certain amount of methodical consideration. Moreover, in the case of the Mahāvrata, as in many other rituals, no single theoretical time exists unless we reduce the polyvalence of the ritual symbols to a single object and purpose.

At any rate, Prajāpati's obtaining of kingship over his creatures, the battle over time, and the culminating feeding of Prajāpati and its attendant celebration (stage n) represent the duration of a paradigmatic mythical year. The ritual itself takes one day and consists of the numerous acts described earlier, as well as many not described. The succession, duration, tempo, rhythm, repetition, abbreviation, and prolongation of these actions are not fixed and are determined, disregarding numerous contingencies, by the musical qualities of the chants and songs that accompany every facet of the ritual.[65] In fact, the entire ritual, with its disparate parts, is strung together along the string of chants, beginning with the Mahāvrata Stotra, which accompanies the assembly of Prajāpati in the form of the altar. Explicit, though terse, musical directions are often provided by naming the *sāman* melody that accompanies a given verse.[66] Other musical elements, for instance the drumming and picking at the one-hundred-string *vīṇā*, are not accompanied by clear instructions. However, I should emphasize that even where the verse meter and *sāman* are known, a great deal of musical freedom remains. The range of speed and rhythm with which the musical chanting was executed and, with it, the freedom of dance movement and gesture were considerable. The temporal drumming structure known later as *tāla* was not specified, and even if it were, a considerable amount of improvisation, as we shall see in the following section, would have been expected. Now, whether or not its purpose was the regeneration of time (the year), the Mahāvrata seeks to produce a unity, or at least resonance, between temporal conception (theoretical time) and experience (performative time). Even the mechanistic Brahmin cannot repress the essential impetus of rituals to place participants within an extraordinary context. This granted, it is extremely difficult to see how the fixed and relatively structured mythical year is mediated experientially by the events of the day. The problem is not the quantitative difference between one day and one year, but the ontological gap between an idea about time and actual duration. It may be helpful to restate the accepted type of explanation which seeks the relation between the ritual and its objects in homologies, analogies, paradigms, or other mystifying terms.[67] However, because we have decided that symbols cannot stand on their own legs, we need a more phenomenological method for looking at the identity, or resonance, between the mythical and performative temporalities of the ritual. In order to do this properly we need, before explaining the mediated temporalities of the ritual, to proceed to a realm of expression that contains only one level of temporality—music.

Musical Time

We have seen that despite the fact that the *Rāmāyaṇa* is characterized by three distinct levels of temporality and the Mahāvrata only by two, both share a similar (musical) peformative time. In both cases, too, performative time consists of profoundly contingent developments, which render the flux of duration lifelike and different from the patterned theoretical time often ascribed to rituals. Consequently, it is significant that in all cases of performative temporality music plays a key role as mediator between experienced duration and theoretical time. I suggest that this is made possible by the monotemporal quality of music and its unique mode of symbolic signification.[68]

Music is a preponderantly nonrepresentational form of aesthetic expression. While artistic meaning in general tends to rest with the sensory percept itself (image), music provides the loftiest example of such a characteristic, which Langer has called the "unconsummated symbol."[69] Music possesses a "logical" form that resembles and evokes certain properties of our inner life—"patterns of motion and rest, of tension and release, of agreement and disagreement, preparation, fulfillment, excitation, sudden change, etc."[70] Music represents the morphology and rhythm of our feelings, not the objects or circumstances with which these feelings may be connected. Consequently it plays a role that verbal and plastic symbolism can never attain. This is particularly true in regards to musical rhythm, which exemplifies the only purely temporal art (dance is also spatial), and the highest aesthetic expression of the temporality of our successive emotional states.[71]

Indians too felt that music reflects and evokes certain moods without representing a conceptual reality. In temporal terms this manifested itself in two primary ways. First, *rāgas* were said to be appropriate to certain seasons or times of day—without exception. The *rāgas* were assigned to fixed times, possibly as a result of dramatic theory, and the moods (*rasa*) ascribed to certain times of day.[72] Consider for example, that "one who sings knowing the proper time remains happy. By singing *rāgas* at the wrong time one ill-treats them. Listening to them, one becomes impoverished and sees the length of one's life reduced."[73]

Second, a far more profound identification exists between musicality and the temporal structure of creation and cosmic life. *Nāda*, or sound which is the essence of music, is also the "life of all things, transformed in the shape of the world."[74] It is hardly surprising that a treatise on music (*Saṅgīta Ratnākara*) (SR) begins with a cosmogony when we consider that ideologically the two etymological components of *nāda* (na-da) are identified with the breath (*prāṇa*) and fire of the primordial Manas in creation.[75] In Daniélou's words, the sounds used in music are those whose mutual relationship forms "an image of the basic laws of the universe as represented by the unstruck sounds."[76] Music reproduces, in a direct and nonsymbolic manner, the rhythm of creation and life. This observation seems to apply, incidentally, to all traditional or primitive music: for instance, the sound of a beaten earth drum is ritually efficacious because it actually resonates with the internal sonority of the Earth.[77] This theme is particularly well developed by Robert Gottlieb in a manner that bears directly on rhythm and temporality. Gottlieb believes that the relation of theme and improvisation in *rāgas* and *tālas* symbolizes creation as a process of expansion (*vistara*—equivalent to the improvised phrase) in relation to the Eternal (theme) as described in *Ṛgveda* 10.149.2.[78]

Indian music draws heavily on the binary characteristic of sound and rhythm. Sound results from manifest or struck qualities (*āhatanāda*) and from unmanifest or unstruck qualities (*anāhatanāda*).[79] Musical time (rhythm, tempo) is itself binary at its origin, which is the syllable length (*yathākṣara*) of prosody.[80] However, the simple binary systems (alternating sound and silence, short and long sounds, etc.) were expanded at the higher levels of the *tāla* system, which was shaped by prefixing, infixing, and suffixing rhythmic (as well as melodic) patterns, along with gesture, cadence, accent, repetition, and other musical elements.[81] This brings us to another binary system in which both fixed melodic and rhythmic themes are counterpoised with improvisation (*ālāp*). Improvisation, as is well known, plays a far more important role in the music of India than it does in classical Western music. It may even be possible to say that improvisation is the heart of Indian traditions of classical music.[82] The rhythmic progression of a musical work is often made possible, and is certainly enriched, by the insertion of improvisational phrases (*vistara*) in a progression that is both melodic and rhythmic. The aesthetic pleasure from a unique performance—and every performance *is* unique—derives from the juxtaposition of "fixed, pre-composed, and traditional phrases with those which are altered, improvised, and non-traditional."[83] This may often manifest itself in a contest or interplay that takes place between the solo and rhythmic instruments.

It is also well known that Indians exhibit an unparalleled sense of rhythm and an innate ability to explore freely its possibilities in performance before landing finally, together, on the first beat of the next period.[84] It is rhythm above melody, in fact, that captures for Indians the essence of musicality and musical temporality, and thereby resonates with the pulse of the universe.[85] Similarly, "the arising, enduring, and disappearance of the three worlds come from rhythm (*tāla*). From the worm onward, all animals move by rhythm. All works in the world depend on rhythm. It is by rhythm that the sun and the planets move."[86] On the subjective side, rhythms and tempo are also expressive of human moods and emotional states.[87] So, if musical time is rhythmic time or, more precisely, tempo, patterns of melodic and rhythmic elements, and the interplay of theme and improvisation, then no culture possessed a richer feel for the complexities of duration that did India. Structure is enriched by freedom; progression is qualified by reversals, repetitions, and cycles; regularity is overwhelmed by acceleration and deceleration (e.g., types of syncopation), and so forth. If we take seriously the identification that Indians posited between music and world process, how subtle and rich must have been their sense of time!

But what about vocal music—music accompanied by "sacred" words—that characterizes rituals such as the Mahāvrata? Would we not expect the referential nature of its language to overwhelm the abstract signification of instrumental music? In fact, although the *tāla* system owes its origin to prosody, no printed version of a poetic text can ever give a clue to the rhythmic sophistication of its performance. The performative rhythmic patterns are linked with the sounds of words, time of day, and desired mood, and not with the sense of words.[88] The same is true not only of Dīkṣitar's kīrtanam's, but of Vedic *mantras* and their ritual chanting. Staal's position on the meaninglessness of *mantra* is familiar, and has not always been kindly received.[89] However, the evidence in favor of desemanticizing *mantras* and verbal expressions used in Vedic rituals is strong. The chant, when sung to a *Sāmaveda* melody, is often subjected to modification of syllables, repetitions, breaking up of words, insertions of apparently nonsensical words or syllables, and so forth. In different terms, "since the essence of Vedic chant is just the combination of words and music and its aim is precisely the establishment of contact with creative power—the effect upon the Unseen of tones sung in a certain way and at a certain pitch in relation to other tones is of great importance."[90] And in fact, meter is often considered the most important musical element, which relates directly to the mood of the stanza.[91] For this reason, above others, meter is commonly associated with a variety of deities.[92]

By now it has become self-evident that music (and dance, as we shall see) mediates, in a sense, between the objective temporality of the ritual and its contingent duration. If music embodies the temporal dialectic that underlies the cosmic process in general, then musical participation generates a definite and concrete level of cosmic identification (resonance). In addition, the rhythmic resonance is enhanced, of course, by the powerful moods that music evokes. Despite these, the musical duration of a one-day ritual cannot produce an absolute and concrete identification, in the imagination, between the duration of an actual day and that of the theoretical year. Consequently, we shall have to look at a subtler musical function in temporal mediation.

Like other mythical elements within the ritual, mythical (theoretical) time, is already spatialized by means of symbols. Ritual symbols act as representations in space of ideas about great cosmic moments such as creation, regeneration, and dissolution. For instance, Prajāpati as the mythical year may be symbolically represented by means of the carefully constructed altar: the year is thus formed brick by brick.[93] Or else, the white circular hide in the Mahāvrata, the Brahmins inform us, represents the sun, which is itself the concrete measure of chronological time. While it is important to note that pure duration can never be "contained" geometrically, or embodied in an object, the ritual nevertheless contains spatial (non-temporal) representations of cosmic time. This fact, in the final analysis, is of no consequence because the mediation (or resonance) between performative and theoretical temporalities can take place in any event. The so-called sacred (mediated) time of the ritual is not a complete transcendence of performative time in favor of theoretical time because, strictly speaking, the latter does not exist: it is only symbolically represented. What happens in the ritual is different: we must recall that performative time is itself formed by the tension (rhythm) between fixed elements (e.g., musical themes) and contingencies (e.g., improvisations). Mediated time, in contrast, is the duration produced by the tension (rhythm) that takes place between fixed elements derived from the spatial symbols of theoretical time and the free preformative elements of the ritual.[94] An experience of a distinct phenomenal temporality is produced by the dancing around the altar. It is a temporality marked by movement (creative, dynamic, "subtemporal"), in relation to a fixed point (static, "eternal," nontemporal). The resulting resonance focuses participants on a duration that is actually constituted by mythical and performative elements alike. Similarly, the carefully timed chanting of verses, synchronized with specific emphatic acts of the ritual participants (e.g., descending the swing) produces the same effect. It juxtaposes the flow of the music with marked stops that are indicated by a specific act. The swinging itself, incidentally, resembles the dance around the altar as movement in relation to a fixed point (*ekarūpa*).[95] The role of music in this mediation becomes clear. Music provides the tempos and rhythms by means of which symbolic themes can always be incorporated into existential duration, in a more or less consistent—but resonant—fashion. Music also provides the appropriate temporal context for dance, by means of which the spatial symbols of the ritual are seized in time, as the body moves across geometrical configurations in a specific temporal sequence and pace.[96]

To restate this important point: haphazard continual dance movement without any spatial point of reference (choreography and staging) or without any fixed temporal point of reference (rhythmic themes) is free "ecstatic" movement; it produces a sensation of timelessness. The choreographed and staged movements of the Mahāvrata vacillate between absolute freedom and absolute stasis to produce a distinct temporal sensation. This is the mediation between the time of the present and the time of the cosmos.

Conclusion

This chapter has shown that focusing on images as the data of religious awareness temporalizes texts and rituals in a variety of manners. No text, however sacred or didactic, is entirely extratemporal. Nor is any ritual entirely contingent and subject to duration. All religious acts exhibit the mediation that takes place between an idea or ideal and a sensory reality. Perhaps a better term than mediation is resonance, as the following chapter will show. For, in order to achieve a simultaneous and meaningful experience of the contingent ongoing present along with the symbolic ideal, a special sensitivity must be cultivated. In other words, the "mediation" I have discussed in this chapter does not take place "out" in the world of text or ritual, but in the embodied consciousness of the text's "reader" and the ritual participant. This refined sensitivity to mediation/resonance is sharpened by a corresponding resonance that takes place between the body—primarily the skin—and the imagination, during the act of purification. The following chapter will describe this process in detail. As we follow the phenomenon of purification, it will become clear that the Cartesian dualism of body and mind, physical and moral, and even signifier and signified must give way to a "phenomenal theater" in which the bather's sensitivity to a powerful environment begins to forge a different type of mind. This is the embodied imagination—or the "ecological Mind," if you prefer something trendy—where perceptions, self-perception, and symbolic ideas resonate together.

Notes

1. *Maitrāyaṇi Upaniṣad* 6.15. See also *Bṛhadāranyaka Upaniṣad* 3.6; *Katha Upaniṣad* 2.14; *Mahābhārata* 12.231.25, 12.267.4, 5; *Atharvaveda* 13.2.39.

2. H. Nakamura, "Time in Indian and Japanese Thought," in J. T. Fraser, ed., *The Voices of Time* (Amherst: University of Massachusetts, 1981), p. 80.

3. H. Oldenberg, *Aus dem alten Inden* (Berlin: Gebruder Paetel, 1910), p. 93.

4. See H. Zimmer, *Myths and Symbols in Indian Art and Civilization* (Princeton: Princeton University Press, 1946).

5. D. Pocock, "The Anthropology of Time Reckoning," *Contributions to Indian Sociology* 7 (1964):28.

6. Ibid, p. 27; Pocock lists a variety of solutions, of which only one will be mentioned here.

7. In the context of dharma, see Robert Lingat, "Time and the Dharma," in *Contributions to Indian Sociology* 6 (1962):14.

8. For this reason no philosophical theories of time will be discussed in this chapter.

9. "Le temps et l'éternité dans la pensée indienne," in *Eranos-Jahrbuch* (Zurich: Rhein-verlag, 1952), p. 220.

10. *Myth of the Eternal Return* (Princeton: Princeton University Press, 1959), p. 35. In contrast, Ninian Smart, "Beyond Eliade: The Future of Theory in Religion," *Numen* 25 (1978):179, altogether voids the distinction between mythical and historical time. I think Smart misses the force of the dilemma that confronts ritual participants, who are not just trying to forget one historical moment in favor of an earlier one. I shall return to this point later.

11. Mary Douglas, quoted in David Kinsley, *Hindu Goddesses* (Berkeley: University of California Press), p. 129.

12. Stella Kramrisch, *The Presence of Śiva* (Princeton: Princeton University Press, 1981), p. 267.

13. See A. Wayman, "Climactic Times in Indian Mythology and Religion," *History of Religions* 4, no. 2 (1965):295–96; for a critique of homologies, see previous chapter and chapter 7.

14. The most sophisticated recent analysis of the "correspondence" between cosmic principles and human conduct (sacrifice) is to be found in Brian K. Smith, *Reflections on Resemblance, Ritual, and Religion* (New York: Oxford University Press, 1989), pp. 69–81 ("The Metaphysics of Resemblance and Connection"): "The sacrifice, as the resembling dynamic counterform of the Cosmic One, represents Prajāpati/Puruṣa's essence," p. 69. Cf. R. Parpola, "On the Symbol Concept," in H. Biezais, ed., *Religious Symbols and Their Functions* (Stockholm: Almquist and Wiksell, 1979), pp. 142–57; see also Louis Renou, "Connexion en vedique, 'cause' en bouddhique," in *Dr. C. Kunhan Raja Presentation Volume* (Madras: Adyar Library, 1946), pp. 43–58, for the science of vedic resemblances.

15. At any rate we need to use caution with such spatial metaphors of time. See, for example, R. Pannikar, "Toward a Typology of Time and Temporality in the Ancient Indian Tradition," *Quarterly of Asian and Comparative Thought*, 24, no. 2(1974):162.

16. Kramrisch, *The Presence of Śiva*, (London: Oxford University Press, 1963), p. 268.

17. W. D. Ross, trans. and ed., *The Student's Oxford Aristotle*, 2:219b; Newton said similarly that "Absolute, true, and mathematical time, of itself, and from its own nature flows equably without regard to anything external." Quoted in A. Friedman and C. Donley, *Einstein as Myth and Muse*, (Cambridge: Cambridge University Press, 1989), p. 59.

18. J. T. Fraser, *Of Time, Passion, and Knowledge* (New York: George Braziller, 1975), p. 20.

19. Thomas Langer, *The Meaning of Heidegger*. (New York: Columbia University Press, 1959), p. 52.

20. Ibid., p. 72.

21. Quoted in Mark C. Taylor, *Deconstruction in Context* (Chicago: University of Chicago Press, 1986), p. 15.

22. E. Minkowski, *Lived Time: Phenomenological and Psychological Studies* (Evanston: Northwestern University Press, 1970), p. 18; in William James's words, clock time is "intellectualism's attempt to substitute static cuts for unity of experienced duration." *A Pluralistic Universe* (London: Longmans, Green, 1909), p. 254; Auden put it far better: "all our intuitions mock / The formal logic of the clock / All real perception, it would seem / Has shifting contours like a dream."("New Year Letter"). *Collected Langer Poems* (New York: Random House, 1965), pp. 77–130.

23. H. Bergson, *Time and Free Will* (New York: Macmillan, 1910), p. 100 According to Bergson, duration is forever incomplete "being always a *fait accomplissant* and never a *fait accompli*; in other words, it is a continuous emergence of novelty." Milic Capek, "Bergson and Modern Physics," in *Boston Studies in the Philosophy of Science VII* (New York: Humanities Press, 1971), p. 90. Augustine also recognizes this fluidity of duration when he describes temporality as "a present of things past, a present of things present. and a present of things future." *Confessions*, trans. R. Warner (New York: New American Library, 1963), p. 273.

24. Martin Heidegger, *Being and Time* (New York: Harper & Row, 1962), p. 337.

25. E. Minkowski, *Lived Time*, p. 38; Bergson, *Time and Free Will.*

26. "When I awoke at midnight, not knowing where I was, I could not be sure at first who I was; I had only the most rudimentary sense of existence, such as may lurk and flicker in the depths of an animal's consciousness; but then . . . memory . . . would come like a rope let down from heaven to draw me out of the abyss of not-being . . . In a flash I would traverse and surmount centuries of civilization." M. Proust, *Swann's Way* (*Remembrance of Things Past*), 1:5.

27. H. Minkowski, quoted in G. J. Whitrow, *The Natural Philosophy of Time* (London: Nelson, 1961), p. 124.

28. Minkowski, *Lived Time*, p. 23.

29. *Of Time, Passion*, pp. 45–46.

30. These are not rhythms in the "objective" world but the rhythmic movement of consciousness itself.

31. Frank Kermode, *The Sense of an Ending: Studies in the Theory of Fiction* (New York: Oxford University Press, 1966), p. 120.

32. See Mark C. Taylor, *Erring: A Postmodern A/Theology* (Chicago: University of Chicago Press, 1981), pp. 39–41, on Hegel's self-conscious reflexivity, which is thoroughly temporal. See also Howard Trivers: "Reflexivity is the primordial ground of time, as it is of the conscious self. The intrinsic rhythm of reflexivity engenders both time and self-consciousness." *The Rhythm of Being: A Study of Temporality* (New York: Philosophy Library, 1985), p. 141.

33. See Paul Fraisse, *The Psychology of Time* (New York: Harper & Row, 1963), p. 157; but time itself is related to velocity in Piaget's Aristotelian thinking. The rhythms of the fundamental reflexivity are grounded in perception and intuition, not in abstract conceptualization and deduction. Richard L. Gregory, *The Intelligent Eye*, New York: McGraw-Hill, 1970); and "The Problem of Temporal Order," pp. 141–49

34. Fraser, *Of Time, Passion*, p. 305, See the poignant and amusing quotation from A. Huxley's *Devils of Loudon* on the timelessness engendered by dance (pp. 305–306).

35. William Condon, "Cultural Microrhythms," in Martha Davis, ed., *Interaction Rhythms: Periodicity in Communicative Behavior* (New York: Human Sciences, 1982), p. 66.

36. Ibid., p. 67.

37. Albert Scheflen "Comments on the significance of interaction rhythms," in Davis, *Interaction Rhythms*, p. 19; cf. Taylor, *Erring*, p. 7.

38. Cf. Eliade, *The Sacred and the Profane* (New York: Harcourt, Brace, 1959), p. 72; Ninian Smart speaks of definite space, indefinite space, and transcendental space—and similarly time ("Beyond Eliade" p. 179). His distinction involves two quantitative temporalities, whereas here there are three qualitative types of temporality.

39. For an opposite view, see J. Brockington, *Righteous Rama* (New Delhi: Oxford University Press, 1984), p. 47.

40. Ibid., p. 42.

41. P. Ricouer, *Time and Narrative*. vol. 2 (Chicago: University of Chicago Press, 1985) chapt 3. Narrative progression may defy, as it occasionally does in the *Rāmāyaṇa*, a simple linear pattern. The latter seems to belong with Euclidean geometry "in which a line may be divided into a series of points," or with the cause-effect determinism of classical thought. Friedman and Donley, *Einstein as Myth and Muse*, p. 135; Or better yet, Virginia Woolf had this to say: "This appalling narrative business of the realist: getting on from lunch to dinner; it is false, unreal, merely conventional." *A Writer's Diary*, ed. Leonard Woolf (New York: Harcourt, Brace, 1954), p. 93.

42. "The Treatment of Time and Location in Uttararāmacarita," *Journal of the Oriental Institute* 32, no. 3 (1983):57–66.

43. The passage (*sarga* 46) concludes with the final illusion of Rāvaṇa disguised as a mendicant (*parivrajaka*).

44. *The Rāmāyaṇa of Vālmīki* (Bālākaṇḍa) (Princeton: Princeton University Press, 1984) p. 54. Boons function in a similar way: they represent a method of moving the narrative forward when no intrinsic or psychological motive exists. See S. Pollock, *The Rāmāyaṇa of Vālmīki*, (Ayodhyākaṇḍa) (Princeton: Princeton University Press, 1986), pp. 26–27.

45. A similar contest between dharma and *adharma* takes place in *sargas* 40–41 as Mārīca argues against Rāvaṇa's designs and loses.

46. See chapter 6.

47. Clearly this point is not as strong for omens as it is for predictions.

48. L. Nathan, "Translating the *Rāmāyaṇa*" in Pollock, pp. 94–95; L. Antoine, *Rama and the Bards* (Calcutta: Writer's Workshop, 1975), pp. 16–17; Pollock, *The Rāmāyaṇa of Vālmīki*, p. 15, quotes the text itself: it was performed "on the streets and royal highways of Ayodhya" (Uttarakanda 84.4); Jack Goody, "Oral Tradition and the Reconstruction of the Past in Northern Ghana," in Jack Goody, ed., *Literacy in Traditional Societies* (Cambridge: Cambridge University Press, 1968).

49. See Jerome Rothenberg, "Beyond Poetics," in OA.Rs no. 1 (Cambridge, Mass.: OA.Rs, 1981), p. 150.

50. See also the numerous repetitions in Sītā's response to Rāvaṇa (45.34–39, 40–45) and the recurring refrain *aham rāmam anuvratā* in 45.29–31; cf.

Nabaneeta Sen, "Comparative Studies in Oral Epic Poetry and the Vālmīki Rāmāyaṇa," in *Journal of the American Oriental Society* (*JAOS*) 8 (1966).

51. The most explicit summary of the ritual is contained in A. B. Keith's appendix to the *Śāṅkhāyana Āraṇyaka*. Numerous details and sequence stages differ from the account given here, which is based largely on the *Pañcaviṃśa Brāhmaṇa*. A bibliography of works on the Mahāvrata is provided in the previous chapter.

52. *History of Dharmaśāstra*. 5 vols. (Poona: BORI, 1930–62), 2.2:1245.

53. See F. B. J. Kuiper, *Ancient Indian Cosmogony* (New Delhi: Vikas, 1983); Jan Gonda, "In the Beginning," in *Annals of the Bandharkar Oriental Research Institute* (*ABORI*) 63 (1982):43–62; Santi Banerjee, "Prajāpati in the Brahmanas," in *Vishveshvaranand Indological Journal*, 19 (June–December, 1981):14–19.

54. Cf. PB 4.10.1

55. PB 4.10.4

56. ŚB 1.7.2.22

57. See Jan Gonda, *Prajāpati and the Year* (Amsterdam: North Holland, 1984), p. 24; see also ŚB. 1.6.3.35; 3.2.2.4; 11.1.1; PB 16.4.12; JB 1.167; cf. B. Smith, *Reflections*, pp. 55–56, especially with regard to Prajāpati as time and space.

58. "The gods took refuge in day, the demons in night; they were of equal strength, and one could not distinguish between them. The gods were afraid of night, darkness, death" (AB 4.5 in Wendy D. O'Flaherty, *Origins in Evil in Hindu Mythology* [Berkeley: University of California, 1976], p. 60).

59. ŚB 1.2.5.1–10

60. We shall return to this theme in the discussion of the spatialization of time (chapter 3).

61. PB 5.2.6, 5.5.1: TS 7.5.8.

62. Compare O'Flaherty, *Origins*, p. 67.

63. PB 5.5.15.

64. Of course, no one claims that the fact of participation explains the mediation between temporalities. But see S. G. F. Brandon, "The Ritual Perpetuation of the Past," *Numen* 6 (1959):112–29, where "magical identification" is described as the mediating principle between the two time levels.

65. PB 5.2.2.

66. E.g., PB 5.4.

67. See comments of Kramrisch, *The Presence of Śiva* and Wayman, "Climactic Times," discussed earlier; for a more emic interpretation (part-whole relationship), see Gonda, *Prajāpati and the Year*, p. 24. Gonda, along with the Brahmin ritualist, addresses the quantitative issue.

68. Nabokov's invented modern poet in *Ada* observes: "Space is a swarming in the eyes, and time a singing in the ears." *Ada; or Andor: a family chronicle* (New York: McGraw Hill, 1969).

69. "A significant form without conventional significance." S. Langer, *Philosophy in a New Key* (New York: New American Library, 1961), p. 204.

70. Ibid., p. 193; See also W. Kohler, *Gestalt Psychology* (New York: Liveright, 1929), pp. 248–49.

71. Avant-garde art in America since 1970, with its emphasis on perishable media and performance, has also become increasingly temporal. See Henry M. Sayre, *The Object of Performance* (Chicago: University of Chicago Press, 1989).

72. H. Powers, "An Historical and Comparative Approach to the Classification of Rāgas," University of California, Los Angeles, Institute of Ethnomusicology, *Selected Reports*, 1, no. 3 (1970), p. 11; Bonnie Wade, *Music in India* (Wellsley Hills, Mass.: Riverdale, 1987), p. 76.

73. *Saṅgīta Ratnākara* (SR) I.1.23–24.

74. SR I.3.1.

75. SR I.3.6.

76. Alain Daniélou, *Northern Indian Music* (New York: Frederick A. Praeger, 1969), p. 22; See Louis Zukofsky:"The order that rules music, the same / Controls the placing of the stars / And the feathers of a bird's wing. / In the middle of harmony / Most heavenly music / For the universe true enough." "A": 1–13 (Garden City, N.Y.: Doubleday, 1967).

77. Marius Schneider, "Primitive Music," in G. Abraham, ed., *The New Oxford History of Music* (Oxford: Oxford University Press, 1957), p. 55.

78. "Symbolisms Underlying Improvisatory Practices in Indian Music," *Journal of the Indian Musicological Society* 16, no. 2 (1985):30; we shall return to this point shortly.

79. For that reason, according to Arnold Bake, it actually corresponds with the creative principle of Śiva ("The Music of India," in Abraham, *The New Oxford History*, p. 198).

80. *Abhinavabhāratī* 31.377; see also Lewis Rowell, "Abhinavagupta, Augustine, Time and Music," *Journal of the Indian Musicological Society* 13, no. 2 (1982):23.

81. Rowell, "Abhinavagupta," p. 25.

82. Wade, *Music*, p. 52.

83. Gottlieb, "Symbolisms," p. 26; on a somewhat different level this is precisely what happened in the narrative time of the *Rāmāyaṇa*.

84. Bake, "The Music of India," p. 218.

85. See *Abhinavabhāratī* 31.3 in which the musical term *kalākālalaya* is identified with the cosmic rhythm of creation, duration, and dissolution.

86. *Rāga kalpa druma* quoted in Daniélou, *Northern Indian Music*, p. 66.

87. Compare *Viṣṇudharmottara* 3.18 and Langer, *Philosophy*, p. 192; Schneider, "Primitive Music," p. 31.

88. Robert E. Brown, "New Perspectives on The History of Tala," *Journal of the Indian Musicological Society* 16, no. 2 (1985):16; Harold S. Powers, "Musical Art and Esoteric Theism: Muttusvāmi Dikṣitar's Ānandabhairavī Kīrtanams on Śiva and Śakti at Tiruvārūr," in Michael Meister ed., *Discourses on Śiva* (Philadelphia: University of Pennsylvania Press, 1981), p. 319.

89. See his early view in *Nambudiri Veda Recitation* (The Hague: Mouton, 1961), p. 16.

90. Jan Gonda, *Vedic Literature* (Wiesbaden: Otto Harrassowitz, 1975) p. 316.

91. Jan Gonda, *Mantra Interpretation in the Śatapatha Brāhmaṇa* (Leiden: E. J. Brill, 1988), p. 176.

92. H. W. Bodewitz trans., *Jaiminīya Brāhmaṇa* (Leiden: E. J. Brill, 1973), p. 87.

93. Kramrisch, *The Presence of Śiva*, p. 268.

94. The reasoning behind these observations is contained in the preceding theoretical section.

95. Compare Kapila Vatsyayan, "Śiva-Naṭeśa: Cadence and Form," in Meister, *Discourses*, p. 191.

96. See Merleau-Ponty, *Phenomenology of Perception* (London: Routledge & Kegan Paul), pp. 100–102, and Jaques Derrida, *Positions*, trans. Alan Bass (Chicago: University of Chicago Press, 1981), p. 27.

3

Why Rivers Purify (And Only Bad Witches Are Ugly)

A common theme that runs through many studies of Hinduism and other religions emphasizes the identity, or at least interconnectedness, of natural and moral conceptions. More specifically, the view that pollution and sin are somehow identical rests on the assumed failure of certain cultures to distinguish between the natural and moral order of being. The ultimate goal of purification, as Van der Leeuw observed in 1933, "is no more liberation from actual dirt in the sense of modern hygiene, but release from evil and the induction of good."[1]

There is much evidence in India to support such an interpretation; one may even wish to add ugliness (as well as disease and foreignness) into the same system of anomalies. The typical literary portrayal of Caṇḍalas, for instance, goes beyond impurity (*aśuddhi*) and sinfulness (*patita*): the Caṇḍala is also deformed, foul smelling , and ugly.[2] The Niṣāda who springs out of the wicked Vena's churned corpse is ugly and impure.[3] Even the goddess Kālī cannot be effectively ferocious and malevolent without her utterly repulsive demeanor. These well-known facts about the Indian imagination seem to caution us against the application of "Western" distinctions—primarily those ultimately resting on the Cartesian dualism—toward the analysis of Indian ideas.[4] However, these rather obvious observations need to be qualified on two fronts. First, the remnants of nondualistic conceptions are far more pervasive in the West than scholarly methodologies seem to acknowledge.[5] When Glinda gleefully anounced to Dorothy that "only bad witches are ugly," she articulated both a tradition and a perception, shared by children and many adults, that beauty and virtue are closely connected. Second, even the most sophisticated modern interpretations of pollution in India are profoundly entrenched within an implicit dualism and positivism that is hardly mitigated by various Kantian qualifications. As we shall see, the result is a serious tautology in our understanding of pollution. In order to trace the topography of an imagination capable of mediating images and symbols, it is necessary to explain pollution in India in a manner that renders its relation to morality and aesthetics more precise. This calls for a somewhat lengthy review of current leading interpretations on the relation of pollution and sin.

Conceptual Approaches to Pollution and Sin

According to Ricoeur, the philosophical phenomenology of sin at its roots forces us to empathetically understand the concept of impurity: "Dread of the impure and rites of purification are in the background of all our feelings and all our behaviour relating to fault."[6] Behind this is an understanding of all objective violations of interdicts as possessing an evil quality not by the imputation of evil motivation to an agent but by reference to a conception that does not distinguish the ethical order from the cosmobiological order. The link is traced psychologically, according to Ricoeur, to a primordial dread of vengeance that can only manifest itself, in this elemental level, through contagion by a quasi-material filth. It is critical to note that even at this level of apperception, defilement is purely symbolic—that is, its relation to the material properties of the organism and its environment is homological or, at best, analogical: "If, from the beginning, defilement were not a *symbolic* stain, it would be incomprehensible that the ideas of defilement and purity could be corrected and taken up into an interpersonal ethics."[7]

Ricoeur's phenomenology here—like Cassirer's—traces thought to its fundamental mythic paradigms, that is, to symbols. But, it does not venture beyond: "reenactment" can proceed no further than elementary thought. His readers are thus left with no explanation for the power of defilement, aside from its contagiousness, to evoke moral dread. The analogical leap from material contagion to symbolic pollution is left unexplained.

Douglas's achievement in elevating pollution to an ideological level of conceptualization takes us a significant step forward. The symbolic hermeneutic of dirt as disorder has opened an enormously broad range of phenomena to a cognitive and sociological mode of analysis. This, of course, has ranked among the most fecund methodological developments in the study of Hinduism, as well as other traditions, over the past few decades. At the root of the conceptual interpretation lie two fundamental assumptions that pertain directly to the distinction I have been drawing between the symbolic and imagistic poles of religious consciousnes.

The first assumption can be described as an overwhelming symbolic tilt, an imperialism of the symbol, if you will: "In chasing dirt, in papering, decorating, tidying, we are not governed by anxiety to escape disease, but are positively re-ordering our environment, making it conform to an *idea*."[8] Purity is understod as an ideological system that orders conceptually and governs symbolically (by rituals) the natural world. It acts as a normative conception that utilizes an organic metaphorical language in order to articulate existing social norms. This theory rests on a key methodological distinction between the relative order of ideas and the relative chaos of experience: "For I believe that ideas about separating, purifying, demarcating and punishing transgressions have as their main function to impose system on an inherently untidy experience."[9]

The second assumption is less basic and follows from the first. The human body presents itself to traditional, as well as modern, awareness as a symbolic system: "The social body constrains the way the physical body is perceived. The physical experience of the body, always modified by the social categories through which it is known, sustains a particular view of society."[10] This theory, when stated more bluntly, emphatically denies a natural way of "considering" the body in a manner that lacks a social dimension.

The two assumptions form an airtight system. If sensory experience is naturally and intrinsically chaotic, but our consciousness is in fact organized through a social-symbolic epistemology, then the body—the primary locus of experience—lacks any experiential structures that are not also social. Society, as Mauss indicated, constitutes the meaning (form)-giving pole of consciousness. Experience, organically considered, merely supplies the "stuff" of coherent awareness. Purity, again, is the "mythical" expression for that form-giving (boundary-setting in phenomenological terms) quality of the human symbolic imagination—a collective force through and through.

It is not surprising that this theory has gained so much currency among historians of religion concerned about materialist reductionism, when we recall earlier, progressionist, interpretations of pollution, which this conception replaced so persuasively. However, a number of factors undermine the thesis that purity is strictly a cognitive system in the manner described here. The first and most fundamental critique must be directed toward Douglas's appropriation of Gestalt psychology —primarily its epistemology. Douglas's basic epistemological approach, at least in her earlier work, is both elementarist and sensationalist—positivistic theories both, and contrary to Gestalt. The postulation that sensory input is chaotic and constituted by random elememts that are only organized by higher conceptual functions, social ones in fact, runs precisely counter to the most fundamental ideas of phenomenologists like Heidegger and Merleau-Ponty, as well as Cassirer, and the Gestalt theories that influenced their thought. As we shall shortly see, the perceptual process, according to phenomenological Gestalt, is constituted even at the most elementary levels, by forms (*gestalten*) that possess both organization and an affective force. Merleau-Ponty also criticizes the sublimation of experience and speaks of restoring the dialectic of "form" and "content" (mind and perception) which is possible only in existence and is independent of the priority of reason.[11] At any rate, the status of purity cannot be addressed in any satisfactory manner without a full consideration of this issue. Otherwise we remain entrapped within an intolerable tautology: if the most basic organizational elements of our experience are symbolic (cognitive), raw (sensory) experience is ex post facto chaotic and (symbolically) defiling. Such an auroboric theory can only be validated by means of a rigorous analysis of perception—not by its internal consistency.

Douglas's debt to Gestalt psychology, though substantial on the system level, is in fact only analogical. The insistence on the symbolic system as a whole, superseding the significance of any of its parts, is taken directly from Gestalt. Consequently, the idea that margins of systems and categories are maintained by zones of paradox, contradiction, or, in this case, pollution derives by analogy from Gestalt theories of perception.[12] However, the radical innovation of the Gestalt theory of wholes rests on its perceptual application. The symbolic and systematic extensions of this phenomenological insight are strictly derivative.

The second critique of purity as a symbolic system is addressed to one of its central practical applications. If pollution is a symbolic expression of cognitive chaos, then purification by bathing becomes superfluous and trivialized. The ritual activity of bathing in rivers fits into the purity system by the logic of symbols only. Washing can never be measured as a subjective or objective process of cleansing because it obtains its meaning strictly within the cognitve symbolism of purity-pollution. However, if the latter is based on a sense of chaos (not filth!), there is no reason why bathing should be regarded as an efficacious "chaos-removing" activity. The fact that bathing actually removes dirt cannot be considered the source of its cognitive meaning because this necessitates a slip from the symbolic reasoning outlined earlier to the crude magicalism that Douglas derided in Frazer. This problem is not left unaddressed, however, and Douglas acknowledges the efficacy of aquatic symbolism in a lengthy quotation from Eliade:

> In water everything is "dissolved," every "form" is broken up. Everything that has happened ceases to exist; nothing that was before remains after immersion in water, not an outline, not a "sign," not an event. Immersion is the equivalent, at the human level, of death at the cosmic level, the

> cataclysm (the Flood) which periodically disssolves the world into the primeval ocean. Breaking up all forms, doing away with the past, water possesses this power of purifying, of regenerating of giving new birth.[13]

Eliade's symbolism fits perfectly into a system of ideas that appropriates all organic activity into the imperialism of symbols. The internal consistency of the system is beyond reproach, but its existential vitality is completely suppressed because it dispossesses the images of organic life. Moreover, Eliade's analysis of water symbolism misses the force and specificity of water in India on the symbolic level as well. There, as we shall see, only hot water is form-dissolving; the cold bathing streams, which are enjoined for purification in the texts, are form-giving in an absolute manner.

The powerful ideological tilt of symbolic interpretations of pollution outlined previously imposes a severe limitation on their application. The cognitive approach grants no noetic force to percepts and to embodied experience. On the contrary, these are the very sources of the chaos that threatens the stability of cognitive structures. Other approaches seem more promising but run up against similar problems. For instance, Victor Turner's astonishing attention to detailed phenomena reflects a conscious stance against the objectivist reduction of symbolic analysis. Turner defines the latter position as the "ideological pole" of cultural symbols. The ideological pole contains a "cluster of significata that refer to components of the moral and social orders of Ndembu society."[14] The symbolism of purity, understood by Turner in Douglas's terms, constitutes the ideological matrix of a normative conception that operates at this pole.

At the other end of experience is the "sensory pole," where "the meaning content is closely related to the "outward form of the symbol."[15] At first glance the sensory pole closely resembles the imagistic pole of symbolic consciousness—as I have described it in an earlier chapter.[16] However, Turner quickly and decisively shifts his analysis of the sensory into a new—nearly metaphysical—locus of symbolism: "The form and substance of sensory experience is inexorably shaped by unconscious motivations and ideas."[17] Unfortunately, Turner recognizes and overly respects an absolute disciplinary boundary between the task of the social anthropologist and the depth psychologist. This boundary is fortified by Medusa's petrifying head, held in the steadfast hand of the psychologist who thus guards the key for unlocking the mysteries of "individual" symbols.[18] The problem, from our point of view, becomes rather obvious: the sensory pole is not sensory at all. It is a thoroughly symbolic perception shaped now not by Mauss's and Durkheim's collective consciousness but by the far more elusive "subcendent" forces of the individual subconscious.

Incidentally, even anthropologists seem increasingly likely to stare Medusa in the face and possibly call Freud's bluff. Obeyesekere's ***Medusa's Hair*** is a splendid example of the analysis of symbols as a dynamic hermeneutic that moves between the poles of the unconscious and the culturally determined rational and cognitive faculties.[19]

The work of Turner and his followers is superior to the purely cognitive modes of analysis in wealth of detail and vitality of evocation. But this work too is predominantly symbolical, even at its empirical best: it provides no map of experience that is not exclusively reductive in that its bearings are taken from other (nonexperiential) dimensions.

To conclude this section, purity remains a comprehensive symbolic system that is locked within its circular logic, accounts for its own lasting vitality only in social terms, fails to explain the practical application of its ritual ideas (purification by bathing), and sometimes turns a deaf ear to the nuances of indigenous languages of pollution. This chapter will redress the ideological imbalance of purity-pollution by grounding the symbolic concept in the experience of pollution and the concrete act of purification. Clearly, an examination of the full range of phenomena that falls under the "category" (a problematic concept for imagistic analysis) of pollution is out of the question here. Nor is it methodologically necessary in order to substantiate the critique of symbolic analysis and to complement it with the lacking phenomenological dimension. These two tasks can be achieved by means of a detailed exploration of ritual (river) bathing in ancient India.

Bathing is that purification ritual that has been left unconvincingly explained by the concept of pollution as cognitive chaos. Only Western intellectuals could reduce the experience of submerging oneself in a dark and cold stream at the crack of dawn to a symbolic paradigm. At the same time, ritual bathing brings together both defilement and sin as distinct, though possibly related, events that are addressed in the same specific context. Therefore, bathing domonstrates the primary epistemological role of embodied experience in the development of the purity symbolism precisely because it is a "remedial"—that is, symbolically efficacious—process, while an overwhelmingly physical one. To put it in simpler terms, we cannot take the actual cleansing properties of water as an analogical source of purification ideas. Similarly, we cannot say that bathing in cold streams is a symbolic experience because this is a tautological explanation and an armchair absurdity. We are left with an obvious need to know precisely in what manner water is said to purify, as well as expiate. Once this agenda is accomplished we shall be in a better positon to evaluate the existential foundations of purity symbolism, at least in India.

Bathing (Snāna)

Purification in rivers, even the Ganges, happens mysteriously. It is not a clamorous onrush of mythical themes but a quiet penetration of subtle images:

It could be
that the old blind flow
creates a field of force across the mind;
their faces blank and waxen, alive in dumb impulse,
drawing of touch to be appeased by mystery.
Is it death which moves the earth? Or birth?[20]

But at the same time, bathing in the river is not always serene. Wading breast deep into the cold morning stream can be an overwhelming experience. Edwin Arnold described the early morning Banaras bathers as "visibly shuddering under the shock of the water and their lips blue and quivering, while they eagerly mutter their invocations."[21] Only a detailed and critical analysis of bathing can explain how such a striking experience becomes transformed into, or subsumed within, the symbolism of purity.

The morning bath in ancient India was meant neither for hygiene nor for sport. Consequently it was presented by normative texts as a relatively complex ritual. And, as usual, variations and differences in the descriptions and prescriptions of ritualized bathing were unavoidable. The following is a brief summary of the *Viṣṇu Smṛti* (VS) and the *Kṛtyakalpataru* (KK), a medieval compendium that owes its account of bathing to numerous sources.[22]

Baths were classified according to their context and function as obligatory (*nitya*), occasional (*naimittika*), and voluntary (*kāmya*). The first category includes the daily bathing, which will shortly be described, as well as those baths that precede sacred rituals. Purification and expiation bathing are occasional (*naimittika*), whereas baths taken on special religious occasions are *kāmya*. Regardless of this classification, all baths possess a utilitarian, "visible" (*dṛṣṭa*) aspect, which is directly related to physical cleansing, and a transcendent, "invisible" (*adṛṣṭa*) dimension. However, the first type possesses a most distinct temporal quality and seems most deeply bound to the passage of time itself.

According to the *Viṣṇu Smṛti*, the best place to bathe is the Ganges, followed by river water in general, fountain or fresh spring water, a tank, a well, and so forth. The general principle is enunciated by the *Vyavahāra Mayūkha*, which states that river water purifies by means of its velocity or the force of its current.[23] Still water purifies less effectively that a flowing river, the confluence (*saṅgama*) of two streams better than just one stream.

The most important and obligatory bath—the routine daily bath—takes place during two or three transitional phases of the day: dawn and noon.[24] The first bath begins shortly before the solar disk emerges above the horizon and ends in time for the morning Saṅdhyā (*homa*). The obligatory bath is universal but women and Śūdras perform it silently, whereas others recite Vedic *mantras*. The bath is accompanied by the use of several items including rubbing earth (*mṛt*), which is prepared on the previous day when light still guarantees its cleanliness. Other items are two or four blades of Kuśa grass, flowers, cow manure, sesame seeds, whole rice grains, and sandal paste. The Kuśa grass and sandal paste are to be used only by Brahmins. The bather may not be naked and must wear two pieces of cloth. In order to possess efficacy, bathing must be undertaken in cold water, except in cases of illness.

As the eastern horizon lights up at dawn, after he has brushed his teeth and before eating, the Hindu goes down to the still darkened river. The sun will rise as the bather stands in the river and proceeds through the ritual at a pace that will insure the performance of the morning *homa* within fifteen to thirty minutes. If the ancient texts are applied, the bather approaches the river in near darkness, his sacred thread hanging from the left shoulder, his right hand clutching a strand of Kuśa grass. With this blade of grass the bather will mark the sacred space (a square) in the water, where he will emerse himself.[25] He has already washed his hands and feet before entering the river, as he would do before entering a particularly sacred place. At the water's edge he sips twice, reciting the *urūṁ hi*: "King Varuṇa has made a spacious pathway, a pathway for the Sun wherein to travel. Where no way was he made him set his footsteps, and warned afar whatever afflicts the spirit."[26] Then the bather cups a handful of water in his joined palms, reciting the Sumitriya to Varuṇa for liberation by means of the lustrous waters.[27] He empties his hands with the water oblation to the sun (Sūrya).[28] Following this, the bather rubs his entire body three times with the dirt he had gathered the previous day.[29] Before entering the water he sips water, bows to the river in the direction of the sun, and recites the following verse: "Through all this world strode Viṣṇu; thrice his foot he planted, and the whole was gathered in this footstep's dust."[30] Facing the rising sun, the bather now walks into the chilly water and immediately submerges his entire body by bowing forward. As he surfaces he may not, according to the texts, wipe the water from his hair with the hand. Standing in the flowing stream, which may possibly be relfecting a golden hue now, he recites: "May the maternal water bestow luster on us, may they purify us with *ghṛta* who make the *ghṛta* pure, the gods drive all stains away, as I came purified from them."[31] Alternatively, or collectively, the bather recites the following verses as well:

> Waters, you are the ones who bring us the life force
> Help us to find nourishment so that we may look upon
> great joy
> Let us share in the most delicious sap that you have,
> as if you were loving mothers.
> Let us go straight to the house of the one for whom
> your waters give us life and give us birth.[32]

Golden of colour, pure, purifying,
In which was born Kasyapa, in which Indra
They have conceived Agni as a germ, of varied forms;
May these waters be gentle and kindly to us.[33]
Whatever sin is found in me, whatever evil I have wrought
If I have lied or falsely sworn, Waters remove it far from me.[34]

Now the bather rises out of the water and massages his entire body with the cow dung he had placed on the bank. As he does this he recites, "We bring these thoughts to the mighty Rudra, the god with braided hair, who rules over heroes, so that it will be well with our two-footed and four-footed creatures, and in this village all will flourish unharmed."[35]

For the second time then, the bather plunges into the stream this time reciting the following, "Let them [healing plants, Soma] free me from the effects of a curse, and also from what comes from Varuṇa, and from the fetter sent by Yama and from every offence of the gods."[36] The alternative or complementary verses this time are:

To the three spheres of light thou goest, Savitar, and
with the rays of Sūrya thou combinest thee
Around, on both sides thou encompassest the
night, yea thou, O God, art Mitra through thy righteous laws.[37]

Order and truth were born from heat as it blazed up.
From that was born night; from that heat was born the billowy ocean.
From the billowy ocean was born the year, that arranges days
and nights, ruling over all that blinks its eyes.
The Arranger has set in their proper place the sun and moon, the sky
and the earth, the middle realm of space and finally the sunlight.[38]

According to the *Snānasūtra* of Kātyāyana, the bather submerges four or five times and recites well over thirty verses repeating several of them three times.[39] According to the much older *Viṣṇu Smṛti*, the process is considerably briefer and the number of verses smaller. This seems consistent with the time constraints placed on the ritual and the concentration required (in cold water!) to complete a recitation properly. The Śāstra versions of the ritual vary greatly, particularly with reference to the verses selected for recitation, but among the universally accepted verses, the themes of the sun, creation, a moral path, and Viṣṇu's three steps are prominent. Moreover, if Staal is correct and the *mantras* are chanted rather nonsensically, then the great stream of mantric syllables and consonants that flow according to the *Snānasūtra* are no more than an auditory burble above the river.[40] Even so, the ever familiar images of the Sun, Viṣṇu, the Puruṣa Sūkta, and

Hiraṇyagarbha cannot fail but impress themselves on the consciousness of the coldest mumbling bather.

If we assume then even a rudimentary level of comprehensibility, the *mantras* produce a simple but powerful mental narrative. The *mantras* evoke rather than actually create a symbolic awareness consisting of two intertwining themes, cosmogonic and sacrificial. The cosmogonic theme is simple and majestic: It consists of the uterine waters, cosmic mother of the flaming seed-embryo, which is Agni the fiery fetus, then Sūrya who bursts out of the primordial waters in order to embark on its dharmic path across the firmament. Can the soft early solar rays in the dark river water suggest any verse more clearly then the following account of Hiraṇyagarbha?: "When the high waters came, pregnant with the embryo that is everything, bringing forth fire, he arose from that as the one life's breath of the gods."[41]

The sacrificial theme emerges more subtly, as the waters turn golden in the growing sunlight. The water now purifies because it becomes the clarified butter and the bather is anointed for his own sacrifice. The sacrificial implements and the verse (TS 5.6.1.1–2) about Agni the golden germ are extremely familiar sacrificial elements.[42] Cosmological and ritual themes are thus closely combined in the Śāstric accounts of bathing to fashion an efficacious locus for the purifying imagination.

We have thus proceeded beyond the symbolic generality of waters that purify, for instance by death and rebirth, to a theater of active religious symbols in which the bather is a participant. The description has already produced a relative wealth of images that seize the imagination of Hindus in a concrete and familiar manner. However, the central question remains entirely unanswered. How do the waters purify? The mere staging of a dramatic reenactment of cosmogony and dharmagony does not explain the need to bathe. Some might even argue, without being facitious, that a warm blanket around the shoulders would enable the Brahmin to focus on his symbol-evoking *mantras* more clearly. The rite of bathing, if we are dealing with symbolic acts, could be dispatched with a dip of the fingers, perhaps an *ācamana*. Why go into the cold dark water? How does the simple yet extreme act of standing in river water become purifying?

In order to answer these questions concretely and exhaustively, thereby, incidentally laying the groundwork for a rudimentary theory of religious perception, a lengthy detour into the phenomenology of perception is necessary. My approach rests very heavily, as does Merleau-Ponty's and Cassirer's (mutatis mutandis), on the phenomenological and empirical theories of Gestalt psychology. Because purification has an irreducible physical component, the lengthy discussion of Gestalt that follows should be read as an essential instrument for the direct analysis of the bathing experience, not as a methodological analogy.

The Phenomenology of Bathing—A Gestalt Approach

According to Gestalt psychology, we are not born with an empirical self that must, like Kafka's Gregor Samsa, become gradually acquainted with the body in which it suddenly finds itself. "He had only the numerous little legs which never stopped waving in all directions and which he could not control in the least. When he tried to bend one of them it was the first to stretch itself straight; and did he succeed at last in making it do what he wanted, all the other legs meanwhile would move the more wildly in a high degree of unpleasant agitation."[43] In fact, the very development of self or ego is itself inseparable from the discovery and manipulation of the body. Still, the bizarre and tragic predicament of Gregor Samsa is not altogether different from the infantile experience of a body neither quite alien nor quite one's own. All cognitions and all symbolic mental operations are inextricably contingent upon the gradual appropriation of that body and its localization in relation to a world and a self.

The most precise phenomenological language to describe the relationship between the concrete experience of bathing and the symbolic imagination of purity will have to draw heavily from Gestalt psychology. Floyd Allport has reduced Gestalt to six fundamental concepts, a manageable starting point for the examination of the basic perceptual forms that constitute the experience of purification.[44]

1. The fundamental units of the perceptual field, as well as (isomorphically) the neurological field, are whole forms (*gestalten*).

2. The wholeness character of a perceptual gestalt form transcends the characteristics of its specific parts. Moreover, the relationship among the parts is an essential aspect of the wholeness of the perceptual experience and its psychological basis.

3. The gestalt perception takes place in a phenomenal field or system that tends to equilibrium or steady state.

4. Such fields of experience are not bound in a one-to-one correlation to the proximal stimulus pattern of the perceived object. Instead they "follow laws intrinsic to the organism."[45] Experiential fields are also flexible and transformable, maintaining only a "topological" relation to the stimulus pattern, that is, the "raw" sensory input.

5. Perceived wholes have boundaries or ground. The bounded configuration is self-closing and simple, balanced and symmetrical. The tendency of these experiential fields is toward "good" form.

6. The experiential field is organized by its dynamic force, "giving rise to segregation, goupings, combinations into subsystems, and articulation."[46] Good forms are strong and well articulated and resist fusion with other weaker forms.

These principles, and related ideas, may be grouped into four pertinent topics for discussion: isomorphism, good form, the phenomenal ego, and proprioception. My goal is neither to repeat what has been said better in other contexts, nor to strain the reader's patience. The four topics are directly applicable to the analysis of purification by bathing. The detailed summary of some Gestalt ideas is a necessary condition for an imagistic interpretation of bathing as a nonsymbolic activity and, in fact, as an introduction to a rigorous phenomenology of Hinduism.

Isomorphism

Historically, Gestalt has taken a middle-ground stance between the positivism and idealism of existing psychological schools. However, the fundamental elements of conscious perceptual experience—percepts—could not be left suspended inefficaciously between the dualistic realms of body and mind, nor could they be monistically reduced to one or the other. The classical Gestalt theorists were thus delighted to discover a close correspondence between the forms of awareness and neurological structures. They named this relation *isomorphism*: "Psychological facts and the underlying events in the brain resemble each other in all structural characteristics."[47] Or, to put it more dramatically, the structural properties of phenomenal and neurological processes are "the same."[48]

This discovery opened a prolific course of empirical and psychological research where previous commitment to one or the other side of the Cartesian dualism seemed to block off progress. It provided an interactionist midlevel theory of great promise. Like the anthropological application of homology, however, the implications were easily overextendable. When the morphological homologies in biological taxonomies were extended to social categories, for instance totemic structures, the hypothetical but testable causal relations that they posited in evolutionary biology were not equally transferable. The underlying, often unstated, causal assumptions remained in much of social and anthropological research, with distorting reductive effects.

Isomorphism too, as an astonishing correlation of perceptual and physiological structures, has been open to severe criticism. The Gestalt forms that have so convincingly been demonstrated at the most elementary levels of perception have, in fact, not been proved to exist in the neurological processes, claim the critics.[49] However, as a phenomenological science Gestalt has been strengthened, not undermined, by the revision of isomorphism. Its theories of perceptual forms remain persuasive. Moreover, even if the human body as a neurobiological organism is "bracketed," the body as a phenomenal body rather than the physical organism remains significant. Isomorphism shifts to the observed relation between "purely mental" states and the perceptual activities of the phenomenal body rather than the physical organism. We shall return to this point shortly.

This limited version of Gestalt as a phenomenology of perception is well suited for the analysis of cultural behavior, even across boundaries. In fact, the use of Gestalt here is not a method borrowed from another field but is part of the theory itself. The theory claims that the perceptual-imagistic experience of bathing is determinative with respect to the structures (for instance, purity) that emerge from ritual. Since the percepts-images are prediscursive by definition, the application of a "European" phenomenology is not invalidated by its extremely etic vocabulary. Gestalt achieves with perception more than psychoanalysis achieves with personal symbols—and there is no Medusa to overcome.

Good Forms in Perception

The basis for the discovery of isomorphism can be traced back to a biological theory (Humphrey's Principle) that the organism, as a dynamic system, tends toward internal and external equilibrium within its environment. In other words, external adaptation to change is regulated by the internal dynamics of the organism, and vice versa.[50] It becomes necessary to abandon the metaphor of the human body as a machine that operates by the adjustment of constraints in order to realize that its physiological activities reflect a natural organization of forces toward equilibrium.[51] The theory of isomorphism then states that these same dynamic processes shape perception in a corresponding fashion.

Regardless of these physiological correspondences, empirical research has amply demonstrated that an interaction does indeed take place in the perceptual field between local perceptual facts and their environment. The emergence of forms is the result of such a dynamic perceptual interaction; "Objects appear in the visual field only if their boundaries are visually preserved. Consequently, the processes which make visual objects emerge in the field are just as much processes which establish certain separations, separations of visual units, as they are processes which make objects unitary entities."[52]

The aesthetic implications of these sensory dynamics were developed by the Gestalt theorists in the fascinating notion of *Prägnanz*: "But in a closed system the action of forces does operate in the direction of equilibrium or a steady state. It is therefore not surprising that during this operation the distributions within the system become more regular, symmetrical and simple."[53] The simplicity and balance of the stimulus response is its "good" form.[54] It manifests itself in the aesthetic-affective quality of objects given to simple perception. The "symbolic pragnanz" as Cassirer calls it, is not a semiotic activity but is the *condition* for the giving of signs and meaning. Cassirer defines it as "the way in which a perception as a 'sensory' experience contains at the same time a certain non-intuitive meaning which it immediatley and concretely represents."[55]

Consequently, not only the works of the artist, but the elements of the perceptual field all around us "communicate" aesthetic qualities such as "tense," "relaxed," "steady," "chaotic," "clear."[56] It is crucial to emphasize that the aesthetic quality of phenomenal structures at this level is not symbolic—not to mention conceptual—but purely perceptual.[57] Cultural symbols will enter the picture as various levels of judgment, but by then a bidirectional dialectic of influences is already at work.

The Phenomenal Ego

We have seen that the form and structure of percepts were related isomorphically to certain physiological processes. However, the same must also be postulated, according to Gestalt, in reference to the perceiving, bodily ego as well as the relation between the object and the subject. All three "are correlated with cerebral processes of a corresponding structure and distribution."[58] The commonsensical view of the body as an ontologically separate and "external" reality to the self is simply incorrect from the phenomenal point of view. In fact, even the very localization of subject and object in an expansive spatial depth is an illusion when the two-dimensional retinal image is taken into account.

It is a veritable "miracle" according to Metzger, one of the crowning achievements of the evolutionary process, that the relationship between the phenomenal subject and object interaction, and the objective organism and environment interaction corresponds so closely.[59] At any rate the phenomenal body, the body of our conscious awareness, is not the physiological organism itself but an aspect of our consciousness of body—our phenomenal ego. And like the other *gestalten* of our phenomenal field, the ego is first and foremost a perceptual structure based on the spatial centrality of the perceiving self between the objects in the sensory field of its surrounding environment.[60]

The cognitive conditions for the development of the adult ego structure are based on the kinesthetic activities of the child. Or, as in the case of adults who are regaining consciousness, the ego "does not become segregated before the [perceptual] field possesses a significant amount of inhomogeneity."[61] The phenomenal ego emerges along with the other structures of perception, which act as a background field. As experiments with pilots and astronauts indicate, the absence of differentiated spatial "contents" or structures results in a profound loss of ego orientation.[62] Thus the same process that accounts for the crystallization of the ego and its world also accounts for the polarized nature of the phenomenal field in which objects are felt to be "out there" in relation to subject. This exteriorizing sensation is reinforced primarily by vision and hearing as will be discussed.

Other senses, most importantly touch and proprioception in general, indicate that the boundary between ourselves and objective experience is not altogether sharp and constant. The objects of touch are sometimes felt as "things and their properties; but they may also be experienced as 'subjective.'"[63] By means of touch more than any other sense, broader spheres of phenomena may be appropriated to the phenomenal ego. "The body belongs to our ego"—this is clear, but the skin need not be its external boundary. Our clothes, cars, and homes, extend the phenomenal ego beyond the body.[64] In some cases of a cultivated religious or mystical consciousness, the ego may encompass the entire world.

To summarize, the physical organism in which we exist, like Gregor Samsa, is not the body of our conscious awareness. The organism is a complicated source of proximal neurological stimuli. The ego-body, on the other hand, is the sum total of these complex sensations which are processed as images or percepts to form conscious perceptual structures. Consequently, the ego-body, as well as its environment, is a gestalt structure since both are aspects of the phenomenal field of ego. This theory has been justly criticized for its failure—regardless of isomorphism—to overcome the interactionist body-mind problem. But despite any theoretical confusion, the practical and empirical evidence for a bidirectional interaction between the organism (as well as its objective environment) and consciousness (the phenomenal ego) is beyond dispute in cases such as psychosomatic diseases, phantom limb pain, and others. Isomorphism may not be metaphysically persuasive but both organism and ego are efficacious in their mutual interaction—as we shall shortly see.

Perception and Proprioception

Sensory activity operates in two directions. When the senses receive stimuli from the "external" world, this is called perception. Perception takes place through the sensory receptors in the surface tissues of the organism. However, according to Charles Sherrington, the deep tissues of the body, located particularly in muscles, tendons, joints, and blood vessels, possess receptors that are unique and specific to themselves.[65] These receptors are adapted to sense the changes occurring inside the organism and are related only in a secondary fashion to the forces of the environment. This sensory activity Sherrington called proprioception. It is the primary sense of a corporeal cohesiveness, the feeling "from within" that the body is a total coordinated system. Loss of this sense results in a severe impairment of physical coordination, tonality and posture, manifesting itself in a "disjointed" or even disembodied feeling as well as an inability to function. Proprioception, however, is profoundly dependent on some interaction with the environment.[66] According to Gibson, who rejects Sherrington's formulation of proprioception as a unique sense, the sense of one's body can even be established by vision due to the ranging of vision relative to a stationary environment. This has been reinforced by clinical cases in which sight compensated somewhat for loss of muscular proprioception.

In any case the proprioceptive and exteroceptive (perceptual) activities are closely interrelated. Even when proprioception is a sensing of one's muscular actions, contraction for instance, the latter may often be a response to the excitation of the surface receptors by the environment. Posture and tonality, both long-term effects of proprioception, are dependent on the stimulation induced by motion (kinesthetics) of the body in its environment and thus, on exteroception as well as proprioception. There is a great deal of empirical evidence that the proprioceptive sense is often triggered by tactile, visual, and auditory stimulation without necessarily an intentional muscular response.[67]

Some senses, primarily vision, are suited for the creation of a phenomenal "outside," whereas touch reinforces a phenomenal subject. Vision gives the illusion of constituting the world at a distance, while in the case of touch, as Merleau-Ponty put it, "I cannot forget in this case that it is through my body that I go to the world."[68] The tactile experience includes a bodily component that vision and hearing seem to lack: "The tactile localization of an object, for example, assigns to it its place in relation to the cardinal points of the body image."[69]

Vision gives us knowledge of objects that are nonego; it creates the forms of the surrounding space. The child owes the differentiation of objects in the space in which it moves to vision. However, neither the sense of its own body as "his" nor, exclusively speaking, the ego are related to vision. On the contrary, the processes that are "aroused in the entero—and proprio-ceptors, form probably, as we have explained, the first material for the organization of the Ego."[70] The development of ego, then, owes to a complex system consisting of local kinesthetic and proprioceptive processes interacting with a larger context of exteroceptive events.

Unlike vision, touch affects the development of ego as subject in an environment far more directly and more comprehensively. It reinforces perception and proprioception equally, and continues to do so non-"discursively" long after vision has been appropriated into a symbolic-conceptual level of (linguistic) awareness: "The unity and identity of the tactile phenomenon do not come about through any synthesis of recognition in the concept, they are founded upon the unity and identity of the body as a synergic totality."[71]

Proprioception, including touch, and perception through vision combine to crystallize the sense of an embodied ego operating in an environment. Vision and touch create the impression of a polarized world with inside and outside, self and environment. The structures of the phenomenal world owe their regularity to perceptual processes even before symbolic thought "elevates" these forms to ideas. Clearly, none of this can account for the actual contents of the religious imagination. Cultural values and judgments, symbols, concepts, language in general, are never reducible to the gestalt structures of perception. Personality, emotions, and motivations—in short, the "person" in general—is never reducible to the structures of the phenomenal ego. The point of the lengthy discussion and the purpose of its application to bathing are to complement the symbolic level of analysis with a purely imagistic level. The latter is particularly well suited for an activity, such as bathing, in which the imagistic and symbolic are clearly distinguished, yet so closely interacting.

The Meaning of Bathing

River bathing—purification in general—is the most important transitional rite in India. Aside from introducing the new day, it precedes and often concludes every other major ritual. In fact, it is a necessary condition for all Vedic rituals. The explanation for the absolute dependence of ritual on purification may be sought in the phenomenal "resonance" that is active between the physical act of submersion in water and the symbolic reconstitution of order. Purity, in other words, is an absolutely synchronized interplay between the physical and mental poles of experience within specific contexts.

The physical acts of bathing are profoundly determinative with respect to the content and force of the symbolic conceptions and vice versa. For instance, the bather begins by thrice rubbing his entire body with dirt. Aside from the symbolic and physical cleansing involved (the two ontological poles), the friction sharpens the bather's tactile perception and the phenomenal effect of the water becomes enhanced. With surface sensitivity increased, skin contact with the water is absolutely focused and all-encompassing. The entire body is touched by a substance of different temperature and consistency and is therefore experienced simultaneously as a whole.[72] This contact achieves two goals; it reinforces a connection with the surrounding, form-giving, environment—the river. Such a perceptual effect supports the symbolic relation of the bather to the river, as we shall see. But, more significant, touch produces overall proprioception along with a coordinated postural response to the external stimulation of the stream. Consequently, submersion becomes an extremely effective method for cultivating conscious proprioception, a necessary condition for the re-emergence of the phenomenal body-ego. At this basic level then, the morning rites begin with a powerful reinforcement of the fundamental phenomenal ego by means of proprioception. All of this takes place strictly in relation to the river. The cold water erases lingering dreams, wandering thoughts, and nagging concerns thereby reducing the phenomenal ego to body (in water).[73] The cold stream also shocks the bather into tactile and kinesthetic focus on the internal and external orientation of his body. Metaphorically speaking, the phenomenal body is "carved" anew within the same cold water that erases the ego's lingering traces.

But this is only half the physical event. While touch establishes a unitary body-self in the water, vision is directed toward the sun. We have seen that vision more than other senses creates the phenomenal impression of constituting a world "out there." The visual creation in this case becomes identified with the emergence and ascent of the solar disk. Visually speaking, the sun is the world creator, and by means of vision it carries the subject into its kingdom: "Rise up, horse in the water, enter this pleasant country. May Rohita (the red sun), who has created this whole world, carry you, who are easy to carry, to that country."[74] Vision, in the symbolism of Indian mythology, is light.[75] In the eyes of an angry sage, vision can be far more powerful than the hot rays of the sun. The polarized "external" effect of vision is heightened during bathing by the phenomenally delimiting influence of the water on the sense of self, and on the unintelligibility of other objects, aside from the sun, in the dark visual field.

To summarize then, the experience of standing in the river at dawn is the creation of a new world. Not the mythic world of Brahmā or Viṣṇu—the absolutely Real World—but the phenomenal world of subject and object in which individuals live. The waters "create" the experiencing subject and the sun "creates" the experienced object of the germinal phenomenal field. Both, moreover, possess "good" form because they are simple, self-enclosed, and balanced. This form, on the symbolic level, of course, corresponds to the purifying power of rivers and fires.

Meanwhile, as we have seen earlier, the *mantras* sustain a symbolic narrative that runs along a parallel course. This is a narrative about cosmic, uterine waters, a golden germ-embryo, Sūrya, Viṣṇu, and the moral path across the sky. The mythic-symbolic level of awareness closely parallels the physical experience. For instance, as the bather looks at the sun, an after image remains imprinted on his retinas even after he closes his eyes and submerges his head in the water. With this act, if he is conscious of the *mantras* about Hiraṇyagarbha or Agni, the bather, phenomenologically speaking, is dunking the sun in the water in order to bring it out again. On the newly recreated slate of his own phenomenal ego, the bather thereby enacts the cosmic theater of creation. But he is the stage and the audience alike. The beauty and propriety of the mythic creation, the "play," correspond directly to the wholeness of the phenomenal forms that are the "stage." The two creations are experienced as one. Consequently, the concept of purity accentuates the phenomenal character of existence precisely because it brings together the subjective and the objective in consciousness.

The śāstric treatment of pollution and purification demonstrates this principle by counterposing symbolic and physical events: purification is always prescribed by means of bathing *after* the physical event—menstruation, a journey, a solar eclipse—had already completed its course.[76] Purification, in short, treats the subjective manifestations of pollution, its phenomenal impact on the self, rather than the physiological contingencies of the polluting act. At the same time, no rite of purification can ever be efficacious unless the objective grounds of pollution have actually been removed.

Bathing, like other rituals, consists of three ontological levels: the purely physical (organic), the phenomenal, and the conceptual ("ideological"). The relation between the three remains problematic. While Gestalt psychology posits an isomorphic relation between the physiological and phenomenal, this cannot be our present concern because the issue of the neurological foundation of consciousness is irrelevant to the question of purity. However, the relation between the sensory—an aspect of the phenomenal—and symbolic levels of experience requires an explanation, if we are to avoid an uncritical extension of isomorphism to these domains. The influence works both ways: sensory experience can become sublimated into ideas by means of metaphoric transformations. On the other hand cultural symbols can strongly influence perception as in the case of Eskimos who name and perceive seventeen white colors, or the cellist who is able to name and hear a dozen sonoric qualities in a Stradivarius.[77] For our purposes the issue can be framed in a number of ways. For instance, how does the tactile proprioception enhanced in bathing "correspond" to the symbolic conception of water as a cosmic womb? Does the mythic imagination stand in relation to experience as cognition stands in relation to images, that is, by abstraction and inference? Is the relation homological? Metaphorical? Or is it donative in simply being given by a leap of intuition from the sensory to the symbolic?[78]

From a purely phenomenal point of view the problem is vacuous. It exists only due to a postivistic misconstruing of experience as a radically empirical representation of reality. But even if one consciously rejected the doctrines of positivism, this assumption is too often taken for granted in our "common sense." Consequently the inevitable Cartesian dualism seems to interpose itself obtrusively and unnecessarily between experience and ideas. However, I believe that Husserl's bracketing can be applied not only to questions of ultimate metaphysical ontologies but to the causal efficacy of one ontological realm over another in the activities of consciousness. As a result it becomes possible to chart a more precise map of phenomenal experience. In the phenomenal field, physical forces and metaphysical forces enter not as movers and shakers, but as players in the same game—resonance.

Resonance, in music and in mechanics, is the synchronized coordination of natural frequencies between two or more objects. In the case of metal wires and horsetail, the result may be a violin concerto. When resonance is achieved between two objects, the natural frequencies of each are increasingly magnified. For instance, the glass that shatters under the pressure of a B-flat note does so only because its resonance with another vibrating force (sound) causes its own natural frequency to increase to the breaking point.

To explain the analogy, the sensory experience of bathing and the mythical narrative of creation resonate simultaneously within the bather's awareness. As this happens both are magnified, sharpened, and even transformed without directly "causing" this change in each other. In the consciousness of the bather, submersion in the river becomes more efficacious on the imagistic level because the simple act resonates with the symbolic significance of the creation narrative. Likewise, the creation narrative becomes animated and meaningful because it is experienced in water. The pure (*śuddhi*), as an adjective applying to persons, is an emic term for the resonance, in the phenomenal field, between the gestalt forms of sensory experience and the perfect structures of mythic imagination. In other words, purity is neither perfect conceptual order not perfect physical cleanliness, wellness, or beauty. On the contrary, purity is the linguistic idiom by means of which the two principles are brought together into one order of being, in a symbolic dialectic that can never lose either of its poles. In India, this vivid but all-encompassing phenomenal condition of existence is registered, first and foremost, on the embodied consciousness of the individual. The manipulations of the body and its interaction with concrete objects are not primarily symbolic actions. They are direct imagistic interactions with religious forces at the very place where these register and assume a meaning.

Concluding Remarks

My discussion has laid the ground for the hypothesis that central cultural symbols like dharma and purity are not rendered meaningful by a transcendental or sociological (functional or structural) a priori made explicit through conventional signs and natural symbols. The unity and coherence of cultural symbols are related within a consciousness that integrates a world of perception with a world of ideas. Phenomenal consciousness acts thus as a prism, which can become objectified by means of epistemological symbols such as the body in the "Puruṣa *Sūkta*" or rituals such as bathing. These symbols and rites provide the locus for an indigenous hermeneutic that is not designed to uncover new facts about the world but to articulate conceptually insights that are already intuited phenomenally. The researcher's task is to track down ideas and symbols to this ground in perception and physical existence. If the path leads through too many landmarks in Western schools, such as Gestalt, the only consolation is that we do not have to track through the jungles of psychoanalysis yet again. And, as we descend from lofty conceptual ideas to concrete experience, we return—again and again—to the human body. How did the Hindus imagine the body as an instrument of resonance, that is meaningful perceptions? Clearly this is a monumental question, which would require a major project to answer, were we to discuss the entire body and all its senses. The following chapter will narrow the focus down to skin and touch, a choice easy to justify because barriers such as the skin play the primary role in the metaphorical homologies of dharma.

Notes

1. G. Van der Leeuw, *Religion in Essence and Manifestation*, vol. 2 (Gloucester, Mass.: Peter Smith, 1967), p. 343.

2. *Rāmāyaṇa* 1.56–1.59; cf. *Manu Smṛti* 3.8,10, According to the *Viṣṇudharmottara* evildoers are to be represented artistically as ugly and dark complexioned. See Kramrisch, p. 20.

3. See the *Mahābhārata* version in 12.59.99–103.

4. These caveats are extremely common these days. See, for instance, McKim Marriott, "Hindu Transactions: Diversity without Dualism," in Bruce Kapferer ed., *Transactions and Meaning* (Philadelphia: Institute for the Study of Human Issues, 1976), pp. 109–42.

5. See chapter 6.

6. Paul Ricoeur, *The Symbolism of Evil* (Boston: Beacon Press, 1969), p. 23.

7. Ibid., p. 28; my emphasis.

8. Mary Douglas, *Purity and Danger* (London: Routledge & Kegan Paul), 1979, p. 2; my emphasis. Cf. Van der Leeuw, *Religion.*

9. Ibid., p. 4.

10. Mary Douglas, *Natural Symbols* (New York: Vintage Books, 1973), p. 93; see also discussion and sources in my chapter 6, n. 43.

11. *Phenomenology of Perception* (London: Routledge & Kegan Paul, 1962), p. 127; cf. Ernst Cassirer, *Philosophy of Symbolic Forms*, vol. 3 (New Haven: Yale University Press, 1985), p. 72; Martin Heidegger, *Being and Time*, trans. J. Macquarrie and E. Robinson (New York: Harper & Row, 1962), pp. 83, 87.

12. Edwin Ardener, Review of *Purity and Danger* by Mary Douglas, *Man* n.s., no. 2 (1967):139.

13. Douglas, *Purity*, p. 161.

14. Victor Turner, *The Forest of Symbols: Aspects of Ndembu Ritual* (Ithaca: Cornell University Press, 1967), p. 26.

15. Ibid.

16. Chapter 1..

17. Turner, *Forest of Symbols*, p. 33.

18. Ibid., p. 46.

19. Gananth Obeyesekere, *Medusa's Hair* (Chicago: University of Chicago Press), 1984, p. 9; the book's name refers to an element in its content but is also a fabulous pun on the Freudians (and Turner). On Turner's methodological poles, see Evan M. Zuesse, *Ritual Cosmos.* (Athens: Ohio University Press, 1985), p. 135.

20. Jayanta Mahapatra, "On the Bank of the Ganges," in *A Rain of Rites* (Athens, G.: The University of Georgia Press, 1982), p. 32.

21. Quoted in Diana L. Eck, *Banaras, City of Light* (Princeton: Princeton University Press, 1982), p. 16.

22. See *Viṣṇu Smṛti* chap. 54, and also the notes by Manmath Nath Dutt in the *Dharam Shastra*, vol. 4 (New Delhi: Cosmo, 1979), p. 940. Cf. *Kṛtyakalpataru*, vol. 3, ed. K. V. Rangaswami Aiyangar (Baroda: Oriental Institute, 1950), with notes on pp. 70ff. See also P. V. Kane's comprehensive discussion in *History of Dharmaśāstra* (Pune: BORI, 1974), 2.2:658–72.

23. III.32.

24. Ascetics, people undertaking vows for a variety of reasons, pilgrims, and the like take a third (optional) bath at dusk.

25. Rai Bahadur Vidyarnava, *The Daily Practice of the Hindus* (New York: AMS Press, 1974, p. 19

26. RV 1.2.4.8.

27. *Vājasaneyi Saṃhitā* (Vāj. Saṃ.) 6.22.

28. Vāj. Saṃ. 6.23.

29. The act is accompanied by the formula to the earth "pervade my limbs (*ārūdya mama gātrāṇi*)" from Tait. Ar. 10.1.1.

30. RV 1.22.17. On the number three and on spatialization of time, see chapters 6 and 3 respectively.

31. RV 10.17.10.

32. RV 10.9.1–3 (O'Flaherty, trans.); cf. AV 1.33: "Behold me with your auspicious eye, waters, Touch my skin with your auspicious body."(4)

33. *Taittirīya Saṃhitā* (TS) 5.6.1.1–2.

34. RV 1.23.22.

35. RV 1.114.1.

36. RV 10.97.16; cf. *Atharvaveda* (AV) 6.81.

37. RV 5.81.

38. RV 10.190.1–3 (O'Flaherty).

39. Quoted at length in Kane, *Dharmaśāstra*, 2.1, p. 662.

40. Fritz Staal, "The Meaninglessness of Ritual," *Numen* 26, no. 2 (1979):20.

41. RV 10.121.7 (O'Flaherty).

42. Arthur B. Keith, *The Veda of the Black Yajur School* (*Taittirīya Saṃhitā* part 2) (Cambridge, Mass.: Harvard University Press, 1914), pp. 453–54.

43. Franz Kafka, "The Metamorphosis," in *The Complete Stories* (New York: Schocken Books, 1971), p. 92.

44. Ibid., p. 114.

45. Ibid.

46. Ibid.

47. Wolfgang Kohler, *The Task of Gestalt Psychology* (Princeton: Princeton University Press, 1969), p. 66.

48. Ibid., p. 90; cf. Floyd Allport, *Theories of Perception and the Concept of Structure* (New York: John Wiley, 1955), p. 128: "All experienced order in both space and time is a true representation of corresponding order in the underlying dynamical context of physiological process."

49. Allport, *Theories*, p. 140.

50. K. Koffka, *The Principles of Gestalt Psychology* (New York Harcourt, Brace, 1935), p. 309.

51. Kohler, *The Task*, pp. 90–93.

52. Ibid., p. 53.

53. Ibid., p. 59.

54. Allport, *Theories*, p. 118.

55. *Philosophy of Symbolic Forms*, 3:202.

56. The Gestalt theorists argue very persuasivley against the projection hypothesis. See, for instance, Kohler, *The Task*, pp. 46ff.

57. See A. Frutiger, *Signs and Symbols* (New York: Van Nostrand, 1989).

58. Wolgang Metzger, "The Phenomenal-Perceptual Field as a Central Steering Mechanism," in Joseph R. Royce and William W. Rozeboom, eds., *The Psychology of Knowing* (New York: Gordon and Breach, 1972), p. 243.

59. Ibid., p. 245.

60. See Cassirer, *Philosophy of Symbolic Forms*, 3:39.

61. Koffka, *Principles*, p. 324.

62. Edward S. Reed, *James J. Gibson and the Psychology of Perception* (New Haven: Yale University Press, 1988), p. 227.

63. Wolfgang Kohler, *Gestalt Psychology* (New York: Liveright, 1929), p. 233.

64. Koffka, *Principles*, p. 320.

65. *The Integrative Action of the Nervous System* (New Haven: Yale Universtiy Press, 1947), p. 132.

66. James J. Gibson, "A Theory of Direct Visual Perception," in Royce and Rozeboom, *The Psychology of Knowing*, p. 126. See also Allport, *Theories*, pp. 201–7.

67. Brian A. Curtis et al, *An Introduction to the Neurosciences* (Philadelphia: W. B. Saunders, 1972), pp. 673, 700.

68. *Phenomenology of Perception*, p. 316.

69. Ibid., p. 315.

70. Koffka, *Principles*, p. 328.

71. Merleau-Ponty, *Phenomenology of Perception*, pp. 316–17.

72. This effect is achieved in a higher degree where the water forms whirlpools, a typical occurrence at the confluence of rivers, which are particularly purifying.

73. See the stories of Nārada's transformations brought about by bathing in river water in Wendy D. O'Flaherty, *Dreams, Illusion and Other Realities* (Chicago: University of Chicago Press, 1984), pp. 81–83.

74. AV 13.1.1, The hymn is meant for the protection of the king and queen who are identified with Rohita and Rohiṇī; Sūrya is depicted in the RV (7.63.1) as the eye of Varuṇa and Mitra. It is also described as the watcher of man (*nṛcakṣaṣāḥ*) (AV13.2).

75. Bachelard, as usual, put it as well as anyone: "The eye is the center of light, a little human sun" *Poetics of Reverie* (Boston: Beacon Press, 1965), p. 183.

76. MS 5.66, 75–76

77. A. R. Luria, *Cognitive Development* (Cambridge, Mass.: Harvard University Press, 1976), chap. 2.

78. Ricoeur, *Symbolism of Evil*, p. 16.

4

Dermatology and Cosmology

No map has been used more widely to chart the terrains of the human imagination than the human body. Consequently, the study of the human body as a symbolic and paradigmatic locus of meaning has been shared by a variety of disciplines. The body has been used to decipher sacred architecture and technology in the study of religion. Corporeal and social homologies have been instrumental in deciphering primitive forms of classification in anthropology and sociology. Mary Douglas has even attempted to demonstrate empirically the direct correlation between body image and social cohesiveness. In contrast to this determinism, historians of religion have emphasized the importance of Puruṣa-like symbolic representations of the social and cosmic organism. And, of course, at the root of the disciplines that study religious phenomena stand the early works of Frazer and Tylor on magic. The concepts of sympathetic and contagious magic are directly related to the experiential primacy of the body in the formulation of causal categories. In light of all this, primarily the lasting significance of theories of magic, it is surprising how little interest has focused on the human skin. I suspect this may be due to the fact that the rather literal, and often derogatory, early theories of magic were later replaced by the conceptual tools of analogy and homology. For instance, the shaving of the head as a stimulant to agricultural fertility, which would have been understood in terms of sympathetic powers of resemblance, is reinterpreted symbolically: hair and plants are now homologous components in two distinct semiotic systems, one of which, the body, acts as a sign for the other. Because the literal-minded talk of power transmission across surfaces has been abandoned, the skin as a boundary between body and world has been rendered insignificant, except as symbol for boundaries in the world.

The following chapter will take the skin very seriously on its own terms, with minimum recourse to semiotics. I shall examine the role of the human skin in the ancient Indian imagination and trace the emergence of the symbolic importance of surfaces and boundaries, out of the "subsymbolic" (sensory) experience of envelopment in a skin. A following chapter will demonstrate the near exclusive symbolic primacy of spatial categories of encompassment, enclosement, and boundedness in early formulations of dharma. Symbolically, dharma has been conceived as a fence of propriety, or a boundary for proper conduct (*maryādā*). These conceptions are not only metaphorically related to the symbolism of the human skin but, more important, the latter rests on the most fundamental tactile experiences of being-in-the-world. This means that the boundaries are significant (signifying) in the way the body senses them, so in a manner of speaking, dharma can actually be touched!

Unfortunately, even the earliest discussions of the human skin in India—usually restricted to skin pathology and therapy—are highly symbolic and articulated in mythical and ritual terms. My task then, after I examine a number of sources on skin pathology and therapeutics, is twofold. I must first explore the experiential basis of these symbolic expressions, then place both the experience and primary symbols in the broader cultural context that they help to shape, and by which they are in turn defined.

Magical systems, therapeutic and others, reflect an empirical cosmology, that is, a world view based on the sensory properties of worldly objects but which, nonetheless, point at a desired state of things, a "concrete ethos" as well. Cognitively, magical systems of medicine, as magic, demonstrate the constitution of a conceptual world along analogical principles that owe their cognitive characteristics to the body image. Thus, my goal in looking at Vedic and Ayurvedic therapeutics is not an explanation of the efficacy of rituals and hymns. Instead, I shall trace the empirical foundations of ancient Indian views of peripheries through their explicit and implicit analogies. The skin will be studied both as the source of tactile awareness and also, with regard to the thigmotropic orientation of humans when they discover the world, as the parameter of all spatial relations at their point of interaction.

At the very edge of physiological periphery (skin) is human hair, which the Hindus regard as a cutaneous member of the body. The Vedas and early Hinduism are fascinated with hair, as are most cultures around the world. Hair is rich with a variety of cosmological and psychological symbolism, and provides the focus for a number of myths and other narratives. Interestingly, since the late Hindu medical texts regard hair (and nails) as an extension of the skin, its absence or premature loss is discussed as skin disease.[1] The human skin must be covered by hair on the head and genitalia, at the very least. A bald head or pubic region is the sign of hopelessly bad luck:

> A bald man suffering from the sun's rays on his head
> sought out the sun-dispelling shade beneath a Bilva tree
> Whereat a Bilva fruit fell down and cracked his skull.
> Wherever the luckless goes he finds calamity.[2]

The famous homeopathic efficacy of plants that cure a variety of skin diseases does not apply here to the Bilva with its heavy fruit. Indeed the loss of hair tested the ingenuity and imagination of gods and physicians from the *Ṛgveda* to the specialized medical texts.[3] Magical homological identifications appear to operate in the Atharvavedic charms for the strengthening and restoring of hair. The ground is often described as the skin (6.21.1), the "down-growing plant" (*nitatnī*) is the opulent and healthy hair, which, when cooked into a concoction and sprinkled on the human hair, promotes its health (6.136.1).[4] Even the black color of the healer's robes and the black-colored food he eats (Kauś. 30.8–10; 31.28; 30.8) are the color of healthy hair.[5] It is frequently compared by means of analogy to the plants of the earth, from whose "skin" these are pulled for medicinal purposes.[6] Such an explicit analogy is played out in rituals such as the first tonsure, in which three blades of darbha grass are placed next to the hair being shorn.[7] Similarly, the *Śatapatha Brāhmaṇa* explores in its usual exhaustive detail the relation between the sacrificial grass and the human hair that it controls by means of ritual manipulations.[8]

Apālā and Indra

A peculiar method for restoring hair, or curing skin diseases, is told in the *Ṛgveda* 8.91.80 in which a young woman named Apālā asks Indra to restore her father's head of hair, and her own pubic hair as well. The story of Apālā is simple yet mystifying and, as usual, it exists in several versions.[9] The earliest version (RV 8.91, O'Flaherty, trans.) is briefest but hardest to decipher.

> 1. A maiden going for water found Soma by the way. She brought it home and said, "I will press it for you, Indra; I will press it for you mighty one.
> 2. "Dear man, you who go watchfully into house after house, drink this that I have pressed with my teeth, together with grain and gruel, cakes and praises.
> 3. "We do not wish to understand you, and yet we do not misunderstand you. Slowly and gently, ever more gently, flow for Indra, O

drop of Soma.

4. "Surely he is able, surely he will do it, surely he will make us more fortunate. Surely we who are hated by our husbands should flee and unite with Indra.

5. "Make these three places sprout, O Indra: my daddy's head and field, and this part of me below the waist.

6. "That field of ours, and this my body, and my daddy's head—make them all grow hair."

7. In the nave of the chariot, in the nave of the cart, in the nave of the yoke, O Indra of a hundred powers, you purified Apālā three times and make her sun-skinned.

The *sūkta* appears to be a simple praise of Indra's miraculous healing powers but it contains much that is not clear. It is further complicated by later versions, including Sāyaṇa's *itihāsa*, as well as by the ritual use to which it is put in matrimonial contexts. Sāyaṇa tells of Apālā who was afflicted with a skin disease and was repudiated by her husband for that reason. She practiced penance at her father's house to which she had returned. In Wilson's translation, the narrative continues in the following manner:[10]

> One day she went out to bathe, intending to make a Soma offering to Indra, and as she was returning, she found some Soma plants in the road. She gathered them and ate them as she walked. Indra, hearing the sound of her jaws, thought it was the sound of the Soma stones, and appeared to her, asking whether there were any Soma stones bruising there. She explained the reason of the sound, and Indra turned away. She called after him, "why dost thou turn away? Thou goest from house to house to drink the Soma, now then drink the Soma ground by my teeth and eat fried grains of barley." . . . Indra then, falling in love with her, drank the Soma as she wished. She then triumphantly exclaimed (v.4): "I have been repudiated by my husband and yet Indra comes to me."

Indra finally granted Apālā's boon by pulling her (*niścakarṣa*) three times through the hole of his own chariot as well as the cart and the yoke. The first layer of skin cast off became a porcupine (*śalyaka*), the second an alligator (*godhā*), and the third a chameleon (*kṛkalāsa*). Apālā was thus left with sunlike skin.

The other versions, naturally, offer variations in detail—often of some significance. For instance, the *Bṛhaddevatā* (6.99) mentions that Indra fell in love with Apālā before the Soma pressing. She went to the river with a pot to fetch water—not to bathe. Apālā's request was for hair, perfect limbs, and a fair skin—all on her own body. Another version (JB 1.220) tells of Apālā Atreyi who, presumably, was not yet wed, who had moles or a bad skin disease. She went to the road, not a river. When Indra pulled her through the holes of the chariot, cart, and yoke, she actually became three different animals in turn. These, and all other variations must be considered in a full symbolic and historical interpretation of the Apālā hymn. However, a note of caution must be sounded here concerning that which Roland Barthes has termed the "massive privilege of resemblance" in the act of symbolic interpretation. Every myth and ritual is a consciously self-enclosed nexus of meaning and form within an extremely broad and interconnected network of symbolic values. If we are committed to a symbolic hermeneutic, then even before the interpretation begins, we find ourselves drawn to an ever widening fabric, which is based on the resemblance of mythical features. The analysis is then broadened to rivers, pots, Soma plants, Indra, Atri, grinding stones, teeth, hair, heads, chariots, wagons, yokes, holes, fields, crops, marriage, kisses, and so on. Each of these forms, symbolically considered, then draws us to additional forms, additional symbols, and new contexts. Reading a text thus demands an encyclopedic erudition in the morphology of mythical consciousness, which postpones rather than sharpens the interpretative act.[11] By focusing on the primary elements of the myth-ritual and carrying them to a limited level of generality, we can manage the scope of interpretation. This still yields interesting insights though it does not provide a method, because the meaning of these associated contexts—valencies, as Eliade calls them, must be determined in some other fashion. I shall return to this point after surveying the results of a symbolic reading of the Apālā text.

The Symbolism of the Apālā Sūkta

Despite a great deal of discussion, few interpretations have been offered for the Apālā hymn and Sāyaṇa's *itihāsa*. The most focused effort, by Ram Gopal, who reads the *sūkta* as a narrative about the Sarasvatī passing through the mountains, has been ridiculed by S. A. Dange.[12] Dange's own interpretation can lead us from the particular to the general along the symbolic hermeneutic path. He notes Apālā's association with Mahānagnī in the *Atharvaveda* (14.1), where the two divine sisters flank the bride in the paradigmatic wedding ceremony. As a younger sister and a *kanyā*, Apālā is thus both unwed and lacking in pubic hair due to age.[13] The "purification" through the three holes is thus not so much a squeezing as a sprinkling, which is equivalent to the matrimonial ceremonies of the Gṛhya Sūtras. The hymn thus becomes a paradigm of fertility by means of which the bride may prevent a potential disaster. However, Dange is forced to concede that the Vedic narrative deals with an existing "sexual defect" so he posits a twofold motif that includes the cure of a postmatrimonial disease as well. Either interpretation forces a rapid move to the general significance of the mythical forms analyzed: Apālā, like Mahānagnī, is the field. She is made fertile by the divine fluid—Indra's rain. The holes (*kha*) through which the the rain passes is the sky or the sun. Apālā's final sunlike brilliance can be attributed to this solar rain and resembles the royal consecration in which the new birth of the king is also enacted by means of the golden waters (*sūryodaka* or *ātaparṣā*) symbol.[14]

All of this takes us quite far afield, for one is now compelled to look at the Rājasuya as a model—that is, a meaning-giving paradigm—for a rite of rebirth and fertilization. In this context, hair (Apālā's and her father's) can be associated with *śrī*, an invigorating vital force (JB 2.204). At the same time, as Heesterman notes, hair is also dead and impure skin to be discarded before the sacrifice.[15] Consequently, shaving may be seen as a discarding of the old skin. The shaving of the sacrificer in the Agnistoma is designed to produce vegetation and the powers of growth in the natural world. The chariot by which Apālā is "shaved"—and Indra's chariot in particular—symbolizes the agricultural year, the seasons of the entire annual cycle of birth-death-rebirth. Chariot races, indeed, were carried out in order to regenerate the productive forces of nature.[16]

We see here the predictable motif of the field, which is regenerated by the cyclical motion of the seasons, enacted here by means of an agricultural rite and myth. The complementary homological aspect of this theme involves symbols of birth seen in the passage through narrow holes and the shedding of symbolic amniotic fluids, which are a discarded layer of skin. The pressing of Soma, too, is symbolically associated with the giving of birth by means of a shared etymology—the shared verbal root *su*.[17] This connection plays a key role in Apālā's relation to Indra in the hymn. The internal Soma offering suggests that Apālā became identical with the oblation itself and so underwent the symbolic sacrificial death and rebirth that concludes with the shedding of embryonic fluids in the form of the animals, which Sāyaṇa and the other texts mention.[18]

The narrative can also be read in a variety of other symbolic manners, one interesting case among which is O'Flaherty's analysis of the split woman.[19] However, the symbols of the fields, birth, and fertility in general are the most obvious. Moreover, the presence of Apālā in the Gṛhya Sūtra wedding ceremony requires a serious consideration of these themes. Hanns-Peter Schmidt reads the Apālā *Sūkta* as a telescoped representation of a girl's maturing into adulthood. Apālā's disease is no more than acne and the purification in the holes is a symbolic ritual of passage, which is also prescribed in some Gṛhya Sūtras for the bride.[20] The relation between the girl's pubic baldness and her father's head and field is an analogy, which Schmidt considers obvious. Consequently, the father's baldness is also not pathological, but caused by seasonal shaving designed to procure the field's fertility.[21] Still none of this enables us to interpret the specific narrative. The preceding interpretations only broaden and deepen the imagination at work behind these various narratives, an imagination we have yet to understand.

A close etymological study obviously deepens our perspective into an intentionally elusive narrative. The *sūkta* hovers in a very narrow zone between devotion and sexuality. Indra's diminutive name, *vīraka*, which O'Flaherty translated as "dear man" is vaguely suggestive of the penis in its Sanskrit connotations.[22] More subtly yet, the fluid produced in Apālā's mouth (*jaṁbhasuta*) can be read as a pun on the love juice produced by oral copulation, and which is contrasted with juice that Indra seeks as he wanders from house to house (*gṛham gṛham*) and which Meyer connects with vaginas. The pun thus contrasts Apālā's oral copulation with Indra to his normal intercourse among women who crush the Soma with stones.[23] This sets the stage for the reversals utilized in Apālā's cure. However, even if we introduce sexuality as an additional level in the narrative, we have merely broadened the parameters of interpretation—not deepened the analysis. Even Schmidt's definitive philological analysis cannot explain the specific form of purification in the holes merely by pointing out that it is shared by features of the matrimonial ritual. To put it more theoretically, whether the case is cosmic fertility and regeneration, auspicious matrimony, or sexual maturation, the symbolic reading requires an emptying of the concrete forms given in the narrative. Hair, field, chariot are all made transparent, so to speak, so that we may glimpse the tapestry of symbolic "meaning" stretching out behind and beyond them. The problem—and this is just one among many—is that one loses sight of the specific occasion of the myth by fracturing the concrete parameters of contingent experience with which a possibly unique insight is circumscribed within an ocean of symbols. Only by wrestling with the contingent "given" does the specific intentionality of the mythmaker reveal itself in a limited—therefore living—fashion.

Even the cross-cultural phenomenology of curing by pulling through holes leaves too many problems unresolved. Wayland Hand collected hundreds of examples from around the world for healing a variety of disorders by pulling patients through holes. These include holes in trees, bushes, vines, earth, rocks, animals, and shrines. The procedure is used not only for skin diseases but for any number of other illnesses. For instance, in Belgium and Luxemburg a child who is slow to walk is made to crawl under a rerooted bramble on Friday. Children in the British Isles who suffer from whooping cough crawl under the belly of a donkey.[24] Researchers have noted early the similarity to snakes sloughing their skins by crawling through narrow apertures. Frazer has applied this observation to a theory that explains the holes as a way of rubbing or scraping off spirits attached to the skin in the form of disease. And indeed, Coomaraswamy regards Apālā as a Naganī who sloughs her skin with the help of Indra. But Hand cautions us that several variations in the performance of the procedure render single theories useless. For instance, the patient is often admonished not to touch the walls through which he crawls, so it appears that scraping is not at work here. The wealth of data, in short, while essential, does not provide the key for understanding the ritual. We must begin with the assumption that the Apālā *sūkta* is precisely what it appears to be, the episodic description of a skin-curing ritual within a specific medical culture. It may be profitable to pause here in order to look at a similar, but more systematic, therapeutical procedure described in the *Suśruta Saṃhitā* (2.9.5ff.).[25]

Skin Therapy

The medical text describes in great detail a therapeutic session involving the use of Soma. The disease (*vyādhi*) in unclear in the text but may include leprosy. I list some of the primary elements in the lengthy therapy.

1. The patient is placed in a room (*āgāra*) surrounded by two others, that is, enclosed by three layers of wall.[26]

2. The patient will spend one month in that inner room after which he or she will move to the next room for ten days, then the third room, and will finally emerge completely.

3. The Soma plant is procured in the customary manner for an Agnistoma, its bulb is pricked with a golden needle, and the juice is collected in a golden bowl.

4. The patient begins the treatment by drinking a measurable quantity (*añjali*) and takes no other food except milk for several days.

5. As the Soma is digested, we are told, the patient first vomits "blood-streaked worm-infested matter." The following (third) day worm-infested stools are observed. On the fourth day swellings appear on the skin and worms creep out of the body.

6. Meanwhile the patient had been lying on a bed alternately covered with black deer skin, silk, dust, and silk again.

7. By the seventh day the patient is reduced to skin and bones. The therapy now reaches a turning point. The patient's body is now washed with tepid milk, and plastered with sesamum, liquorish (*yaṣṭi madhu*), and sandalwood. A similar treatment follows the next day.

8. Shortly thereafter, the results begin to appear: as the patient's muscles begin to grow "the skin cracks, the teeth, nails and hair begin to fall off."

9. Anu-taila oil, the very same ointment used for newborn infants, is rubbed on the skin. The patient is bathed in Soma-vaka. After the tenth day the skin becomes firm and by the seventeenth day perfect new teeth will have appeared.

10. As the patient's diet is strengthened new fingernails grow in, "fixed, glossy and coral colored . . . resembling the new rising sun in lustre." Hair grows back in abundance. The skin assumes the soft hue of a blue lotus and the disease is finally expelled from the body.

The similarities between this therapeutic ritual and the enigmatic

Apālā *sūkta* are numerous and striking : the three layers (skins, walls), the threefold expunging of disease in animal form, the combination of liquid and gold, the imbibing of Soma, the resulting brilliant skin, and others. The historian might seek a common therapeutic origin, an ancient Aryan magical rite possibly. The phenomenologist would focus primarily on a shared symbolism of death and rebirth. Both are valid and necessary approaches but stop short of explaining a series of unique qualities and dynamics attributed to the skin as a human boundary. The concrete practical science of the Saṃhitā points not only to a symbolic world view but is also based on a specific conception of envelopment within a skin. In order to understand this we must delay interpretation still further.

Dermatology

The Vedas, particularly Ṛg and Atharva, are greatly interested in human skin, primarily its pathology and health, but also in the ritual use of ointments, washings, massage, cooling, and so forth. For a physiognomic description of the skin, however, we must turn to the medical texts such as the *Suśruta Saṃhitā* (Su.S.) and *Caraka Saṃhitā*, which still owe a good deal of their general orientation to Vedic ideas.

The *Suśruta Saṃhitā* distinguishes external skin (*tvac*) from the tissues (*kalās*) that envelope the body's internal elements (*dhātus*). The former is divided into seven layers (4.3) though some limbs are covered with two or three layers only. From the outside in these layers are *avabhasini*, *rohita*, *śveta*, *tāmra*, *vedini*, *rohiṇi*, and *maṇsa-dhara*. As ususal, the names are revealing. The first layer, the "brilliant" or "irradiating one," is said to reflect both the colors of the external world and the five hues of the body's elements (*dhātus*). The five bodily elements are identical with the cosmic elements: *ākāśa* (ether), *vāyu* (wind), *teja* (heat), *āpas* (water), and *pṛthivi* (earth). Each element determines the nature and function of perception organs, internal organs, and the entire body's disposition and energy level. The five colors are representative of the combination of the three *guṇas* (material strands) within the *dhātus* (internal elements).[27] The luminosity of the external skin layer is related to its reflectivity and translucence, which are indications not of transparency but of a unique power to mediate between the internal and external dimensions of the lived world.

Vedic conceptions of the skin or rather skin pathology, on which the Saṃhitā may ultimately rest, tell as much about the Vedic imagination and cosmology as about the skin itself: "Born by night art thou, O plant, dark black sable. Do thou, that art rich in color [*rajanī*] stain this leprosy, and the gray spots."[28] If leprosy is a discoloration of the skin, reflective in the later medicine of a *guṇa* imbalance that originates in the bones and reflects an inner corruption (*doṣa-kṛta*), then the multicolored coloring plant (the black *rajanī*) is an appropriate homeopathic treatment. Curing is identical with coloration in a system where health and propriety are interconnected and both become manifest in skin color.[29]

The seventh skin layer inside is the "flesh supporter" (*maṇsa-dhara*).[30] Because this layer serves a purely functional role, it is described as altogether inwardly turned. It resembles in name the seven *kalās* or internal skins that are characterized as the supporters (*dhara*) of whichever internal organ they envelope—for instance, the *meda-dhara* is the abdominal fat supporter.[31] It is most indicative, therefore, of the skin's subjective or internal connection. Not surprisingly perhaps, the seven layers of skin are replicated in Hindu mythology and in village folklore, with the seven layers of the earth, through which trees and grass seeds are spread when the earth is impregnated by its husband, the bull.[32] The copulation takes place by the insertion of his horns into anthills and, as we shall see, both possess medicinal value for skin disease.[33]

In contrast with this reflective-luminous dermatology, an entirely distinct conception is articulated in the *Ṛgveda* 10.97, which is particularly instructive of the moral and cosmological nature of diseases. The hymn is a praise of herbs, whose king is the Soma plant: "O all you various Herbs whose king is Soma, that overspread the earth, Urged onward by Brihaspati, combine your virtues in this plant" (10.97.19). The "king plant" cures the body as the king rids the kingdom of crimes (12).[34] Illness, indeed, is closely linked to the moral dimension of life and may be described as Varuna's curse or Yama's fetter. Disease steals into the body like a thief, breaking through the skin, and so must the curing herbs: "Over all fences have they passed, as steals a thief into the fold," in order to drive out the malady (10). The upshot of this outstanding example is that the body is a battleground for an ongoing dramatic cosmic conflict; it is a fenced-in kingdom, so to speak, which is invaded by evil-disease, then restored to wholeness by the martial powers of curative plants. Wellness is equated with wholeness or the inviolability of the body, surrounded as it is by the skin.

A related metaphor is utilized in the conceptualization of seven varieties of smallpox. The disease is not mentioned in the Vedas and is regarded as minor in the *Suśruta* and *Caraka Saṃhitās*, where it is known as Masurikā. Śītalā is only first mentioned in the twelfth century in Ḍalhaṇa's commentary on Su.S. 2.13.38.[35] It is described in seven varieties, most of which are incurable and all sharing a very high fever. Remedies, if they are to work at all, consist in lowering the body's temperature by applying cold (*śīta*) water and ash of cow dung, and fanning with Nimba leaves. The "śītalā stotram" from the *Skanda Purāṇa* may also be recited.[36] Like invaders of a city, a village, or the body, the fever must be kept out. This tradition reflects the homology established between the village, house, and room, which are respectively penetrated by the sisters, and the human body as it is invaded by the fever.

Given these factors and considering also the pervasive theory of karma, it is not surprising that the skin is a primary register of the fruition of sins committed in previous births.[37] A newborn baby's wet nurse must be examined for moles or stains on her skin in order to protect the nursing child (Su.S. 10.18). The baby herself is rubbed with Vala-taila cream and is bathed in an infusion of the Kṣīri tree barks, in Sarvagandha drugs, Kapittha leaves, or water in which red-hot gold or silver had been immersed (10.12). Because the skin "records" internal as well as external processes, creams and oils in Ayurvedic and Vedic medicine possess salutary effects for more than just skin conditions and diseases. The skin, as we shall see, can act either as the transmitter of the medicine's potency or as the locus for its effects.

It may be interesting to digress briefly in order to note, by means of a comparison, the temporal quality of the skin among the Trobriands, in the following myth told by Malinowski:

> it is told to explain the fact that after a span of spiritual existence in Tuma, the nether world, an individual grows old, grey, and wrinkled; and then he has to rejuvenate by sloughing his skin. Even so did human beings in the old primeval times, when they lived underground. When they first came to the surface, they had not yet lost this ability; men and women could live eternally young.
>
> They lost the faculty, however, by an apparently trivial, yet important and fateful event. Once upon a time there lived in the village of Bwadela an old woman who dwelt with her daughter and grand-daughter; three generations of genuine matrilineal descent. The grandmother and granddaughter went out one day to bathe in the tidal creek. The girl remained on the shore, while the old woman went away some distance out of sight. She took off her skin, which carried by the tidal current, floated along the creek until it stuck on a bush. Transformed into a young girl, she came back to her grand-daughter. The latter did not recognize her; she was afraid of her, and bade her begone. The old woman, mortified and angry, went back to her bathing place, searched for her old skin, put it on again, and returned to her grand-daughter. This time she was recognized and thus greeted: "A young girl came here; I was afraid; I chased her away." Said the grandmother: "No, you didn't want to recognize me. Well, you will become old—I shall die." They went home to where the daughter was preparing the meal. The old woman spoke to her daughter: "I went to bathe; the tide carried my skin away; your daughter did not recognize me; she chased me away. I shall not slough my skin. We shall all become old. We shall all die."[38]

Like most myths, this one is overflowing with meanings, many of which compare with our own material: the emergence into the sunlight made vision replace touch and rendered identification problematic at the very least; it was the skin that registered the passage of time and had to be sloughed for renewal and change; bathing played an important role in the process of rejuvenation.[39]

Interpretation

I now propose the following hypothesis, which is based on the material we have seen and additional material to follow. The body in ancient India was conceived as an enclosed container enwrapped by a boundary that distinguishes and separates inside from outside. This familiar metaphorical conception is so fundamental that it is virtually inseparable from its experiential basis. However, it is never articulated in such a basic and unitary manner and recourse is always had to related metaphors. Two fundamental metaphors underlie most conceptions relating to the human body. The first basic metaphor, previously seen in the *Suśruta Saṃhitā*, describes the body as a microcosmic reflection of the world. It is a symbolic and actual "locus of intersection of the life-process of human society and the world of wild nature."[40] The body thus constitutes a cosmological map of the macrocosmic as well as social order, as illustrated in the famous Puruṣa *sūkta*. The second metaphor, as we have seen in the *Ṛgveda* 10.97, appears to contradict the first. It describes the body as a kingdom fortified within borders and sealed from the outside world by the king's forces. More generally, the body is a self-enclosed space (fort, house, room, pot) situated rather antagonistically within a surrounding world. This metaphor is seen at work in Manu's conception of crime (*adharma*) as a thorn stuck in the body of the kingdom (MS 8.12).

Predictably, the conception of the skin varies with the broad metaphor in which it is situated. In the first instance, the skin mirrors both the cosmos and the body. As it faces the world, it shines because it reflects the brilliance of the sun, which is taken as a normative paradigm of wellness. As it faces inward, the skin reflects the physiomoral constitution of the body. Thus, its interior colors are related to the appropriate *dhātus* and *guṇas* and the colors these represent. The skin here is related to the experience of transitivity and communication, basic to its tactile sensory properties. Tied to this spatiocosmological conception is the temporal metaphor of the skin as a map of character and moral predisposition. Essentially, the temporal order is merely subsumed within the spatial properties of the skin as a mirror of physical as well as moral properties in the world and the encompassed individual.

Within the second fundamental spatial metaphor, the skin acts like a wall. It separates and protects inside from outside. The penetration of the skin is not a sensory encounter or exploration—it is invasion. Contact is acceptable as sensory engagement, but its effect on the inside can never be direct.

For two primary reasons, it is not possible to state specifically the nature of a given skin disease according to each metaphorical conception. First, there is no necessary correlation between a disease and a dermatological conception. Leprosy and its treatment, for instance, can be described by both metaphors. Moreover, most texts reject an exclusive unitary perspective and employ both. Second, most skin diseases are described in a sketchy manner, if at all, and with a minimal number of symptoms given. Broader conceptual concerns are seldom stated, or even implied, where a specific skin disease is discussed. Still the diseases I have described and those to follow permit the formulation of the following basic hypothesis.

1. A skin disease that falls within the first metaphorical conception involves, above all, a loss of reflectivity and transitivity. The cure for such a disease would involve actual and symbolic reversal of spatial relations: inside and outside are reversed.

2. A skin disease conceptualized by means of the second basic metaphor entails the loss of protection, the weakening of a surface, and the penetration of the body proper by the disease. Curing involves expulsion of foreign substance and the fortification of the skin from the inside out ("growing out"; dietary manipulations) or from the outside in (amulets, cream rubs, baths). Again, both conceptions are usually combined so most diseases would involve both idioms.

We shall now see how these basic considerations affect the interpretation of the Apālā narrative. Apālā's skin disease, whatever it actually was, rests on a predominent, but not exclusive, dermatological conception of the skin as a reflector of the world. Her pubic baldness was associated with her father's bald pate and his barren field not homologically but paradigmatically. Her skin reflected the universe around her, a universe pervaded by barreness in all regions. As Sāyaṇa put it, her condition was due to some action of her own. The story of the cure contains two primary stages, each involving a reversal—the first posseses symbolic significance, the second therapeutic.

We are told in the *Ṛgveda* version that Apālā went to the "water" (*vāra*). It is reasonable to assume, as Sāyaṇa does, that she went to bathe (*snānārtha*). Her intention to wash her skin is juxtaposed with the drinking of Soma, which is pressed by her teeth (*jaṃbhasuta*). External washing is replaced by internal Soma oblation.[41] The second reversal is therapeutic. The disease manifests itself by an absence of growth so one might have expected a fortification and fructification of the skin by means of herbs, ghee, or other medicines. Instead three layers of skin are removed by scraping, though the *sūkta* only speaks of a threefold "purification" (*pūtvya*) in the holes. Given the fact that humans are said to possess between three and seven layers of skin, Apālā's cure is a movement of an inner skin layer to the outside. The fourth layer was healthy, that is, it was able to reflect the brilliance of the sun (*sūryatvac*). What did the other skin layers reflect? This is not clear but could be answered if we knew what Sāyaṇa meant by his porcupine, alligator, and chameleon. Their symbolic significance notwithstanding, there is an apparent movement here from the gross and prickly, to a skin that is already capable of external reflection (the chameleon) though not the reflection of the sun, and is still too crude of texture. The story of Apālā, then, illustrates and substantiates the hypothesis relating to the first dermatological metaphor. However, the choice of animals in Sāyaṇa's version, and the "pushing out" of internal skin layers, are related to the second fundamental metaphor, that is, the skin as shield. As the conclusion of this chapter will show, more is at stake here than the qualities of skin and skin diseases. The dynamics of the spatial relations described in our hypothesis will extend to other domains, including dharma, which rest on fundamental metaphors of space. These spatial dynamics are far more basic than symbolic values such as birth, which are often said to explain this and similar rituals. These are not mutually exclusive options but two levels of hermeneutic discourse, the first of which underlies various symbols and makes their empirical resemblance possible.

Kṣetriya *and Jaundice*

The two fundamental body metaphors are operative in several diseases described in the *Atharvaveda* and *Kauśika Sūtra.* Two diseases that are said to reside in the skin are jaundice and Kṣetriya. The charm against jaundice (AV 1.22) emphasizes the skin's yellow color as a symptom-locus of the disease. The cure involves removal of the color both to the sun and to three yellow-feathered birds. Simultaneously: "The cows whose divinity is Rohini, they who, moreover, are themselves red [*rohiṇī*]—(in their) every form and every strength do we envelop thee" (I.22.3).[42] The practices associated with these formulas are described in *Kauśika* 26. 14–21: The patient is given water mixed with hair from a red bull to drink. He also drinks water that had been poured over a red bull. The patient sits on a bed made of stretched bull hide wearing an amulet, apparently of red bull hair and gold. He is then fed porridge made of turmeric or curcuma. He is smeared with the remaining porridge, which is subsequently washed off his body and onto three birds (parrot, thrush, yellow agtail) that had been tied to the bed.

The washing off of the disease is generally regarded as the therapeutic act in this ritual, the return of the patient's yellow color to its natural location.[43] However, there is also a massive "injection" of redness into the patient's body by means of a drink and amulet. In later medical texts there are two red-skin layers (Rohiṇī and Rohita), second from the inside and second from the outside. I suggest that the successful washing of the yellow skin is made possible by the fortification of an inner skin layer that "pushes out" the existing (ill) external layer. The consumption of the yellow porridge precedes its smearing on the skin. It is thus symbolically pushed out from within by the healthy (red) skin layer, which is imbibed with bull hair. This conception is based primarily on the skin's reflective powers, but also, in a less significant manner, on a concept of expulsion that is linked to the "body as container" metaphor.

This order of significance is reversed in another Atharvavedic source (3.7). The illness in case is the Kṣetriya, a hereditary skin disease of uncertain characteristics. The Kṣetriya and an elaborate cure will be shortly discussed in detail. The following formula, however, is a splendid example of the body as kingdom metaphor. The *Atharvaveda* formula states: "Upon the head of the nimble antelope a remedy grows! He has driven the kshetriya in all directions by means of the horn . . . The kshetriya that has entered into thee from the prepared [magic] concoction, for that I know the remedy: I drive the kshetriya out of thee" (3.7.1; 6). The curative ritual associated with the verbal fomula is described in *Kauśika* 27.29–31: the patient wears an amulet made from the horn of an antelope, drinks and rinses himself with water, then he is sprinkled with water warmed by antelope skin. The patient is finally fed with barley.

The metaphorical language leaves little doubt about the corporeal conception being employed here. The antelope itself is also extremely significant. Bloomfield notes in *Hymns* the pun on the animal's horn (*vi—ṣyati*) which relates to the sense of loosening or freeing from a disease (p. 337). However, the (black) antelope is also the major paradigmatic animal for establishing the sacred geography of India. The land where the black antelope (*kṛṣṇa mṛga*) roams is defined as Aryavarta or the area fit for sacrifices. The metaphor suggests a spreading equivalent to a loosening of the disease. The use of the horn is utterly obscure, but if my proposals are on track, it may be related to the "military" limb of the antelope, and the one that protrudes out of its body.

The disease called Kṣetriya (pertaining or belonging to the field or womb) presents additional interesting, but difficult, problems of interpretation. This is a disease of uncertain symptoms, which may or may not be a type of leprosy. Its treatment, along with the appropriate hymns, is given in the *Atharvaveda* (2.8) and in the *Kauśika Sūtra* (26.41ff.). The cure begins with two washings outside the house, the first apparently at night, and the second at dawn. With the first washing the healer blesses the Vicṛtau ("twin looseners") stars and beseeches them to cure the Kṣetriya (AV 2.8.1) With the second washing he asks the night and the plant to destroy the disease and the witches (*abhikṛtvarī*) (AV 2.8.2) He ties an amulet of barley and sesame prepared with wood from the Terminalia Arjuna, having first allowed it to sit for three days. He also puts some straw and mud from an anthill, which he had beat to powder, into the skin of a freshly slain animal. As he does this he recites, "With the straw of thy brown barley, endowed with white stalks, with the blossom of the sesame—may the plant, destructive of kshetriya, shine [*ucchatu*] the kshetriya away" (AV 2.8.3). Then he pours the dregs of ghee placed in a water container over the yoke of a spanned plow that is suspended over the head of the ill person, while he pays homage to the plows, wagon poles, and yokes.

Next, he pours what remains of the ghee into a pot full of water, and places the pot in an empty (clay?) hut. As he does this, he pays reverence "to those with sunken eyes [*sanisrasākṣyebhyo*] . . . to the indigenous [*saṅdeśyebhyo*] . . . to the lord of the field [*kṣetrasya pataye*]." Finally, he places straw from the roof of the hut within an old pit or ditch in which the patient is standing, sitting, or lying. The patient is given the liquid to drink, and is finally washed with the remainder.

Several interpretations have been proposed for this ritual: according to Bloomfield, the disease is being washed into the ground out of which it had emerged.[44] This may be consistent with another obscure illness of the skin—sores apparently—caused by Rudra's arrow of one hundred points.[45] This skin disease, if it actually existed, was cured by a washing with *jalasa*, which Bloomfield takes literally, Geldner symbolically, as urine.[46] Unlike leprosy with its strong moral underpinnings, Rudra's disease apparently describes a skin ailment that can spread into the internal organs but is curable by washing off the skin onto the ground (AV 6.57.3). Another interpretation of the Kṣetriya disease emphasizes its spiritual characteristics and explains the birth symbolism with reference to "another body" (*para kṣetra*); for since leprosy is incurable, the treatment is karmic and pertains to the emergence of a new body.[47]

Two additional factors, which can be taken into consideration, also complicate an effort to interpret the Kṣetriya therapy by means of its obvious agrological context, and the less obvious but strongly suggestive embryological nuances. First, according to the *Atharvaveda* (3.7.1), as we have seen, the same leprosy (Kṣetriya) can also be treated with the horn of an antelope by which it is said to be scattered in all directions. Second, both Atharvavedic hymns refer to the twin stars (Vicṛtau), which are literally the "looseners" of fetters (*pāśa*), calling to mind Varuṇa's fetters. Like the dropsy of classical Hinduism, the Kṣetriya suggests the moral (*adṛṣṭa*) characteristics of congenital diseases, possibly because it is both incurable and uterogenic. However, it is hard to see how these observations help us interpret this elaborate therapeutical ritual in any concrete fashion. While the ritual clearly enacts a new birth, its spiritual efficacy is hardly rendered obvious by the agricultural symbols involved.

The recited text is interesting, but it is the sequence of ritual actions that is therapeutic and ultimately meaningful. To review the symbolic narrative: the patient under the plow is "poured" into the earth with the liquid that flows off the plow. He is thus ritually ejaculated from the male organ (plow) into the mother (earth). The same ghee that had been poured over his head (it is the flaming liquid—the sperm) is now poured into a water container within an empty (clay) hut.[48] The association of clarified butter with birth is evident in numerous sources, including the *Ṛgvidhāna* (17.1–2): a woman who fears fatal premature birth pours a burnt offering into the fire with clarified butter. She anoints herself with the remaining ghee, then gives birth. After delivery she drinks from the remaining ghee and the child is finally anointed with the remains (18.4).[49] A continuity has been established in the Kṣetriya ritual between seed and embryo within the womb, which is the earth (clay) impregnated. This ritual continuity is sustained when straw from the roof is placed in a ditch, pit, or furrow—which is now *yoni*. The patient in the *yoni* is given to drink from and is bathed with the (amniotic) fluid from the hut, thus establishing his identity with the fetus.[50] And, it is well known that immediately after delivery the child's mouth should be rinsed with clarified butter (and rock salt). The *Caraka Saṃhitā*, (Śārīrasthana 8.46) prescribes that ghee mixed with honey should actually be given orally.[51] According to the *Suśruta Saṃhitā*, a linen pad soaked with clarified butter is applied to the head of the newborn. After the umbilical cord has been severed, the baby is given a mixture of herbs, gold dust, and clarified butter to drink. It is then rubbed with Vala taila ointment and bathed in an infusion of the barks of Kṣīri trees, or trees with milky sap (Su.S. 10.11–12). The entire ritual sequence of sexual symbolism is not surprising and is immediately suggested by the name of the disease—Kṣetriya (uterine; agrological). Since the disease is uterogenic, it is treated both physically and morally as congenital diseases must be. Phenomenologically, too, a new birth is expected to produce a newborn's pure skin. However, this is still too general because the new birth enacted here for the Kṣetriya illness could characterize a wide variety of ritual, religious, and therapeutic contexts alike. Rebirth too often symbolizes the transition or passage into new spiritual, social, or physical states. The symbol of the new birth, thus, does not explain the specific narratival elements employed. In this instance we have a specific skin disease that the ritual needs to rectify in a concrete manner. The symbols of rebirth fail to illuminate this specific agenda. The symbolic level of the ritual contains a penetration of germ (sperm) into the earth (womb) followed by a period of germination (pregnancy), then growth (birth). These are the fundamental structural symbols, but the locus of the disease is the patient's skin.

Nonsymbolic Analysis of Disease

We are not given sufficient detail to make very specific judgments, but the ritual utilizes skins and other surfaces, as well as passage across them, in a very significant manner. There are four important spatial surfaces or boundaries, and one temporal (the dawn). First is the patient's skin, then the earth surface, the empty hut, and the skin pouch used as amulet. The latter is particularly important for this specific skin disease. It is made of emphatically fresh hide—in order to retain the qualites of healthy living skins, which are primarily their transitivity and reflectivity.[52] Within the pouch are four items, among which the anthill dirt stands out incongruously (the other three are the "healing plants" of the verse). Now while straw, barley, and sesame grow out of the earth and are regarded in certain contexts as curative, and the anthill dirt had also been churned out of the earth, the ant also carries seeds into the earth. Ants impregnate the earth, so to speak, they are travelers across surfaces and their primary quality, in the present context, is a dynamic power of osmosis. Pulverized in the skin pouch, that is, refined into powers, the regenerative and transitive objects "percolate" through the pouch into the patient's skin. As he is "reborn" he is also cured by means of his skin's characteristics because it is injected with the curative amulet. According to the *Ṛgvidhāna*, amulets transfer powers obtained both naturally and ritually from trees (e.g., Banyan—Ficus indica), ghee, and other objects, such as clothes. The pregnant woman wears such an amulet, which has been fertilized (by clarified butter) and fortified (by the tree). On the third month she carries it on her stomach for a direct transference of powers to the womb (*Ṛgvidh.* 17.3–18.2).

The concrete therapy in the *Kauśika Sūtra* involves two external elements—clarified butter and amulet. Both are first manipulated externally, then penetrate the patient's body, the first orally, the second, as we have seen, by "injection" through the skin.[53] The same transitive dynamism is retained with regard to the symbols in the ritual. The butter is poured out, then put in a hut, then out again, and into the patient, and finally rubbed on him. These spatial orientations are more fundamental than symbols and would exert an experiential (magical) effect independent of any symbolic ramifications. The factual, therapeutic movement of curative substances across the surface of boundaries such as skins is made to resonate with the "mythical" birth symbolism. In such a magical system, however, the therapy is efficacious or, more important, meaningful, before it becomes mythical. This is due to the essential purpose of the ritual: to restore the skin's transitivity and translucence. The skin disease can only be called "agricultural" (Kṣetriya) or "uterine" because it effects the skin's ability to act like a field and a womb. Obviously, the skin neither gives birth, nor does it produce crops from a seed. When it is healthy, however, the skin absorbs sensory input from the external world, processes data creatively, and returns it reflectively to the outside through growth, luster, and interaction. The Atharvavedic rite is not about fields or wombs; it is about the human skin, which is experienced and imagined by means of a combined metaphor: the metaphor of the enveloping shield around a self-contained body but a porous shield, which places the body squarely within its environment and acts as a sensitive and transformative locus of the world's forces.

The material we have looked at indicates a keen awareness of the skin's significance for placing the individual in a spatial and heuristic context. Health and disease are terms of relation or balance between interiority and exteriority. The skin becomes the primary organ of relation, and touch is its principal action. The type of experience that can give rise to these symbolic insights is consistent with psychology's understanding of touch and other sensory functions, and their importance for the development of symbolic thought. From the earliest stages of infancy, sensorimotor interaction with the environment enhances the development of human intelligence. The early stages include proprioceptive coordination of sensory input and performative response; progressive sensory intermodal integration followed by action; mobility, balance, posture, and object permanence as conditioned by maternal contact. These and others are elements in infant cognitive development that enable the child to acquire language and symbolic functions.

The unique properties of the skin and tactility establish their relational primacy. Tactile perception opens itself to objective properties but, unlike vision, for instance, includes a bodily component: "The tactile localization of an object, for example, assigns to it its place in relation to the cardinal points of the body image."[54] Unlike the illusion that vision creates of constituting a distant world, tactility functions only by localizing our body in the world and the world in our body, so to speak.[55] The infant learns the foundations of appropriate spatial relations by means of the reproduction of the uterine tactual closeness in the exterogestational state. This renders the cognitive and emotional conditions of learning possible.[56]

We can not tell on the basis of the given material whether the intensive tactile stimulation that Indian babies undergo affects their cognitive development in an entirely unique manner. It is clear, however, that the symbols of skin surfaces, and the principles of their functioning, are closely related to the central role of tactility in situating humans within the world. The experience of the skin in the world simultaneously places the world—experientially, not symbolically—upon the skin. We have seen this in a previous chapter with the enormous power that cold river water exercises over the bather's state of mind.[57] Apālā's relation with her father, his field, or Indra's chariot is grounded in experience before it can become symbolically and homologically meaningful. Dermatological health is the skin's simultaneous ability to register the universe and protect us from its dangers. The mythical and ritual symbol, for once, have not been entirely separated from the most rudimentary impact of experience.

Animal Skins (Carman)

We have already seen a number of instances where animal skins are used in ritual and therapeutic contexts. While human skin defines the boundaries of the empirical person and his sense of a surrounding world, animal hides are not likely to carry the same meaning. The texts' interest in animal skin was never zoological, it was always "homologized," as Eliade would put it. In the medical texts animal skins were significant heuristically when, for instance, they retained the osmotic powers of a living membrane in amulets. However, the ritual texts were interested in hides in a variety of different, and far more symbolically loaded, roles.

Every *śrauta* ritual utilized skins in numerous manners. The Rājasūya for instance, includes rituals in which the appointed king steps, then sits, on tiger skin and the texts themselves are quite explicit about what this means: "Yourself a tiger step on the tiger [skin], into these great lands."[58] Thus, according to Bloomfield, following the explicit identification of king and tiger, the skin of a tiger is a mark of royalty because the tiger, as well as lion, is the king of animals.[59] But the situation is apparently more complicated in the case of bull or cow hide, which is used with far greater frequency. Instances abound, of course, but the marriage *saṃskāra* as well as the *upanayana* show the initiate (bride and student respectively) sitting on red cow (or bull) hide with hair side up. The Rājasūya, too, specifically the "Truth Messenger (Satyadūta—Haviṃsi) Iṣṭi," utilizes a dry skin bag, which is mentioned as containing "heavenly fluids and abundance" to be released in the form of rains.[60] The mythological associations make the meaning of such a skin bag abundantly clear as symbol for the rain-holding clouds or, in other instances, the water-packed earth.[61] Heesterman observes: "viewed against this background the dry skin bag in this *iṣṭi* seems to me to be the same vessel of heavenly fluids, the heavenly fluids having been released and put in motion again at the beginning of the new year . . . In other words it is the emptied womb or amniotic sac which is left over after the new birth has occurred."[62] Similar but distinct gestational symbols are used in other *iṣṭis*, including the broad cosmological identification of the king with the sun—both emerging out of an embryonic state in the Maitrabarhaspatyan Iṣṭi.[63]

Indeed, with ritual subjects huddling under animal skins in various fetal postures, no other explanation seems so obvious, and so the skin becomes analogous to the uterine walls. Still, it is not clear whether this analogy develops out of the ritual syntax or out of some intrinsic quality attributed to the skin itself.

More than either the tiger or cow skin, the black antelope's skin is typically associated with the Vedic ritual. It may be used as mat, cover, screen, container for the grains to be offered, and other functions. The Darśapūrṇamāsa contains a very elaborate manipulation of the entire hide including both the neck and anus, accompanied by explicit references to the skin of Aditi.[64] The black antelope was used as the gauge for the boundaries of India's sacred geography: "Where the black antelope ranges by nature, that should be known as the country fit for sacrifices."[65] The *Śatapatha Brāhmaṇa* (1.1.4.1?–2) tells of *yajña*—the sacrifice—taking the shape of a black antelope in order to escape from the gods.[66] Due in part to this identification, the Brahmin initiate to studentship must wear a garment made of antelope skin (*kārṣṇa*), while the Kṣatriya and Vaiśya are to wear spotted deer skin (*raurava*) and he-goat skin (*bāstāni*) respectively.[67] The text (Manu) prescribes some form of identity between the caste status of the students and dress material, just as it does in the case of the staff (*daṇḍa*) they are to carry. This implies that aside from the meaning attributed to hides strictly by means of a ritual syntax, animal skins are said to possess certain characteristics that derive from the animal itself. Morevoer, the act of wearing or coming into tactile contact with the skin is extremely significant. This line of ienquiry opens up new possibilities for understanding the ritual use of skins. Consider the following *Jaiminīya Brāhmaṇa* tale (2.182–83; translated by O'Flaherty):

> In the beginning, the skin of cattle was the skin of a man, and the skin of a man was the skin of cattle [i.e., cattle then had the skin that men now have, and the reverse]. Cattle could not bear the heat, rain, flies, and mosquitoes. They went to man and said, "Man, let this skin [of ours] be yours, and that skin [of yours] be ours." "What would be the result of that?" [man asked]. "We could be eaten by you," [the animals said], "and this [skin of ours] would be your clothing." So saying they gave [man] his clothing. Therefore, when [the sacrificer] puts on the red hide, he flourishes in that form. Then cattle do not eat him in the other world [if he wears the skin, they think he is one of them]; for cattle do eat a man in the other world [otherwise]. Therefore, one should not stand naked near a cow, for it is liable to run away from one, thinking, "I am bearing his skin [and he may try to get it back from me]." And this skin has got a tail, which makes it complete.[68]

According to O'Flaherty, the text is both a justification for the exploitation of cows and a foreshadowing of later karma theories. For our purposes it may be equally profitable to look at the absolute reversal of identity engendered by the exchange in skin. It is because of this exchange in this world that men eat cows. If the exchange had not taken place, in other words, if men still possessed the hairy hide they had originally owned, the cows would be eating men, because "cattle do eat a man in the other world." Men and cattle, in sum, exchange not only their outer wear but also their places in the food chain—a clear mark of identity. Indeed, the idea that wearing a given animal's skin confers an actual ontological transformation is characteristic of so-called magical thinking and shamanic practices around the world.

In a sense, it is almost as though the skin is the source of the animal, its defining quality (more than its flesh or bones): "Out of a skin, O'Ṛbus, once you formed a cow and brought the mother close to her calf again . . ."[69]

Undoubtedly, two perspectives play distinct and often complementary roles: a given skin may act both "semantically" and "syntagmatically" due to the animal powers it retains and its role in the ritual context. Occasionally the skin takes a life of its own, so to speak, when it is used in a third—independent—effect. This is the case of the drum, for instance, which is made of wood but constructed with the aid of the hide of cow or antelope.[70] Such a drum produces a living force, a sound, which owes its existence neither to the animal nor to the ritual in which the drum is used.

The skin, in conclusion, whether human or animal, is the primary relational organ of the body. It places the world on a corporeal map, which can help eliminate the distinct separation from the territory "out there." And unlike visual images it defines relations in the world in terms of subjective perceptions. We shall see in chapter 5 below that this is an important quality of the dharmic agent—though hardly sufficient yet. This book will eventually explain how individuals—using the term guardedly—become transformed by the landscape in which they move. This will be done in the marriage chapter. But we must first describe the topography of such a landscape, which is conceived as a physical world of dharma, that is, marked by meaningful boundaries.

Notes

1. See for instance MS 11.49; Nār. 1.184.

2. "Bhartṛhari Collection," in D. Ingalls, *Sanskrit Poetry*, pp. 262–63. On the private and public, sexual and nonsexual symbolism of hair, see E. R. Leach, "Magical Hair," *Journal of the Royal Asiatic Society* 88 (1958):147–65; Paul Hershman, "Hair, Sex, and Dirt," *Man*, n.s., 9, no. 2 (1974):274–99; Raymond Firth, *Symbolism: Public and Private* (Ithaca: Cornell University Press, 1973). The most comprehensive recent article is Alf Hiltebeitel, "Draupadi's Hair," *Purusartha*, 5 (1981):179–214.

3. RV 8.91; AV 6.21, 136, 137; Su.S. 25.18.

4. On hair and land homology, see the story of Candra who pulls out her hair and the land begins to burn, as told by M. Bloomfield in "The Art of Stealing in Ancient India," *American Journal of Philology* 54, no. 3 (1923): 193–229 (see my chapter 8).

5. See Kenneth Zysk, *Religious Healing in the Veda* (Philadelphia: American Philosophical Society, 1985), p. 88.

6. AV 6.21.1; Kauś. 30.8–10.

7. *Jaimini Gṛhya Sūtra* 1.11; Vāj. Sam. 2.1–2.

8. Ś.B. 11.14.1.14: " . . . and inasmuch as he then throws after it all the

sacrificial grass of the altar-ground, therefore, in the last stage of life, one again becomes gray all over." See also 9.3.1.4.

9. *Bṛhaddevatā* 6.99–107; *Jaiminīya Brāhmaṇa* 1.220; Sāyaṇa's commentary on RV 8.91; Ṣaḍguruśiṣya and a similar tale in TMB 9.2.14. The story has been discussed in numerous secondary sources including H. Oldenberg, "Ākhyāna Hymnen in *Ṛgveda*," *Zeitschrift der Deutschen Morgenslandischen Gesselschaft* (*ZDMG*) 39 (1885):76; H. Oertel, "Contributions from the Jaiminiya Brahmana to the History of Brahmana Literature," *Journal of the American Oriental Society* (*JAOS*) 18 (1897):26–31; Theodor Aufrecht, *Indische Studien* (Leipzig: Brockhaus 1878), 4:1; M. Muller, *Rigveda*, 3:33; H. H. Wilson, *Rig Veda Sanhita*, 6:173–75, and several others including some that will be cited later.

10. H. H. Wilson, *Rig Veda*, 6:173.

11. Cf. Jonathan Smith, *Imagining Religion* (Chicago: Univesity of Chicago Press, 1982), p. 25.

12. Ram Gopal, "A Non-Legendary Interpretation of the Apala Sukta," *Visveshvarananda Indolgical Research Journal* 2 (1964), critiqued in Dange's *Vedic Concept of the Divine Fructification* (Bombay: University of Bombay, 1971).

13. *Vedic Concept*, pp. 12, 68ff. According to L. Sternbach a *kanyā* (cf. also *nagnikā*, *śyāmā*, *gandharī*) is probably older than ten or twelve, but has not yet matured sexually; *Juridical Studies in Ancient Indian Law* (Delhi: Motilal Banarsidass, 1967) pt. 2, p. 36.

14. Dange, *Vedic Concept*, p. 76. According to the *Śatapatha Brāhmaṇa*, gold was Prajāpati's strength that went out of him and became the sun. The skin's relation to the sun is enhanced by contact with gold, as seen in Apālā's cure, the bride's purification, and by the infant's intake of ghee rubbed by gold. See Sindhu S. Dange, *Hindu Domestic Rituals* (Delhi: Ajanta, 1985), pp. 25–29; moreover the sunlike skin relates Apālā to Atri—whose daughter she was. Atri protects the sun against the eclipse in AV 13.2.12; RV 5.40.

15. Jan Heesterman, *The Ancient Indian Royal Consecration* (The Hague: Mouton, 1957), p. 216.

16. Jan Gonda, *Visnuism and Sivaism: A Comparison* (London: Athlone, 1970), p. 47; ŚB 5.4.3.26; TB 1.3.61.

17. See M. Bloomfield, *Hymns of the Atharvaveda*, Sacred Books of the East (SBE) vol. 42 (New York: Greenwood Press, 1969), p. 243. See further discussion.

18. In the *Ṛgveda* (9.41) Soma is described as a cure for dark skin.

19. Wendy D. O'Flaherty, *Origins of Evil in Hindu Mythology* (Berkeley: University of California Press, 1976), p. 350. Coomaraswamy identifies Apālā, along with other manifestations of Indra's consorts, with Earth, who possesses reptilian characteristics such as sloughing off her skin ("On the Loathly Bride" *Speculum* 20, no.4 [1945]):391–404. See also AV 12.1; RV 10.22.14, 1.185.2; SB 4.6.9.17.

20. This interpretation follows Haradatta's reading of *Āpastamba Gṛhya Sūtra* 2.4.8 as a ritual performance of Apālā's purification.

21. Hanns-Peter Schmidt, *Some Women's Rites and Rights in the Veda* (Poona: BORI, 1987), lecture I.

22. J. J. Meyer, *Sexual Life in Ancient India* (New York: E. P. Dutton, 1930).

23. On the explicit sexual associations of grinding stones (*sil* and *nora*), see Lina Fruzzetti and Akos Ostor, *Kinship and Ritual in Bengal* (New Delhi: South Asian Publishers, 1984), p. 169.

24. Wayland Hand, *Magical Healing* (Berkeley: University of California Press, 1980), chap. 11; cf. Victor Turner, *The Ritual Process* (Ithaca: Cornell University Press, 1969).

25. Kaviraj Kunja Lal Bhishagranta, ed., *The Sushruta Samhita*, 3 vols. (Calcutta: S. L. Bhaduri, 1907–16).

26. The treatment of skin disease (*kuṣṭha*) in the *Caraka Saṃhitā* is far more detailed and less spectacular. It is based on the homeopathic relationship between the diagnosed *doṣa* and the curative plants. But therapy also consists of a combination of purgation, elimination, and bloodletting on the one hand, and various forms of injection on the other. See Cikitsāsthāna 7.

27. *ākāśa* = *sattva*; *vāyu* = *rajas*; *teja* = *sattva/rajas*; *āpas* = *sattva/tamas*; *pṛthivi* = *tamas*; see Su.S. 1.20; the *Caraka Saṃhitā* lists six layers of skin and names them after the pathological symptoms they manifest (Śarīrasthana 7.4). On the pathological relation (*kuṣṭha*) of the skin layers with the internal elements, see Nidanasthana 8.

28. ŚB 1.23.1 in M. Bloomfield, *Hymns*, p. 16.

29. Coloration is a primary feature of skin pathology and diagnosis in the *Caraka Saṃhitā* (Nidānasthāna 5). Color is not just symptomatic, it possesses an ontic and etiological nature. Cf. Heinrich R. Zimmer, *Hindu Medicine* (Baltimore: Johns Hopkins University Press, 1948), p. 6.

30. See MS 5.55 for a fanciful and moralistic interpretation of *maṇsa*.

31. Su.S. 4.5–21.

32. See *Viṣṇu Purāṇa* 2.5.1–27 on the seven *pātālas* or lower regions of the earth. The number seven recurs in other contexts suggesting spatial fullness or completion: "Fill full . . . seven wombs with butter"(Vāj. Sam. 17.79). The seven wombs are apparently the seven layers of the altar in the Agnistoma. See also the seven hairs left by the renouncer who shaves *Nārada Parivarjak-opaniṣad*, A. N. Bhattacharya, ed., *One Hundred Twelve Upanisads* (Delhi: Parimal, 1987), p. 269.

33. P. Jayakar, *The Earthen Drum: An Introduction to the Arts of Rural India* (New Delhi: National Museum, 1980), p. 76.

34. Cf. AV 8.7: "With Avaka as their hull, With the waters as their nature, May the sharp horned herbs rend distress asunder"(9). The metaphor is still military, though naval; see especially vs. 15 for the expulsion of the disease. Cf. Zimmer, *Hindu Medicine*, pp. 12–13

35. Julius Jolly, *Indian Medicine* (Delhi: Munshiram Manoharlal, 1971), p. 138.

36. On the cult of the seven smallpox sisters, see William Crooke, *Popular Religion of Northern India* (London: Oxford, 1896), 1. 125–36; Lawrence Babb, The Divine Hierarchy (New York: Columbia University Press, 1975), pp. 129–32.

37. See MS 11.49. Cf. Ariel Dorfman's Dr. Marivelli in *Mascara*: "My operations have such an incredible degree of success because along with the old skin, they eliminate old habits, the past." (*Mascara: a novel.* New York: Viking, 1988) Moral pathology registers on the skin no less than physical disease. For instance, *kuṣṭha* is due, among others to "*viprān gurūn dhār-*

ṣayatam pāpam karma ca kurvatam"—insulting brahmins and teachers, and committing other sins (*Caraka*, Cikitsāsthana 7.8).

38. B. Malinowski, *Myth in Primitive Psychology* (New York: W. W. Norton, 1926), pp. 103–5; I am grateful to Wendy Doniger for bringing this myth to my attention.

39. For lack of time and space, this intriguing myth cannot receive the attention it deserves. Malinowski's own comments are not very useful; the myth will be discussed in Doniger's forthcoming book on doubles. For a dramatic possible interpretation, see William I. Thompson, *Imaginary Landscape* (New York: St. Martin, 1989), chap. 1.

40. David Landy, ed., *Culture, Disease and Healing* (New York: Macmillan, 1977), p. 280; According to the *Caraka*, "metaphor" may not be the best term to describe this relationship: *pūruṣo 'yam lokasanmitaḥ*—Man resembles this world because what is present in the one is present in the other and vice versa; the two are alloformic (Śārīrasthāna 5.3).

41. The force of the internal pressing is strengthened by the contrast with *gṛham gṛham vicākaśat*, referring to Indra's practice of gathering the Soma from the households to which he wanders.

42. For a detailed analysis, see Zimmer, *Hindu Medicine*, pp. 3–6; Zimmer understands the magic involved in healing as a psychosomatic approach, which preceded the "rational" methods of the later texts. This view represents an intermediate position between earlier derogatory readings of magic and contemporarly cognitive-semiotic interpretations.

43. See James G. Frazer, *The Golden Bough* (New York: Macmillan, 1935), vol. 1; Bloomfield, *Hymns*, pp. 566–67.

44. *Hymns*, p. 287; cf. Weber, *Indische Studien*. (Leipzig: Brockhaus, 1878) V, 145. On the controversy regarding the meaning of the name "*Kṣetriya*" see, Jean Filliozat, *The Classical Doctrine of Indian Medicine* (Delhi: Munshiram Manoharlal, 1964), p. 113.

45. See Zysk, *Religious Healing*, pp. 93–95.

46. Filliozat, *Indian Medicine*, p. 132; Zysk, *Religious Healing*, p. 93, n. 2; according to Zysk, the remedy is rainwater and the reference to urine is metaphorical (p. 94).

47. Kāśikāvṛtti quoted by Filliozat, *Indian Medicine*, p. 113

48. On the use of ghee as amniotic fluid and on a pot as uterus, see for instance the story of Yudhiṣṭhira's birth in Mbh. 1.107. On the clay hut see AV 5.30.14; RV 7.89.1.

49. See RV 10.162.

50. Notice that identity and continuity are established by means of contact between concrete objects and cannot be sustained strictly by the referential qualities of symbols.

51. The ghee is administered with the following formula, according to the Aśv. G. S. (I.15.1): "I give you the Veda of honey and ghee, produced by the bountiful Savitri; protected by the gods may you, of long life, live a hundred autumns in this world."

52. For the general qualities of animal hides, see subsequent discussion.

53. Note that the symbolic interpretation shifts the reading of ghee from sperm to fetus to amniotic fluid and embryonic tissue. The imagistic reading has no such difficulty.

54. M. Merleau-Ponty, *Phenomenology of Perception* (London: Routledge & Kegan Paul), p. 315.

55. Ibid., p. 316.

56. Ashley Montagu, *Touching: The Human Significance of the Skin* (New York: Harper & Row, 1986), p. 294; E. L. Lipton et al. "Swaddling, a Child Care Practice: Historical, Cultural, and Experimental Observations," *Pediatrics.* 35 suppl. (1965): 519–67.

57. See also Anzier Didler, *The Skin Ego* (New Haven: Yale University Press, 1989).

58. AV 4.8.4; Kauś. 17.3.

59. *Hymns*, p. 380.

60. Heesterman, *Royal Consecration*, p. 206.

61. RV 5.83.7, 1.85.5; the year itself is often compared to a dry skin bag: JB 2.396; PB 5.10.2; TS 7.5.6.2.

62. *Royal Consecration*, p. 207.

63. Ibid., pp. 58–62.

64. ŚB I.1.4.5; JB 11.4.42; see also Kane, *History of Dharmaśāstra* 2: 1026ff.; Vāj. Sam. 1.19.

65. MS 2.23.

66. Cf. AV 10.9.2: "May your skin be the sacrificial altar [*vedi*], may your hair be the sacrificial grass."

67. MS 2.41.

68. Wendy D. O'Flaherty, *Tales of Sex and Violence* (Chicago: University of Chicago Press, 1985), p. 40; cf. the widely circulated story of the man who dressed his old ass in tiger's skin so he could graze in someone's field. One day the ass mistook the field owner, who was crouching behind a bush, for a female and came charging and braying. The owner was able then to identify the animal and kill it. *Hitopadeśa* 3, kath. 2; *Pañcatantra* 3, kath. 1.

69. RV 1.110.8; cf. RV 1.161.7, 3.60.2.

70. AV 5.21.3; 7.

5

Boundaries in Space and Time

Dharma Metaphors

Previous chapters have repeatedly emphasized the phenomenological obligation to concentrate on images in our study of religious symbolism. Symbols, we have seen, derive their force from the resonance between a temporal ideational and experiential levels of awareness. This resonance takes place because sensory images contain a prefigured meaning imparted by the most elementary acts of consciousness and perception.

If one were to select a fundamental religious symbol, the method just described would imply that the significance of the symbol is largely fashioned by the metaphors that constitute it, taken literally! The significance of the cross, for instance, is prefigured, at the most primitive level, by the structure of the imagination in relation to verticality and horizontality. Among the observations that could be made about the simple structure of the cross is the following: "the horizontal is a concrete which can be dominated, controlled and paced out . . . In contrast, everything that falls on the earth follows a vertical movement and is therefore something that happens . . . rather than is."[1]

Dharma, of course, is a highly abstract conception and symbolic complex. However, a brief lexical examination of the language employed in the Smṛtis reveals a fairly consistent set of spatial metaphors that signify the meaning of dharma as well as its violation and observance. Verbs most often used in association with dharma are *stha* (stand), *car* (go), *kṛ* (do), and *vṛ* (proceed) as in obeying dharma: *anutiṣṭha* (MS 2.9); consistently discharging dharma: *vartamāna* (MS 2.1); following dharma: *acarati* (MS 12.20); good conduct: *sadācāra*; or transgressing dharma: *atikramya* or *atikrama* (K160, 181; MS 3.63); keeping on the path of dharma: *dharme vartamani tiṣṭhata* (MS 9.1); deviate from *svadharma*: *svadharmāt carāṇi* (MS 7.15); keeping within the norms of conduct: *maryādāyāḥ pratiṣṭhāra* (literally, staying within the boundary; *Kūrma Purāṇa* 1.27.47); violation: *ullaṅgha* (literally, leaping over; S.74; 12.57); *Yājñavalkya Smṛti* (2.5) describes departure from the law of Smṛti as *ācāra vyaptena mārgeṇa*, and upholding the law as *dharmaśāstra dhārayipyanti* (3.330).[2] Restraining from violation of dharma is invariably described as *niyama* (MS 8.122; 10.59; 9.213), which is a prevention of going out beyond certain limits. A famous and markedly different metaphor depicts dharma as an organism injured (*viddhas*) by the dart (*śalya*) of *adharma*. Such a metaphor derives from the penetration of the organism's boundary, the skin.

Of course, not all terms draw on spatial metaphors. *Vidhi*, the injunction to perform dharma comes from the verb to do (*vidhā*), but such examples are fewer. The spatial metaphors may be related to an original conception of a very specific and concrete nature, pertaining possibly to the protection of enclosed property. However, the wide-ranging scope of dharma in the imagination of Hindus requires that the study of images focus on the notion of boundedness in a comprehensive and nonhistorical manner. Consequently this chapter will discuss a variety of boundaries: from the simple outline that bounds a pictorial representation to the picture frame itself; from house and temple walls to fences, agricultural boundaries, and the natural boundaries of sacred India itself. It will become clear from the very outset that all boundaries in space possess an irreducible temporal component and that boundaries, in the final analysis, are meant to be crossed.[3]

Perception and Forms in Space

The deepest and most persistent mystery in the history of culture must be the meaning of those enigmatic cave drawings which the paleolithic man left in numerous sites throughout the world. Of course, there is nothing primitive about the Altamira bisons or the Lascaux bulls. Their very size, let alone the sophisticated stylistic formulas, attests to a tradition of artistic work going much farther back in time.[4] But for twenty thousand years or more even these masterpieces remained silent in the inaccessible depths of absolutely dark caves. Suddenly, in one century, they have come to life and have begun to shout frantically. Their shouts are actually only the echoes of the voices coming from the rambunctious modern observer. First came theories of magic and magical manipulations to increase the hunt. Then we discovered hidden languages, structural masterpieces in the bowels of the earth. Needless to say, these paintings and drawings will continue to be as eloquent or as dumb as we wish them to be, for as long as we ask them to mean something.[5] But long before meaning emerged for the artists, long before conscious representation became an artistic goal and before the Magdelenian masterpieces were created, early artists merely played with their bodies and with the media around them. There may have been just the "dot," a trace of touching the dirt with a stick, then perhaps a scratch on the wall.[6] Then, quite simply, the dot became a line because, as we know with some confidence, "every linear expression consists of a dot set into motion."[7] The first line, that is the simplest and most natural, was an arch, due to the mechanics of the arm. A straight line involves a series of operations that requires more conscious will.[8] Two basic, but hardly trivial, things happened when primitive man moved his hand and traced a line out of the dot. First, a surface emerged out of mere sand or rock, a surface that is an "activated" empty space. Instantly, foreground became marked off from background, and background became divided into areas or zones.[9] Second, the line that followed a dot in motion became a record of an act in time, a record or trace that very clearly outlined the act itself—not unlike the footprint of a passing animal. Without treading too far into this aesthetic wilderness, let it just be said that the next major revolution in representation was probably the simple outline. For while spontaneous and haphazard lines evoke only the abstract schema of perception and fantasy, enclosed areas take the viewer into the realm of elementary mimesis and begin to awaken memories and "perception" of objects.[10]

If all this can be said about a simple outline, what can we say about the stunning cave art, which, by the way, is nearly always constituted by a filled out outline? These art works depict, by means of such outlines, the presence of a temporally existing creature against a background of solid rock. Of course, while the outline was a primary conceptual and stylistic instrument for depicting three dimensional objects in a two-dimensional space, it was not the only one. The cave artists recognized the effects of light and shade, color tonalities, the textural properites of their medium (rock), perspective, and so forth. Still, the outline, like every boundary that encloses a space within a space, was so basic because, as Heidegger has put it, it is "that from which something begins its presencing."[11] In other words, the boundary creates a relationship by establishing an aesthetic dualism. And like the fundamental existence that it evokes, the sign of the outline is grounded first and foremost in the simple images of perception with which the artist (in Joyce) recognizes, then depicts, the contours of his world: "In order to see that basket, said Stephen, your mind first of all separates the basket from the rest of the visible universe which is not the basket. The first phase of apprehension is a bounding line drawn about the object to be apprehended . . . the esthetic image is first luminously apprehended as selfbound and selfcontained."[12]

Like Joyce and his classical predecessors, the primitive artistic creator of profoundly realistic animal figures fashions not just a beautiful imitation of nature but reflects at a prearticulated level a human imagination already once removed from nature.[13] The artist is no longer conscious only of his objects and figures: he now begins to be aware of himself as creator. Even if primitive man does not seek symbolization or even representation per se, his art gradually becomes an elementary and unconscious metaphysic: it arrests becoming—the spontaneous interaction of his undivided attention with nature, and establishes rudimentary being as the trace of artistic creation. In the words of Charles Wentinck, this is a "magical act of possession." In the trace left on the cave wall primitive man for a moment (and for the first time) "has halted the passing of his life and produced a lasting and permanent work. Out of time he has fashioned space; he has enclosed it within an outline . . . He has created order, a unity, an equivalent form to his feelings."[14] This may already be saying too much but certainly the spatialization of time that takes place in primitive cave art is an unintentional and unconscious by-product of the simple drawing as it is of more complex designs and great masterpieces.[15] At its elementary level, incidentally, this art shares with children's drawing not the absence of beliefs and technique, but the surrender to the basic structure of the imagination in relation to an emerging sense of self.

Being and Becoming—Time and Space Reversed

Students of religion and philosophy know that our very conception of time is largely determined by spatial considerations and is quite distinct from our perception of time, that which Bergson calls *durée.*[16] Few descriptions of the distortion that takes place between chronology (spatialized time) and *durée* can match Benjamin Lee Whorf's astute remarks:

> Our awareness of time and cyclicality does contain something immediate and subjective—the basic sense of "becoming later and later." But in the habitual thought of us SAE [Standard Average European] people, this is covered under something quite different, which though mental should not be called subjective. I call it *objectified,* or imaginary, because it is patterned on the *outer* world. It is this that reflects our linguistic usage . . . Concepts of time lose contact with the subjective experience of "becoming later" and are objectified as counted quantities, especially as lengths, made up of units as a length can be visibly marked off into inches. A "length of time" is envisioned as a row of similar units, like a row of bottles.[17]

The traditional Hindu calender, like many others, is a quantified calculation of astronomical movements across certain distances. For instance, "Every day the sun traverses those zones in due order. Just as the outer rim of the potter's wheel comes back quickly, so also the sun functions quickly during his southern transit. Hence he traverses a major portion of the Earth in the cause of a shorter period." (And the days are consequently longer.)[18] This correct astronomical observation reflects the impossibility of reckoning calendrical time in any but a quantifiable recurrence of movements in space. But calendars aside, time may be spatialized (and space temporalized) in other manners, for other purposes. Unfortunately these may often stay buried in the confusion that myths about time communicate to us. Consider for instance the myth of Viṣṇu, the dwarf in the *Śatapatha Brāhmaṇa* (1.2.5.5). This is one among several versions of the fight between the Devas and the Asuras over the earth. The latter won the earth and began to divide it by means of oxhide curtains from west to east. The Devas took Viṣṇu the dwarf to the Asuras and struck a deal that as much as Viṣṇu covers with the length of his body will be theirs. But to the gods Viṣṇu was the sacrifice itself, so they laid him facing east and surrounded him in a three-sided outline consisting of the three meters: Gāyatrī, Triṣṭubh, and Gagati.[19] They thus completed the entire sacrifice (enclosing Viṣṇu with Agni on the east side) and obtained the whole earth. Later Viṣṇu buried himself three *aṇgulas* under the earth of the sacrificial space and had to be dug out so the sacrifice could be performed again. The three-lined enclosure was drawn again so the six lines became the six seasons of the year. The three meters (consisting of two half-lines each) were recited again, so the twelve sacred "words" became the twelve months of the year. In this narrative, space (earth) was taken by the Asuras and divided linearly. But it was then usurped when the virtually spaceless (dwarfish) and temporal (sacrificial) Viṣṇu was surrounded by lines. The linearity of the Asuras was replaced by encircled time. Moreover, the lines around the sacrifice were temporal because they were identified with metrical sounds, the very manifestation of time in the world. The confluence of temporal principles in a spatial arrangement resulted in the annual cycle of seasons and months.

It is clear from a reading of the sacrificial instructions that the authors were completely conscious of the correspondences they were establishing between ritual boundaries and cosmological ideas. In the *Śatapatha Brāhmaṇa*'s version of the preparation of the burial ground, for example, the enclosing stones around the fire hearth are of indeterminate number because the "other world" is indeterminate (13.8.2.2); the six oxen that plow the furrows marking the boundary are the six seasons (one year) and the furrowed square is the world with its four regions. Thus the burial ground is an elementary spatial and temporal unit in this world set off by stone-lined boundaries from the other world. This self-conscious formulation does not lend itself particularly well to an interpretation of the elementary (nonmetaphysical) act of enclosure. Still, the conscious manipulations of spatial and temporal elements do seem to reflect a complex psychological reading of the geographical world and a recognition that changes in time can be charted by means of markers in the ground. This insight is crucial for understanding rites of passage, such as the marriage of the girl.

The *Rāmāyaṇa*, which has been discussed at some length in a previous chapter, contains a number of rudimentary techniques for spatializing time and temporalizing space on the narrative level. One is the juxtaposition of simultaneous events. Rāvaṇa was deceiving and preparing to kidnap Sītā at precisely the same time that Rāma met with Lakṣmaṇa. In the story's chronology these two events are simultaneous. However, in the act of telling the story, or reading it, in other words, in the narrative and performative sequence, the meeting of the brothers takes place after the abduction. The narrator may further manipulate the tempo of each event in order to exploit its various possibilities and meanings. This subjugation of natural time-perception of simultaneity into a linear structure is one example of spatialization.[20] The tacit cooperation of a single omniscient narrator and prescient audience contributes to another method of spatialization. The events of the *Rāmāyaṇa* are in fact a repetition of a few fundamental themes ranging over an ever widening geographical circle. The sense of novelty, which is necessary to impel the characters forward, is fused with the story's spatial sites: the palace, Ayodhyā, the forest, and so on. The journey across the boundaries between city and wilderness, forest and hermit dwelling, India and Laṅkā directly embodies the temporal transformations that the characters undergo.[21]

Other traditional methods of spatializing time will be discussed in due course. These sketchy notes were intended to make it clear that boundaries may be studied as nonsymbolic contours of the topography of a self defined not by self-consciousness (or individuation) but by nearly absolute exteriorization. Such lines and boundaries should be distinguished from the symbolic lines of *maṇḍalas* and *raṅgolis*.

Where chronology serves only a superficial function in recording the temporal dimension of personal transformations, it is the spatialization of time, which utilizes movement across bounded spaces, that expresses "inner" growth or changes. The absence of clearly articulated internal landscapes indicates, perhaps, not a lack of suitable metaphorical language so much as the weakly crystallized distinction of inside and outside as a defining characteristic of the "person." This subject will be explored in a subsequent chapter, but it is important to note now as a caveat against reading the following sections in a symbolic frame of mind.[22]

The Picture Frames of Tribal India

Every culture produces, at different periods, various modes of aesthetic expression that reflect an imagination and style unique to itself. Even an artistically diverse context such as the Mauryan period, with its known sources in Mesopotamian, Achaemenid, and Hellenistic artistic traditions would show its own distinct stamp.[23] Clearly, nothing short of a detailed historical study would suffice in defining such unique, "typical," stylisitc features. Since our goal here is to analyze the way in which the basic spatial perception operates in India in relation to boundaries, a far more limited and somewhat crude approach has been undertaken.

The creation of visual arts, specifically the decoration of house walls, has been taking place for thousands of years. Those familiar with Indian painting of various ages may immediately recognize its one formal characteristic, shared with Western painting, of marking off the "fictional" space by means of a frame. Contemporary tribal art in India, that of the Bhils, Bhilolas, Warlis, Gonds, at once rudimentary and sophisticated, allows us a close look at frame making and its meaning.

As we shall see in a subsequent section, the clay and mud walls that are used as canvas to depict mythical motifs do in fact mark time just as much as space. The care that attends the frame making, in frequently elaborate rituals, is therefore telling. The Rathavas in the Chuli area of Gujarat mark the frame by means of a cotton string (*hutar* or *hutarni dori*) dipped in red liquid pigment drawn tightly against the wall by two painters, one of whom pulls the string away from the wall, then allows it to snap back. A parallel line is similarly marked, and thus around the four sides of the frame. At the center of the bottom border an opening, "the entrance," is created with a guardian figure next to it. Three or four artists then begin the work of decorating the frame.

The decorating motifs used inside or along the frames of wall paintings appear to be independent of the subjects depicted within the frame.[24] Moreover, a relatively small number of universal forms are utilized everywhere. By calling these forms ornamental, scholars usually assume that no representation as sign or symbol is intended.[25] In Rathava art only the lesser artists engage in this ornamentation work and are barred from working on the painting itself. The most commonly used forms are triangles, diamonds, chevrons, bone patterns, and wavy lines. Occasionally, when greater space is available and care is sought, cobra heads are used, or fish scales, or even vegetative-growth signs. Even *toraṇa*-like gate images may be drawn along the exterior lines of the frames (see figures 2 and 3).

The simple triangles and chevrons are most interesting from my point of view because they appear to be most purely ornamental and abstract. Their meaning seems to emerge only in relation to the function of the frame as a whole. The frame marks one space from another: it establishes a dialectic of inside and outside as two spaces where only one existed before. Without such a dialectic, the one space is utterly meaningless and "blank"; it is unactivated space. Aesthetically, the frame marks a perceptual Gestalt which the mind can incorporate

Figure 2 Corn Goddess (Kanasarai) drawing from a Maharashtra. From P. Jayakar, *The Earthen Drum*, p. 173; by permission of the National Museum in Delhi.

and develop into categorical distinctions. Semiotically, the frame establishes a relationship on the representational level between the events of the inside and the events, or sheer chaos, of the outside. Thus, figure 3, drawn to protect a widow from the ghost of her husband, depicts a threatening space around a protected enclosure. Figure 2, on the other hand, depicts an extremely auspicious and fecund environment surrounding the principal figure in the work—Kansarai, the corn goddess. (Note that in both works the frame is inside the work itself.) It may be far too facile to conclude that triangles or chevrons pointing "outside" represent a protective motif suggestive of sharp objects. Taken as purely abstract images these figures could equally evoke, or somehow relate to, growth and fertility. According to Adrian Frutiger the rows of triangles are a stylized representaion of grain and tree life (figure 4).[26] This finds unexpected substantiation in the drawing of figure 2. The central image, the goddess, is constituted by means of two triangles with lines that do not intersect (⧗). Human figures, on the

Figure 3 Saora picture to divert the ghost of a man which pestered the unhappy widow. From V. Elwin, *The Tribal Art of Middle India*, p. 202.

other hand, are formed by two triangles with intersecting lines (⧗) marking two separate and enclosed spaces of the lower and upper parts of the body. (Note that the horse is equivalent to a horizontal human figure.) The human and divine are thus distinguished from each other on the basis of the transitivity of upper and lower regions. Regardless of the symbolic values intended (e.g., harmonious coexistence of heaven and earth; infinity), the triangles indicate a growth or movement in the direction of the triangle's point, a limited growth in the case of humans. Consequently, while the frame in figure 2 seems to resemble a prison wall, it also places inside and outside within an interactive context. The growth motifs make the frame transitive. The same effect is rendered by means of the diamonds, which are symmetrical triangles pointed in opposite directions.

This very brief survey has shown that the frame not only separates one space from another, but also brings the two spaces into a relationship. The frame separates and joins with the very same act. At the same time the frame itself is transitive: it marks (aesthetically and perhaps symbolically) the potential movement of outside in and inside out. Whether the former may be a threatening invasion and the latter an auspicious growth depends not on the frame itself but on forces

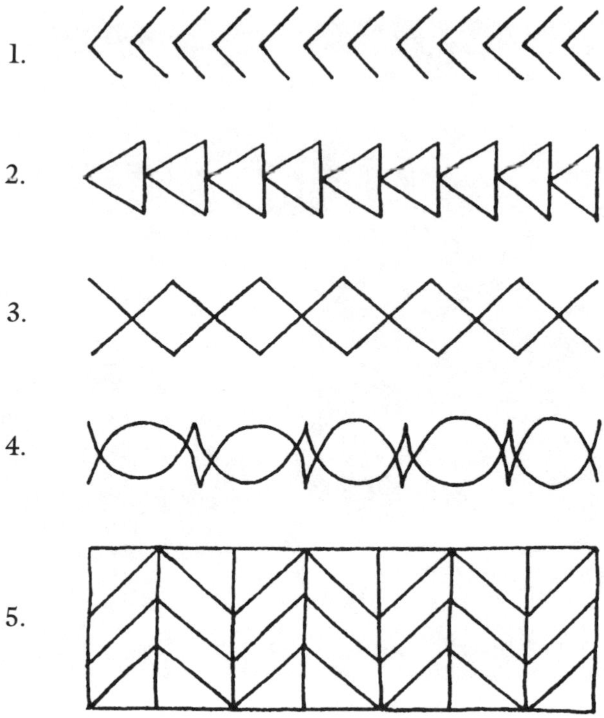

Figure 4 Rows of abstract and ornamental figures. From A. Frutiger, *Signs and Symbols*, p. 286; 1, 2: "The chevron motif and the row of triangles are stylized representations of grain." 3, 4: "The symmetrically aligned patterns carry a sense of duality or complementarity and may be interpreted as meaning fertilization." 5: "Fishbone and scale patterns probably appear most often for purely ornamental purposes, but one may also read into them the meaning of protection from without."

symbolized in the work and its context. The shapes of the frame itself merely indicate the dynamic nature of elementary distinctions between inside and out by means of an ornamentation that pleases the eye because it leads it in both directions. It may also suggest a flexibility in cognitive categories that separate cosmological and social spaces, but, of course, we would be getting ahead of ourselves.[27]

House Walls

The Indian rural and urban landscape was marked by arrangements and divisions that were meant to correspond with social and cosmic ideas. Cities and villages were planned to match the structural roots of the imagination and to mark the space for the social categories.[28] Indian houses, like houses everywhere in premodern times, were built primarily along ecological considerations. Principal among these were availability

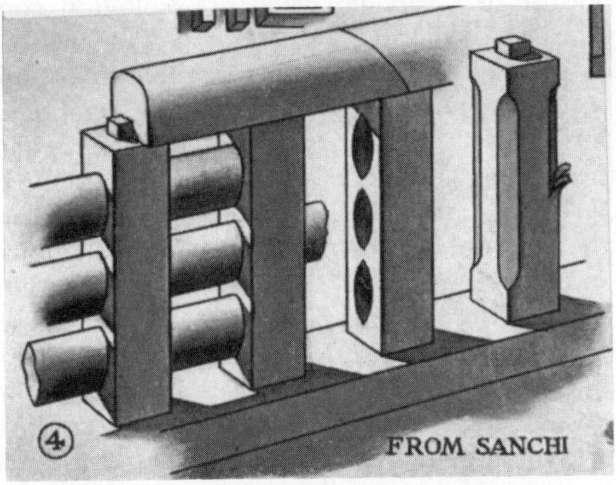

Figure 5 Rail section from the Sanchi Stupa. From P. Brown, *Indian Architecture*; by permission from D. B. Taraparevala Sons.

of building materials and skill in their utilization, climactic conditions, terrain, natural enemies, and others.[29] Balancing or usually complementing these were social considerations, such as nature of economic activity, location and strength of economic rivals, and structure of social organization. Poised somewhere between the two levels of consideration, depending on one's own assumptions, is the cosmological and sociological belief system, which places the house in a self-conscious symbolic space and time.[30] The present discussion is limited to the wall only and will attempt to situate the wall within an appropriate level of analysis.

The changes in construction material recorded (obscurely) in the texts, and more clearly in archaeological remains, traces the movement of the Aryans through a variety of ecological terrains as well as technical and conceptual innovations. Houses were built of wood, bamboo reeds, palm leaves, and grass in some areas, baked mud bricks, clay, husk, lime, cow dung, or plain mud in other areas and times. The material itself was used regardless of wealth, the primary manifestation of social hierarchy being design and size of structures.[31] Rudimentary principles of design, however, were often governed by construction material. For instance, the roof of the typical "Vedic" house (according to the sketchy material available) was constructed with ribs of flexible bamboo cane (*vaṃśa*) bent to form a distinct looking canopy. This, in turn, determined the shape and design of the house's floor plan and general shape, just as the Renaissance capella and dome had to match before the round dome could be fitted on angled structures. We shall see later that these design patterns were often retained in construction utilizing stone or rock carving, when no ecological considerations continued to exist.

The floor plan and orientation in space followed (and continues to follow) both ecological and sociological considerations. The need to shelter cattle and sheep from natural and human enemies might determine the number and size of rooms and their configuration (RV 7.56.16; AV 1.3, 4; 9.3, 13; RV10.106; AV 3.3). Historians and archaeologists have noted the spatial orientation of houses in their ancient urban context and remarked on the absence of windows in the street-facing walls. More sociological work, steeped in a semiological hermeneutic explains the distinction between open and closed design in the following manner: "These mansions are designed to look out onto a world that invites human, secular intervention in contrast to the traditional Hindu house whose exterior walls were windowless and looked inwards toward the world's cosmic center."[32] A rich literature has analyzed the Hindu house in the imaginative cosmos of the Hindu mind. In such analyses the wall, wood, mud, bamboo or whatever is a conceptual boundary between symbolic cosmological categories of inside (e.g., cosmic center) and outside (secular world). Its mental function, so to speak, rests strictly on its location within a cosmological space.

However, the wall itself is often manipulated artistically in such a way as to render it phenomenologically "transparent." This is achieved through aesthetic and symbolic means.[33] The hut wall paintings of tribal India tend to obscure the natural color of the substance used for consructing the hut. The clay may be plastered white, which is then painted over with red and black (Gonds); or white and gerua red may be painted over the clay's natural pigments (Warlis, Bhils).[34] The wall surface, framed or unframed, may be further subdivided by means of horizontal and vertical lines (decorated with the usual frame motifs) into subsections within which subsidiary themes can be depicted. The artwork may be ornamental only or representational, but in either case the spatial divisions of the village world may be replicated in the spatial orientation on the wall. If the contours of the house are ignored, the framed wall art creates an illusion of autonomous space, occasionally utilizing depth perspective.[35] In other instances, the densely rich ornamentation, consisting of only horizontal lines with frame motifs like triangles, chevrons, fishbones, or clearly vegetative signs, simply obscures the wall as a perceptual block and transforms it into the canvas of a compelling design.

Along with these aesthetic considerations representational themes, often possessing a chronological significance, are used to render the wall transparent. The subjects drawn are often mythological, cosmogonic, or sociogonic. The Bhils of Maharastra and Gujarat record the "descent from the high places, from the freedom of cave and mountain to the enclosed space of the hut built on flat lands."[36] The wall becomes the canvas in which the enclosed spaces of the agricultural domicile and life have fallen off from the open spaces of the forests and mountains. In a sense the wall acts like the celluloid on which the events of a journey are recorded. The time in which the journey is reexperienced is the time of the celluloid, but its space (depth) disappears in verticality and horizontality. Of course, not all themes are chronological: they may depict magical objects and implements, fertility motifs, guardians, and so forth. Either way the wall is never just an aspect of a cosmological symbolism because it takes part in a broader conceptual system. Like the human skin itself (but not homologically so), the wall acts as a living membrane between the inside and outside and between the past and the present. It reflects (literally, like a mirror) the fenced world of agricultural settlements, and it also records its own biography, its own "wrinkles."

Temple Walls

Like the walls of tribal mud huts, temple walls exist dynamically, and remember the past.[37] Long after Indian builders moved away from using wood and bamboo for the construction of buildings, they retained the textural and mechanical properties of wooden construction. The earliest examples of rock-cut architecture in India, the sanctuaries north of Gaya, are in some cases "exact copies in the rock of existing structures in wood and thatch."[38] The walls are lined by perpendicular grooves that imitate the upright battens of wood or bamboo. As Percy Brown puts it, "it is an exact lithic copy of a beehive hut."[39] Similar features are found around the doorway where a precise reproduction of the gable end of a wooden frame is chiseled in the rock. Even the tie-rods holding down the old wooden planks of the roof are depicted ornamentally in the stone. The stone cutters simply imitated every detail of the carpenter's work, still very much in use around the time of Aśoka.[40]

A similar reproduction of carpentry techniques in stone work is manifest in the stone railings around the Sanchi stupa (figure 5). The general design seems to resemble the older (Vedic?) village fencing with its three broad horizontal bars stretching between posts and leaving a fairly narrow space for any creature to get in or out. The shapes of the bars and the end joints were accurate reproductions of carpentry. Clearly the builders were interested in sustaining a continuity with an ancient tradition of temple and house construction marked by the use of wood, which embodied significant powers in and of itself. This conservative approach infused the walls and fences of temples with a symbolic power that included a strong temporal component. The rock ceased to exist as mere construction material and lost its most distinct lithic properties: silence and atemporality.

The living arboreal qualities of the new building materials were reinforced by the aesthetic transitivity of the temple's stone walls in relation to the divine residents within. Despite the massive thickness of the temple's walls, prescribed as one-quarter of the width of the inner sanctum, they are conceived as the body of a living organism.[41] As is well known, the building is "charged with life" through a complex symbolic ritual. Regardless of this, the stone wall is rendered three dimensional as it is furrowed by chaises and recesses, and projects with the images of gods and goddesses who are, from a visual point of view, coming out of the temple through the walls.[42] Kramrisch has actually studied the chronolgical development of several architectural examples and demonstrated that the temples' buttresses display an outbound "motion" from the inner sanctum out to the world. It is this outbound movement of the wall that carries the deity on the *ratha* (vehicle), through the wall and away from the center toward the four directions. This is not just a symbolic movement; it is an aesthetic expansion, and it places the walls in a far more interesting perspective than mere homology with the structure of the cosmos would. Since the effect is accomplished on the visual level, it actually renders the wall's cosmological significance redundant because the wall, seen through a prolonged time exposure, is itself animated.[43]

Fences

Like the urban environment, the agricultural landscape was checkered by means of dividing lines, preferably but not always natural: rivers, hills, trees and shrubs, tanks, wells, roads, and so forth.[44] In other instances the boundaries may be reinforced by means of stone markers, often inscribed with warnings and curses against trespassers. But the most effective, if expensive boundary was the fence. Fences played a key role in the economic life of the Aryans as soon as they began settling down to an agricultural existence in the spaces cleared out of the jungle. The thatched huts that probably consituted the "Vedic" communites (*grāmas*) were usually surrounded by a fence built out of the same materials as the homes. For obvious reasons, little is known about these fences, but their survival in later stone rails allowed Percy Brown to render the following hypothetical description: "This fence took the form of a bamboo railing the upright posts (*thabha*) of which supported three horizontal bars called *suchi* or needles, as they were threaded through holes in the uprights."[45] (See figure 5.) The cattle and other livestock spent the night within the fenced area of the *grāma*. The fencing was designed to keep the livestock in and wild animals out. It was also intended to protect against thieves, though this task was more effectively performed by dogs.[46] These fences acquired a significance that exceeded their economic function because, as noted earlier, their construction methods were imitated closely in the stone railings of temples and stupas. Fergussons's description of the rail at Sanchi makes it clear that the architectural logic behind its fabrication was entirely wooden: "The pillars, for instance, could not have been put up first, and the rails added afterwards. They must have been inserted into the right or left hand posts, and supported while the next pillar was pushed laterally, so as to take their ends, and when the top rail was shut down the whole became mortised together as a piece of carpentry."[47] Decorative motifs displaying a profound respect for tree worship, Nagas, and a great variety of trees as well as other plants in Sanchi, Bodh-Gaya, and Bharaut indicate that the rails are more than a tip of the hat to the carpenter. The wood itself, or the tree with all it represented to the Buddhist builder, was being fashioned out of stone. The fence around the sacred site, in other words, was not just an emblem of protection and a barrier between sacred and profane zones. It marked off two regions in space by means of the ancient fence that indicated the dynamic interplay of village life with its surrounding forest. This relationship has yet to be discussed, but the boundary itself brings together more than it separates, and it brings together both in space and in time.

In the settled, king-dominated rural life, fields were also marked by means of boundaries, though rarely actually fenced. The Dharmaśāstras spend far more time on the boundaries of fields than on prescribing activities that ought to take place in the fields. A careful look at the boundaries that mark one field from another reveals an interesting fact: the boundary markers are not only meant to prevent land disputes among present and future owners: they also represent a public domain that looks back at the settlement of agricultural land out of the forest. Possession of land in ancient India, when no prior ownership was established by purchase or inheritance, depended legally and in practice on the "law of the waste land" (*bhūmi chidra nyāya*). In effect, the law states that anyone who brings a plot of nonagricultural land under cultivation by clearing away the forest (for instance) becomes owner of the land. Since most of these forest-cutting operations were undertaken under royal initiative, often following new conquests, it was the king who was the owner or master of such land.[48] Consequently, while the choice of boundary markers indicates a concern for permanence—surviving floods, for instance—others are closely related to the royal possession of the land as a whole. The choice of milk-bleeding trees (*kṣīri*) places the cultivated land in a relationship with the primordial, precivilized forest. The terms for this relationship are defined by Manu on the basis of the myth of Pṛthu and Pṛthivī: "(Sages) who know the past call this earth (Pṛthivī) even the wife of Pṛthu. They declare a field to belong to him who cleared away the timber" (MS 9.44).

The paradigmatic royal possession of the earth is not only a function of his ancestry, or even his own righteousness. It dervies from the forceful and sexual possession of Bhūmī, the earth who took refuge in the shape of a cow. To save her life, she asked Pṛthu to provide her with a calf in order to produce milk. She then asked him to level her, "so that the milk that flows out shall spread everywhere equally."[49] Pṛthu did not create irrigable land by clearing forest: he flattened mountains and cleared away rocks. Where no defined boundaries existed between villages and towns, and within land utilized in a variety of manners, he marked the separate domains by means of boundaries. The plants and vegetables were then "milked" out of the earth by Pṛthu or, in other versions, by farmers and herbivore animals.[50]

The myth of Pṛthu and Pṛthivī, particularly in its later versions (e.g., *Bhāgavata Purāṇa*) combines a variety of political and religious doctrines. For instance, the obvious identification of Pṛthu with Viṣṇu, in addition to retaining the myth's other meanings, grants the king a profound cosmogonic role, thereby depriving the forest of its primordial force and reducing its opposition to the field to a matter of royal convention. The boundary trees are not signs of an ancient forest but signs of royal dominion, complemented by the fertile liquids of his escort—Śrī. But this is only one perspective.

The relation of forest and field is profoundly complex, a situation hardly alleviated by the wealth of recent analyses.[51] Certainly it is easy to regard the forest as *adharma* to the village's dharma, and the crossing a devotional baptism of fire involving a potentially antinomian rapprochement with the god. My purpose here is not to provide any alternative symbolic reading of the mythic forest. Undoubtedly the crossing over from settlement to forest (wildernes to be precise) derives its meaning from the respective significance of both. As I discuss crossings in general, however, it will become clear that the movement across all boundaries, not just going to the forest, shares important characteristics. At any rate, it is interesting to note in passing that India's heroes did not merely travel away from settlement into the forest. Rāma had to cross the river Sarayū before the exile was valid. Nala and Damayantī stayed outside the city walls where Nala described the numerous paths he could take across the Vindhya range and the river Payoṣṇī, or alternatively the road to Vidarbha, to Kosala, and so on.[52] Yudhiṣṭhira and his brothers left the city through the (northern) Vardhamāna gate and formally crossed into the forest at no less a boundary than the Gaṅgā by the great Banyan tree called Pramāṇa. In short, no journey takes place across an empty, unmarked landscape and even the wilderness has a gate.[53]

Doors

India's ancient city and palace gates were a place of explicitly noted activities, such as congregations, begging, meeting honored guests, gathering for special anouncements, councils, and even passing judgments. Such places included not only the gate itself, but often the space in front of it, or the bridge leading to it.[54] Often guarded by anthropomorphic guardians, or by abstract protective devices, the door seems to serve as the locus for the coalescence of symbolic ideas about man in his universe:

> The doorways should never be blocked with anything. The exits and entries should not be hindered by anything. These being blocked by a thoroughfare, tree, corner of another house, are inauspicious. By its being blocked up by a lane means [*sic*] the annihilation of the family; by being blocked up by raised earth, it brings jealousy; by being blocked up by moist soil or mud, it brings misery; by being blocked up by a well it gives epilepsy; by being blocked up by a waterfall, it brings some evil; by being blocked up by some nails, it brings in danger from fire; by its being blocked by any Deva, there is danger of destruction . . . The doorway being blocked by a filthy drain or other impurities causes sterility to women.[55]

David Shulman describes the ***kolam*** as "a reflection of some inner labyrinth externalized here at the boundary, the line dividing the inner and the outer, the pure from the chaotic. The boundary is dangerous: a division in the heart . . . Space and consciousness intersect at the threshold of divinity."[56] In short, the ***kolam*** is a symbol, located on the house's threshold, of the threshold between the perceptual world and all worlds of invisible potencies. Unfortunately, the symbolic intuitions that illuminate the deepest regions of Indian consciousness must somehow be explicated as nothing less and nothing more than mere door.

If, for instance, the doorway derives its symbolic significance from the simple fact of marking the opening in the boundary between inside and outside, what do we make of its relation to the walls? We have seen that walls, much like the human skin, possess reflective, transitive, and temporal characteristics, which, on a symbolic level, ***minimize*** the distinction between inside and outside! Interestingly, even the wall paintings of the Rathavas are marked with "doors" in the frame. As the frame is elaborately created, a gap is left in the center of the lower horizontal frame line. The gap is left protected by a guardian deity.[57] Predictably the Śilpaśāstras and Vastuśāstras devoted entire chapters to the door. The texts were predominantly interested in correct proportions and freedom from obstruction in front and around its proximity: "A door which causes the death of a brahmin as a result of his being struck by the vault when entering or leaving mounted on an elephant, such a door leads to the death of the king."[58]

In much of India's village architecture, doors merit the greatest amount of attention and are lavished with elaborate decorations, either on the door itself or on its frame. As usual, the decorative motifs are revealing. In their most abstract design they resemble the picture frames described earlier: a wooden door may be divided into a dozen or so panels separated by means of frames, which are decorated with herring bone, zigzag, rows of lozenges, diamonds.[59] Or else, the door may be decorated with a stylized cobra (guardian of hidden treasures); the door could be flanked by elephants carrying lotuses, or framed with semi-permanent abstract designs around its frame.[60] The classical architectural texts also insist on decorating the door with auspicious designs, such as leaves, creepers, fruits, animals, in addition to entirely abstract patterns.[61]

The temple or stupa gateway (*toraṇa*) reveals similar elements. We have already remarked on the preservation of wooden construction methods in stone. But there is more. The artists who worked on the Sanchi stupa have left numerous relief panels used for decorating the porticals, *toraṇas*, and other parts of the building. Due to their essentially conservative, backward-looking style and orientation, these representations provide a fairly reliable source of insights on a variety of older architectural designs.[62] We noted that wooden and bamboo fences constructed around villages tended to possess three horizontal bars fixed to the ground posts. The gateway into the village enclosure was constructed "by projecting a section of the bamboo fence at right angles and placing a gateway in advance of it in the fashion of a barbican, the actual gate resembling a primitive portcullis (*gamādvāra*)."[63] This gateway and gate, most historians believe, have survived with remarkable precision, in the design of the stupa *toraṇa* (gate). The *toraṇa* has been defined as "an arch, a canopy, a gate-way of a temple or stupa, a peg, a mechanical arrangement of blocks of any hard material disposed in the line of some curve and supporting one another by their mutual pressure." *Toraṇas* are employed as an architectural object, an ornament to a building, thrones, pedestals for images, boundary walls and over gates and vehicles.[64] The stupa *toraṇa* is remarkable from our point of view for the following reason: the portcullis design involves turning the three horizontal bars ninety degrees to a vertical attitude and using a simple mechanical device to raise and lower the bars. The top of the Jala *toraṇa* in stupa 1 and Sanchi, for instance, is an elaborately decorated representation of a rail section, turned at a right angle and raised up.[65] While the *toraṇa* is embellished with numerous symbolic designs, many of them protective and auspicious in nature, the fundamental orientation is established by the simpler, even crude, design observations made earlier.[66] The entrance has no existence apart from the fence, it is a modification or manipulation of the boundary. In the simplest possible terms, horizontality is replaced by verticality. Verticality itself operates in two ways: first, the bars have been turned into a vertical attitude, and, second, the entire "section" of the fence has been raised up. In simple terms again, one can either climb over a fence or crawl beneath it: the *toraṇa* invites us to assume the second posture. At the same time, the turning of the fence section changes an illicit act of stealth into a formal invitation. This is a unique feature of the *toraṇa* and distinguishes it from, say, the bridge. The *toraṇa* utilizes an architectural knowledge of the arch as a way of bridging spaces, but only for passage below.[67] It is interesting, and somewhat unusual, that arches and overhanging structures such as *toraṇas* were reserved exclusively for passing under. Despite the existence of technology for constructing spans, the bridge was conceived along entirely distinct lines. The term usually employed was *setu* (more rarely *salila*), which means causeway in the *Rāmāyaṇa* (6.15.9; 11 and passim). But it also refers to the boundary between two fields, an elevated earthen ridge, which is described in Manu.[68] The technique used in the *Rāmāyaṇa* to cross the ocean is significant because trees and huge boulders are described as having been dumped into the water to form a causeway—not a bridge. In a sense, the enormity of the construction materials created a peninsula out of Laṅkā. This indeed is how the *Bhaṭṭikāvya* imagines this episode. The level of the water arose, indicating that the waters were not spanned and the ocean was said to be overcome by a land bridge (*lavaṇa salila*) (13.30). Apparently, Indian architecture did favor horizontal forms over arch work in bridge construction.[69] We have too little to go on for any sweeping conclusions, but it is significant that boundaries may be crossed by a "downward" movement, for instance, by walking under the *toraṇa*, but not by traveling above, as crossing a span bridge would seem to allow. But his may already be saying too much.

No specific gateway, door, or *raṅgoli* can fully be interpreted—if it is even meant to be—by means of simple and sweeping principles. The point is to emphasize that the door itself falls within a concrete (nonsymbolic) spatial context determined by basic attitudes toward space in general and walls or houses specifically. The linear designs of various passages are an elaboration of intuitions that are prefigured at the more fundamental and prosaic levels of domesticity and passage.

It would be too easy to fall into the homological-analogical trap in relating the spatial boundaries to the conceptual boundaries of dharma. Are we not, after all, trying to show that the conception of norm as boundary is modeled on actual boundaries in the world? Some Indian myths lend themselves easily to interpretation based on homologies: when Arjuna set out to conquer the world (Mbh. 2.25), he proceeded to defeat every kingdom in his journey north. He crossed all the natural boundaries until he reached the ultimate boundary of Harivarṣa. There Arjuna encountered two gigantic gatekeepers who informed him that no human eye can see what lies beyond the walls, in the land of the Kurus. If ever a clear homological allusion to the boundary between the mundane and transcendent world existed in mythical form, this is it. Arjuna settled for tributes given to Yudhiṣṭhira, which consisted of "divine textiles, divine ornaments, and divine skins and hides." At the outer edge of his world-embracing kingdom, the king of dharma receives divine skins and garments. But despite such explicit homologies, physical boundaries are not just metaphorical tools in a conceptual workshop. The physical encounter with a wall or fence is somehow transforming in and of itself. But this is a thesis that must still await the elaboration of the following chapter.

Crossing Boundaries

There are many ways to cross a boundary—the simplest and most obvious is to be invited through the door. This does not make crossing a door entirely simple, of course: "To open, the sage holds the leaf with his left hand and lifts the bar with the right; whether the door has two leaves or just one, attention should be paid to the noise it makes when it is opened or closed by hand; if it is like a drum beat, like trumpeting or like roaring or like a note on a *vīṇā* or flute, that is good; on the other hand, if it is like the clearing of a throat, a cry, an inarticulate sound or other noise of that kind, this is not appropiate."[70] Still, this is hardly ever the most interesting passage, and it accounts for few narratives indeed. India's mythmakers and storytellers were deeply fascinated with the variety of manners for getting to the other side of a boundary without being invited to do so. Interestingly, this usually involves breaking into an enclosed space, not out of it. The reasons for breaking and entering also vary. The two usual reasons are wealth and love, not necessarily in that order. India's greatest thieves were as likely to steal love as any amount of wealth. As far as means are concerned, in simplest possible terms, there are only three ways to cross a boundary illicitly: above, below, and through. The first path necessitated some vehicle of air travel: a flying chariot, an airplane, or a magical ability to fly al fresco. Crossing below barriers usually involved the far more prosaic art of tunneling. Traveling through a boundary meant crashing or boring through if you were a fighter, dressing in drag if you were a lover, or making yourself disappear altogether. In any case, the implements used were many and varied: a black cloak (for night work), sword, scoop ("cobramouth"—*phaṇimukha*), whistle (*kākali*), tongs, a fake head (*puruṣa śīrṣaka*), magic powder, measuring string, compass (*karkaṭaka*), rope, lamp case, bees in a box (for putting out the light).[71] The use of some of these implements is nicely demonstrated in a famous passage in the *Mṛcchakaṭika*:

> Erudition and energy opened a hole that allowed easy ingress, and thereby the way to easy success! And now I crawl through, groveling in the gravel like a snake wriggling out of its old skin . . . Now in what precise location do I make the breach? Where is the wall weakened by seeping water? Where will the noise go unheard? Where do I risk no gaping holes that demand to be noticed? Where is the mansion's clay emaciated by the corroding effect of saltpeter? . . . First stage: I must now create a hole. But what kind of hole? The Lord of the Golden Lance has addressed himself to this problem and suggests four methods, to wit: baked bricks are to be pried out, unbaked bricks are to be broken, clay elements are to

> be watered, wooden elements are to be hacked. Here we have an instance of baked bricks—the bricks are to be pried out. Next point: the nature of the hole. Lotus Cup? Sun-Shaped? Crescent? Oval? Cross? Conic Pitcher? What spot is most suitable to exhibit my craftmanship and astonish on the morrow the staring citizenry? It is a baked-brick wall, therefore the Conic Pitcher looks best.[72]

And if digging failed, the art of disguise, raised to a lofty level of creativity, could be used to keep the king's wives moderately satisfied during the long hauls between shifts.

India's most powerful and sacred religious figures engaged in highly touted adharmic conduct of an erotic and nonerotic nature. The following are lesser known stories selected in order to illustrate an obvious relish for breaking into structures and across the bounds of acceptible conduct. The stories lack any theological pretension and reflect the simple joy of telling the exploits of overachievers in the highly scrutinized game of love.

The Weaver as Viṣṇu

Two close friends, a weaver and a carpenter, once lived in the city of Pundhravardhanam.[73] During a festival one day the weaver caught a glimpse of the princess in a window of the royal palace. He became hopelessly smitten with love, as the narrator tells it poetically: "Whenever one enters in to dwell / He strengthens and protects it well; / But, cruel! to my heart you came / And waste it with a burning flame."[74] Of course, his infatuation was hopeless for, as the carpenter pointed out, the separation between the princess, who belonged to the warrior caste, and his own craftsman caste was too wide to bridge without violating dharma. Still, the carpenter agreed to help the weaver and constructed an airplane shaped like Viṣṇu's bird—Garuḍa. The weaver disguised himself to look like Viṣṇu and flew onto the princess's balcony at the palace. It was easy to win her, and by their joyful coition a Gandharva marriage was established. Before long, the king and queen discovered that their daughter was receiving nightly visits, but were delighted that the amorous intruder, and their son-in-law, was none other than Viṣṇu. The king immediately undertook to remove his kingdom from the yoke of King Vikrasena's rule. Vikrasena, in rage, invaded the kingdom and layed siege to Pundhravardhanam. The weaver resolved to fight in defense of his new family, though he expected to die. But Garuḍa took to the courageous weaver and argued before Viṣṇu that should the weaver die in his disguise all the worshipers would assume that Viṣṇu himself died and the sacrifices would fall into neglect. The god then entered the body of the weaver, Garuḍa entered into the flying machine, and the power of the discus entered the weaver's replica. Thus fortified, the weaver proceeded to rout Vikrasena's army while the other gods watched in bewilderment, wondering why Viṣṇu would become involved in a minor skirmish: "When the deception is complete / Brahmā himself sees not the cheat; / By donning Viṣṇu's shape and dress / The weaver sports with the princess."[75]

The Vidyā-Sundara of Bhāratchandra

In contrast with the weaver and all other protagonists fortunate enough to travel the skies, Bhāratchandra's hero, Sundara, had to settle for digging. In this Bengali version of a very old tale, the hero, a prince, falls in love with a princess named Vidyā.[76] The obstacle this time is not caste difference but, as in so many other instances, mistaken identity. Sundara must gain access to Vidyā's quarters in the palace and is assisted by a woman named Hira who sells flowers, and by Kālī. Interestingly, Vidyā herself is infatuated with the prince, whom she has never seen, and hopes that he will somehow—magically perhaps—gain entry into her room the way water enters the coconut. Or else, since she knows him to be a poet, she hopes that the magical power of his words will somehow open doors the way they opened the door to her heart. However, the goddess Kālī is more practical and she drops a pickax at Sundara's feet, then leaves him a few *mantras* to instruct him, like a treasure map, into the palace. When the prince nearly completed his digging, he returned to Hira's house and put on his best clothes, doing his best to look like Kāma. Meanwhile, Vidyā was still fantasizing that he would show up in a chariot from the sky.

A short time later the beautiful bridegroom materialized in the princess's well-guarded apartment. And no sooner had he broken into her quarters, and layed eyes on Vidyā, Sundara began plotting his next break-in, this time into her clothes. His wit stood him well, for when she accused him of being a thief, he accused her of stealing his heart. He then vanquished her in a lengthy debate on the *śāstras* and finally accepted her unconditional surrender—a marriage by debate![77] In fact, like the weaver and other romantic thieves, this was a Gandharva marriage, established by the consummation of the thief's conquest. The tunnel is a familiar, if demanding, means of crossing a boundary. An entire Jātaka (Mahā-Ummagga) is dedicated to the tunnel, but, of course, that was no ordinary tunnel: "Come see, O king, a tunnel well made, big enough for elephants or horses, chariots or foot soldiers, brightly illuminated, a tunnel well built."[78]

Sharing this romantic genre is the suitor who enters his beloved's quarters by means of disguise or even invisibility. Obvious examples are Nala, who enters the royal palace and inner apartments thanks to his invisibility, granted as boon by Indra.[79] In contrast, Rāvaṇa approaches Sītā in the disguise of a mendicant, a redundant—possibly ironic—device, considering that he intended to abduct her forcibly anyway. A plethora of true lovers in disguise inhabit India's ancient folklore and mythology in lesser-known contexts. Such is the story of

Vasutaka, who won Vāsavadattā after entering the royal palace magically transformed to look like a deformed monstrosity.[80] In the story of the "Laughing Fish," a king stops short of killing an innocent Brahmin when he discovers that half the women in his harem are lovers in drag.[81]

In sum, when some form of heroism or prowess is not involved in breaking and entering, then magic and trickery are just as effective. In ancient Greece it was Hermes, the god of commerce, who initiated traffic across boundary stones and lorded over trade activities, which were as often furtive and transgressive as not. Indian attitudes toward commerce across boundaries particularly the ocean, were ambivalent at best. Although ocean faring was widespread in practice, it was deeply condemned by those whose considerations for pollution were probably matched by a vested interest in a self-contained economy.[82] The ocean presented the type of final boundary that one did not cross unscathed. Even Rāma, whose magnificant "bridge" took him to Laṅkā, did not return unchanged.

Crossing rivers, by contrast, represented a geographical passage on the way to the wilderness, from the wilderness, or most any other place of significance in Indian literature. However, it could still be a tricky undertaking as numerous versions of a *Pañcatantra* tale testify. This, of course, is the tale of the monkey or jackal who tricks the crocodile to ferry him to the other side of a river, usually for food.[83] The oldest versions (probably) merely illustrate the power of cunning. The more moralistic, and less interesting versions, such as the Jātaka's, illustrate and praise the victory of the virtue of wisdom.

The last section of this chapter has described several instances of crossed boundaries without fully explaining the consequences of passage. My interest has been limited to the crossed boundary rather than the crossing agent. As we have seen with the most rudimentary markers, space is divided in order to mark movement or passage, to "homologize" motion if you will. It would therefore be misleading to expect space markers to act as barriers: it is precisely at the point where a boundary is marked and crossed that the crosser experiences passage and becomes transformed. This fact is recognized and utilized in rites of passage, for instance, in the passage of the girl into the status of wife, as we shall see next.

Notes

1. A. Frutiger, *Signs and Symbols* (New York: Van Nostrand, 1989), p. 25.

2. The verb (*dhṛ*) rests on a vertical metaphor; see my final chapter.

3. See Victor Turner, *The Forest of Symbols: Aspects of Ndembu Ritual* (Ithaca: Cornell University Press, 1967), p. 109.

4. André Malraux, *The Voices of Silence* (New York: Doubleday, 1953); cf. Robert Layton, *The Anthropology of Art* (New York: Columbia University Press, 1981).

5. Obviously they do "mean" something: their structures reveal systematic redundancies, which are the defining features of meaning. But if, as Gregory Bateson notes, the meaning is in the relationships rather than the objects, then no single interpretation would ever exhaust the range of meaning.

6. The evolutionary scheme that seems to be implied should not be taken as more than common sense. Even Michaelangelo began by scribbling circles as a child.

7. Frutiger, *Signs and Symbols*, p. 24.

8. Rudolf Arnhiem, *Art and Visual Perception: A Psychology of the Creative Eye* (Berkeley: University of California Press, 1974).

9. The line was in the foreground, and surface was "behind" it. Ibid. p. 138.

10. Frutiger, *Signs and Symbols*, p. 34; Of course, lines are not necessarily "primitive." The lines of *yantras* are a "graphic expression of a conceptualized relationship" and are saturated with signification. Heinrich Zimmer, *Artistic Form and Yoga in the Sacred Images of India* (Princeton: Princeton University Press, 1984), p. 123. For this reason *yantras* are not discussed in this book.

11. Martin Heidegger, *Poetry, Language, Thought* (New York: Harper & Row, 1971), p. 154. In India the sage Nārāyaṇa once created the beautiful nymph Urvasī by drawing her outline with Mango juice, as her name indicates, on his thigh (*Viṣṇudharmottara*, 1.29, 1–19.

12. James Joyce, *A Portrait of the Artist as a Young Man* (New York: Penguin, 1976) p. 212.

13. Cf. William Blake: "Nature has no outline, but Imagination has./Nature has no tune, but Imagination has. / Nature has no supernatural, and dissolves. / Imagination is eternity." "The Ghost of Abel," *The Prophetic writings of William Blake*. Edited by D. J. Sloss and J. P. R. Wallis (Oxford: Clarendon, 1964), p. 646.

14. Charles Wentinck, *Modern and Primitive Art* (Oxford: Phaidon, 1979), p. 15.

15. See H. A. Groenewegen-Frankfort, *Arrest and Movement: Space and Time in the Art of the Ancient Near East* (Cambridge, Mass.: The Belknap Press of Harvard, 1987).

16. See chapter 2 on time and duration.

17. John B. Caroll, *Language, Thought and Reality: Selected Writings of Benjamin Lee Whorf* (Cambridge: MIT Press, 1956), pp. 139–40; Evans-Pritchard was acutely aware of this distinction and apologized for his inability to record the more elusive time perception in his discussion of Nuer chronology.

18. *Brahmāṇḍa Purāṇa* 1.2.21.87–88

19. Cf. VS 1.27.

20. Cf. Sharon Spencer, *Space, Time and Structure in the Modern Novel* (New York: New York University Press, 1971), p. 156; Spencer does not note that the traditional narrative sequence is also a spatialization process, which merely takes place in an opposite direction.

21. Jack Goody, "Oral Tradition and the Reconstruction of the Past in Northern Ghana," in Jack Goody, ed., *Literacy in Traditional Societies* (Cambridge: Cambridge University, 1968), p. 293.

22. For examples of such a subjective-contextual logic, see A. K. Ramanujan, *Interior Landscape* (Bloomington: Indiana University Press, 1967),

discussed in my chapter 6, and Alice Boner et al., *Vastusūtra Upaniṣad: The Essence of Form in Sacred Art* (Delhi: Motilal Banarsidass, 1982), pp. 5–6.

23. See Irene N. Gajjas, *Ancient Indian Art and the West* (Bombay: Taraporevala, 1971), chap. 4.

24. But in ancient art, according to the *Viṣṇudharmottara* the frame depended on the picture, at least in shape. The frame was oblong, square, round, and mixed if the picture was realistic (*satyā*), lyrical (*vainika*), urban (*nagara*), and mixed (*miśra*) respectively. See Kramrisch, trans., *Viṣṇudharmottara*, p. 8.

25. For a critique of this view, see Ananda K. Coomaraswami, *Figures of Speech or Figures of Thought* (New Delhi: Munshiram Manoharlal, 1981), chap. 3.

26. Frutiger, *Signs and Symbols*, p. 287.

27. On the relation of perceptual and aesthetic outlines and social norms, see Donald N. Michael, "A Cross-cultural Investigation of Closure," in D. Beardslee and M. Werthermer, eds., *Readings in Perception* (Princeton: Van Nostrand, 1958), pp. 160–70.

28. See *Mānasāra* 9.126–159; *Mayamata* 9.87–91: "The cow shed should be to the south, the flower garden to the north and the dwelling of ascetics either near the eastern gate or to the west . . . .The quarter for vaisya is to the south and that for sudra on the periphery."

29. H. D. Sankalia, *Some Aspects of Indian History and Archaeology* (Delhi: B. R. Publishing, 1977); John Marshall, *Taxila: An Illustrated Account of Archeological Excavations* (Cambridge: Cambridge University Press, 1951).

30. See for instance Caroline Ifeka, "Domestic Space as Ideology in Goa, India," *Contributions to Indian Sociology*, n.s., 21, no. 2 (1987):307–29. Most sociologists would regard the latter distinction as a false one, but that is an old debate which will not be resurrected here.

31. Sankalia, *Aspects*, p. 238.

32. S. Grover, *The Architecture of India* (New Delhi: Vikas, 1980), p. 5; Melinda A. Moore, "The Kerala House as a Hindu Cosmos," in McKim Marriott, ed., *India through Hindu Categories* (New Delhi: Sage, 1990), pp. 169–202. An opposing but still cosmological reading can be found in *Matsya Purāṇa* (255.7–9), which prescribes that the four doors in a house should be located in the cardinal directions and named after the Lokapalas (guardian deities: Indra, Yama, Varuṇa, Soma).

33. On the symbolic power of artistic motifs on a temple wall, see David Shulman, *The King and the Clown in South Indian Myth and Poetry* (Princeton: Princeton University Press, 1985), pp. 407–8.

34. P. Jayakar, *The Earthen Drum; An Introduction to the Arts of Rural India* (New Delhi: National Museum, 1980), p. 172. Palace walls and the walls of wealthy merchants in ancient India were also decorated with paintings or at least plastered. A. Coomaraswamy, *Early Indian Architecture* (New Delhi: Munshiram Manoharlal, 1975), p. 3.

35. Kanwarjut Singh Kang, *Wall Paintings of Punjab and Haryana*, (Delhi: Atma Ram & Sons, 1985), p. 104; See also Kramrisch, *The Hindu Temple*, p. 260 for "outward" perspective.

36. *Earthen Drum*, p. 172.

37. On the temple as organism, see Percy Brown, *Indian Architecture*

(Bombay: Taraporevala Sons, 1954), p. 76; Kapila Vatsyayan, *The Square and Circle of the Indian Arts* (New Delhi: Roli Book International, 1983), p. 79.

38. P. Brown, *Indian Architecture*, p. 13; Coomaraswamy, *Early Indian Architecture*, pp. 7–10.

39. Ibid., p. 14.

40. Similarly, Manorama Janhari links the rock-cut caityas with their facades, and barrel-vaulted roofs to the gabled end of a wooden structure, and the wooden, beam-supported roofs of much earlier construction styles. *South India and Its Architecture* (Varanasi: Bharatiya Vidya Prakashan, 1969), p. 30.

41. *Agni Purāṇa* 61.23–25; ŚB 13.8.1.1; see also Kramrisch, *The Hindu Temple*, pp. 253–54.

42. See Kramrisch, chap. 14.

43. George Michell, *The Hindu Temple* (Chicago: University of Chicago Press, 1988), p. 71.

44. Manu 8.246–52.

45. P. Brown, *Indian Architecture*, p. 4.

46. RV 7.55.

47. J. Fergusson, *History of Indian and Eastern Architecture* (Delhi: Munshiram Manoharlal, 1967) bk. I, p. 111. H. Zimmer sees the wooden technique as an acknowledgment of the cosubstantiality of the built structure with the organic universe (*Indian Architecture*).

48. See Mirashi, ed., "Inscriptions of the Kalachuri-Chedi Era," in *Corpus Inscriptionum Indicarum*, vol. 4, pt. 1, no. 7 (p. 21) no. 11 (p. 36); S. D. Singh, *Land System and Feudalism in Ancient India* (Calcutta: Calcutta University, 1966), p. 28.

49. Brah. Pur. 1.2.36.194.

50. In the *Bhāgavata Purāṇa* version. Interestingly, some versions of the myth describe the world immediately after Pṛthu's coronation as a perfect state of economic plenty, where agriculture was redundant (*Viṣṇu Purāṇa*; *Bhāgavata Purāṇa*). For no stated reason Pṛthu's subjects suddenly approach him to complain of overwhelming famine. This narrative glitch looks like the stitch between two distinct traditions.

51. The prevailing interpretation of forest owes more to depth psychology than any other single discipline. Similarly, no other part of the landscape, excluding the ocean, has been more thoroughly psychoanalyzed. See, for instance, Van Buitenen, *The Mahābhārata*, 2:173–76; S. Pollock, *The Rāmāyaṇa of Vālmīki*, (Ayodhyākaṇḍa) (Princeton: Princeton University Press, 1986), pp. 3–4; Nancy Falk, "Wilderness and Kingship in Ancient South Asia," *History of Religions* 13, no. 1 (1973): 1–15, and David Shulman "The Crossing of the Wilderness: Landscape and Myth in the Tamil Story of Rama," *Acta Orientalia* 42 (1981):23. See also my chapter 6.

52. Mbh. 3.58.

53. Madeleine Biardeau reads the episode in *Viṣṇu Purāṇa* 22–23, in which Kṛṣṇa transfers Mathurā's population to Dvārakā, as a significant transition from the midlands to "the outer limits of the earth, to a city whose name implies that it is an "entrance" a "gate"; but a gate to what?" She answers her own question metaphysically, but, of course, the gate between land and ocean is very significant on its own terms. See "The Childhood and Adulthood of Krishna," in Bonnefoy Yves, ed., *Mythologies* (Chicago: University of Chicago Press, 1991), 2:860–61.

54. See, for instance, *Mṛcchakaṭika* III.3; Coomaraswamy, *Early Indian Architecture*, p. 2.

55. *Matsya Purāṇa* 255.10–14. According to the *Caraka Saṃhitā* protective amulets must be tied around the necks of the newborn child and the mother as well as the upper beam of the door to the maternal house immediately after delivery (Śārīrasthāna 8.47).

56. David Shulman, *The King and the Clown*, pp. 2–5

57. Jyotindra Jain, *Painted Myths of Creation: Art and Ritual of an Indian Tribe* (New Delhi: Lalit Kala Akademi, 1984), p. 48.

58. *Mayamata*, 30.41; see also T. Bhattacharya, *A Study of Vastuvidya* (Patna: Bhattacharya, 1947), p. 235.

59. Verrier Elwin, *The Tribal Art of Middle India* (Oxford: Oxford University Press, 1951), p. 100.

60. Stephen Huyler, *Village India* (New York: Harry N. Abrams, 1985), pp. 164–65; Elwin, *Tribal Art*, p. 98.

61. The elephants are already to be found in the *Mānasāra* 39.79, along with Gaṇeśa and Sarasvatī, on both sides of the door. Cunningham reports, in reference to temples of the Gupta period, the existence of the figures of Gaṅgā and Yamunā guiding the entrance door (*Arch. Surv. Rep*, vol. 9, pp. 42–44). The practice substantiates the prescription of the *Agni Purāṇa* (21, 33) where the two river goddesses/door guardians are to be worshiped before the primary deity.

62. K. Murthy, *Early Indian Secular Architecture* (Delhi: Sundeep Prakashan, 1987).

63. P. Brown, *Indian Architecture*, p. 4.

64. Prasanna Kumar Acharya, *An Encyclopedia of Hindu Architecture* (Delhi: Oriental Reprint, 1979), p. 216; note that *toraṇas* were for passing under, not bridging spaces for crossing above!

65. B. N. Misra, "Early Toraṇa-Gateways as Predecessors of Temple-Doorways in Ancient Malavadesa," in Krishna Deva et al., eds., *History and Art* (s.l.: Ramanand Vidya Bhawan), Pl. 2

66. On the formulaic prescriptions for decorating *toraṇas*, see *Mānasāra*, 46.37–62.

67. See *Mānasāra* 46.

68. 8.245: "If a dispute about a boundary has arisen between two villages, [the king] should determine the boundary in May or June, when ridges of earth [*setu*] that divide the fields are clearly visible."

69. Jean Delouche, *The Ancient Bridges of India* (New Delhi: Sitaram, 1984), p. 4.

70. *Mayamata*, 30.33–35.

71. *Daśakumāracarita*, second story.

72. *Mṛcchakaṭika*, act 3 (van Buitenen, trans.).

73. *Pañcatantra* 1.8; abbreviated retelling of Alfred William's translation in *Tales from the Panchtantra*. See also L. Sternbach, *Juridical Studies in Ancient Indian Law* (Delhi: Motilal Banarsidass, 1967), 2:69–73.

74. *Tales*, p. 190.

75. Ibid., p. 202. See also A. M. Hocart, "Flying through the Air," *Indian Antiquary* 51 (1923):80–82, on flying as a mark of royalty and divinity.

76. E. Dimock, trans., *The Thief of Love* (Chicago: University of Chicago Press, 1963).

77. In the *Prabandhacintāmani* (p. 67), a thief entered the quarters of King Bhoja just as he was in the middle of composing a stanza to the moon. The thief could not restrain himself and finished the stanza, getting himself caught. However, instead of having him impaled, the king rewarded him handsomely.

78. E. B. Cowell, trans., *The Jataka, or Stories of the Buddha's Former Births* (London: Luzac, 1957), 6:235–36: the tunnel was furnished with eighty large doors and sixty-four small doors, it contained one hundred one bed chambers, and several hundred lamp niches. See also T. B. Yatawara, *The Story of the Tunnel* (London: Luzac, 1898).

79. *Naiṣadhacarita*, canto VI and Mbh.

80. "The Magical Transformation", in *Kathāsaritsāgara* (Kath.) p. 135.

81. Ibid., pp. 47–48.

82. A. L. Basham, "Notes on Seafaring in Ancient India" in A. L. Basham, *Studies in Indian History* (Calcutta: Samadhi Publications, 1964), pp. 73–81.

83. See for instance, Brenda Beck et al., eds., *Folktales of India* (Chicago: University of Chicago Press, 1987), pp. 256–58.

6

Passage to Marriage—The Dharma Agent

When Yudhiṣṭhira and his brothers left the city of Elephants through the auspicious northern gate called Vardhamāna, they set off for their forest exile. The dharmarāja's last concern before entering the forest was sending back his Brahmin followers, whom he feared he would not be able to feed properly when he himself became a mere food gatherer. The forest in that episode posed the ultimate dilemma for a man stripped of his status but determined to obey the injunctions of royalty. But inevitably, reluctantly, even Yudhiṣṭhira succumbed to the forest's reality and agreed to let the Brahmins scavenge.[1]

The theme of the king who leaves his domain, for a variety of reasons, voluntary or not, and enters a forest is pervasive in Indian literature.[2] There may be here, as Heesterman suggests, an initiatory ritual element associated with the establishment of royal legitimacy, or with the achievement of royal status.[3] The mythical or ritual passage to the wilderness—a more appropriate term than forest—consisting in explicitly specified obstacles, such as walls that must be crossed, is clearly initiatory in structure.[4] The wilderness assumes the liminal phase of the passage because it is characterized, on a variety of levels, by the complete loss of the subject's previous identity as prince. The forest, in contrast with the village or city, is not just a place of brutality and terror; it is also a place of romantic love and ascetic aspirations, and therefore the complete other side of dharma.[5]

We seem to stand on solid ground when we claim that royalty

must incorporate the forest's forces of chaos and that initiation requires separation, "exile," and reincorporation. Moreover, such a passage characterizes a variety of other transitional phases in the life of Hindus aside from the king's enthronement. This chapter will look at the ritual of marriage as such a process, especially for the bride. Such discussions usually owe their parameters to van Gennep and Victor Turner, but these men have also bequeathed to us a conceptual orientation that will require closer scrutiny with reference to our Indian material.

The Marriage Ritual

No attempt to describe the marriage ritual according to a normative text can ever do justice to the wealth of detail evident in even the simplest actual performance. Nor is that problem remedied by using several texts because of numerous incongruous details, inconsistencies, and varied sequences. The "marriage" to be described here, following primarily the oldest text—the *Āśvalāyana Gṛhyasūtra* (Āśv.)—is to be taken as a text about marriage rather than the detailed reproduction of the ritual.[6] The reader should avoid seeking an ethnographic abundance and precision of detail, because the texts limit their prescriptions to general guidelines. Moreover, it is not the marriage ceremony in its totality that interests me. The whole contains a variety of symbols pertaining to the purchase of the bride, the groom's journey, *mantras* and songs voiced by numerous participants, and other details that contribute to the meaning of marriage as a social institution of great importance. However, I shall focus on the narrower theme of the bride's passage from *kanyā*—a mere object in social terms—to the status of a married woman. For if we are not to regard the marriage solely in functional terms as the joining of social units (and thereby reduce the adult woman into a passive object), then we must assume that the passage from childhood to the status of married woman involves a serious transformation in the subject herself. It therefore becomes incumbent to see what this transformation entails and how it is brought about. Those aspects of the wedding ceremony that bear most strongly on the transformation of the bride will be examined.

The bride enters the events of the ceremony as a young girl, a guarded daughter, and in legal terms, as J. J. Meyer put it, a chattel. The early events of the ritual take place without her participation: the negotiating party's arrival, the negotiations, the *kanyādāna*, by means of which her fate had been decided. But then the girl emerges into the light of the sūtra's ritual attention. She emerges in a natural fashion, of course, that is with her body receiving an extraordinary purificatory washing.[7] This unusual bath, which utilizes more than just water, takes place at midnight (*niśākāle*) and involves herbs, fruit, and scents (*surā?*) as well. The purification is thorough and includes the head, as well as (according to Gobhila G.S. 2.1.9) the bride's vagina (*uttarā-*

bhyaṃ). It is carried out by female relatives of the bride, but there will be another purification (before departure to the groom's house), which will be performed by the groom. According to other texts, the bathing is performed by the groom and differs completely from the description given in Āśvālayana.[8] The groom places a round braid of Darbha grass on her head. On that he places a piece of gold. He pours the water through the yoke hole over her head after which he dresses her with the new dress.

Following her scented washing the bride is given a new garment (*ahataṁ vāsaḥ*) to wear, which according to the same text (but later on) the bridegroom gave her.[9] But as Gobhila's risqué version describes it, the groom himself actually dresses the young bride. In some contemporary versions of this rite, the mother of the groom gives him a white cloth, which he puts around the bride's body over her dress. He then leaves the room and she changes privately into the white sari he had given her.[10] A short time later, just before the groom or the bride's relatives tie her garment to his, he places a number of objects in her hands. In the right hand he places a quill of porcupine (*salalīṃ*) and a three-threaded cord. In her left hand he places a mirror (*ādarśaṃ*). According to Mānava it is the priest who then ties the clothes of the girl with those of the groom by means of a cord of Darbha.[11]

Following these opening rites (I have omitted a few), the bride and the groom begin to act in some unision. The *pāṇigrahaṇam* (taking of the hand) is the first among the following central rites, and one that may have been the original sine qua non—the consumation of the purchase, if you will.[12] As the bride sits, the groom stands facing her and takes her right hand.[13] He holds only her thumb if he wants sons, her other fingers for daughters, or all if he wishes for both. The bride then rises and he leads her around the fire and a new water pot (*udakumbha*) in which the priest had placed the following items: a limb from a milky sapped tree that has a masculine name (*punnāmno*), *kuśa* grass, and gold. The couple proceeds in a clockwise fashion (*pradakṣiṇā*), the groom to the right of the bride, and they complete three full circles. In Bengal the woman walks, or is carried, around the groom seven times. At the completion of each round she greets the groom like a deity.[14]

On the northern side of the fire and pot, a stone (*aśmāṇam*) had been placed along the orbital path of the bride. With every completed circle the groom leads the bride to step on the stone with the tip of her right foot.[15] Between each circumambulation the bride joins her hands while a brother, or other male relative pours fried grain (*lājā*) over them and she makes the oblation. When this procedure is completed the groom unties her two hair locks, if these had been tied.[16] With her hair loosened, again led by the groom, the bride takes the seven northeasterly steps (*saptapadakramaṇam*) with which the wedding is often identified.[17] Each step is accompanied with an invocation for a different wish. According to *Kauśika Sūtra* seven lines are drawn north of the fire and the couple place their feet on the lines as they recite the *Ṛgveda* verse (10.5.6) about the seven *maryādās* (boundaries).[18] The steps, Manu tells us, mark the legal culmination of the wedding. The heads of the bride and groom, joined together, are now sprinkled with water from the pot (*udakumbha*).

The bride will now spend her first night away from home, at the house of a married Brahmin woman. The following day, preparations for the trip to her new home will be made before she departs with her husband. The bride anoints the axle of the vehicle in which they will travel with clarified butter (*upānjanaṃ kurūte*).[19] She then also anoints the two wheels and the two bulls, *usrau*. The axle is held in place by two pins, which, on this occasion, are made of a fruit-bearing tree (*phalvato vṛkṣasya*), and the bride places these pins in their holes. With these preparations complete, the bride mounts the chariot and the couple departs to the groom's house. In Sri Lanka, the bride passes through a "ceremonial gate," specially constructed for the occasion, before departure.[20]

The trip is not passive or silent for every notable landmark or every manmade and natural boundary is noted and punctuated with a separate Vedic verse. The list of noteworthy landmarks includes a burial or burning ground (*śinaśānaṃ*), a large tree, a river (boarding the boat, crossing the river, and disembarking) (Śāṅkh.), road intersections (*caturpatheṣu*), every house (*vāse vāse*) (Āśv.), trees with milky sap (or others that serve as boundary markers), deserts, and others.[21]

The arrival and entry into the groom's house are carefully orchestrated to coincide with the sun's completion of its own journey in explicit synchrony with the cosmological identifications, which are established by means of the verses throughout the wedding. The couple must enter the village at sunset, along with the cows, and the bride's entrance into the house coincides with the setting of the sun (*saṇdhyā*).[22] She enters the house right foot first and she avoids stepping on the threshold.[23]

Her journey now complete, the bride assumes the role of a resident in her new home. Several rituals of some significance follow, but none of these are essential to the girl's passage because her status as wife has already been established. The nuptial fire that the couple had been transporting is now established in the groom's house. The new wife offers her first oblations in this fire while sitting on a red bull's hide east of the fire. Particularly interesting among the various observances following the bride's arrrival to her new home is the three-night abstention (*trirātravrata*) from sexual intercourse. Before they go to bed together on the first night, though not to consumate the marriage yet, the husband shows his wife the polar star (*dhruvadarśanam*).[24] The couple lie down on the ground and place between them a staff (*daṇḍa*), which is anointed with perfume and is dressed with a garment (*vāsa*) or a thread.[25] During the three days and nights of continence, they avoid salty and spicy foods, and probably anything with even remotely aphrodisiac qualities. On the fourth night the husband removes the staff, washes it, and leans it against the supporting pillar of the house. The next day it is thrown into water. On this fourth night the wedding is consumated sexually, if all goes well.

These then are some of the more notable events the girl undergoes in the course of the wedding. As indicated earlier, the actions are accompanied by a constant recitation of Vedic hymns that links the ritual to a broader cosmological context and reveals the broad social and religious meaning invested in the joining of individuals and families. It is virtually certain, however, that the *mantras* mean little to the young bride—aside from familiar references to the sun or Indra—and that her subjective "passage" does not build on a conceptual comprehension of the words.[26] Far more important are auditory rhythms, pitches and volume, the sights and smells of the ritual, the touching, dressing, perfuming, and other sensory manipulations of her body, the reactions of her relatives, the age and appearance of her husband. She may, of course, be familiar with mythical and literary models for the marriage, but these can never illuminate the process in its full breadth and depth.

The Marriage as a Rite de Passage

Van Gennep's seminal work on the threefold structure of rites of passage requires no restating. In the present context two points, which are not often singled out, should be discussed. First, the rite of passage is never solely a symbolic event but usually requires an actual passage in space:

> It seems important to me that the passage from one social position to another is identified with a *territorial passage*, such as the entrance into a village or a house, the movement from one room to another, or the crossing of streets and squares. This identification explains why the passage from one group to another is so often ritually expressed by passage under a portal, or by an "opening of the doors." These phrases and events are seldom meant as "symbols"; for the semicivilized the passage is actually a territorial passage.[27]

Furthermore, since the transition takes place in actual space, it can only be efficacious because the landscape has a magical impact on the subject: "Whoever passes from one to the other finds himself physically and magico-religiously in a special situation for a certain length of time: he wavers between two worlds."[28] The door, for example, is a boundary between the domestic and outside worlds, and crossing such a threshold produces an actual transformation or a unity with the new context.[29] Bruce Lincoln was correct to claim that all rites of passage do not necessarily involve the crossing of boundaries in space.[30] We shall return to this point shortly. Note however, in the following passage from Kuper, the preponderance of boundaries, which may be conceived in far broader terms than landmarks and doors:

> The entire population is also temporarily in a state of taboo and seclusion. Ordinary activities and behavior are suspended; *sexual intercourse* is prohibited, no one may *sleep late* the following morning, and when they get up they are not allowed to *touch* each other, to *wash the body*, to sit on *mats*, to poke anything *into the ground*, or even to *scratch their hair* . . . The king remains *secluded* . . . all day he sits *naked* on a *lion skin* in the *ritual hut* of the harem or in the *sacred enclosure* in the royal *cattle byre*.[31]

This paragraph makes it clear that passage and crossing need not entail geographic movement across boundaries, but they nonetheless require an explicit awareness and manipulation of "edges." Poking a stick into the ground can also be a (dangerous) crossing of boundaries in space. However, the more interesting and fundamental point that van Gennep was making was the denial of the boundary's symbolic ontology. This point requires a more fundamental approach than Lincoln's empirical observation, because it assumes a magical world view that has been reconsidered since 1908.

Turner's elaboration of the liminal state at the heart of the transition is equally familiar.[32] Our present focus is its implicit rejection of van Gennep's magicalism in favor of an essentially structural semantic: "The symbolism attached to and surrounding the liminal persona is complex and bizzare. Much of it is modelled on human biological processes, which are conceived to be what Levi-Strauss might call 'isomorphism' with structural and cultural processes. They give an outward and visible form to an inward and conceptual process."[33] To be more specific, the subjects of rites of passage, as they enter the liminal state lose their previous conceptual sense of identity and therefore act according to symbolic models taken from the processes of gestation and parturition.

What now is the relation between the boundary and the neophyte who crosses it? Van Gennep's magic has been replaced by Levi-Strauss's "isomorphism" or, in other instances, "homology."[34] Where the symbols employed in rites of passage are said to be isomorphic or homologous with cultural or natural phenomena, the subject who undergoes the ritual passage participates in a conceptual process that allows him or her to proceed from one state to another. The prince can become king and the daughter can become wife as a result of a powerfully transforming, symbolic learning process.

But the terms *isomorphism* and *homology* are just as confusing as *magic* and must be reconsidered in this context.[35] Moreover, the notion of a subject who undergoes passage is itself problematic, certainly in ancient India, and consequently we shall see that the efficacy of passage across ritual boundaries emerges without recourse to methodological concepts of relation, which have been borrowed from the life sciences.

Following the binary structure of Saussure's linguistics (primarily phonetics), Levi-Strauss posed homology as a system of equivalencies between pairs of oppositions taken from different planes such as geography, meteorology, zoology, economy, and technology. For instance, a set of equivalencies might contain pure or sacred with male, superior, fertilizing, and bad season in contrast to impure (profane) with female, inferior, fertilized, good season.[36] These phenomena are described as homologous. Following this example, Bruce Lincoln has analyzed a large number of homologous phenomena in Indo-European languages. These phenomena represent a correspondence between microcosmic and macrocosmic levels of reality: human hair, for instance, corresponds to plants, and house walls correspond both to cosmic and social categories.[37]

But there is more in Lévi-Strauss's analysis to shed light on the boundary-crossing act. He argued that a fundamental isomorphism exists between the (unconscious) structure of the mind and the variety of cultural phenomena that exemplify the homologies listed earlier. Homologies owe their value to the fundamental structure of the mind, a mind that acts not causally but isomorphically. This is not the place to deal with isomorphism in a systematic fashion, though it is hardly an improvement over saying that phenomena are magically related. Perhaps all that needs to be said in this context has been voiced by Derrida's critique of the essential atemporality of Saussure's structural linguistic and his recognition of the primacy of the temporal process over the structural-conceptual correspondences in Lévi-Strauss's isomorphism.[38]

For Lévi-Strauss the primary datum for research required a movement from the specific to the general and, therefore, from the conscious to the unconscious.[39] Boundaries in space are isomorphic with the mind's structure because they define the relation between in and out, here and there, sacred and profane, as well as other binary oppositions. The binary logic overrides the consciousness of concrete passage in space and time. Note in contrast that boundaries conform at the most elementary level to a tripartite structure (if any at all) because they assume transition (not mediation!) between the two sides. The third "morpheme" here is consequently irreducibly temporal and consequently specific and even irrational. It corresponds, as we shall see later, with the structure of consciousness, that is, with the spatiotemporal configuration of our awareness of a world. In other words, the meaning and effect of crossed boundaries can never be fully gauged by their relation to social and cosmic phenomena: the boundaries and the crossing must somehow signify in the conscious awareness of the individual crosser.[40]

Sociological and Cosmological Meaning of Passage

Nonetheless, cosmological and sociological models dominate our interpretation of marriage, as indeed of all rites of passage. The meaning ascribed to such rituals rests either on nonconscious social principles that render emic awareness irrelevant, or on complex cosmological ideas (homologically related to the former!), which render individual experience trite.

Examples of the first type abound in the literature on Hindu marriage: every major ethnographic study of a community contains significant portions on marriage, and there are several monographs that focus on marriage, among which Fruzzetti's work stands out. In the most basic terms the wedding "very clearly symbolizes the giving of a woman by one 'group' to another."[41] More specifically, the purpose of the wedding is the continuation of the line blood by means of a woman who belongs to a different line. The wedding makes her a receptacle and transmitter of the male blood in an appropriate manner.[42] The ritual as a whole is a complex expression and reinforcement of the principles that structure kinship, alliance, and, according to some studies, caste. The passage of the girl is defined by the structural semiotics of the ritual: functional signification is all there is. Some schools of thought would carry this even further: According to Mary Douglas, even the elaborate cosmology built into the symbolism of the ritual—or, more strongly, even the perception of the ritual—are merely the expression of social control ("grid" and "group"):

> Most values and beliefs can be analyzed as part of society instead of as a separate cultural sphere. The endless argumentation filling all the gaps in the conception of the cosmos. Theories of the nature of man and his place in the universe are developed to justify the argument maintained. There is nothing natural about the perception of nature; nature is heavily loaded with political bias.[43]

Most historians of religions would regard such observations as profoundly reductionistic, but obviously there is no way to settle that old argument. Still, some of the most widely accepted cosmological interpretations of the wedding substantiate the argument that cosmology only validates empirical social forces. The most common reference to marriage is in terms of a field and the seed in the field, or some related metaphor of fertility. In Fruzzetti and Ostor's study the "woman is the field [*khettra*], the cultivator provides the seed and 'cultures' the field."[44] This metaphor, already cosmological, places the bride in the paradigmatic context of Sītā, who was born of the earth, both as perfect wife and as mother earth.[45] Such a pervasive agrological metaphor is shared by numerous phenomenological studies and has recently been criticized by William Harman, who regards the ritual and mythical marriage of Śiva with Minakṣī as a devotional metaphor "expressing the dynamics of a devotee's relationship with a particular deity or a group of deities."[46] Since the relation of such a cosmological ritual and the "real thing" is homological or metaphorical, we are left with the marriage relegated again to the hermeneutics of kinship and alliance.[47] Perhaps I have already said too much about the cosmology of the wedding passage, not having first looked at the verbal narrative that accompanies the classical version of the ritual.

The Wedding in Verbal Formulas

As already noted, the wedding is accompanied by a constant recitation of Ṛgvedic and other *mantras*, which are rarely spoken (or understood) by the bride herself. The oral narrative follows the well-known marriage hymn of Sūrya and Soma in the *Ṛgveda* 10.85 and *Atharvaveda* 14.2. The hymn, of course, tells the story of the giving away of the Sun's daughter to the Moon (Soma), and the couple's journey across the sky to the groom's abode.[48] But even given the paradigmatic role of Sūrya's and Soma's wedding, the Gṛhyasūtra versions draw mostly benedictory formulas from the Veda and little of its mythical narrative. As the groom purifies the bride he recites RV 10.85.47: "Let all the gods and the waters together anoint our two hearts together. Let Matarisvan together with the Creator and together with her who draws the way join the two of us together." As the bride looks at the mirror in her hand, RV 6.47.18 is recited: "In every figure he has been the model: this is his only form for us to look on. Indra moves multiform by his illusions; for his Bay Steeds are yoked, ten time a hundred." The *pāṇigrahaṇa* (taking the hand) is accompanied by the following familiar formula: "I take your hand for good fortune, so that with me as your husband you will attain a ripe old age" (10.85.36).[49] As the bride smears the chariot or vehicle before departure, the cosmological context is invoked with "the sages luminous in themselves have praised you with their latest hymn. Now Indra, yoke your two Bay Steeds" (RV 1.82.2). Finally, when the bride enters the groom's house, this *mantra* is chanted: "Stay here and do not separate. Enjoy your whole life-span playing with sons and grandsons and rejoicing in your own home" (10.85.42). This, of course, is an abbreviated version of the oral accompaniment to the ritual. Additional recitations draw on *mantras* that are not Ṛgvedic, but are equally efficacious in placing the ritual within a broader context:

As the groom pours the golden water over the bride's head, he recites: "Of golden colors, pure, purifying, the waters have started on their way after destroying the evil. In these are spread a hundred purifiers. With them may the god Savitṛ purify you."[50] This and other *mantras* recited at the wedding, are used in other rituals such as the Somāvastana and even the Soma sacrifice (Hiraṇyakeśin G.S. 1.10.2; Āp. Ś.S. 10.6.1). They are used as tools in a toolbox, so to speak, that serves a large—though not unlimited—number of functions. Another *mantra* that may be used for this purification is taken from the same source: "In whom that are of golden color, pure, purifying, is Kaśyapa born, is Agni born, who have held Agni as embryo, who are of good color, let those waters be gentle and friendly to you."[51] As the groom ties the bride's garment to his own, this *mantra* is recited: "The cord of Indrāṇī. May Pūṣan tie a knot for you; let that knot of yours rest in me; I hold you up with the arms of Indra; with the head of Bṛhaspati I seize you; traverse the wide atmosphere. I shall place you on the surface of Aditi."[52] As she puts on the new dress, the following *mantra*, used also in the Upanayana ritual, is said: "The goddesses who have spun, woven, (and) spread out, the goddesses who have stretched out the skirts on both sides, may those goddesses weave about you (a cloth of) long life. O, woman of long life, you put on this garment."[53]

One of the most revealing *mantras* is recited as the groom gives the bride the quill of porcupine (*salalīṃ*) and the threefold cord (*trivṛt*): "May this protect you N.N. here as it (protected) Śacī the beloved one, and Aditi the mother of excellent sons, and Apālā the non-widow."[54] Then, as the bride's hair is combed, with a comb or the quill, the groom recites: "This well-made comb with one hundred teeth shall remove the impurities of her hair, (scratch) away (the impurities) of her head."[55] These texts, the reference to Apālā, and the scratching away of impurities, revive the association of the bride with a sloughing symbolism, though the allusion is certainly oblique enough to keep it esoteric.[56] Among the best-known marriage *mantras* is the one that accompanies the circumambulation of the fire: "This I am, you are that, you are that, I am this, I am heaven, you are earth, I am Sāman, you are Ṛk, come then, let us marry, and beget offsprings, dear to each other, may we two live a hundred autumns".[57] A clear linking of the couple to cosmic and sacred principles in a complementary union of opposites suggests a lofty conceptual state. The *mantra* is also reasonably easy to follow due to its musical repetitions. Still, I think it is just as significant for linking the circular motion around the fire with the idea of longevity and with the offsprings who punctuate the years (and the orbits). This provides an example of time that is ritually spatialized or, in other words, the spatial experience of walking around the fire resonating with the idea of the years and children. Such a conjunction of space and time will figure prominently in the manner that the ritual will be read perceptually in a subsequent section. Indeed, while these and other verses are critical for understanding the values embedded in the wedding ritual for social and religious purposes, only the conscious resonance of spoken word and perceptual experience can help us understand the passage of the bride. If the cosmological and the sociological interpretations share one shortcoming, it is the assumption that the wedding can be meaningful as a signifying totality—in other words, that the ritual acts as a complex semiotic "container" (of one sort or another) and that the participants are persons who may partake of different "quantities" of meaning according to their levels of comprehension. The passage of the bride is both society's functional reassignment of a new role to the girl, and the girl's growth into that role by her ability to absorb some of the meanings articulated ritually. Both assumptions fail to acknowledge the residual "imagist" power of any existential event (however ritualized) and, more important, the radical difference of the Hindu person.

The "Person" in Passage

The Indian girl who passes from her village to that of her husband, and from one social status to another is not an individual or person in the Western sense of these terms and therefore "signification" means in a different fashion for her. We must take account here of Dumont's important distinction between the ideological and empirical individual.[58] The former is "the independent, autonomous, and thus (essentially) non-social moral being, as found primarily in our modern ideology of man and society. The latter is the empirical subject of speech, thought, and will, the indivisible sample of mankind, as found in all societies."

Clearly it would be a serious error to confuse the two senses of the term and then attribute to the Indian person ideological components taken from our notion of the individual.[59] But this is only a beginning. For a variety of cultural reasons, the empirical individual, the person, in India, is markedly different from us. McKim Marriott has called the Indian an "open person" and quoted the following observations from one of his students: "The person is a more or less open flower, or an open 'vessel' characterized by what it contains at a given moment—the quantities, powers, and actions of its coded substance."[60] An open person is an empirical individual who lacks the sense of a rigidly enclosed body and a distinctly separate ego. This is a transactional self who possesses personal fluidity ("unctousness"—*sneha*, as Marriott puts it) and is characterized by a social transitivity and absence of clearly demarcated boundaries with other such persons.[61]

The open person, empirically speaking, is a phenomenon that characterizes a variety of cultures including modern ones such as the Israeli kibbutz. R. Moffit tells of an incident that happened to him in South Africa as he was preparing medicine for a woman to take to her sick husband. He instructed the woman to give the drink to her husband in two separate doses hours apart. But when she asked whether the medicine could not be taken in one drink, he agreed that it could. The woman then promptly swallowed the entire bottle. She was astounded to learn that her drinking the medicine would not cure her husband.[62] A person who believes and possibly feels such a link emerges into a sensory world characterized by intensive and prolonged tactile stimulation.[63] The structure of the Indian family encourages constant contact—the child is always carried by someone, and as the sense modalities develop they are enhanced by the sensory stimuli that are transmitted by means of these many carriers.[64] No single and isolated nexus of stimulation is formed in conjunction with a developing differentiated self. As Erikson noted in his direct observation of Indian child play patterns, children create

> a play universe filled to the periphery with blocks, people, and animals but with little differentialtion between outdoors and indoors, jungle and city, or, indeed, one scene from another. If one finally asks what (and, indeed, *where*) is *the* "exciting scene," one finds it embedded somewhere where nobdoy could have discerned it as an individual event and certainly not as a central one . . . Significant moments embedded in a moving sea of unfathomable multiformity: does not life on the street or at home anywhere offer such an overall configurational impression? . . . If, in all this, I should endow one word with a meaning which unites it all, the word is *fusion.*[65]

The effects of rearing and early childhood sensory motor stimulation occupy a vast area in cognitive psychology. Speaking in very general terms, child-rearing practices in India seem closely correlated with concrete and contextual thinking. Erikson's observation seems to corroborate what Valentine Daniel calls a "person-centric" orientation, taking the term *person* in its unique Indian sense. This results in a fluid and shifting perception of any standards, including dharma, according to time, place, and context.[66] In logical terms, no relationship is ever exhausted by the logic of either/or and by a subject with predicates, who passively records the interaction of objects in an external world. Consequently, no object can ever, properly speaking, act as a sign or symbol for another as signifier to signified. All elements of the natural and man-made world act as indexical signs because they belong in the same context, which is determined by the perceiving subject.[67] Only such a logic can explain India's long and bewildering lists, which constitute so much of what is taken as philosophy, jurisprudence, and so forth. The logic resembles the stunning dexterity of imagination that surely underlies the following taxonomy cited by Foucault (out of Borges) from a Chinese encyclopedia: "Animals are divided into: (a) belonging to the Emperor, (b) embalmed, (c) tame, (d) sucking pigs, (e) sirens, (f) fabulous, (g) stray dogs, (h) included in the present classification, (i) frenzied, (j) innumerable, (k) drawn with a very fine camelhair brush, (l) *et cetera*, (m) having just broken the water pitcher, (n) that from a long way off look like flies."[68]

But this is not to say that ontological and logical distinctions do not exist. Just as this list owes its existence to the alphabetical index that holds it together, so Indian taxonomies owe their existence to conventional signs, which are relational, and rules of dharma. It would be an exaggeration to describe the boundaries of the physical person as completely porous or fluid, and altogether deny the distinction of inside and outside. We have seen in the case of Apālā that the skin is both transitive and protective. Disease is often an invasion of the enclosed organism and, as Deborah Bhattacharya has shown, "madness" (*pāgalāmi*) is a phenomenon "which involves the disintegration of the boundaries separating outside and inside."[69]

Still, the conventional design that allows a Tamil poet to evoke the emotion of constant love by means of signs such as earth, sky, and water is based on the contextual imagination of an open person.[70] The landscape of mountain slopes and hummingbirds could never affectively signify inner states, as it does in an *akam* poem, unless the empirical agent experienced internal states by means of external events. This is the psychology at work in the power of omens, which is a way of reading the course of events based on the "subjective" registering of external events: "Changeable winds are blowing, harsh and grating, the sky is covered with an ashen darkness, the clouds look rough-textured and are strange to behold, our various weapons are falling from their seaths! Jackals are howling, grisly there on the burning horizon, the horses are shedding tears, and the flags are fluttering in the stillness."[71] All these portend the arrival of Arjuna to Bharadvaja, and the likely consequences of fighting him. The omen is not significant in the way the world behaves but in the way it registers on our senses. As one witch in Macbeth puts it: "By the prickling of my thumbs, something wicked this way comes."

It is important to emphasize that while cultural variations in child rearing and body manipulation result in different ways of conceptualizing the world, the very act of conceptualizing, the nature of thinking itself, varies too. Here again is Marriott's lacuna. The point is not that Hindus possess different conceptual categories from our own, but that thinking itself is deeply affected by the ongoing inputs from the body. The body still does much of the thinking in the way it registers the world sensorily. The open person with his body's *nadis* and metaphorical hydraulic mechanisms is not a different (indigenous) construct—a body in the mind.[72] It is not enough to observe that some Hindus believe that they share the substance of the soil on which they live and from which they derive nutrients.[73] This too is a conceptual notion that is not validated by perception as such. At the very least, we must discover the body image, as Kakar puts it, the unique phenomenological experience of the body-self.[74] No amount of discourse in any language on the subject of phantom limbs can capture the sensation of a missing limb. The phenomenon exists in nondiscursive experience and is, indeed, one extraordinary aspect of the body image as a whole.

Consequently, the mere replacement of one set of conceptual categories with another set, though important, is not a sufficient condition for exploring what the person-body undergoes while passing through sensory environments. Kakar's emphasis on the body image draws attention to perception as an ongoing factor in the definition of the empirical individual.[75] In simple terms, and in a limited fashion, this sets another agenda in the study of rites of passage. We limit our focus to the experiential and sensory dimension of the marriage ceremony in order to see what the girl actually undergoes and how she attains a new social status by means of the rite. Why, for instance, does the rite proceed with the insistent emphasis on boundary crossing?

The notion of the open person—or, in the case of a young girl, nonperson—requires that we study a passage with an eye toward the following hypothesis: the nature of a young girl's persona is amorphous (extremely fluid in Daniel's terms) and interactive. It is characterized by an unceasing flow of sensory, emotional, and cognitive stimulation and a near complete absence of self-consciousness or rather a rigid sense of self-identity. Passage is not an acquisition of knowledge or a gain of status by means of conceptual-symbolic indoctrination. It is a carefully controlled manipulation of the girl's perceptual awareness designed to forge a self-consciousness that is extratemporal and on which her new sense of identity can rest.

Such a hypothesis depends on a number of implicit assumptions that cannot be fully elaborated here.

1. The girl's sense of identity is closely related both to the level of interaction with her social (and physical) environment and to a sense of a segregated body: "People with a relatively high field-dependent way of perceiving have a less developed sense of their identity and of their separateness from others than do more field-independent perceivers."[76]

2. In other words, perception correlates closely with social practice—child rearing, play, economic activity, to mention some factors.[77] The perceptual manipulations of passage have strong implications for members of societies whose nature is profoundly interactive ("field dependent").

3. At the same time there is strong empirical evidence that suggests that body image is shaped by the experience of the body's surfaces and skin sensations in particular.[78] Consequently cutaneous responses to passages, following the paradigm of river bathing, engender strong effects on the body image, and the ritual, as indicated in the quote from Kuper, would capitalize on this fact. Such activities as bathing, anointing, or wearing of skins and special garments seem to confirm such an assumption.[79]

The Perception of Passage

As we shift the focus of the inquiry from social and cosmological significations to the girl's perceptions, it is difficult to believe that a very young, hungry, and tired (if elated) bride undergoes a serious conceptual transformation. Consider the following testimony of a much older (college graduate) bride:

> I broke down with sobs; someone from the crowd came and held me and wiped my eyes, I do not think I cried because I was particularly sad, but I felt very emotional and light as if nothing mattered anymore. I was also very tired from the whole day's ceremony and fasting, I guess. This was a feeling, I suppose, no woman ever feels again.[80]

Briefly recounted, the events of her marriage tell an interesting story of expanding boundary crossing, which significantly supports van Gennep's theory. The obvious boundaries are those crossed on the couple's journey to his house. But the first boundary crossed is the girl's skin, which is bathed in scented water, thus overcoming that first critical border between nature and culture. Her scented skin is now, at least ambiguously, not exclusively her own: it also belongs to those who washed her and to the herbs that have given her a new scent. This holds even if the washing is the highly symbolic ritual (according to Mānava) carried out through the yoke hole and utilizing a piece of gold. Even if the girl is oblivious to the sexual or solar symbolism of the yoke and the golden waters, she is still being washed by a strange man (the bridegroom) for the very first time in her life. In a sense, he is taking charge of her very body! This step is expanded when he gives her a new dress to wear and is further strengthened when this dress is tied to his garment. When Nala abandoned Damayantī, they had just one skirt between the two of them. He had to cut it in half and found a sword to do this. After cutting the skirt, he ran off but (in van Buitenen's translation) "his heart held its string, and he went back to the lodge and looked upon Damayantī as she lay." But his own heart was "cut in two," torn between his love and Kālī, and he abandoned his wife.[81]

If as a young girl the bride's attention tends to waiver, it now seems literally tied to this new figure who takes her hand and leads her to three circles around a center. Technically, the seizing of the hand (*pāṇigrahaṇa*) is a critical act that solidifies the groom's claim over the bride, and can even render the girl unmarriable to anyone else.[82] In the girl's outbound journey it is a logical step to follow the tying of her garment. The bride recognizes the domestic fire, but as she walks around it, the man who holds her is interposed between herself and that fire. He is closer to the center of her focused attention and acts as an intermediary through whom her sense of the fire must extend.

The circular and horizontal movement is interrupted at the completion of each circle for the low but still vertical ascent on a stone onto which the groom guides the bride. Again, she may have heard what the stone means, or caught a word or two about its symbolic firmness.[83] The important point is that she now does something that her guide does not do, she moves vertically, she may even be taller than him as she treads on the stone. The stone imparts to her a sense of distinction and importance. The three circles punctuated by three steps on the stone are thus much more likely to evoke feelings related to the birth of three sons, which are often regarded as the ideal number. In the words of Kuntī(!) to Pandu, after three sons a woman "is loose, after four she is a harlot."[84] With the perimeter around the fire thus established as the girl's appropriate space (and time), her locks are loosened and seven increasingly distant boundaries (*maryādās*) from the fire are stepped on. Since the fire belongs to her parents' residence, her orbit around the domestic sphere is broken and she will spend her first night away from home, but not yet at the groom's house. However, I believe that more than domesticity has been broken: in punjabi and other contemporary Hindu practices the mother will have applied a reddish mixture of oil and turmeric on her daughter. She places seven applications of the mixture while other kinswomen jokingly try to remove her hand.[85] We have seen in the Apālā chapter that the body is covered by seven layers of skin, which are reddish when healthy. The *saptapadī* are related to the notion of envelopment within seven boundaries, and, though the bride may not be "stepping out of her skin," she is certainly stepping out of her natural condition as daughter into the acquired role of wife.

Note that, as the bride breaks out of childhood and acquires a new persona, this is never internalized. Her newly acquired "center" is always kept in the horizontal space around her and is always mediated by the groom. The groom becomes her new "self," a self that exists outside of her but is closer to the center of her new orbit. The mirror (*ādarśaṃ*) that the groom gives to the bride is perhaps a striking illustration of this effect. Hillebrandt believes it is merely instrumental in helping her comb her hair, but clearly more is at work.[86] According to the *Kāṭhaka* G.S. (38.5), a mirror is the fee at the ritual occasion of a newborn child's first (forced) glance at the sun and moon. S. S. Dange cites the *Skanda Purāṇa* suggesting that a projected image, or shadow is the "very soul" of an individual.[87] This may be too strong, but the alignment of a visual image of one's self with the giver of the mirror (the groom) certainly seems consistent with the hypothesis that the person can find a locus in external space. The bride's only "centered" act is mounting the stone, but this too is only periodical and hardly sets her free from her new center of gravity.

During the journey to the groom's village the couple explicitly notes every boundary on their way and recites a variety of protective hymns, though these are not meant exclusively for married couples. Having thus either symbolically or literally stepped on every centrifugal mark between her parents' domestic fire and her husband's house, she now gingerly steps over the threshold, careful not to step on the newest and most potent boundary.[88] The trampling and marking of boundaries on the way "out" signifies their annihilation, whereas the respect for her new home's integrity marks her own new identity. Paul Hershman records the following observations concerning the reception of the young wife at the new house in contemporary Punjab: the groom's mother performs with her female relatives the *kacci lassi* (buttermilk) rite where they all dip their toes in a mixture of milk and water. The mother of the groom drinks the thoroughly polluted liquid. Hershman cites H. A. Rose and concludes that the rite is meant to establish the status superiority of the older married women over the new mother-in-law. But clearly there is more here: "Following the drinking of the liquid the mother of the groom bathes and washes her hair, and has it bound by the barber's wife, as if she were leaving a time of ritual impurity, such as following chilbirth."[89] This ritual act of self-pollution resembles a new childbirth, the delivery, perhaps, not of an individual, but a social entity—the married couple conceived as one. The rite is duplicated, in general terms, in Bengal, where a pot of milk is made to boil and overflow just as the bride crosses the threshold.[90] The rite may indicate auspiciousness, of course, but it also suggests a similar idea of new birth.

The bride, however, is still not altogether the groom's yet—that is, her own "new" physical boundary is still inviolable. For three nights she lies protected by the boundary protector par excellence, the *daṇḍa*. As the final chapter (9) will show, *daṇḍa* is a vertical force in a horizontal world, an ambivalent, androgynous, and dangerous power. The girl may know that the staff is the Gandharva Viśvāvasu, but this is beside the point. For three nights the only male companionship she will have will be made of Khadira wood. The three nights of abstention are obviously significant.[91] The new *brahmacārya* also has to mark three days of mortification at the conclusion of his initiatory process (Upanayana). Indeed the number three plays a pervasive role in *saṁskāras* and in the wedding ceremony in particular. Aside from the Triratra *vrata* (three nights of abstention), we have already counted the three circles around the fire and *aśmārohanam*, the three-threaded cord (*trivṛt*), the three (Mahāvyāhṛti) oblations that the groom makes (Śāṅkh. 1.12.11), the three *Ṛgveda* verses that "loosen" the bride from her house (Śāṅkh. 1.15.1), and others, including, incidentally, the three days of seclusion following the *tali* tying ritual for premarried girls.[92] According to the *Jaiminīya Gṛhya Sūtra* (1.7) the porcupine quill already mentioned must have three white spots (*tri śuklayā śalalyā*). The text also contains what may be among the most fundamental physiological grounds for the importance of the number three, namely the three phases of breathing (*prāṇam*, *apānam*, *vyānam*) stated in the formula that accompanies the combing of the hair.

It is easy to see that such an emphasis on three is not coincidental by comparing the *vivāha saṁskāras* with the Upanayana (investiture of sacred thread). That ritual often follows tonsure on the third year of the boy's life when three bunches of sacred Kuśa grass are placed on his hair (Āśv. 1.17.8). As the boy's hair is split into a right half and a left half, and each half is sprinkled with water (three times), the father recites the following verse: "May the waters moisten you for life, for old age, and splendor. The threefold age of Jamadagni, Kaśyapa's threefold age, the threefold age of Agastya, the threefold age that belongs to the gods, that threefold age I produce for you, N.N." (Śāṅkh. 1.28.9). In the boy's rite of passage the introductory formula (Śāṅkh. 2.2.1) is repeated three times as the girdle is tied around the initiate's body three times. Before that he wipes his own face thrice while reciting: "With splendor I anoint myself" (Āśv. 121.2). The student is also sprinkled three times and, three days after the ritual began (at least), he may recite the Gāyatrī for the first time (Śāṅkh. 2.5.2). After the major recitations the teacher makes the initiate sip water three times.

At its most obvious level the number three is the quantitative embodiment of van Gennep's scheme of separation, liminality, and reincorporation.[93] It is easy to criticize an interpretation, which seems so obvious, that everything has a beginning, a middle, and an end. Such a reading, however, is not so alien to Indian thinking on the connection of the number three with the boy's passage: "When the teacher takes on a disciple he makes him an embryo [*garbha*] within. He carries him three nights in his stomach. The gods gather to see him born."[94] The hymn itself contains the temporal meaning of three as acceptance, residence, and emergence accordioned into three nights, as the metaphor for the student's career as a whole. The pervasive use of threefold repetitions in initiatory rituals may represent a strong example for the schematic temporalization of the elementary acts of perception and consciousness in space. The initiation is a passage from one state of existence, of awareness, to another. Passage from childhood to adulthood in particular seeks to replace the free-flowing, unselfconscious, and little differentiated awareness of childhood with a relatively fixed and firmly determined social persona and self-awareness. This can only be carried out effectively by utilizing, in a ritual fashion, the underlying perceptual Gestalt processes by means of which awareness fashions, and is fashioned by, a world. Just as the most fundamental structure of perception is tripartite—an object set against its background by means of a boundary or outline—the most fundamental act of perception sorts out visual and other sensations in a corresponding (isomorphic) fashion.[95] Obviously, the three nights of abstention are far too semantically rich to be reduced to elementary acts of consciousness. My point is that the pervasive use of the number three in passage rituals points back to fundamental intentionalities because the rite of passage seeks explicitly to forge a new sense of awareness.[96]

The Dharma Agent: Intention by Extension

If the marriage *saṁskāra* transforms the young girl into a dharma agent, it is clear that agency is not a matter of moral individuality. The young wife does not acquire an internal orientation, a moral depth to which she can turn in order to determine her intention in dealing with matters of dharma. Instead, she becomes attached to an external center—two of them, in fact. One is the domestic fire and the other her husband; dharma is determined strictly by reference to such a compass point: "This only is what the good call the oldest law: what the husband says to the wife, whether right or wrong, that she must do exactly; thus do the knowers of the holy knowledge know."[97] Her moral "self" awareness simply exists in external space and deliberation on any course of conduct is not a matter of intention but extension.

Still, this is not the exclusive domain of women in India. Feeling, reasoning, and moral judgment by reference to an external agency are typical of its interdependent society and characterize some of India's greatest heroes. Consider Rāma for instance, as a dharma agent, not as a literary character. The *Rāmāyaṇa* runs its lengthy course tracing Rāma's pursuit of his abducted wife. It follows the man's heroic journey and magnificent deeds in overcoming obstacles—including even the ocean. But then, when his wife is rescued, her purity is established in the fire, what does Rāma do? He asks Vadra, one of his counselors, how the word on the street goes about Sītā![98] Now the gossip about his wife is not good: as the city folks see it, Rāma took back a woman who cohabited with Rāvaṇa (willfully or not—we saw in the wedding that will is not particularly determinative in the ritual so the citizens have a point). After years of exile and warfare, his own "passage" ostensibly, Rāma now takes two hours—maybe less—in narrative time to decide and then plan the abandonment of his wife. In effect, the decision to get rid of her followed no internal deliberation at all.[99] The text narrates Rāma's profound sorrow and even shame at betraying his wife. But the decision to do so was automatic and contingent entirely on the gossip of his subjects. What Western readers often find deplorable in Rāma's lack of loyalty to Sītā is precisely the result of the dharmic preparation seen in rites such as marriage, or coronation (Rājasūya) in the case of kings. If the exile in the wilderness is an initiatory motif, as many scholars have claimed, then the passage from prince to king, like the physical journey, is not a process of internalization but of establishing new external "centers" of orientation, which are conditioned by the journey.[100] Show me where you have been and I'll tell you who you are, so to speak. If the epic poem was meant for listeners who resembled its charcters, then the geography was not symbolic but paradigmatic. As king, Rāma's locus of intentional action was "out there" in his city, the locus of his royal persona.

Much later in the history of the *Rāmāyaṇa*'s evolution in various literary, regional, and sectarian contexts, Rāma's motive will become increasingly internalized. The Jain *Rāmāyaṇas* and various Bengali versions, or else the *Bhaṭṭikāvya*, explain Rāma's motive as jealousy. Though hardly more forgivable, such a motive at least gives the character an internal landscape in which resentment conflicts with duty and even love. The *Rāmāyaṇa*'s hero lacks this depth and his sorrow fails to move us because the loyalty to his royal persona is knee-jerk and utterly conditioned.

Needless to say conflicts in dharma may often place the hero in a position of having to choose between two or more exterior centers. But invariably even these cases do not involve an application of some internalized standard in relation to which alternatives are gauged. Instead, dharma options are determined with reference to their own intrinsic "gravitational pull," or in the manner they compete with each other independent of the subject's interests.

For the married woman the locus of dharmic dilemmas is not her interest weighed against any external factor, but rather the weighing of two or more competing options in relation to an external center—the husband: Vāsuki the snake (Naga) gave his sister to Jaratkāru the seer.[101] After their marriage was consumated Jaratkāru made his wife promise never to say anything displeasing or he would leave her. One day, after a child had already been conceived,

> the ascetic lay his head in her lap and fell asleep like a man who is tired. While the princely brahmin was sleeping, the sun went down to the mountain of its setting; and as the day drew to its end, O brahmin, she began to worry, Vāsuki's sister, mindful and afraid that her husband might decrease in the merits of the Law. "What should I better do—awaken my husband, or let him sleep? For my melancholy husband is devoted to the Law. . . . How can I fail to wrong him? Either he will grow angry, or he will lose merit as he lives by the Law. Surely the loss of merit must weigh heavier," thus she decided. "If I awaken him, he will of a certainty be angry; but of a certainty he will decrease in the Law, if he transgresses the Twilight." She woke him up to light the agnihotra and Jaratkāru flew into a rage and anounced that he was leaving her.[102]

Note that while the wife experiences this conflict in purely external terms, the seer has internalized the whole universe: "The sun does not have the courage to set at its appointed time while I am asleep!" he declares pompously, but reflecting a deep truth. Similar examples, incidentally, are not limited to women. Paraśurāma, who was teaching Karṇa archery (the latter pretending to be a Brahmin) once fell asleep with his head on Karṇa's lap. An insect bit Karṇa painfully but he remained perfectly still for fear of waking his teacher. But the blood that dripped out of the wound woke Paraśurāma who immediately read Karṇa's strength as a mark of a Kṣatriya and cursed him for the deception.[103]

Perhaps the sharpest literary device for depicting the righteous wife's identification with her husband is to represent her as altogether invisible—at least to some beholders. When Utanka wanted to give his teacher a present, he was instructed to bring a pair of earrings from Pauṣya's wife.[104] On the way "he saw an oversized bull and, mounted on it, an oversized man. The man addressed Utanka: "Utanka, eat the dung of my bull!" He refused. Once more the man spoke : "Eat it, Utanka, do not hesitate, Your teacher himself has eaten it in his time." So Utanka ate the dung and drank the urine, then went to Pauṣya. He begged Pauṣya for the earrings and was sent to the women's quarters to ask them. However, he could not see Pauṣya's wife until he purified himself from the journey's meal.

This story is interesting for illustrating a very concrete point about wives, rather than Utanka. While Utanka had no difficulty seeing Pauṣya in his polluted state, Pauṣya's wife was altogether invisible. Her body vanished or completely merged with that of her husband at a rather critical moment of pollution. This bonding is the precise goal of the wedding, and the ideal for successful marriage. From a natural and unmarked girl the path leads to an absolute phenomenal identification with the husband. This, at any rate, is the ideal of dharma. Paradoxically, the ideal is attained after a systematic centrifugal movement away from her parents' home, across numerous boundaries, to her husband's home. The dharmic wife cannot come into existence without the eradication of an old world by trampling on boundaries. So while the girl becomes a man's property, a field (*kṣetra*) or chattel (*vasu*), she also comes to experience herself as a boundary crosser. The seeds of *adharma* are planted in this fine line between the girl's perception of herself through the eyes of others, and an ever deepening subjective experience. We shall examine this volatility in the conduct of a mythical character named Daṇḍa, who changes as he moves across boundaries, and vacillates between his assigned role and his nature.

This book's exclusive focus on the sensory orientation of the empirical individual may seem somewhat arbitrary. If we have argued in the present chapter that the broader social unit (family, caste) is the decisive ideological category, should we not then proceed to examine the type of social "consensus" that develops on the basis of perception? Indeed, the conceptual framework of dharma remains rooted in the metaphorical language of spatial perception, as we have seen in chapter 5. However, a fully developed perceptual sociology—if one is possible—transcends the parameters of a phenomenological project. Instead, we shall continue to focus on the more fundamental implications of a dharmic world view that is grounded in space and time.

Notes

1. Mbh. 3.29.1.

2. David Shulman, *The King and the Clown in South Indian Myth and Poetry* (Princeton: Princeton University, 1985), p. 294.

3. Jan Heesterman, "The Conundrum of the King's Authority," in J. F. Richards, ed., *Kingship and Authority in South Asia* (Madison: University of Wisconsin Press, 1978), pp. 1–27. But note the comments of S. Pollock, *The Ramayana of Valmiki* (Ayodhyakanda) (Princeton: Princeton University, 1986), p. 4: the journey into the forest may equally characterize abdication of the throne.

4. Nancy Falk, "Wilderness and Kingship in Ancient South Asia," in *History of Religions* 13, no. 1 (1973): 1–15.

5. van Buitenen, *The Mahābhārata*, 2:173–76.

6. I have also greatly relied on the *Śāṅkhāyana Gṛhyasūtra* (Śāṅkh.G.S.) and *Mānava Gṛhyasūtra* (Mānav.).

7. The precise sequence of rites is uncertain because the texts disagree on several details. My reconstruction is based largely on Āśv.

8. Mānav. 1.10.5–7; Āp.G.S. 2.4.8.

9. Āśv. 1.11.3; 1.12.3.

10. Nur Yalman, *Under the Bo Tree* (Berkeley: University of California Press, 1971), p. 166.

11. Mānav. 1.11.5–6.

12. This is the rite with which Āśv. begins the description of the wedding.

13. Āśv. 1.7.3.

14. Manisha Roy, *Bengali Women* (Chicago: University of Chicago Press, 1975), p. 86.

15. Śāṅkh. 1.13.12.

16. Āśv. 1.5.16.

17. Manu 8.227.

18. *Kauśikasūtra* 76. 21–22: *Sapta maryādā uttato 'gneḥ sapta lekhā likhati prācyaḥ. Tāsu padāny utkrāmayati.*

19. Śāṅkh. 1.15.3.

20. Yalman, *Under the Bo Tree*, p. 167. Such gates are a universal feature of Hindu weddings to this day.

21. Āp. G.S. 2.6.5.

22. Mānav. 1.14.1.

23. *Na ca dehalīm abhitiṣṭhati*; Āp. G.S. 2.6.8–9

24. This sequence conforms to Śāṅkh. but not the others.

25. Āp. G.S. 3.8.9, A similar arboreal practice is described by K. B. K Singh among current Rajputs as the "Aam-vivaha" or the marriage of the Mango tree. Before the bride's departure either she or the groom marks the lower portion of the tree with five spots of vermillion after which five married women make five rounds with cotton yarn in a knitting fashion around the tree (*Marriage and Family System of Rajputs* [New Delhi: Wisdom Publications, 1988], p. 49).

26. See, for instance, Yalman, *Under the Bo Tree*, p. 166.

27. A. van Gennep, *Rites of Passage* (Chicago: University of Chicago Press, 1960), p. 192.

28. Ibid., p. 18.

29. Cf. Shulman, *The King*, pp. 3–9.

30. Bruce Lincoln, *Emerging from the Chrysalis* (Cambridge, Mass.: Harvard University Press, 1981), p. 100.

31. H. Kuper, *An African Aristocracy* (London: Oxford University Press, 1947, pp. 219–20 (my emphasis.)

32. Victor Turner, *The Forest of Symbols: Aspects of Ndembu Ritual* (Ithaca: Cornell University, 1967), chap. 4 ("Betwixt and Between: Liminal Period")

33. Turner, *Forest*, p. 96.

34. C. Lévi-Strauss, *The Savage Mind* (Chicago: Chicago University Press, 1966).

35. The use of the term *homology*, which had been borrowed by anthropologists from evolutionary biology (comparative anatomy) through linguistics, is quite distorted. Homology ought to indicate common ancestry among corresponding elements, but no necessary similarity at all!

36. Lévi-Strauss, *Savage Mind*, p. 93.

37. Bruce Lincoln, *Myth, Cosmos and Society*, (Cambridge, Mass.: Harvard University Press, 1986); Melinda Moore, "The Kerala House as a Hindu Cosmos," in McKim Marriott, ed. *India through Hindu Categories* (New Delhi: Sage, 1990), pp.169–202.

38. T. K. Seung, *Structuralism and Hermeneutics* (New York: Columbia University Press, 1982), p. 152.

39. Lévi-Strauss, *Savage Mind*, pp. 20–21. Unconscious refers not to a Freudian realm but to the conceptual structure of the mind.

40. This is not intended as a critique of structuralism but as a phenomenological alternative.

41. Yalman, *Under the Bo Tree*, p. 167.

42. L. Fruzzetti, *The Gift of a Virgin* (New Brunswick, N. J.: Rutgers University Press, 1982).

43. "Introduction to Grid/Group Analysis," in Mary Douglas, ed., *Essays in the Sociology of Perception* (London: Routledge & Kegan Paul, 1982), p. 7. These observations contradict the principles of Gestalt psychology and are directly challenged by experimental studies on perception and culture. See, for instance, Donald Michael, "A Cross-cultural Investigation of Closure," in David Beardslee and Michael Wertheimer, eds., *Readings in Perception* (Princeton: van Nostrand, 1958), pp. 160–70.

44. "The Seed and the Earth: A Cultural Analysis of Kinship in a Bengali Town," *Contributions to Indian Sociology*, n.s., 10, no. 1 (1976):96.

45. Fruzzetti, *Gift*, p. 24.

46. *The Sacred Marriage of a Hindu Goddess* (Bloomington: Indiana University Press, 1989), p. 3.

47. Harman, *Sacred Marriage*, p. 96.

48. See W. O'Flaherty's translation in *The Rig Veda* (Harmondsworth: Penguin, 1984), pp. 267–71. The hymn is not a model of subsequent weddings but rests on the basic practices known to its author, and provides a verbal *context* for later versions.

49. This, perhaps more than any other verse indicates that the RV hymn contains material that was already used as standard ritual formulas in ancient weddings.

50. *Mantra Patha* (MP, Winternitz, ed.)1.2.1; See also, P. K. N. Pillai, *Non-Rgvedic Mantras in the Marriage Ceremonies* (Trivandrum: Travancore

Devaswam Board, 1958). Not only does the sun purify, it also binds the couple as it binds all objects in the world: ŚB 6.1.1.17, 8.7.3.10; AV 9.8.38.

51. MP 1.2.2.

52. Mānav. Ś.S. 1.1.2. This formula is shared with the tying of the sacrificial straw in the Darśapūrṇamāsa sacrifice (Āp. S.S. 2.1.4.12).

53. *Sarva Mantra Brāhmaṇa* 1.1.5. On the relation of clothes and Earth, see Alf Hiltebeitel, "Draupadi's Hair," *Purusartha* 5 (1981): 179–214.

54. Śāṅkh. 1.12.6.

55. AV 14.2.68.

56. See A. Coomaraswamy, "On the Loathly Bride," *Speculum* 20, no. 4 (1945): 391–404, and my chapter 5.

57. Āśv. 1.7.6.

58. *Homo hierarchicus* (Chicago: University of Chicago Press, 1977), p. 8.

59. However, it is too easy to exaggerate the ideological emphasis on the individual in the West and overlook the range and depth of Western traditions on the relational quality of the person. See, for example, Anselm Strauss, *Mirrors and Masks* (Glencoe, Il.: Free Press, 1959), particularly with reference to the Pragmatists.

60. "The Open Hindu Person and Interpersonal Fluidity," in Marriott, *India*, p. 2; citing also Ronald Inden, *Marriage and Rank in Bengali Culture* (Berkeley: University of California Press, 1978).

61. One lacuna this theory does not address is the distinction between the (indigenous) conceptual notion of the open person and the actual experience of existing as an "open person," which is empirical and can never be captured by means of conceptual categories.

62. R. Moffit, *Missionary Labors and Scenes in Southern Africa* (London: Seow, 1904), pp. 591ff.

63. See *Caraka Saṃhitā* on child rearing, and my chapter 4.

64. Sudhir Kakar, *The Inner World: A Psycho-Analytic Study of Childhood and Society in India* (Delhi: Oxford University Press, 1978).

65. *Gandhi's Truth: On the Origins of Militant Non-violence* (London: Faber and Faber, 1970), p. 40.

66. E. Valentine Daniel, *Fluid Signs, Being a Person the Tamil Way* (Berkeley: University of California Press, 1984), pp. 70–71.

67. See A. K. Ramanujan, "Is There an Indian Way of Thinking?" in Marriott, *India*, p. 50.

68. M. Foucault, *The Order of Things* (New York: Vintage Books, 1973), p. xv.

69. *Pagalami: Ethnopsychiatric Knowledge in Bengal* (Syracuse: Maxwell School of Citizenship, 1986), p. 151.

70. A. K. Ramanujan, *Interior Landscape* (Bloomington: Indiana University Press, 1967), pp. 108–9.

71. Mbh. 4.37.3ff. If omens are a way of reading the world as it registers on our body, then "bad" omens (according to the author), greeted as good omens (by an idiot like Agniśraman), can become good ones with some success (*Kathāsaritsāgara* 171).

72. M. Marriott, "Constructing an Indian Ethnosociology," in Marriott, *India*, pp. 1–40

73. Daniel, *Fluid Signs*, p. 63.

74. Sudhir Kakar, *Shamans, Mystics and Doctors* (New York: Alfred A. Knopf, 1982), p. 232.

75. This area has become increasingly focused in anthropological research; see, for instance, M. Spiro, "Ifaluk Ghosts: An Anthropological Inquiry into Learning and Perception," in Robert Hunt, ed., *Personalties and Cultures* (Garden City, N.Y.: Natural History Press, 1967) pp. 238–50; and Mary Douglas, *Essays in the Sociology of Perception* (London: Routledge & Kegan Paul, 1982).

76. H. A. Witkins, ed., *Psychological Differentiation, Studies of Development* (New York: John Wiley and Sons, 1962), p. 5.

77. Jan Deregowski, "Illusion and Culture," in R. L. Gregory and E. H. Gombrich, eds., *Illusion in Nature and Art* (New York: Charles Scribner's Sons, 1973), p. 179.

78. K. von Fieandt, *The Perceptual World* (London: Academic Press, 1977), p. 400. Cf. John Updike's decidedly unscientific remarks about his psoriasis: "Having so long carried a secret behind my clothes, I had no trouble with the duplicity that generates plots and surprises and symbolism and layers of meaning; dualism, indeed, such as existed between my skin and myself, appeared to me the very engine of the human. And with my changeable epiderm came a certain transcendent optimism; like a snake, I shed many skins: I had emerged relatively spotless from many a summer and holiday, and the possibility of a 'new life' in this world or the next, has been ever present to my mind." *Self-Consciousness* (New York: Fawcett Crest, 1989), p. 77.

79. See my comments on RV 8.90 and the story of Apālā in chapter 5.

80. Roy, *Bengali Women*, p. 85.

81. Mbh. 3.32.59.

82. See the story of Bhīṣma's abduction of Ambā in Mbh. 1.7.96 and 5.60.172. As Śālva points out later in the story, the hand contact rendered her Bhīṣma's property (*vasu*). Talmudic law regards the handling of merchandise as the moment of possession, and chess players, according to international rules, cannot withdraw a hand that has touched a piece.

83. See *Atharvaveda* 14.1.47.

84. Mbh. 1.114.65.

85. Paul Hershman, *Punjabi Kinship* (Delhi: Hindustan Publishing, 1981), pp. 63–64.

86. *Rituallliteratur* (Strassburg: Trubner, 1897), p. 65.

87. *Hindu Domestic Rituals* (Delhi: Ajanta, 1985), p. 32.

88. See William Crooke, "The Lifting of the Bride," *Folklore* 8 (1902): 238–42.

89. Hershman, *Punjabi Kinship*, p. 168.

90. Roy, *Bengali Women*, pp. 89–90.

91. The Gandharva Viśvāvasu kept the stolen Soma for three nights before the gods could recover it (TS 6.1.6.5). See my chapter 8.

92. On tying the girl with the threefold Muñja grass cord by the Adhvaryu, see Ralph T. H. Griffith, *The Texts of the White Yajurveda* (New Delhi: Munshiram Manoharlal, 1987), p. 9, n. 30.

93. For Dumezil, incidentally, the tripartite functions are always conceptual—never psychological, let alone perceptual (*L'idéologie tripartite des Indo-Europeèns* [Brussells: Latomus, 1958], despite his comments pp. 24–25.

94. AV 11.5.3. The metaphor of the guru as father was extremely familiar. See Āp. 1.1.1.15–17; Gautama 1.8; Manu 2.146: "Between the one who gives him birth and the one who gives him the Veda, the one who gives him the Veda is the more important father" (Doniger, trans., *The Laws of Manu*).

95. This fact is utilized by film makers and animators in establishing the timing for repeated events used for comic or similar effects.

96. The threefold repetition is not limited to *saṁskāras*, of course. On the Darśapūrṇamāsa, for instance, see P. V. Kane, *History of Dharmaśāstra* (Pune: BORI, 1974), 2:1027.

97. Mbh. 1.113.2; Cf. J. J. Meyer, *Sexual Life* (New York: E.P. Dutton, 1930), p. 351, and Julia Leslie, *The Perfect Wife: The Orthodox Hindu Woman According to the Strīdharmapaddhati* of Tryambakayajvam (Delhi: Oxford, 1989), p. 312.

98. *Rām.* Uttara. 53–55.

99. According to Goldman, "Rāma and his brothers rarely show any of the inner ambivalence that lends such psychological reality to the finest portions of the *Mahābhārata*. (*The Ramayana of Valmiki* [Princeton: Princeton University Press, 1984], p. 53).

100. Ibid., p. 28.

101. Mbh. 1.43. Cf. Mbh. 12.148 on the woman who would not wake her husband to stop her son from going into the fire.

102. This theme became pervasive in much later popular literature in a variety of forms. See *Bhojaprabandha* in which the king saw a woman sitting with her sleeping husband's head in her lap. Her young child, meanwhile, was approaching a fire and the woman could not move. She pleaded with Agni, who saved the boy from burning. (Louis H. Gray, trans., *The Narrative of Bhoja* [New Haven: American Oriental Society, 1950], p. 82).

103. Mbh. 12.2–3.

104. Mbh. 1.3.105. Contrast with Gāndhārī who covered her eyes with a cloth so she would not enjoy sight while her husband Dhṛtarāṣṭra suffered from blindness.

7

Playing the Field: Adultery as Claim Jumping

by Wendy Doniger

A man who steals lamps becomes blind, and a man who extinguishes lamps, one-eyed; a sadist is always sick, and an adulterer is rheumatic.
The Laws of Manu[1]

When the bride has crossed the boundary into marriage, and is fully identified with her husband, she has still not reached the end of her journey nor crossed the final boundary line. The dharmic construction of her real self is incomplete until she bears her husband a son. Indeed, even then it is not over; ideally, the perfect wife will die before her husband (hence the perception of widows as, at best, failures, and, at worst, murderers), having lived her whole life in complete faithfulness to him as a *pativratā*, a woman who keeps her vow to her husband and is hence regarded as chaste. This is the cultural ideal of Sītā.

But what if she does not have a son? Or, perish the thought, what if she is not faithful to her husband? For much of the *Rāmāyaṇa*, Rāma fears that both of these things have happened to Sītā, though he is wrong in both cases. Thus, the Dharmaśāstras and Epics recognize that these problems do arise, and they propose elaborate solutions: other ways of procuring male heirs, and appropriate punishments for the straying woman.

But folklore, Sanskrit romances, and *Kāmaśāstras* suggest that, sometimes, adultery is the solution, not the problem. The solace of fantasy was available to women as well as men, regardless of the gender of the hand that actually wrote down the texts. For these texts offer not a practical solution but a fantasy that may make unadulterous marriage viable; they offer the vision of new boundaries that may be crossed safely in fantasy—and crossed, not so safely but still crossed, in reality. The fantasy of adultery is particularly important when the woman's will is so fully subordinated to her husband, her natural emotions so repressed, that the only outlet for both her individualism and her passion is a perfect stranger—a lover or a god. Let us begin with the human lover and move on to the god.

The Appeal of the Human Lover: The Kāmasūtra

The *Kāmasūtra* of Vātsyāyana, though written, like the Dharmaśāstras, ostensibly from the man's point of view, is also able to imagine the woman's point of view. Friedrich Wilhelm has noted the ways in which the textbooks on *kāma*, dharma, and artha (the triple path or *trivarga*) cite one another and vie for supremacy.[2] Manu himself grants the importance of desire (*kāma*) at the very outset of his work: "Acting out of desire is not approved of, but here on earth there is no such thing as no desire; for even studying the Veda and engaging in the rituals enjoined in the Veda are based upon desire."[3] Perversely, when the *Kāmasūtra* tells us about the merits of adultery, desire is *not* a significant factor, as we shall see.

The *Kāmasūtra* tells us that Śvetaketu Auddālaki abbreviated the text.[4] In glossing this statement, the commentator tells us about the origin of the view that adultery is a crime:

> Formerly there was adultery [*paradārābhigamanam*] in the world, as it is said:
>
> Women are all alike, just like cooked rice, O lord of men; therefore one should not get mad at them or get attached to them or delight in them (or have sex with them [*rāmate*]). But this state of affairs was forbidden by Auddālaki, and thus it was said:
>
> Drinking wine is forbidden for Brahmins by the Guru's son [the son of Bṛhaspati or Uddālaki, i.e. Auddālaki Śvetaketu], and other peoples' wives are forbidden for common people by the sage Auddālaki. Therefore, with his father's consent and because of the state of affairs in which people had sex with people that one should not have sex with, Śvetaketu, rich in inner heat, happily constructed the text.

Thus, in the good old days, adultery did not matter, since women did not matter; if all cats are gray in the dark, there is no reason for a tomcat to make a fuss if another tom strays onto his turf. But Auddālaki changed all that and distinguished between women that one can and cannot have sex with; and if the cats are different, you can get badly scratched for messing with another tom's lady.

The *Kāmasūtra* passages on adultery show how seriously it was taken, and how carefully the author(s) of the text understood the good reasons for it. It goes into great detail in all of these passages, in part because it is a manual (how to commit adultery) and in part because, like all *śāstras*, it strives to give an encyclopedic coverage of its subject, which must take into account all possibilities, all points of view. Its rules involve a hierarchy of rationales that are brought into play by the author in a structured series so that he ends up proving what he wants to prove.

First, the text expresses to woman's reasons for doing it and her (much fewer) reasons for not doing it.

The Wife's Reasons for Committing Adultery

Explicitly, this portion of the text, like the text as a whole, is addressed to a man, the would-be corruptor of the married woman: it tells him how to do it. But indirectly it presents us with a most sympathetic image of a series of unhappily married women, expressing, through male scribes, their point of view:

> The following are women who can be gotten without any trouble, who can be had by means of mere perseverance: a woman who stands at the door; who looks out from her porch onto the main street; who hangs about the house of the young man who is her neighbor; who is always staring (at you); a woman who is sent as a messenger but throws sideways glances at you; one whose husband has taken a co-wife for no good reason; who hates her husband, or is hated by him; who has no one to look after her; who has no children; who is always in the house of her relatives; whose children have died; who is fond of society; who is addicted to pleasure; the wife of an actor; a young woman whose husband has died; a poor woman fond of enjoying herself; the wife of the oldest of several brothers; a woman who is very proud; a woman whose husband is inadequate; a woman who is proud of her skills; a woman who is distressed by her husband's foolishness or by his lack of distinction or by his greediness; a woman who was chosen as a bride when she was still a young girl, but somehow was not obtained by that man, and now has been married to someone else; a woman who longs for a man whose intelligence, nature, and wisdom are compatible to her and not contrary to her own personality; a woman who is by nature given to taking sides; a woman who has been dishonoured (by her husband) when she has done nothing wrong; one who is put down by women whose beauty and so forth are the same as hers; whose husband travels a lot; the wife of a man who is jealous, foul-smelling, too clean, impotent, a slow-poke, unmanly, a hunchback, a dwarf, deformed, a jeweler, vulgar, sick, or old.[5]

It needs no Indologist come from the grave to gloss this passage, though it might help to know that Manu says that sex with the wife of an actor is not a sin[6] and that jewelers in the ancient world used chemicals that might have rendered them impotent. Most of the reasons make perfectly good sense to a contemporary Western reader (even reasons for the jeweler's wife to commit adultery: seeing the rich gifts that other men gave to their women, but that never came to her). And, by and large, these reasons express a woman's point of view.

The Wife's Reasons for Not Committing Adultery

This part of the text reverts to the more male, indeed gynophobic, point of view, but still in the service of the hero, the would-be adulterer: if all women are keen to give it away, why shouldn't one of them give it to him? In this context, the woman's virtue or, more often, her fears and misgivings are regarded as mere obstacles to be overcome. Yet here, too, there is remarkable empathy, and a woman's voice is heard from time to time:

> A woman desires whatever attractive man she sees, and so does a man desire every attractive woman. But for various considerations, the matter goes no farther . . . Here are the reasons why a (married) woman rejects a man: affection for her husband, regard for her children, the fact that she is past her prime, or overwhelmed by unhappiness, or unable to find an opportunity to get away from her husband. Or because she gets angry and thinks, "He is propositioning me in an insulting way." Or because she lacks imagination and thinks, "This is unthinkable." Or because she thinks, "He will soon go away" or "He has no tie to me; he is attached to someone else." Or because she is frightened and thinks, "His face cannot keep a secret," or, "His affection and regard are all for his friends." Or because she fears that his attachment to her is light. Or because she is diffident, regarding him as glamorous. Or if she is a "deer-woman" of slight built and little passion she may fear, "He is too passionate and forceful." Or she may be embarrassed when she thinks, "He is a man about town and accomplished in all the arts." Or she may feel, "He has always treated me just as a friend." Or she may be displeased with him for his lack of knowledge of the right time and place, or despise him for his low status. Or she may be disgusted when she thinks, "Though I have given him hints with my face and gestures, he does not understand." Or if she is an "elephant-woman" of large build and strong passion she may think, "He is a 'hare-man' of weak passion." Or she may feel pity for him and think, "I would not want anything unpleasant to happen to him because of me." Or she may become depressed when she sees her own shortcomings, or afraid when she thinks, "If I am discovered, I will be thrown out by my own people." Or she will not respect him because he has grey hair. Or she may worry that he has been employed by her husband to test her. Or she may have regard for dharma.[7]

For some of this, one does need an Indologist, to tell us that the *Kāmasūtra* classifies men and women into animal types, according to the intensity of their passion and the size of their sexual organs; men are (in descending order) stallions, bulls, and hares; women are elephants, mares, and deer. But this physiological factor is by far outweighed by the subtle attention to more universal psychological and even sociological factors. Almost any one of the sentences in this paragraph could serve as the thumbnail sketch of the plot of a soap opera. But it is worth noting that among these many possible reasons for crossing the boundaries of marriage, the concern for dharma is merely a casual, last-minute consideration—the very last reason cited. It is also worth noting that the woman in this passage is said to experience various sorts of affection—regard for her husband, obsessive passion for her lover—in dramatic contrast with the man's allegedly cold-blooded reasons for becoming involved with her.

Then, the text expresses the lover's point of view: the man's reasons for doing it, or not doing it.

The Lover's Reasons for Committing Adultery

> He thinks, "This woman does whatever she wants to do, and has ruined her virtue with many other men. Even though she is of a class higher than mine, I can go to her as I would go to a whore, without squeezing my dharma." Or he may think, "This woman was widowed as a virgin and remarried; she has been mounted by other men before me. There is no reason to hesitate toward her."[8]

Here the commentator adds that the man thinks, "Since her womb has been spoilt (or at least broken open, the maidenhead gone), there would be no *adharma* in going to her." The text continues:

> Or, he thinks, "This woman has her husband under her thumb, and he is a great and powerful man who is very close with my enemy. If she becomes intimately attached to me, out of affection (for me) she will turn her husband away (from my enemy)."[9] Or, "Her husband, a powerful man, is in her power. If she gets him to break from me, she will get him to join with my enemies, or she herself will join with them."[10]

The commentary spells it out. The man thinks, "She has her husband under her thumb, and when her affection (for me) has grown great because of sexual union, she will act so that he will have special concern for me. If not, taking refuge with his great and powerful friend, he will kill me, and I have not yet accomplished the four goals of a man." Thus *kāma* is set in the service of the other, more respectable goals of a man (success, religion [dharma], and release [*mokṣa*]. But the would-be adulterer continues to imagine the indirect benefits of adultery:

> "She will cause (her husband) who is disposed against me and is powerful and wishes to harm me, to change his attitude." Or, "If I make him my friend through her, I will be able to do favors for my friends or something against my enemies or accomplish some other thing that is difficult to accomplish."[11]

Again the commentary attributes an altruistic motive to the adultery. He thinks, "For one should give up one's life's breaths or enter hell for the sake of something to be done for a friend."

But then the adulterer reverts to sex as power, as he continues to meditate: "If I become intimately attached to her, and kill her husband, I will come to possess his great wealth and power, which should be mine."[12] Still the commentator equivocates. The hero thinks,

> Having made an alliance with her who has become full of affection for me as a result of sexual union, and whose husband hates me, I will kill him silently with a stick, but only if he is killing our family or is even crazy. I will cut him down suddenly, violently, and then I will get it (his power). And as a result of the fact that he is one who has drawn his bow to kill me (i.e., is attacking me), even killing him will not cause *adharma.*

Here the commentator has helpfully had his hero cite the famous passage in Manu that allows killing in self-defense.[13] But the adulterer may be nothing but a gigolo:

> Or he thinks, "There is no danger in my having this woman and it may involve a lot of money. Since I have no property and little means of making a living, this is the way that I will get a great deal of money, from her, with no difficulty."[14]

Still the commentary insists that he acts out of altruism, thinking

> I am not able to support my family, and so my sexual connection is a means of achieving dharma and so forth; the wealth will be given out of affection. For the sake of the family even what is not to be done is to be done. And so it is said: "An old mother, a father, a good wife, and a young engendered son, are to be supported even by doing a hundred things that are not to be done; this is what Manu says."

Manu does not say this in so many words. What he does say is, "If a Śūdra is unable to engage in the service of the twice-born and is on the brink of losing his sons and wife, he may make a living by the innate activities of a manual laborer."[15] He also says, "A man should save money for an extreme emergency; he should save his wife even at the cost of his money; he should always save himself, even at the cost of his wife and his money."[16] But, moving right along, the adulterer fears that he will be ruined if he does *not* commit adultery:

> Or he thinks, "She is madly in love with me. If I don't want her she will ruin me by publicly exposing my faults, for she knows my weak spots. Or she will hurl in my face a fault which I don't in fact have, but which will be easy to believe of me and hard to clear myself of, and this will be the ruin of me."[17]

The commentator suggests that the woman scorned will say, "He desires the kingdom," or "He does unwholesome things to the king," or that she will accuse him (deservedly, one would think) of being an adulterer, or that she will engage with the adulterer's enemies to kill him. But the adulterer, too, is capable of revenge.

Or he may think, "Her husband has defiled the women of my

harem. So I will pay him back by defiling his own wives."[18] And in defense of this, the commentator cites the age-old sexual version of Hammurabi's code: "For it is said, 'Cruelty is to be used toward an enemy in order to pay him back appropriately.'"

The text continues to list nonsexual motives for adultery: in order to kill an enemy of the king inside the target woman's house (the commentator suggests that the man may be employed as the king's spy and have no other way to get inside the house), and the less respectable (and also less realistic) motive of seducing the woman in order to get access to a *different* woman with whom he is genuinely in love.[19] And the conclusion is that the only inadmissible reason to commit adultery is for the sake of sex: "This is how one should think, but (the excuse should) not be just the rashness that comes from passion."[20] In contrast with the Western tradition that looks the other way when a *crime de passion* is committed, the *Kāmasūtra* insists that adultery (and, indeed, most sexual acts) should only be committed in cold blood. Indeed, the passion that motivates the adulterer is not love (or even lust) for the woman, but hate for the man. The act of cuckolding is a ball game between two men; the woman is just the field on which they play.

The Lover's Reasons for Not Committing Adultery

Finally, after all those reasons for doing it, Vātsyāyana lumps together in one verse the relatively few counterindications:

> But the following women are not to be approached for sex: a leper, a lunatic, a woman who has fallen from her caste, or who tells secrets, or who begs (for sex) publicly, a woman whose youth is almost entirely gone, one who is too light or too dark, bad-smelling, a close relative, a friend, a female ascetic, or the wife of a relative, a friend, a learned Brahmin, or a king.[21]

And the commentary unpacks the list:

> The meaning is, "Even when there are things to be done, these women should not be approached." A leper indicates a disgusting disease; as for a lunatic, whatever she does, it does not make anyone happy; she will do anything, but she does not give pleasure. By contact with a woman who has fallen from her caste because she has committed some great sin, he would fall too. A woman who tells secrets embarrasses the man by telling a secret in public. A woman who openly lusts for the man makes him ashamed and does what is counter to her aims. In servicing a woman whose youth is almost entirely gone, one's health and glory are destroyed. When a woman smells bad in her secret parts and in her mouth during sex she causes a man to turn away from her. A woman friend of one's wife would be impeded (by that friendship).
>
> A female ascetic, who has taken a vow in some discipline or other, (should be avoided) because of the destruction of *dharma* and *artha*. The

> wife of a pupil or a teacher, the wife of a brother, etc. (should be avoided) because of the destruction of *dharma*. The wife of a friend is to be avoided because of the danger of such things as *adharma* and making him your enemy. For it is said [by Manu]: "Discharging semen into women born of the same womb as oneself, virgins, women of the lowest castes, or the wife of one's friend or son, is regarded as equal to the violation of the guru's marriage-bed."[22] The wives of a learned Brahmin are called blazing fires, because of the destruction of *dharma*. And in this matter *all* the wives of other men are not sexually approachable, with the exception of those that have been spoken of.

The commentator begins with the self-interest of the adulterer, but then he turns to dharmic reasons against adultery and even finishes with dharma as a kind of fallback position: if there is no really good reason *to* commit adultery, don't.

The Appeal of the Divine Lover: Bhakti *Texts*

But there *is* one really good reason for a woman, if not a man, to commit adultery in India, if by "good" we mean sanctioned by religious texts: and that reason is if her lover is a god. Clearly we move now from the practical world of the *Kāmasūtra* to the visionary world of devotional texts (*bhakti*), but we are still in the realm of Sanskrit texts, the world of intertextuality.

One remarkable Purāṇic text invokes the god Kāma as the patron saint of adultery:

> One day Kāma caught sight of Pūrṇakalā, the wife of the Brahmin Hārīta, and pricked his heart with his own flower arrow. She, too, was pierced by one of Kāma's arrows and lusted for him. As Kāma was wooing her, her husband caught them and cursed Kāma to become a leper and Pūrṇakalā to become a broken stone [*khaṇḍa-śilā*, a pun on "broken virtue"]. Kāma propitiated the Brahmin and was freed from his disease, but Pūrṇakalā remained in the form of a stone. And if a man worships her in this form on the thirteenth day (of the month), there will be no offense either for the man or for his lover when adultery occurs. And a woman who is being neglected by her husband should offer flowers to her.[23]

As Cathy Benton points out, there are obvious links between this myth and the paradigmatic story of the adultery of the god Indra and Ahalyā, including the pun on "stone/virtue" (*śīla*). What is significant for the present argument, however, is the way in which the text condones, indeed abets, adultery.

Adultery is attributed to the mortal women, married women, who leave their husbands' beds to join the god Kṛṣṇa. Kṛṣṇa helpfully provides multiple doubles of himself in order to commit adultery simultaneously with sixteen thousand married women; he also provides, conveniently, doubles of *them* to remain at home in bed with their husbands while they cavort with him: "The cowherd men did not get jealous with Kṛṣṇa, for they were deluded by his magic power of illusion and each one thought that his own wife was lying beside him."[24] (Later commentaries, embarrassed by the bad example set by the god, argued that the real women remained at home with their husband, while Kṛṣṇa made love to the doubles.) Thus, where Western tales of adultery have a mere eternal triangle, the Hindu myth gives us an eternal *maṇḍala*. Edward Cameron Dimock has explored at great depth the theological implications of the love of the adulterous god who is the great "thief of love."[25] Dimock demonstrates how Bengali Vaiṣṇavism scorned the smugness of married love (like the bastard Edmund in Shakespeare's *King Lear*, who scorned those who "within a dull, stale, tired bed / Go to th' creating a whole tribe of fops, / Got 'tween asleep and wake")[26] and emulated, rather, the passionate commitment of adulterous love, fraught with dangers and the constant threat of social ostracism for lovers who are tormented by separation and the knowledge that union can never become realized once and for all. And David Tracy has argued that, for contemporary political theologians and liberation theologians, religion is regarded as an interruption that upsets bourgeois complacency, that scorns the traditional forms of Christianity in which "the eschaton is boredom."[27]

The *bhakti* myth of Kṛṣṇa represents a revolutionary view of both marriage and the love of god. In this view, adulterous love is a suitable metaphor for the love of an otiose god whom one could only love in separation, through unfulfilled longing, *viraha*: the longing for a lover (often an adulterous lover) from whom one is separated. God is not with me, the abandoned mistress of Kṛṣṇa says, because he is making love to some other woman instead. God comes to her with some other woman's lipstick on his collar (or the Hindu equivalent: the scars of her nails on his back).

The Vedic sacrifice, a public event, corresponded to a strictly regulated marriage. But after the revolutionary impact first of the Upaniṣads and then of *bhakti*, the worshiper internalized the sacrifice and internalized the center of his or her existence: the *ātman* is the person, not society. For a woman in the *bhakti* period, this went one step further: she moved the center of her being from her husband to the god she loved, external once again, and was faithful to him, though he was never faithful to her. It was necessary to reject the husband and the conventional world, in order to give herself wholeheartedly to her lover and his transcendent world—only to find her love for him, in turn, rejected. As Professor Godbole puts it, in E. M. Forster's satire of this aspect of Hinduism,

> The God refuses to come. I grow humble and say: "Do not come to me only. Multiply yourself into a hundred Krishnas, and let one go to each of my hundred companions, but one, O Lord of the Universe, come to

> me." He refuses to come . . . I say to Him, "Come, come, come, come, come, come." He neglects to come.[28]

But adultery remained only a metaphor; or, to put it differently, the female worshiper was still not allowed to commit adultery with any male other than God.

It is surely significant that Indra and Kṛṣṇa are part of a polytheistic pantheon or, more precisely, one that F. Max Müller in his *Lectures on the Science of Language* rightly characterized as henotheistic or kathenotheistic: the worship of each of a series of gods as the supreme god, the theological equivalent of serial monogamy ("I love you, Indra/baby, and have never loved any other god/woman." "I love you, Viṣṇu/baby, and have never loved any other god/woman."). Avishai Margalit and Moshe Halbertal discuss the use of adultery as a metaphor for idolatry in monotheistic religions, particularly ancient Judaism, where "whoring after foreign gods" is a common way of referring to idolatry.[29] They argue that one must first establish that adultery is a sin in the text in question, and they examine what sort of a sin is attributed at different times to the idolator who is likened to an adulterer:

> It is possible that the feminine representation of God [in later texts] makes the sin of idolatry less severe, as in this framework it is perceived as the addition of a co-wife to the beloved wife, which is not a sin in a society where polygamy is permitted, although it is difficult for the first wife to tolerate—in contrast to the representation of idolatry [in earlier texts] as the wife's betrayal of her husband, which is a sin punishable by death.[30]

Clearly it matters a great deal whether god is perceived as masculine (as in the early texts) or feminine (as in the later texts). A polytheistic religion, by this argument, might be expected to be more tolerant of idolatry—and, by extension, perhaps, more tolerant of the adultery of the man, who may have many wives, though not of the woman. This would suggest a correlation between a system wherein there are many male gods and the (apparently inverse) system wherein men can have lots of wives but women can't have lots of husbands.

The Indian evidence, as we have seen, supports this correlation. The lesson that the adulterous god teaches the worshiper is twofold: God cannot belong to any one person, and true love (whether of God or of a human lover) respects no boundaries, particularly possessive boundaries. The worshiper may be "possessed" by god in a trance, but God is never possessed.

The divine escapades thus shed light upon the human dilemma of adultery; but, beyond that, the human situation helps us to understand what it means to worship a god who cheats on his worshiper. Margalit and Halbertal have demonstrated how human adultery is used as a metaphor for the betrayal of God. But God's abandonment of his worshiper is also used as a metaphor for human adultery. Thus A. K.

Ramanujan has pointed out how Tamil and Telugu love poems are enlisted in the service of poems for the love of God; but then those devotional poems are recast as poems sung by courtesans about their customers—or, perhaps, about God.[31] Sex may begin as what is signified (with its symbols that signify it), but then it is religion that is signified (by sex and its symbols, as well as by the symbols of religion), and finally, in a kind of second naïveté, sex is signified by religion and its symbols, which is in turn signified by sex and its symbols, as well as by the symbols of religion, and so on, until we find ourselves in an infinite *mise en abîme*, and it is impossible to distinguish between signified and signifier.

The Appeal of Theft: The Romance of Adultery

The orthodox tradition says that the woman is the field, the land; this is the tradition of landed, aristocratic, conservative religion. In this bourgeois view, theft is a terrible sin, and tragedy is noble. Against this rather monolithic view, the dharmic view, India sets a number of different traditions; here, as elsewhere, *adharma* is more complex than dharma; if there is only one way to do something right, there are infinite ways of doing it wrong. The counterdharmic line is expressed in books like the *Kathāsaritsāgara* (and the folktales on which it is based), which is by and for people such as merchants, who do not have land but may have movable property. The contrast is not between economic classes, for merchants were often as wealthy as, or wealthier than, landowners. Rather, it is a contrast between what F. Scott Fitzgerald called "old money" (rich people who lived in big houses that were handed down from generation to generation) and "new money" (rich people who ran up astronomical bills living in the Ritz in Paris). Old money is tied down, and male; new money is mobile, and female.

Indeed, the *Kathāsaritsāgara* itself tells many different sorts of stories expressing different points of view, some based on the society of a merchant economy, some from other parts of Indian society. But, by and large, in this upwardly mobile world, the woman is no longer the passive field but is an active agent, and adultery is just fine if you can get away with it, as is theft. The thief, of property or love, hopes that all will end in success; tragedy is stupid. Despite this cynicism, love, which is given short shrift in the dharmic texts on marriage, comes into its own in the romances of adultery.

Often, the *Kathāsaritsāgara* (like the *Arabian Nights*, with which it shares many stories) tells stories from the standpoint of the lover, the adventurer, the thief of love who seeks the princess who is forbidden to him. (Many of these stories overlap with themes of theft, such as the story of "The Weaver and Viṣṇu" and "The Three Thefts," that will be related in chapter 8.) A folk variant of the *śāstric* idea of the woman as field and the question of the ownership of the crop (which we shall soon explore) is told in the many versions of the *Twenty-five Questions of the Vampire.* Here is the version from the *Kathāsaritsāgara*:

> A prince encountered a tricky problem when he went to make an offering to his dead father. His grandmother had been left a widow while still very young, with a young daughter. She came upon a thief who had been impaled and left to die. He wished to marry the little daughter, in return for which he told the woman where a great treasure was hidden. The marriage took place, the thief died, and the mother and daughter had a great fortune. Eventually the girl fell in love with a handsome young Brahmin, who was in love with a courtesan but consented to sleep with the girl for pay. The girl bore the Brahmin a son and left the baby, with a thousand pieces of gold, at the doorstep of a king who was childless. The king brought up the foundling as his son and heir.
>
> When the king had died, the young prince wanted to make an offering to his departed father, but as he made the offering three hands reached out to take it: that of the impaled thief, the Brahmin, and the king. Who deserved the offering? The answer is: the thief. The Brahmin sold himself and the king received payment in gold. The thief, however, gave the money for the child to live and was the only one legally married to the child's mother.[32]

The complexity of this story is reminiscent of the intricacies of a hypothetical case in a law school textbook. In this case, the romantic tradition supports Manu: the owner of the field is the owner of the child. But the thrust of the tale is clearly antinomian, giving the criminal and worker, the thief, a status above the two ruling classes of priest and king.

In Sanskrit texts more closely tied to the folk tradition, the clever woman who actually commits adultery comes into her own. In folksongs sung even today in Rajasthan, women sing stories about women whose husbands failed to give them children, and who took this matter into their own hands by taking lovers who made them pregnant.[33] As Ann Gold remarks,

> There is of course an ironic tone in these congratulations to an adulterer, who would by village custom be culpable and punishable. But . . . men themselves so desperately desire progeny that, at least as some popular folk traditions along with rumors have it, they may allow themselves to be deceived if the result is the desired birth of a boy.[34]

Moreover, some of these songs specifically refer to the lover as the "husband's brother," inviting resonances with the levirate. But, as Gold cautions us, "The implication of the reference is *not* that one's lover *is* one's husband's brother; rather, by saying the word for husband's younger brother one may with a very slight degree of discretion allude to a lover." Folk traditions the world over laugh about adultery; it is the landed classes that take it seriously.

Of course, women in India, as elsewhere, were never officially allowed to be promiscuous. But official texts do not cover the full gamut of human invention. After the *bhakti* revolution, a woman might have a (divine) lover instead of a husband, but adultery remained, in *bhakti*, only an ideal, rather than a reality. In the *Kāmasūtra* and the *Kathāsaritsāgara*, by contrast, adultery was real, and now it was, at the very least, acknowledged and, at the most, celebrated. Even among these texts, however, adultery was real in very different ways, and within the different currents in any single text the reality, as well as the fantasy, of adultery had very different implications for the different players in the drama.

Breaching the Boundary: The Husband's Nightmare

Having made the case for the defense, as it were, we must give equal time to the case for the prosecution—the cuckolded husband. More precisely, it remains to explore the metaphor of the seed and the field (the field being a place marked by boundaries), and of the woman as a bounded field, nature reclaimed for culture, a basic trope found in ancient Greece[35] as well as ancient India.[36]

This metaphor is invoked as a reason not to commit adultery in several different parts of the *Śatapatha Brāhmaṇa*. The basic metaphor of the womb as earth and the semen as seed is first stated in an agricultural context:

> "Yoke the ploughs, and stretch across the yokes!" Indeed they yoke the plough and stretch the yokes across. "Into the ready womb here cast the seed!" It is for the seed that that womb, the furrow, is made; and if one casts (seed) into unploughed (ground), it is just as if one were to shed seed elsewhere than into the womb.[37]

But the human implications of this view are brought out in the ritual of the horse sacrifice, where the priests make obscene jokes at the expense of the queen, and one of them says, "When the deer eats the barley, (the farmer) does not hope to nourish the animal; when the low-born woman becomes the mistress of a noble man, (her husband) does not hope to get rich on that nourishment."[38] The implication of the metaphor of the deer in the field seems to be that the farmer is unhappy about the loss of his crops, not happy that he has accidentally fed an animal; so, too, the husband is sorry that his wife has been defiled, not glad that she has cuckolded him with a richer man.

Manu breaks down the image of the deer in the field into two separate metaphors for the adulterer: a man who sows seed in another man's field, and a man who shoots an arrow into a wounded deer. This metaphor is nastier in Manu than in the Brāhmaṇa: "Just as an arrow is wasted if it is shot into the wound of an animal already wounded by another shot, even so seed is immediately wasted on another man's property . . . They say that a field belongs to the man who clears it of timber, and the deer to the man who owns the arrow."[39] This is a metaphor with heavy mythological resonances: in a pivotal episode in the *Mahābhārata*, Arjuna shoots an arrow into a boar, but another hunter claims that his arrow had hit the boar first. They fight, and Arjuna discovers that the other hunter is Śiva, God.[40]

But the way in which Manu develops the metaphor of a field is far more complex, and needs a bit of introduction. We have seen that the marriage act transforms the woman by drawing her across old boundaries and creating new boundaries for her. The act of adultery might then be seen as yet another crossing of bounds, an intensification of the marriage act itself, but this time it is unacceptable. The basic argument is that there are two forms of adultery: a man's adultery, called *pāradārya* ("another man's wife"), and the more general sexual misconduct of a man or a woman (called *vyabhicāra*, "straying"). Both forms of adultery considered by our texts are regarded as an injury to the husband rather than the woman, and both involve legal problems for inheritance. The concept of an injury done to a woman by her husband's unfaithfulness is never treated, for a man is allowed to have several wives; and the minor crimes that a man might commit in defiling women (sexual misconduct, *vyabhicāra*) matter less, since they are not regarded as productive of children. A man with several women still poses the legal problem of dividing up the inheritance (which is implicit in the normal form of adultery: the wrong son gets the inheritance), and Manu uses the metaphor of the field to describe these problems, too, but polygyny is not a crime. Paternity is the primary gauge, because the bottom line is procreation and inheritance.

The first instance (*pāradārya*, adultery with another man's woman) means that a man takes the woman of another man; this man is primarily another husband, but if the woman is a maiden, the adulterer is regarded as stealing her from her father. In this view, the man is adulterating, as it were, someone else's wife. The second instance (*vyabhicāra*, sexual misconduct) means that the woman is, again, injuring her husband by being unfaithful to him. The negativity, and cynicism, of Manu's attitude to fidelity in marriage is clear throughout: "'Let there be mutual absence of infidelity until death'; this should be known as the supreme duty of a man and a woman, in a nutshell."[41] (And how could Manu not be cynical, when, as I will suggest, he was moonlighting as the author of texts in praise of adultery?) But it is in the development of the double-edged metaphor of the field that the full extent of his dilemma becomes apparent. For in *The Laws of Manu* there are two different, conflicting models of paternity, expressed through a single agricultural metaphor: the sower of the seed is the biological father, who may or may not be the legal husband; the woman is the field, and the owner of the field is the legal husband. The son born in the field (the wife) by a man other than her legal husband is known as the *kṣetraja*, literally "born in the (husband's) field," the wife's natural son.[42] But there are two ways of looking at this metaphor.

First, the man who owns the field (i.e., the wife) owns whatever crop is sown in the field. Manu assumes that the field is entirely neutral, and that the crop (son) sown in it will always resemble the seed (the father). Therefore you should never waste your seed by shedding it in another man's "field" or wife, but you are not harmed if another man sheds his seed in your wife (in that you own the son resulting from that act). Manu thus forbids a man to commit adultery in another man's wife but encourages him to let a brother produce a levirate heir in his own wife, through the Indian practice of *niyoga*, in which the widow of a man who has produced no male heirs is appointed to have a son by that man's younger brother. This argument—that the man owns the woman—prevails in India.

But, on the other hand, it might also be argued a second way, that the man who owns the seed, and who in any case determines the characteristics of the crop, owns the crop. This supplies a reason why a man might want to shed his seed in someone else's field, but it now also argues that a man should make sure that only his own seed is sown in his own field. This argument—that the man owns his own seed—takes a secondary place, as it would both encourage adultery (you would produce legitimate sons in all sorts of women) and make levirate marriage meaningless (since the son that your brother produced in your wife would be his son, not yours).

Manu begins by defining his terms:

> The following discussion about a son was held by good men and great sages born long ago; listen to it, for it has merit and applies to all people.
>
> They say that a son belongs to the husband, but the revealed canon is divided in two about who the "husband" is: some say that he is the begetter, others that he is the one who owns the field. The woman is traditionally said to be the field, and the man is traditionally said to be the seed; all creatures with bodies are born from the union of the field and the seed. Sometimes the seed prevails, and sometimes the woman's womb; but the offspring are regarded as best when both are equal. Of the seed and the womb, the seed is said to be more important, for the offspring of all living beings are marked by the mark of the seed. Whatever sort of seed is sown in a field prepared at the right season, precisely that sort of seed grows in it, manifesting its own particular qualities. For this earth is said to be the eternal womb of creatures, but the seed develops none of the qualities of the womb in the things it grows. For here on earth when farmers at the right season sow seeds of various forms in the earth, even in one single field, they grow up each according to its own nature. Rice, red rice, mung beans, sesame, pulse beans, and barley grow up according to their seed, and so do leeks and sugar-cane. It never happens that "One seed is sown and another grown"; for whatever seed is sown, that is precisely the one that grows.
>
> A well-educated man who understands this and who has knowledge

and understanding will never sow in another man's wife, if he wants to live a long life. People who know the past recite some songs about this sung by the wind god, which say that a man must not sow his seed on another man's property.[43]

People who have no field but have seed and sow it in other men's fields are never the ones who get the fruit of the crop that appears. In the very same way, men who have no field but sow their seed in other men's fields are acting for the benefit of the men who own the fields, and the man whose seed it is does not get the fruit.[44]

If no agreement about the fruit is made between the owners of the fields and the owners of the seed, it is obvious that the profit belongs to the owners of the fields; the womb is more important than the seed. But if this (field) is given over for seeding by means of an agreed contract, then in this case both the owner of the seed and the owner of the field are regarded as (equal) sharers of that (crop). Seed that is carried by a flood or a wind into someone's field and grows there belongs to the owner of the field, and the man who sowed the seed does not get the fruit.[45]

The basic argument seems sensible enough; Manu acknowledges that the quality of the field does influence the quality of the crop (crops grow better in a well-plowed or "good" field), but he argues, correctly, that the basic characteristics of the field do not influence the basic characteristics of the crop (barley, rather than mung beans, grows in any field in which it is planted). The "contract" for seeding would presumably be the levirate, in which the "equal" claims to the child do indeed produce problems in the mythology.

But Manu also discusses the question of the ownership of the crop (the son) in terms of a pastoral image, the point of which is not quite so obvious. Now, as we have seen, the image of the deer is used in the Brāhmaṇa text as part of the agricultural image: the deer is regarded as a factor in farming, not in hunting. In Manu, however, the deer is separated from the agricultural metaphor, made into a hunting metaphor, and used in an independent image, in which the question, "Who owns the crop?" is extended to ask, "Who owns the deer?" Now he asks, "Who owns the cow, the horse?"

Just as the stud is not the one who owns the progeny born in cows, mares, female camels, and slave girls, in buffalo-cows, she-goats, and ewes, so it is too (with progeny born) in other men's wives. If (one man's) bull were to beget a hundred calves in other men's cows, those calves would belong to the owners of the cows, and the bull's seed would be shed in vain. This is the law for the offspring of cows and mares, slave girls, female camels, and she-goats, and birds and female buffalo.[46]

These pastoral verses appear in Manu interspersed with the agricultural metaphor of seed and field and are used in support of the prevailing argument, that the one who owns the female, rather than the one who owns the seed, owns the offspring. But, as we shall see, the commentators on Manu acknowledge the difference between the two arguments, and imply that the female animal does at least influence the characteristics of the offspring, if not its legal status, in ways that the earth or plowed field does not.

And Manu himself elsewhere acknowledges the equal contribution of the mother and the father into the nature of the child when he discusses mixed marriages, again in terms of the mixed agricultural-pastoral metaphor:

> An unknown man, of no (visible) class but born of a defiled womb and no Aryan, may seem to have the form of an Aryan, but he can be discovered by his own innate activities. Un-Aryan behavior, harshness, cruelty, and habitual failure to perform the rituals are the manifestations in this world indicating that a man is born of a defiled womb. A man born of a bad womb shares his father's character, or his mother's, or both; but he can never suppress his own nature. A man born of the confusion of wombs, even if he comes from a leading family, will inherit that very character, to a greater or lesser degree.[47]
>
> But if this (question) should arise: "Which is higher, someone born by chance from a priest father in a non-Aryan mother, or from a non-Aryan father in a mother of the priestly class?", this is the decision: "Someone born from an Aryan father in a non-Aryan woman may become an Aryan in his qualities; but someone born from a non-Aryan father in an Aryan mother is a non-Aryan." The law has been established: neither of these may undergo the transformative rituals, because the birth of the former is deficient in (Aryan) characteristics, and the latter is born "against the grain." Just as good seed, sown in a good field, culminates in a birth, so the son born from an Aryan father in an Aryan mother deserves every transformative ritual. Some wise men value the seed, others the field, and still others both the seed and the field; but this is the final decision on this subject: seed sown in the wrong field perishes right inside it; and a field by itself with no seed also remains barren. And since sages have been born in (female) animals by the power of the seed, and were honored and valued, therefore the seed is valued.[48]

Thus Manu moves into increasingly complex areas of speculation. Even the relatively simple agricultural image proved ambiguous; the pastoral image introduces further complications, especially when, as Manu admits in the last line of the passage cited, humans mate with animals; and when it comes to human beings, a third factor is introduced: the behavior of the child, which must be regarded as a factor separate from the genetic contribution of either of his parents (let alone the genetic contribution of the "owner of the field" in the case of an adulterous connection). Moreover, elsewhere, such as in the discussion of inheritance in chapter 9, Manu assumes that a Brahmin with wives of various classes produces children whose status is in part determined by their mothers' status. And, finally, the human genetic pool is entirely transformed by culture, by the ritual transformations of the *saṃskāras*, so that a child obtains what McKim Marriott calls his "coded substance" not only from his parents but from his teachers and priests, as Manu also argues (2.169–71).

In later Indian thinking about the woman's contribution to the child, it was often argued that the woman had seed, too, like the man; her seed, physically incarnate in her menstrual blood, contributed the soft parts of a child (the flesh and blood), while the man contributed the hard parts (bone and sinew).[49] Manu does not take account of this tradition, but it may well be that it underlies many folk beliefs, and folk stories, about human sexuality. The agricultural model remains a referent to this day in India, but it is not always accepted. Lina Fruzzetti and Akos Ostor have demonstrated the variants that Bengali villagers ring on the basic theme,[50] and E. Valentine Daniel has recorded a wonderful conversation in which Tamil villagers cynically reject the whole concept of the seed and the field in favor of the concept of female seed.[51] The idea of the levirate, too, has been problematized, as Sudhir Kakar has demonstrated in his analysis of a novel in which a brother forced to marry his older brother's wife is deeply troubled.[52]

But a final caution is in order when we equate the ownership of a woman with the ownership of land. In Indian thinking, what is at stake is not the woman at all, but the male child that the woman will bear. Thus a woman is a funny kind of property, well summarized by the statement that "a chicken is an egg's way of making another egg." So, too, the farmer does not really own the land but merely the crop (or, rather, the right to a portion of the crop): the king has rights to the land, and so does the the tax collector, and sometimes others as well.

Conclusion

In contrast with the relatively consistent view of the dharma texts, the interacting stances expressed in the other genres are more complex. They cannot, moreover, be reduced to a simple contrast between the points of view of a man and a woman (for husband and lover are competing, as are wife and mistress). And they are further enriched by the different human investments in other competing genres, such as law and myth. Indeed, we must never forget that we are talking about a single culture, in which an educated individual could certainly be expected to be familiar with several genres. More than that: to the extent that we are dealing primarily with Sanskrit texts, the preserve of a highly limited, élite class of men, a single individual may well have composed texts in several genres. Thus, when such a man wrote a Dharmaśāstra he would imagine the point of view of the husband (which he could do well, since he was almost certainly someone's husband); but when he composed the *Kathāsaritsāgara* or the *Kāmasūtra*, he put on (or, perhaps, took off) the hat (or pants) of the lover, which was also his own hat; and, having talked to his wife (and his mistress), he was able to express the woman's point of view. There is no special caste of lovers who were the custodians of a genre that lobbied for adultery. With one hand (presumably the right), our educated Brahmin wrote the dharma texts; with the other (presumably the left), he wrote stories in praise of adultery. It would be interesting to speculate as to why the man who took such a rigid stance when he wrote a dharma text sang such a different song in the other genres. Perhaps, like his wife, he sought the solace of fantasy, or expressed in the narratives the limits (or flip side) of his official point of view. Or is this just another way of saying that *adharma* is the flip side of dharma?

Notes

1. Manu 11.52. From *The Laws of Manu*, translated by Wendy Doniger with Brian K. Smith (Harmondsworth: Penguin Classics, 1991). There is much confusion in the manuscripts about this verse, and it is one of only two verses in all of Manu that many commentators omit. The verse has many things to recommend it to us, however, such as the link between theft and adultery and the double entendre (in English) of the sick sadist and the rheumatic/romantic adulterer. (In Sanskrit, the last line in the version used here reads *hiṃsārucih sadā rogī vātāngaḥ pāradārikaḥ*.)

2. Friedrich Wilhelm, "The Concept of Dharma in Artha and Kāma Literature," in Wendy Doniger O'Flaherty and J. Duncan M. Derrett, eds., *The Concept of Duty in South Asia* (Delhi: Vikas Publishing, for the School of Oriental and African Studies, 1978), pp. 66–79.

3. Manu 2.2.

4. *Kāmasūtra* of Vātsyāyana, with the *Jayamangala* commentary of Yasodhara (Bombay: Laksmivenkatesvara Steam Press, 1856), 1.1.9.

5. *Kāmasūtra* 5.1.52–54.

6. Manu 8.362–63.

7. *Kāmasūtra* 5.1.8, 17–43.

8. *Kāmasūtra* 1.5.5–7.

9. *Kāmasūtra* 1.5.8.

10. *Kāmasūtra* 1.5.16a.

11. *Kāmasūtra* 1.5.9–10.

12. *Kāmasūtra* 1.5.11.

13. Manu 8.350–51.

14. *Kāmasūtra* 1.5.12.

15. Manu 10.99.

16. Manu 7.213.

17. *Kāmasūtra* 1.5.13–15.

18. *Kāmasūtra* 1.5.16b.

19. *Kāmasūtra* 1.5.17–19.

20. *Kāmasūtra* 1.5.21.

21. *Kāmasūtra* 1.5.29.

22. Manu 11.59.

23. *Skanda Purāṇa* (Bombay, 1867), 6.134.1–80. This text is translated and analyzed by Cathy Benton in her 1991 doctoral dissertation for Columbia University. I am grateful to her for allowing me to cite it here.

24. *Bhāgavata Purāṇa* 10.34.38.

25. Edward C. Dimock, *The Place of the Hidden Moon* (Chicago: University of Chicago Press, 1966).

26. Shakespeare, *King Lear*, I.ii.13–15.

27. David Tracy, in a lecture, Kansas City, November 20, 1991.

28. E. M. Forster, *A Passage to India*, Abinger Edition (New York: Holmes and Meier, 1979), p. 72.

29. Avishai Margalit and Moshe Halbertal, *Idolatry: A Conceptual Analysis* (Cambridge, Mass.: Harvard University Press, forthcoming).

30. Ibid., p. 64.

31. See the Afterword to *When God Is a Customer*, by A. K. Ramanujan, David Shulman, and Velcheru Narayana Rao (Berkeley: University of California Press, forthcoming).

32. *Kathāsaritsāgara* of Somadeva (Delhi: Motilal Banarsidass, 1970), 93 [12.26].1–102.

33. Ann Grodzins Gold, "Sexuality, Fertility and Erotic Imagination in Rajasthani Women's Songs," in Gloria Goodwin-Tomar and Ann Grodzins Gold, eds., *Songs, Stories, Lives: Listening to Women in Rural North India* (unpublished manuscript, 1991).

34. Gold, "Sexuality."

35. See Page du Bois's discussion of *field* and *furrow* as metaphors for the female body in ancient Greece, in *Sowing the Body: Psychoanalysis and Ancient Representations of Women* (Chicago: University of Chicago Press, 1988).

36. Indeed, it is hardly limited to Indian and Greek texts, and may constitute something very like a natural metaphor. Cf. Carol Delaney, *Seeds of Honor, Fields of Shame* (Berkeley: University of California Press, 1990), for the metaphor in Turkey.

37. *Śatapatha Brāhmaṇa* 7.2.2.5.

38. *Śatapatha Brāhmaṇa* 13.2.9.6–9.

39. Manu 9.43–44.

40. *Mahābhārata* 3.40.

41. Manu 9.101.

42. The *kṣetraja* is defined by Manu at 9.167.

43. Manu 9.31–42.

44. Manu 9.49 and 51.

45. Manu 9.52–54.

46. Manu 9.48, 50, and 55.

47. "That" character may be the character of both parents, of his father, or the bad character of the confusion of classes.

48. Manu 10.57–60, 66–72.

49. Wendy Doniger O'Flaherty, *Women, Androgynes, and Other Mythical Beasts* (Chicago: University of Chicago Press, 1981), pp. 21, 35–39, 50–51.

50. Lina Fruzzetti and Akos Ostor, "Seed and Earth: A Cultural Analysis of Kinship in a Bengali Town," *Contributions to Indian Sociology*, n.s. 10, no. 1 (1976):97–132.

51. E. Valentine Daniel, *Fluid Signs: Being a Person the Tamil Way* (Berkeley: University of California Press, 1984), pp. 163–170.

52. Sudhir Kakar, *Intimate Relations: Exploring Indian Sexuality* (Chicago: University of Chicago Press, 1990).

8

Thieves and Dharma in the Story Literature

The thief, unlike the adulteress, is a professional crosser of physical and social boundaries. He is not tragically trapped between social expectations and natural self-awareness, but instead he toys with the system of dharma as a whole. We have seen throughout chapter 5 and in the conclusion to chapter 6 that the social consensus that informs textual conceptions of dharma cannot remain directly embodied in a sensory orientation. A prohibition is not a wall; the two belong to distinct and separate ontologies. The concept of dharma, transformed and transmuted metaphorically, is many times removed from the fundamental perceptual intentionalities examined in the early chapters of this book. Similarly, the Dharmaśāstras and subsequent texts pursue a social and juridical agenda that requires a highly structured and fixed notion of proper conduct, which they ground in the Veda for ultimate authority. But we have also seen that the contingent images of everyday life could never be set aside. Because of its thoroughly embodied epistemology, dharma continues to be informed by perception even as a sociojuridical system. The wall gives a prohibition its "feel" and possibly even a door. The storytellers who relished telling the exploits of India's fabled thieves were exploring precisely this flexible joint in the structure of dharma, namely, the point where temporal images softened the rigidity of an ideological structure. We shall shortly see that the thief is different from other criminals, say the robber, not because he is nonviolent. He is different because he teases our perceptions like a magician, and by magically transforming himself he shows that the fixed social roles that the Dharmaśāstra upholds are still highly vulnerable to the uncertainties of perception.

Few topics have aroused the concern of lawmakers and the fascination of storytellers in India as the topic of thieves. If Manu can serve as a reliable guide for the actual state of affairs, then thieves must have lurked behind every corner, and anything that was not nailed to the floor was fair game.[1] Anything could, and probably was, stolen at one time or another: rope or bucket from a well, grain, any item measured by weight, garments, people (kidnapping for ransom), large and small livestock, medicines, thread, cotton, agents of fermentation, cow dung, molasses, yogurt, milk, buttermilk, water, grass, baskets made of bamboo or split cane, salts, clay, things made of clay, ashes, fish, birds, oil, clarified butter, meat, honey, other animal products, cooked rice and other cooked foods, flowers, green grain, shrubs, creepers, trees, unwinnowed grain, vegetables, roots, fruits.[2] But there is something surprising about theft because it is rarely about wealth: In contrast, for example, the topic of adultery also occupies a great deal of space in Manu, which leads us to expect that this form of illegal sexuality would find expression in other sources. And indeed, both *kāvya* and *katha* literatures—not to mention Kāmasūtra—reflect a profound interest in a variety of sexual activities. Romantic and physical love are the chief interest, and probably a fascinating antidote to the sexual boredom of traditional married life, in fantasy if not in practice. Should we then, not also expect, based on Manu's obsession with stolen property, an equivalent interest in wealth by other literary sources? Now, although the story literature and oral folktales are indeed as interested in the act of breaking and entering as in love, wealth is somewhow not as fascinating as sex. Among the eighty stories I have been able to locate, few if any reflect a strong interest in the material objects of thievery, either on the part of the thief or the author.[3]

This contradicts a sociological or economical reading of theft as a literary phenomenon in India, as elsewhere. Such a reading might see theft, cattle rustling for instance, as an expression of changing modes of social relationships and social controls governing economic exchanges.[4] Sheep and cattle are best stolen by a group of criminals: distracting, or physically overcoming, the shepherd and driving the animals —usually over long distances off the main paths—require team work, perhaps a sophisticated relay method. The animals then have to be kept safely by another party, or butchered professionally, or sold to a regular buyer. Such work in India often involves entire castes who specialized in criminal teamwork.[5] In this context, the distinction between theft (steya) and armed robbery is real and important because, whereas robbery (*sāhasa*—violent crimes) may involve the communal aspects of great or minor social upheavals, theft shows another face of crime. Theft is understood as the removal of another's property without his knowledge and permission.[6] Of course, in the case of theft too, the economic aspects are by definition best left for the analysis of sociologists. However, the fascination that this crime inspires in storytellers cannot be completely reduced to the glee of disadvantaged nonlanded classes over the humiliation and slow bleeding of the wealthier landed or merchant groups. In contrast to the organized activities of illicit large scale property transfer, the thief of the *Kathāsaritsāgara* and other sources is a loner whose indifference to wealth is almost ascetic. At the very most he works with one or two accomplices, usually a father or son. Moreover, the stories seldom betray an interest in the economic consequences of the crimes, or in the manner of disposing of the stolen goods. The thief fascinates storytellers precisely because he is nonsocial and scorns the status that property often confers. He provides the literary occasion for an extended exploration of the psychology of individuality in a profoundly communal society.

But there is more. Criminals in ancient India, particularly thieves, did not operate against a code of laws. The political system in which they moved in the city or countryside, was governed by a king, but without the existence of a fixed criminal code. The so-called code of Manu and other Dharmaśāstras is a practical fiction, given prominence by the British rulers of India. The thief is rather a direct enemy of the king, not just as an enforcer of laws but as the embodiment of Law. Among the central motifs in the stories on theft is this explicit confrontation between the sovereignty of dharma (and *artha*) and the sovereignty of "permanent transcience"—the individualist scoundrel.[7] The symmetry between the two characters—king and thief—and two types of power emerges in the many stories in which the thief seeks to deceive the king, and the king in turn bypasses his entire enforcement apparatus to take on the thief by himself. Incidentally, the tally of score between the two ends up in a draw, a sign perhaps of the storytellers' ambivalence. Unlike other criminals, highway robbers for instance, who act in a communal fashion and therefore reflect more accurately the true sociology of crime, the thief's individuality makes him as free and, in the storytellers' fantasy, as powerful as the king. Like the king, he is the only individual who embodies a juridical principle—in this case absolute lawlessness—and is therefore more of a threat to the personal authority of the king than to the validity of enforced laws.

The other major motif that fascinates the storytellers is the quasi-magical power of transformation involved in the act of theft above any other crime. The stories we shall encounter are often more about exploits of deception and sleight of hand than obtaining property—the ostensible purpose of theft. No full understanding of thieves, and perhaps of dharma and *adharma*, is possible without looking at this magical psychology of boundary crossers, human as well as divine.

Thieves and Kings

The stories about thieves are not myths and should not be read with an eye for subtle complexities or unresolvable paradoxes. On the other hand, a wealth of invaluable information on the psychology of choice and freedom is available in this material. Thieves, and those who catch them while disguised as thieves, defy the relatively static and rigid identity imposed on social actors in Hindu society.

A thief (*caura*) was terrorizing the city of Ayodhyā during the rule of King Vīraketu.[8] When the secret police and city guards failed repeatedly to catch the thief, Vīraketu decided to try by himself. Armed and dressed like a thief, he roamed the city at night until he met the thief and identified himself too as a thief. Together they went to the thief's hideout. Later, when the thief stepped out of the room, his female servant, who had recognized the king by his noble demeanor, warned the king to leave, fearing that he would be treacherously killed. The following morning, a large force surrounded the place and the thief was captured after fighting heroically. As he was being taken to the execution ground, a merchant's daughter, who had never loved any man, fell in love with the handsome thief. She tried to ransom the condemned man but the king insisted on executing him. As the thief was dying on the stake, he was told what had happened. In response he cried for a moment, then he laughed a little.[9] His body was taken to a funeral pyre which the young woman ascended with him.

The story is interesting for a number of reasons: it insists that only thieflike trickery can fool a thief—it does indeed take a thief to catch one. Furthermore, the thief was unable to spot a king behind the disguise but a woman servant was able to do so. We shall encounter this theme again shortly. The thief's enigmatic behavior on the stake may be due to this. He was dying because he had been betrayed by a lowly woman who saw a king in the thief's clothing. Now he was nearly saved by a noble woman who recognized some worthy quality behind his own criminal demeanor.[10]

In the city of Beṇṇāyaḍa, where Vikramarāja (Mūladeva as king) ruled, a beggar named Maṇḍiya used to operate.[11] During the day he was a sickly old pan-handler, but at night he changed into a ruthless thief who would bore holes in house walls and steal whatever he could. On top of this, he always found someone to carry the loot to his house, in the middle of which was a deep well. The thief would instruct his sister to wash the guest's feet, and as the unsuspecting victim sat on the edge of the well, the two pushed him to his death. When the king's agents consistently failed to capture the thief, the king donned a black cloak and set down near a gambling hall. Soon Maṇḍiya saw him and asked who he was. The king identified himself as a beggar and was invited to accompany Maṇḍiya on his rounds. Later, at Maṇḍiya's house Vikramarāja sat at the edge of the well like all the other victims, but Maṇḍiya's sister recognized the feet of a nobleman and warned him. The king took off immediately with Maṇḍiya close behind, sword in hand. As the thief closed in on him, Vikramarāja hid behind a Śiva phallus and the thief decapitated the *liṅgam*, mistaking it in the darkness for a human figure. The next day the king invited Maṇḍiya to the palace and asked for his sister's hand. The thief delightedly consented and even contributed a large dowry. When the king later asked for a loan the thief agreed, and little by little the entire stolen wealth was restored to its owners until none was left. At that point the king executed Maṇḍiya.

It is interesting to note in these stories that only the king, the man at the head of the political hierarchy, possesses the ingenuity and freedom to deal with the thief on his own terms. The agents, even disguised secret agents, somehow lack the ability to change a persona and completely abandon (for a short duration) their own role. But the king does not always succeed because the key to the success of a great thief is an uncanny ability to read and predict the actions of those who are pursuing him, and to change identity at will. One story about such a thief, surprisingly a Brahmin, is told in McCulloch's *Bengali Household Tales.*[12] This thief was not only lucky, he was astonishingly resourceful. Having once been caught and tied to the impaling post for execution in the morning, he spotted a hunchback and called him over. "Is there a hump on my back?" he asked, and responded joyfully when he heard there was none. He explained that he had been a hunchback too but that the post had magical curative powers just as he had heard. In no time the two traded places and in the morning the king was outraged to find a hunchback tied to the impaling post. The Kotwal took it as his mission to punish the Brahmin and restore the king's honor. Meanwhile the Brahmin found a hiding place in the house of a garland weaver, to whom he promised wealth and respectability in exchange for her help, primarily in procuring information. The next evening he dressed to look like the Kotwal's son-in-law and wended his way into the daughter's bed where he complained of being scratched by her jewels. She took them off and soon was asleep. Without touching her or bothering anyone else in the house, the Brahmin took the jewels and brought them to the garland weaver. This direct assault so enraged the Kotwal that he recruited all the household men to search for the Brahmin and thereby exposed the women to another ploy. This time the Brahmin, disguised as a Śiva devotee, managed to literally steal the hair off the heads of the Kotwal's wife and daughter by telling them about a magical tank that gives shaven bathers new and lustrous hair.[13] Finally, the king decided, like King Vīraketu, to go after the thief himself. But he too was completely taken in by the thief's series of disguises, and even exchanged places with what he thought was a holy man, only to have his wife robbed in bed and himself arrested. Finally, when the king desperately offered half the kingdom to anyone who could catch the thief, the Brahmin came forward, confessed his identity and claimed half the kingdom and the king's daughter.

Other kings, who regularly practice the art of disguise, have been more successful at the game of anonymity when taking to the city streets, dressed as thieves or beggars: Mṛgāṅkadatta was once visiting Māyāvatu, and spent the night roaming the city streets dressed like a thief.[14] He collided with another man and both identified themselves as thieves. The stranger led Mṛgāṅkadatta into a secret tunnel, which ended in the harem of the king. There, in the lamplight, Mṛgāṅkadatta recognized his companion as Caṇḍaketu, the king's warder, who was having nocturnal visits with the king's wife.

Another king (prince) who actually became quite accomplished at stealing was Apahāravarman.[15] Once in his travels he came across an ugly Brahmin who had been reduced to utter poverty by a prostitute named Kāmamañjarī. The prince took pity on the man and resolved to restore his wealth. He entered the city of Campā, which was governed by scoundrels and set out to rob the wealthy in order to give to the poor. He started out at the gambling hall where he humiliated the local sharks at their own game. At night he roamed the city with all the tools of the trade of thieves and bore through the walls of wealthy homes. By means of his stealing he even managed to unite a couple that had been betrothed in youth but separated by the man's poverty and the greed of his fiance's father. But the height of his achievements was a magical weighing bag that seemed to fill with jewels whenever emptied—the jewels came from his nocturnal thieving, of course. By means of this bag, which Apahāravarman gave the young man, he achieved both ends. The girl's father gave away his daughter, and the prostitute Kāmamañjarī purchased the bag with all the money she had taken from the homely Brahmin.

In another story, King Bhoja on one of his nightly journeys through the streets of his city, came across an entirely different experience.[16] He chanced to hear two thieves who had just finished a successful job and were now discussing the distribution of the loot and what they were going to do with their respective shares. The first said that he planned to give his entire share to a knowledgeable Brahmin so that he would not have to beg. He strongly felt that this was his duty (dharma) as thief, following his father's and grandfather's example. The second said he would give his share to finance his father's pilgrimage to Banaras now that the old man renounced his profession as thief. Of course, this kind of a story shows the *Bhojaprabandha* as a pious exception to the literary rule. It is meant for the glorification of the king himself, in whose kingdom even thieves are dharmic. Still, while surprising, it is still not altogether absurd that thieves follow some standard of righteousness, one, however, that does not interfere with their ability to slip in and out of houses.

The Theft of Identity

India's king among thieves, the arch deceiver and master wit was Mūladeva.[17] However, he too once fell victim to theft and trickery—by his own son. After Mūladeva left his wife, their marriage unconsumated, he returned to Ujjayinī in order to test her ingenuity at finding him. The young wife, who had vowed to Mūladeva that his own son would bring him back to her, came to Ujjayinī disguised as a courtesan and seduced her husband. Of course, he did not know he was sleeping with his wife. After a while she abruptly left and returned to her home in Pāṭaliputra, where she bore a son. Years later, at the age of twelve, Mūladeva's son came to bring his father home. Presumably, we are not told, he had gone to a master of theft and trickery because he now entered a gambling hall and outplayed his father and everyone else there. At night he entered his father's quarters and stole his bedstead right from under him, easing him down on a heap of cotton. The following day when Mūladeva saw the boy selling his bed in the market and wished to buy it back, the boy insisted on exchanging riddles instead. If Mūladeva solved the riddle given to him he would get his bed back. Otherwise he would lose his freedom and become the boy's slave. Mūladeva failed to solve a riddle about Viṣṇu and had to accompany the boy back to the boy's mother and his own wife.

There is no better way, apparently, to win a thief's confidence than to identify yourself as a colleague. But this is not always easy. Discretion and a passion for anonymity are at the heart of several striking thief stories. A thief and his son broke into a king's bed chamber where, aside from great wealth, tempting food was found.[18] The thief ate so much that on his way out through the hole he became stuck. The son and loot were already outside, and at his father's command the boy cut off the thief's head and took it away in order to avoid recognition and collective punishment. The king had the corpse dragged throughout the streets of the city on the assumption that the man's relatives would not be able to contain their grief. But as the corpse came nearer, the boy climbed a tree, then fell off intentionally. As the body was passing by, the thief's wife clasped her son and both wailed openly and safely.[19]

Similar ingenuity can be found in the case of two thieves who broke the wall of the royal palace into the bed chamber of the princess.[20] One was named Karpara (Pot) the other Ghaṭa (Kettle). While Ghaṭa guarded outside, his friend dallied with the princess, who fell in love with him. These nocturnal visits became regular until one morning Karpara overslept and was discovered. At his execution he managed to communicate to his friend that the princess was to be taken away and maintained.[21] So when a few days later the princess disappeared the king suspected a partner of the dead lover. He left Karpara's corpse in a public place and had it watched. But Ghaṭa anticipated this and dressed himself as a Pāśupata ascetic carrying a pot of boiled rice and milk. In such a manner he approached his dead friend and then "accidentally" dropped the pot. When he then cried "O Karpara, full of nectar" (*hā karpara amṛta bhṛta*) nobody bothered him. Later he was able to subdue the guards and burn the corpse and spread the ashes in the Ganges.

Karpara went looking for money and found love, then death, instead. One of the best-known stories in the *Kathāsaritsāgara* involves two thieves who set up such a complex and elaborate scheme that it left no room for mere chance.[22] Śiva and Mādhava were two thieves who targeted Śaṅkarasvāmin, the chaplain for the king of Ujjayinī, in an elaborate con job. Śiva disguised himself as an ascetic while Mādhava posed as a Rajput (*rājaputra*) and settled just outside the city. After some time, when both had established a certain reputation, Mādhava approached Śaṅkarasvāmin, confessed his own wealth and offered him gifts in exchange for an introduction to the king toward possible employment. The greedy chaplain arranged the meeting and even invited Mādhava to live with him. The thief gladly accepted and moved into the chaplain's house, bringing with him a large trunk full of fake gems. A short time later he pretended to fall gravely ill and refused to see any healer, except the ascetic Śiva to whom he promised all his wealth if a cure was found. Śaṅkarasvāmin worried about losing such an opportunity for great riches and quickly offered his daughter to the ascetic, while the latter reluctantly agreed to compromise his vows. As the sick Mādhava was gradually recovering, Śiva began selling the fake jewels to his father-in-law and the two thieves found opportunities to spend their money. Eventually the host ran out of cash so he went to sell one of his gems in the market. To his shocked surprise, he discovered that all the jewels were fake, so he quickly took his case to the king. The king reviewed the case in all its details and concluded, amazed and delighted, that no law was actually broken. The sick Mādhava *gave* the jewels to the ascetic and the ascetic, who had just come into their possession, had no way of knowing they were fake when he sold them to his father-in-law.

Achievements of the Best in the Trade

Aside from the technical skill that is clearly called for in breaching walls and fences, the art of thieves is remarkable in another way. The power and ingenuity to become successful imposters in a society that values strict status and role observance is considerable. Stealing successfully requires a sense of self-confidence, a self-assurance that is to be found only among ascetics, kings, and gods. That may be the reason that a king would make three undetected thefts the task for winning his daughter.[23] A prince was accompanied by three of his best friends, including the minister's son, on a lengthy journey after they had all been rebuffed by their fathers for being lazy and careless. They came to a kingdom whose king proclaimed that the man who could commit a triple theft without being detected would marry his astonishingly beautiful daughter. The thefts had to take place at the ferry, the market, and the palace. The task was made doubly difficult by the presence of a great astrologer who managed to solve every crime commited in the city. The prince duly fell in love with the princess, and his friend, the minister's son, promised to help. His plot entailed numerous clever identity changes (by changing clothes and appearance), constantly changing residence among several homes they had rented simultaneously, and a number of sophisticated deceptions. The theft at the palace, for instance, followed a secret meeting with the astrologer, who did not know their identity, of course. They confessed to being petty thieves and promised the old man bribes if he would ignore their activities, which he promised to do. Before departing, the minister's son swiftly cut off the tip of one of the astrologer's fingers and disappeared. At night he managed to cleverly breach the palace wall and entered the royal bedroom with jewelry on one hand, the other hand free of it. He placed himself between the two beds and with the jeweled hand removed the king's ring. The king stirred, but when he felt the jewels he assumed it was his wife and returned to sleep. With his other hand the minister's son had meanwhile removed the queen's jewelry. Before departing the thief placed the tip of the astrologer's finger on a stick and stroked the king. The king woke and assumed there was a thief in the dark room. With one stroke he chopped off the finger in the dark, then went to get his guards, while the minister's son escaped as he had come. In the morning the king instructed his police to search the city for anyone with a chopped finger, and eventually the astrologer, the king's favorite, was detected and accused of theft. At that point the prince intervened and confessed to the thefts, which he described according to the instructions of the minister's son. In such a manner he won the hand of the princess and eventually returned home to rule wisely. The choice of the tasks imposed by the king, and the manner in which they were performed, make it clear that theft was a profession of great personal power and charisma, both physical and psychological.

Clearly this is a justifiable source of pride. As the thief Sarvalika was working to breach the wall of Maitreya and Cārudatta in the *Mṛcchakaṭikā*, he reflected on the conditions and his own qualifications:[24] "Ha! The moon is down. And Night, obscuring the Stars behind a Veil of Clouds , covers like a mother the world's greatest Hero whose noctural sallies, when he is bent on the Plunder of his Neighbors, moves the King's Constabulary to panic! . . . Let people decry our handiwork that flourishes during sleep, let them protest that a confidence trickster is a robber, not a clobber—but if we have a bad name, at least, it is better to be free than to kneel to a Master."

Of course, the special skills of thieves are often the product of schooled training, for which there are several accounts. In Day's *Folk-Tales of Bengal* two thieves send their sons to a master for instruction. In the course of their progress, the teacher tests them in the following manner. One had to steal a gourd, which was being carefully watched on top of a thatched roof of a dilapidated hut. The roof was so unsteady that even a mouse would shake down bits of straw. The boy gently climbed the roof holding a cat, a string, and a knife. When the woman woke up due to the rustling on the roof, he squeezed the cat's throat making it meow. Then he cut the gourd, tied a string to it, and threw the cat down. In the commotion that ensued, he lowered the gourd and got away. The next test was stealing the gold necklace off the neck of the queen, which he accomplished by means of a complex operation.[25]

But even the best of thieves must recognize the force of chance and show some respect for religion, his own religion of course. Sarvalika, like other thieves, worshiped and prayed to the god of thieves Skanda:

> I bow to thee, granter of Wishes, Kumāra Kārttikeya!
> I bow to thee, God of Golden Lance, Subrahmaṇya,
> That art vowed to the Gods,
> I bow to thee, Son of the Sun!
> I bow to thee, Master of Magic whose first pupil I am![26]

The thief, even at the earliest times known to us from India, had at his resources more than just invocations. He had in his arsenal magical spells for putting to sleep the occupants of a target house, especially the guard dog. Such a spell would be magical not just, or even primarily, for the belief in the ability of the word to communicate power, but for the effect of lullaby music on those who hear it sung:

> 1. Lord of the House, you who drive away diseases and permeate all forms, be a gentle friend to us.
> 2. White and tawny son of Saramā, when you bare your teeth they gleam like spears in your snapping jaws. Fall fast asleep!
> 3. Bark at the thief or at the marauder, as your run up and back again, O son of Saramā. But you are barking at those who sing Indra's praises; why do you threaten us? Fall fast asleep!
> . . . .
> 5. Let the mother sleep; let the father sleep; let the dog sleep; let the master of the house sleep. Let all the kinsmen sleep; let our people all around sleep.[27]

Idiot Thieves

Few characters in Indian fiction are more comical than simpletons who decide to become thieves. Despite the well-known wariness of thieves, occasionally they will take an apprentice who would be far more successful as the victim of theft, not its perpetrator. In one story six thieves took such a student on several of their jobs.[28] They left him standing guard outside the house into which they broke. As he was standing in the dark waiting for the six, he began thinking that he too should steal something. With his hand he felt around in the dark, until he discovered a large grinding stone. However, due to its weight the thief could not lift it so he woke up a man who was sleeping on the veranda and asked for help. The seven outlaws barely escaped the mayhem that ensued. The next time waiting outside, the would-be thief shook the post that was holding an ash-pumpkin creeper, and a fruit fell on his head. The fool then yelled in terror, "They killed me!" and again the seven barely escaped. After this episode, the six thieves decided to send our hero on his own job, and told him to steal some food. In the house of one old woman who was sleeping, he found some pulse, but he felt that he should fry it before taking it away. Then, to check if it was sufficiently cooked, he put a spoonful in the mouth of the sleeping woman. Needless to say, the idiot barely escaped, and left his treasure behind.

Similar wit was displayed by a weaver who decided to join three thieves in order to supplement his income.[29] The first time out his task was to find a pole, in order to lift the thatch. As he could not find a pole he woke one of the household men asking for such a tool. On the second job, the weaver was told to stay outside but he crawled through the hole in the wall and began to grope in the darkness of the house. He found some vermicelli and sugar and began to cook. Now in her sleep, the woman of the house accidentally dropped her hand under the weaver's nose, and he imagined that she was asking for some food, so he put a spoonful of hot vermicelli in that hand. In the noise that erupted, the weaver, whose name was Kadra ("God" in the local dialect) jumped and hid in the rafters. Meanwhile the husband was yelling at his wife whom he suspected of cooking for a lover. The frightened woman, eyes raised to the rafters, appealed to Kadra to attest to her innocence. So he (the weaver, not the other) did, and the thieves were apprehended.

The humor in such stories comes from the absolute parody of a profession known for sophisticated deception, total lack of trust, and self-reliance. The thief who is a moron is one who takes everything at its face value and lacks every grain of suspicion. Such a thief, in short, is no better than the average householder who usually finds himself on the other side of the wall.

Brahmin Thieves—A Digression on Dharma Itself

Not only kings but, on a rare occasion, Brahmins too steal. One Brahmin stole in order to test the source of his esteem and social standing:[30] He was

> maintained by the king of Kosala, and sought the Three Refuges; he kept the Five Commandments, and was versed in the Three Vedas. "This is a good man," thought the King, and showed him great honor. But that Brother thought to himself, "The King shows honor to me beyond other brahmins, and has manifested his great regard by making me his spiritual director. But is his favor due to my goodness or only to my birth, lineage, family, country and accomplishments? I must clear this up without delay." Accordingly, one day when he was leaving the palace, he took unbidden a coin from a treasurer's counter, and went his way. Such was the treasurer's veneration for the brahmin that he sat perfectly still and said not a word. Next day the brahmin took two coins; but still the official made no remonstrance. The third day the brahmin took a whole handful of coins. "This is the third day," cried the treasurer, "that you have robbed his Majesty"; and he shouted out three times—"I have caught the thief who robs the treasury." In rushed a crowd of people from every side, crying, "Ah, you've long been posing as a model of goodness." And dealing him two or three blows, they led him before the King. In great sorrow the King said to him, "What led you, brahmin, to do so wicked a thing?" And he gave orders, saying, "Off with him to punishment." "I am not a thief, sir," said the brahmin. "Then why did you take money from the treasury?" "Because you showed me such great honor, sir, and because I made up my mind to find out whether that honor was paid to my birth and the like or only to my goodness. That was my motive, and now I know for certain (inasmuch as you order me off to punishment) that it was my goodness and not my birth and other advantages, that won me your majesty's favor."

Indeed, perhaps only a Brahmin would consciously reflect on the ambiguity in dharma between status and personal morality. It is also telling that he chose theft to clear up the matter. Another Brahmin, Sarvilaka, may have been more typical of actual thieving Brahmins or, indeed, thieves in general.[31] He is the thief in *Mṛcchakaṭikā* who forgot his measuring tape on his way into Cārudatta's and Maitreya's quarters: "No matter, my Brahmin's thread will replace it. Indeed a Brahmin's thread is a tool of many uses for a Brahmin, especially for one like me. If one makes a professional hole in the wall, one can use it to measure with. If one wants to lift a jewel off a body, one can use it as a lasso. If one wants to open a bolted gate, one can use it to pull the bolt. If one's bitten by an insect or a snake, one can use it as a tourniquet."

The most notorious instance of a Brahmin thief is cited by Manu as an example of *āpaddharma*. According to Bhīṣma there was once a time at the end of the Treta and the first twelve years of the Dvapara when all the conditions materialized for a Brahmin to follow the rules of *āpaddharma*. Viśvāmitra, the great Brahmin sage, who was dying of starvation along with his family, spotted a piece of dog flesh inside a Caṇḍāla's hut in a Caṇḍāla hamlet. Even in his condition, he was painfully aware of the two violations of dharma in what he had to do: steal from another and eat forbidden food. Moreover, stealing was an art he was untrained in and even an unlocked door proved too much for him. The Caṇḍāla who was lying awake inside heard the door latch noise and immediately threatened the intruder with grave violence. Viśvāmitra reacted by trembling with extreme fear and shame for what he had been about to do.[32] The Caṇḍāla, hearing Viśvāmitra identify himself, became equally terrified. However, he regained his senses when he heard the Brahmin admit that he was about to commit the sin (*pāpa*) of stealing and eating the dog meat. The debate that ensued is a sophisticated, but repetitive, review of Dharmaśāstra literalism versus the legal provision for times of extraordinary distress and extenuating circumstances. The heart of the debate is perhaps encapsulated best in the following representative statements. According to Viśvāmitra, "Whatever is needed for living should be done without scruple. Life is better than death, by living one can obtain dharma" my act is justified on the grounds of extreme distress and I shall have the meat. (*Yathā yathā vai jīveddhi tat kartavyam apīdya, jīvitam maraṇāt śreyo jīvan dharmam avāpnuyāt* 61).

According to the Caṇḍāla, "That which is done by an evil man is not eternal dharma. Improper conduct must not be done, do not commit a sin by deception" (*Asatā yat samācīrṇaṁ na sa dharmaḥ savātanaḥ, nāvṛttam anukāryaṁ vai mā chalenārtaṁ kṛthāḥ* 70).

The two went at each other for several rounds, but the Caṇḍāla finally fell silent and allowed Viśvāmitra to take the dog meat. The sage returned to his family in the forest and prepared the meat according to all the rules. As the preparations were underway, rains began to fall and the world started to regenerate. Still, Viśvāmitra and his family ate the dog meat and later he returned his merit and burned away the sin.

The story of Viśvāmitra is rarely cited as an example of theft—it was a bungled amateurish attempt—but as the most notorious case of dharma in times of adversity (*āpaddharma*).[33] It is useful for our purpose, not because it demonstrates how not to steal, but because it illustrates the most fundamental principle that is explored by the notion of *āpad*, namely that dharma is, in principle and fact, subject to time. This despite the fact that dharma is often portrayed as the very foundation of cosmic structure, and it aspires to the time-transcending status of Veda. We may be forgiven a digression into this issue, both because it is intrinsically important, and also because it helps explain the ambivalent fascination with thieves, who appear to break the law of dharma at will, and yet are never depicted as absolutely adharmic.

The principle of *āpaddharma* seems to stipulate that in times of adversity one may find subsistence by means of work, or by eating food, normally forbidden.[34] The principle strikes us as a commonsensical relaxation of law for extraordinary times, or the reasonable rule that the interpretation of the law is "never complete unless the surrounding circumstances of the alleged offender had been taken into account."[35]But more is at stake here: the stories cited by Manu and told in the *Mahābhārata* and other sources begin by describing circumstances so severe that they could never mitigate the strict application of the letter of the law in practical terms. They are meant, in other words, to illustrate the very dramatic point that, since Brahmins are the embodiment of dharma, they can "violate" it only when dharma itself disappears altogether in a mythical sense. But where does this leave everyone else? Is the difference between Brahmins and non-Brahmins only quantitative or is there a difference in principle? I think some of the answers are found within different stories in the *Mahābhārata* and other texts that try to deal with the issue of dharma in a contingent world. Only by looking at this issue can we come to terms with the unique status of, and facination with, thieves.

A wise mouse named Palita lived at the foot of a huge Banyan tree in the middle of a forest.[36] On one of the branches lived a cat, Lomaśa, who subsisted on birds. A Caṇḍāla trapper moved to that part of the forest and set numerous traps nearby. One day the cat became ensnared in one of the traps. Palita immediately began to act overconfidently and to feed near the trap, while completely ignoring the cat. In his heedlessness, he failed to notice that Harita, a mongoose who was a more dangerous enemy than the cat, was quietly approaching from one side. Meanwhile an owl named Candraka was also approaching from another side, and getting ready to swoop down. By the time Palita realized what was happening, it was too late to escape. He concluded that his only hope of escaping with his life was the cat. He reflected that in times of distress one must sometimes befriend one's worst enemy, and he hoped that the cat too knew that dharma of time and place, namely when to fight and when to make peace. And so, the two struck a deal for the mouse to free the cat, while the latter would shield him from Candraka and Harita. Seeing this newly created alliance, the owl and the mongoose took off, and now it was time for Palita to free his friend from the bonds of the trap. However, to the cat's distress, Palita gnawed at the net very deliberately and slowly. He explained that his work was timed to free the cat just as the trapper arrived, and not before, because only then could he feel safe that Lomaśa would not betray him. The frightened cat implored Palita to rush on grounds of the pact they had made. But the mouse stuck by his own prudence and said: "No one is another's friend and no one is another's well-wisher; people become friends or enemies only from self-interest"(104). In the morning, just as he had promised, the mouse cut the last string as the hunter approached and both animals escaped safely. Later the cat came around to Palita's way of seeing things: "No condition deserves permanently the name of either friendship or hostility. Both friends and enemies exist due to considerations of interest and gain"(121). Still, Lomaśa wished to remain friends out of sheer gratitude. The mouse, however, recognized the contingency of their relationship, and since the special threat had passed, he felt that the basis for any friendship was gone too.

This story (and many others like it) illustrates the contrast between the temporality of dharma, its precarious subjectivity to time on the one hand, and the fluid nature of action itself. This is an ancient debate on the relation between time and action, a debate that finds its expression in the sad story of King Brahmadatta and the bird Pūjaṇī.[37] The bird lived in the palace with her son who was born on the same day as the prince. One day when she returned from gathering food and found that the prince (a baby) had killed her son, she pecked out the boy's eyes and prepared to leave the palace. Brahmadatta heard of what happened and rushed to keep the bird from leaving. A debate ensued between the two as the bird explained her reasons for leaving while the king tried to prevent her departure.

Brahmadatta argued that their account was squared by her revenge, so there was no reason to leave. He explained that all actions are manifestations of time, that time is the author of all events and the cause of the bird's and his own grief. There is no point in blaming anyone for such events, therefore she should stay. Pūjaṇī argued that if time was indeed the cause of all things, what was the point of medicine, or for that matter religious acts that are designed to produce merit. It was the prince who killed the chick and she, Pūjaṇī, who deprived him of his sight. To put both positions in our own terms, although the king was arguing compassionately, his position is essentially anarchistic. It subjugates all norms and all conduct to absolute temporality and therefore to the subjectivity of a purely situational perspective. The bird's position is traditional: it does not deny the influence of time, but it refuses to relinquish the notion of agency (and with it propriety and culpability) to time.

It would probably be prudent to look for the "normative" position about dharma somewhere between these two. Time is not incidental and external—a mere background—for actions and norms. It is a pervasive reality that renders the very authority of dharma problematic. Though ideologically consistent—even rigid—dharma can never completely transcend the contingencies determined by time, place, and the particulars of the agent. Bhīṣma narrates a "story" (actually an apodictic discourse) about a robber named Kāvyaya who was born of a Kṣatriya father and a Niṣāda mother.[38] This was a ferocious and powerful criminal who also worshiped his aged parents and venerated Brahmins. Despite his ruthless professional excellence, this man was so righteous that Bhīṣma was certain he would go to heaven after his death. When Kāvyaya was approached by other robbers in order that he may lead them, he set down numerous rules of conduct, by which they had to abide: women and anyone shying from a fight must not be killed. Brahmins are always to be honored. Truth can never be violated and marriages were sacred. No house should ever be robbed in which gods, ancestors, and guests are worshiped. As noted, it is much more fitting for a leader among robbers—a group crime—to maintain such values than it is for the thief. However, such narratives are instructive not for the reality they portray, of course, but for the absolute flexibility in the notion of dharma which they imply. First, there is the often discussed distinction between occupational norms (*svadharma*) and absolute norms (*sādhāraṇa dharma*). This part is clear and requires no particular exertion on our part: we know that even the Mafia follows certain self-imposed prohibitions. The subtler point is that there is nothing adharmic about Kāvyaya's ruthlessness either. There is no conflict, no paradox, between two dharmas—one higher, the other lower. Everything he does is absolutely appropriate to who he is. We and Brahmins may be conscious of an apparent conflict, which is "resolved" by the encompassment of one type of dharma (*svadharma*) by a broader and higher kind.[39] Everyone else in India, and probably the Brahmins too in moments of sobriety, were acutely aware of the temporality of existence and the very contingency of dharma. The Brahmins never lost the sense of unease about *āpad* (understood both as danger and contingency) as a source of dilemmas, but to everyone else given a voice in the story literature, dharma is intrinsically a matter of time and place. In other words, *āpad* is an everyday occurence.

A crow named Laghupatanaka once saw a fowler approaching his part of the woods, and taking this as a bad sign, he uttered the following bit of wisdom:[40] "Whenever one awakens he should be aware of a danger that will take place, which will befall today, death, disease or sorrow?" Wise people (*paṇḍita*), the crow reflected, recognize emergencies always and everywhere around them. This is illustrated by a very large number of stories in the *Hitopadeśa*, which must have been written by authors who were intimately familiar with Dharmaśāstra but believed, above all, in its contingency in the face of danger, as the following example shows.

An old tiger once preyed on travelers by offering them a gold bracelet that he held in his paw.[41] A certain greedy traveler wanted the bracelet but mistrusted the tiger. The beast reassured him by means of a lengthy and beautiful speech about dharma. He said that sacrificing, studying the Vedas, generosity, penance, honesty, patience, forgiveness, and absence of greed are the eightfold path of dharma in the Smṛtis. One who sees his own mother in a neighbor's wife, a lump of earth in another's wealth, and his own self in all creatures, is a wise man. These and other noble thoughts convinced the traveler that he can go into the lake nearby, as the tiger suggested. There he became stuck in the mud and was seized by the tiger. His last thoughts, before being devoured, were that learning in Smṛti and Veda does not warrant placing one's trust in a villain (*durātmana*). "In such a case it is one's nature that prevails" (*svabhāva evātra tathātiricyate*). One must never trust rivers, people with weapons, animals that have claws or horns, women (all!), and royal families (*rājakula*). It is natural disposition above other qualities that determines how these will behave.

A similar fate befell an old vulture who was assigned to guard the young birds in a certain Parkaṭī tree.[42] One day a cat approached and began to build trust in Jaradgava's old and suspicious heart. He uttered words of great learning about dharma and about nature. In ironic accord with the famous Brahmin in the Jātaka tale, the cat asked: "Should anyone be killed or honored only because of their caste [*jāti*])? One should be either killed or honored when his actions [*vyavahāra*] are known."[43] Later, after a discourse on the importance of guests, the cat continued to emphasize the importance of dharma with the familiar maxim that dharma is the only friend [*suhṛda*] that accompanies man at his time of death. Everything else is destroyed along with the body"[44] Having won the trust of the old vulture with his wise words, the cat ate the young birds and then disappeared. When all the birds returned and found their young ones gone, they suspected Jaradgava of the crime and killed him.

These stories, whether from the *Mahābhārata*, *Pañcatantra*, or any other source, demonstrate an acute nonidealized predominance of *svabhāva* (nature) over dharma, and an emergency behind every rustle in the woods. But even granting such a perspective, it would be misleading to label this a world-weary cynicism and generalize about a certain "mentality." In fact, we have already seen that even individuals possessing an apparently ferocious *svabhāva* may follow dharma under certain conditions. More important, it is often one's conduct in relation to dharma that determines one's identity—even one's nature. In other words, just as dharma is not absolutely fixed and static, a person's character or nature—one's very identity—is fluid and changing. The crossing of boundaries, as we have seen with the bride, and certainly the crossing of rules provide the means for transforming identity. Such a pattern determines the ritualized conduct of weddings, and is, in the final analysis, the source of the Brahmin's embarrassment in cases of *āpad*, as well as the need for his penance.

Divine Thieves: The Theft of Soma, Vedas, Amṛta

The multiple theft of Soma is a very familiar episode associated with the acquisition of the plant for the sacrifice.[45] It begins with the earth-bound gods wanting the celestial Soma for the sacrifice. So they produced two female illusions (*māyās*) Kadrū and Suparṇī/—the first Earth, the second Speech. The two females began to argue over eyesight and decided that the one whose eyesight was better would take over the self (*ātman*) of the other. Suparṇī lost the contest but was given the chance to redeem herself by bringing Soma down for the gods. She then produced the metric forms in the shape of birds and they took turns trying to steal Soma, starting with the shorter meters first. The shorter meters were unable to reach Soma but managed to bring down *dīkṣā* and *tapas*, then the *dakṣiṇā*—all essential sacrificial elements. Soma himself was enclosed between two sharp golden cups that snapped every twinkling of an eye.[46] Getting through would have challenged the best of thieves. Still, the *gāyatrī* meter managed to steal Soma from his guardians by means of a Khadira staff and she took him to the gods. However, on her way back, the Gandharva Viśvāvasu, who was responsible for guarding Soma, stole him right back, though it is not clear how. The Gandharvas then kept Soma for three nights. During that time, according to RV 9.113.3, they placed the semen in Soma, and made him fecund. The gods then concluded that since Gandharvas love women, they should send Vāc (Speech) to finish the job, which she did in the shape of a one-year-old woman. As she returned to the gods with Soma, the Gandharvas followed her and demanded that the gods exchange her for Soma. Vāc was allowed to decide for herself and chose to go to the gods because they offered her music and dance, whereas the Gandharvas merely recited the Vedas.

This bare-bone retelling overlooks a large number of details that purport to link the myth to specific elements in the sacrifice. For instance, the myth is said to explain the exclusion of the Gandharvas from the sacrifice, except as Soma's "guardians" in the form of the hearths. The Adhvaryu is prohibited from passing between the hearths with the pressed Soma in order to avoid losing a single drop into the gaping mouths of the Gandharvas.[47] Thus precariously part of the sacrifice now, the Soma is better guarded by Agni and Rudra, who are the gods' experts on theft.

Clearly, the ritual cannot explain the myth, nor can the myth explain the full ritual. Elements of the myth have been explained in a variety of ways beginning with the familiar naturalistic allegories of earlier scholarship.[48] In contrast, according to Malamud, the purchase of the Soma is "the prototype of the eminently profane social practice known as commerce."[49] In other words, the ritual practice and mythical narrative are not outstanding but reflect a norm of acquisition that may have been widespread. And given the fact that the early sacrifice was preceded by looting raids, as well as the widely held hypothesis that early commerce was a ritualized form of theft, Malamud's observation rings quite true.[50] Still, I doubt that sociological and historical explanations are enough. The myth is not about a military or quasi-military raid, but about deception and subtle theft. Twice the gods used females to steal Soma, and the first pair (Kadru and Suparṇī) was explicitly described as deceptions (*māyā*). Moreover, while the Gandharvas were willing to settle for an exchange of the feminine (Vāc) with the masculine (Soma) and the narrative seemed headed in that direction, the gods ended with both, though not through violence.[51]

The gods Agni and Rudra, who were placed in charge of Soma following the successful theft, are no strangers to thievery. Of course, as fire— sacrificial or other—Agni is usually addressed for protection against theft: "With missles of this Agni, his who looks afar, will we lay low the thief in combat for the kine."[52] The reference to cattle draws attention to Agni and Soma who stole back the cattle that the demon Paṇi had stolen in the first place.[53] So even if the cause is justifiable, Agni the guardian can be a thief when necessary.[54] Moreover, on completion of the fire altar for the Śatarudriya, Agni becomes identified with Rudra who is the Lord of thieves and robbers: "Homage to conquering, piercing Lord of assailing bands, homage to the towering sword bearer, to the Lord of thieves homage."[55] Perhaps it is not altogether surprising that the guardian and the thief are one and the same, even if not at the same time. We shall shortly see this in the Gandharva Viśvāvasu. A recent series of articles highlights this outstanding feature in the personality of a South Indian god, Kāttavarāyan.[56]

The Gandharvas too are not altogether simple. Viśvāvasu managed to steal Soma back from the gods, but he is not just a thief. As the Soma sacrifice is being set up, that is, as the enclosing sticks are placed in a circle around Agni's fire, it is Viśvāvasu who is addressed as the guardian of the fire.[57] Better yet, Viśvāvasu is the staff (*daṇḍa*) that is placed between the bridegroom and the bride during the three nights that the couple is to abstain from consumating the marriage (*triratra vrata*).[58] At the end of the period, Viśvāvasu is asked to give up his claim on the bride and join the Apsarases instead. It is not clear whether the Gandharva is a competitor for the bridegroom, as this verse suggests, or the protector of the bride from the eager young man. The identification with *daṇḍa*, which carries associations of boundary markers and protection, suggests that Viśvāvasu may be both. In the myth of Soma, due to the specific character of the stolen object (Soma), and to the ambivalent nature of the participants (gods and Gandharvas), it is clear that the mere reference to commerce is inadequate to explain the meaning of the crime involved—theft. Other mythical episodes bear out the conclusion that theft is interesting not for the economic forces involved, but for other reasons.

The *Mahābhārata* (12.335.21–65) tells the story of the theft—actually robbery—of the Vedas by the demons Madhu and Kaiṭabha, and their restoration by Viṣṇu. The two demons emerged out of two drops of water at the instigation of Nārāyana (Viṣṇu) at the time of creation. The two were armed with maces and they saw Brahmā emitting the four Vedas. They violently (*sahasā*, perhaps suddenly) grabbed the Vedas and dived into the ocean. Brahmā was struck with grief, and beseeched Viṣṇu to restore the Vedas, which were his eyesight. Viṣṇu agreed to get the Vedas back and with his lordly power (*eśvarena prayogena*) he assumed a second form. He became bright as the moon, took on an equine head (*hayaśira*). The entire universe with its stars and constellations, earth, rivers, oceans, the Om syllable, the *pitṛs* who drink Soma, and so on became his body with its many parts. Then, he controlled his voice in the *śikṣa* manner and he began to chant Vedic *mantras*. The two Asuras became fascinated by this voice and left the Vedas in order to see where it was coming from. Waiting for this chance Hari (Nārāyaṇa) took the Vedas and returned them to Brahmā.

The story contrasts the theft of the Vedas by Madhu and Kaiṭabha, an act of armed violence, with the deception used to restore them. This deception fits the model of theft we have seen elsewhere and also resembles the theft of Soma in a remarkable manner. Here too the loss of sight is linked to the impetus to steal, just as Suparṇī's inferior eyesight was the reason for her obligation to go. The *Mahābhārata* story also has *māyā* or illusion (the god's self-transforming powers) as the necessary condition of divine involvement, which is indirect. Just as Suparṇī and Kadrū are *māyās*, Nārāyaṇa's visible form is a second body (*dvitīyām tanum*), in fact the manifest immanental world. In his restorative work, the god does not operate by fiat, or by an application of great force, but by stealth. Finally, Suparṇī obtained Soma by means of voice or at least the Vedic meter (*gāyatrī*), and similarly Nārāyaṇa deceived Madhu and Kaiṭabha by means of the *śaiksa svara*, a voice regulated according to the science of Vedic recitation.

We saw that Namuci, who stole the soma from Indra, ended up beheaded by foam. The demon (Dānava) Rāhu met with a similar fate when he attempted to steal *amṛta* from the gods.[59] After the churning of the ocean the gods fought with the Daityas and Dānavas over the nectar of immortality, but there was no clear winner. Viṣṇu then took on the form of a feminine illusion ("*māyāmāsthitah mohinīṁ prabhuḥ*") and he mesmerized the demons who gave him the nectar, which he then brought to the gods. The Dānava Rāhu saw the gods drinking and wished to become immortal too. He disguised himself as a god ("*vibudha rūpeṇa*") and began to drink. However, the sun and the moon recognized him and drew the gods' attention to the pretender. Just as the *amṛta* was reaching into the throat of the demon, Viṣṇu beheaded him.

The difference between god (Viṣṇu) and demon (Rāhu) in this simple narrative is certainly not ethical—both steal *amṛta* for their own purpose. The clear difference is that while Rāhu was only capable of disguising himself, and was consequently recognizable, Viṣṇu actually became the *māyā* lady who stole the nectar. This is where the draw between gods and demons is broken: not power but deception—the ability to become transformed into something altogether different, an inner transformation governed by will. The gods win immortality due to an ability to fashion "inner" change rather then just assuming a deceptive facade, which is all that demonic and human thieves can do.

One is easily led to conclude that divine theft is a metaphor for *māyā*, the god's operation in the manifest world. This seems to be confirmed by John Hawley's informants on the thievery of Kṛṣṇa. As a thief, Kṛṣṇa could be seen in all his "naturalness" (*svabhāviktā*), that is, as an immanental—human like—rather than transcendent force.[60]

The choice of theft over other crimes is dictated, therefore, by the deception and transformations involved rather than the material benefits of stealing. This has certainly been the case with the folkloristic narratives about human thieves. Thieves interest writers on dharma because, unlike other criminals, they do not threaten or violate a structure that is imagined in spatial terms. Instead they expose by their conduct the essential transparency and temporality of dharma as social norm. Their absolute freedom of movement across barriers and through different social types makes them "magical" or almost invisible, because they are too individualistic to identify. This magic is not used for amassing wealth in order to dominate their social environment, but for the pleasure of changing their identity at will, a seductive fantasy in a controlled caste society. Consequently, thieves demonstrate—they almost embody—the idealized possibilities of living as an individual in a world where dharma continues to exist but is temporalized. Unlike the *sannyāsin* who abandons dharma, or the king who enforces it, the thief lives within the world of dharma but moves about as though dharma were completely transparent.

At one point or another, the thief will probably end up being impaled or, more likely, tied to a post and starved to death. But how is dharma itself restored? The next chapter will examine the mythical representation of punishment—conceived again in spatiotemporal terms—as a force that is particularly well suited to restore dharma as we have described it. In order to do this, we shall have to "deconstruct" a form that is given to us, at best, in a symbolic fashion—the royal scepter—or more frequently in a conceptual (ideological) formulation of punishment. Of course, most religious data are given in one of these two forms. Reducing them to more concrete and natural spatiotemporal terms is essential to an imagistic mode of analysis. In the process we shall look at a character, Daṇḍa, who embodies the mythical way of articulating the tension between a social persona and natural self-perception, as well as the transformations induced by this tension and triggered by passage across boundaries.

Notes

1. Technically, the concept of theft (*steya*) extended far beyond breaking and entering for the purpose of removing property. It included cheating in commercial transactions (see stories on blacksmiths), withholding salary, and so forth. For a recent technical review of theft, see Chanchal Bhattacharya, *The Concept of Theft in Classical Hindu Law* (New Delhi: Munshiram Manoharlal, 1990). This chapter will confine itself, arbitrarily perhaps, mostly to those thieves we normally call burglars.

2. Manu 8.319ff., trans. Wendy Doniger; on the logic of lists, see my chapter 6.

3. Stith Thompson and Jonas Balys (*The Oral Tales of India*

[Bloomington: Indiana University Press, 1958]) list 220 submotifs (under "Thefts and Cheats"), many of them with numerous versions. And, of course, thieves surface in other motifs as well (e.g. deceptions, escapes). The 80 stories I have read cover many of the submotifs, but the 30 or so told or cited in this chapter should be viewed against such an imposing background.

4. See, for instance David Moss, "Bandits and Boundaries in Sardinia," in *Man* 14 (1978): 477–96. Several recent articles have been written on the subject of cattle raiding, including Ruth Katz-Arbegian, "Cattle Raiding and Bride Stealing" *Religion* 14 (1984); and Bruce Lincoln, *Priests, Warriors and Cattle: A Study of the Ecology of Religions* (Berkeley: University of California Press, 1981).

5. M. Kennedy, *The Criminal Classes in India* (Delhi: Mittal, 1985).

6. Bhattacharya, *The Concept of Theft*, p. 17. Strictly speaking, theft is a broader category, but this definition shall suffice in the present context.

7. The term *permanent transcience* is taken from Alf Hiltebeitel ed., *Criminal Gods and Demon Devotees* (Albany: SUNY Press, 1989). See my subsequent discussion.

8. *Kath.* 88 vetala 14 (pp. 436–38); Maurice Bloomfield "The Art of Stealing in Hindu Fiction," *American Journal of Philology* 54, no. 3 (1923): 195–96, 222–23.

9. *aśru muktvā kṣaṇaṁ tataḥ, hasan sa cauraḥ kim api, Kath.* 88.14.43.

10. On the laughter and crying motif, see Maurice Bloomfield, "On Recurring Psychic Motifs in Hindu Fiction," *JAOS* 36 (1914): 68ff. Bloomfied owes his explanation to King Vikrama's own (p. 74), but it is not very interesting from a psychological point of view.

11. *Kath.* 112, 147ff. (pp. 429–32); cf. Devendra's Prakrit story about thief Maṇḍiya in Jacobi's *Ausgewahlte Erzahlungen in Maharastri*, pp. 65ff.

12. "The Lucky Rascal," William McCulloch *Bengali Houshold Tales* (London: Hodder and Stoughton, 1912), pp. 152–74; the narrated version is recent, but it contains numerous older and quite common motifs.

13. Such a ploy could only work where these tanks are known of course. See "The Bald Wife" in Lal B. Day, *Folk Tales of Bengal* (London: Macmillan, 1912) (cf. my chapter 5).

14. *Kath.* 71, 22ff. (pp. 367ff.). On the theme of kings in disguise, see A. Weber, *Indische Studien* (Leipzig: Brockhaus, 1878), vol. xv. 344, 354, 357, 381, 393, 417, 421; Hemavijaya, *Kathāratnakara*; story 178 (p. 170). See also the Sultan Mahmoud of Ghazni in Charles Swynnerton, *Indian Nights' Entertainment* (New York: Arno, 1977), pp. 242–44.

15. *Daśakumāracarita*, story 2; Bloomfield ("Art of Stealing") compares him with Robin Hood, p. 218.

16. *Bhojaprabandha* (Louis H. Gray, trans. *The Narrative of Bhoja* [New Haven: American Oriental Society, 1950]), p. 34.

17. *Kath.* 124 ("Mūladeva Saśina Katha"); see Bloomfield, "Art of Stealing," p. 202; also Bloomfield, "The Character and Adventures of Mūladeva," *Proceedings of the American Philosophical Society* 52 (1919): 624ff.; Other versions of the story can be found in J. Knowels, *Folk Tales of Kashmir* (London: Trubner and Sons, 1893), p. 104; Maive S. Stokes, *Indian Fairy Tales* (London: Ellis and White, 1880), p. 216; Henry Parker, *Village Folk-Tales of Ceylon* (Dehiwala: Tisara Prakasakayo, 1972) 2:75ff.; Natesa Sastri, "Story of Madana Kama Raja," in *Indian Folk Tales* (Madras: Guardian Press,

1908), p. 246 (see also Doniger's retelling of the story in chapter 7). A close second in quantity, if not antiquity, is Sharaf Tsur (the thief) whose many exploits are told in Knowels, *Folk Tales* pp. 338–54.

18. Parker, *Village Folk-Tales*, 3:43ff.; Bloomfield, "Art of Stealing," PP. 208–209; William Goonetilleke, *The Orientalist*, 1 (1884): 59.

19. Cf. the ingenious boy and the weaver-thief in William R. S. Ralston, *Tibetan Tales* (London: G. Routledge, 1926), pp. 37ff. It was common for thieves to enter legs first so their head could be removed by a partner if they became stuck or discovered.

20. *Kath.* 64, 43ff. (pp. 336ff).

21. For a different view of the passive female victim, this time as cunning and ruthless, see "The Seven Thieves," in Verrier Elwin, *Folk-Tales of Mahakoshal* (New York: Arno, 1980), pp. 249–51.

22. *Kath.* 24, 82 (p. 96). Indeed, as we can see from the thief Sarvalika's comments in *Mṛcchakaṭikā*, one of the considerations for selecting a place to break in was avoiding the opportunity to see women.

23. "The Triple Theft," in William McCulloch, *Bengali Household Tales* (London: Hodder and Stoughton, 1912), pp. 175–205.

24. Act 3; J. A. B. van Buitnen, trans., *Two Plays of Ancient India* (New York: Columbia University Press, 1968), p. 85.

25. Day, *Folk-Tales*, pp. 171ff. See also, Bloomfield, "The Art of Stealing" p. 204.

26. van Buitenen, *Two Plays*, p. 86.

27. RV 7.55 (O' Flaherty).

28. Parker, *Village Folk Tales*, 2:71–74.

29. Swynnerton, *Indian Nights' Entertainment*, pp. 139–42; cf. Ralston, *Tibetan Tales*, pp. 37ff.

30. "Sīlavīmaṁsa Jātaka" (no. 86) in *The Jataka* trans. E. B. Cowel (Cambridge: Cambridge University Press, 1895) 1:213.

31. van Buitenen, *Two Plays*, p. 86.

32. Mbh 12.139.44. vss. According to some versions, his face was transformed with shame (*vrida kulamukhaḥ*).

33. Manu 8.105–8 also cites the cases of Ajīgarta who tried to sacrifice his son, Vāmadeva, who wanted to eat dog flesh, and Bharadvaja, who accepted cows for eating. See *Aitareya Brāhmaṇa* 7.13–16, Mbh 13.94–95, *Skanda Purāṇa* 6.32.

34. The issue is more complicated because the texts disagree on particulars. For instance, some texts (Gaut. 5.6, 7, 26; Baudh. 2.2, 77; Manu 4.95; Vas. 2.23) allow members of higher castes to engage in the work of lower castes, but not vice versa. In contrast Nārada and Yājñavalkya allow lower castes, even Śūdras, to engage in the work of upper castes, excluding tasks unique to Brahmins.

35. J. D. M. Derrett, *Religion Law and the State* (London: Faber & Faber, 1968), p. 96.

36. Mbh 12.136.19–204.

37. Mbh 12.137. 4–109.

38. Mbh 12.133.

39. The metaphorical terminology of *higher* and *lower, encompassing* and "encompassed" clearly betray the limitations of our own spatial thinking in relation to dharma.

40. *Hitopadeśa*, (Hit.) Kath. 4 ("Mitralābha").

41. Hit., Katha 1.

42. Hit., Katha 3.

43. 3.58; cf. "Sīlavīmaṁsa Jātaka," trans. Cowel.

44. 3.66.

45. ŚB 3.6.2.2ff.; TS 6.1.6.1ff.; Ait. Br. 3.25.

46. ŚB 3.6.2.9–12.

47. ŚB 3.6.2.20.

48. See for instance Alfred Hillebrandt, *Vedische Mythologie.* (Breslau, 1927–29), 1:377–83, on the three moonless nights before the new moon. But note also ŚB 12.7.3.6, which prescribes that the Soma plant must sit for three nights after acquisition.

49. "Soma as Sacrificial Substance and Divine Figure," in Yves Bonnefoy, compile, *Mythologies* (Chicago: University of Chicago Press, 1985) 2:804.

50. See J. Heesterman, *The Inner Conflict of Tradition* (Chicago: University of Chicago, 1985), and Norman O. Brown, *Hermes the Thief* (Great Barrington, Mass.: Lindisfarne, 1990).

51. Unlike the Gandharvas, who were protecting their property (Soma), the Asura Namuci got Indra drunk by means of *surā* in order to steal Indra's Soma (RV 10.131; TB 1.4.2.1; ŚB 12.7.3; MS 3.11.4, 4.12.5). This qualifies as an excellent theft technique, especially when we consider the vow Indra made to avoid killing Namuci. See also Maurice Bloomfield, "Contributions to the Interpretation of the Veda" *JAOS* 15 (1893):143–63.

52. RV 8.64.7; cf. Vāj. Saṁ. 11.77–80 where Agni physically destroys thieves and robbers.

53. RV 1.93.4; 1.65.1.

54. See esp. RV 5.15.5.

55. Vāj. Sam. 16.20; and see comments by T. H. Griffith, *The Texts of the White Yajurveda* (Delhi: Munshiram Manoharlal, 1987), p. 154.

56. Hiltebeitel, *Criminal Gods and Demon Devotees*; the tricks and deceptions of this god read like a résumé of the best of thieves whom we have encountered in this chapter. Similarly, Rudra is both the inflicter of severe diseases and best among physicians: AV 11.2.22; 6.90.1; Āśv. 4.8.40; Kauś. 51.7.

57. Vāj. Sam. 2.3.

58. RV 18.85.21, 22; AV 14.2.33. See my chapter 6.

59. Mbh 1.17.1–10, MP 251.5–16; VP 9.

60. *Krishna the Butter Thief* (Princeton: Princeton University Press, 1983), pp. 267–68.

9

The Adharmic Force of Punishment (*Daṇḍa*)

Vertical Space

Up to this point we have looked at the implications of horizontal spatial metaphors in imagining dharma and its violation. This chapter focuses on punishment and the restoration of dharma so ably violated by thieves and lovers. It will become evident that since the notion of punishment is embodied in the royal staff, we shall have to explore this switch to metaphors of verticality. In chapter 5 we have seen that horizontal space is clearly related to human existence and action in the world, to will, change, and even contingency. In short, metaphors of horizontality even include spatialized time as a context for action, both dharmic, and nondharmic. However, even there, verticality played a subsidiary role to horizontal movement: the thief or devotee must crawl under a fence or climb over it; Rāma had to get above the ocean (unless he were to dry it up—which he threatened to do), and so forth. The movement up or down seems merely instrumental for getting across. Even the religious crossing of *tīrtha* takes place mainly in horizontal space, though the climbing of stairs and mountains plays a key role. Absolute verticality, in contrast, is the movement up or down without any corresponding travel in horizontal space. The tree stays fixed and

This Chapter was previously published as the following article: "The Royal Scepter (*Daṇḍa*) as Legal Punishment and Sacred Symbol," *History of Religions*, 28, no. 2 (1988).

so does the mountain, the boundary marker, the mast (in relation to the ship), and the royal staff.

This simple observation seems to invite a myriad of interpretations ranging from the metaphysical or paradigmatic (axis mundi), to the psychological and usually sexual. The explicit connection between the boundary marker and phallic representation, for instance, is widely known. But even aside from the easy slide into simplistic Freudianism, there are empirical caveats to be noted, such as the observation by van Gennep that very seldom in such cases does the idea of the fecundity of the territory and its inhabitants prevail. The so-called phallic symbolism of landmarks, he emphasizes, has almost no truly sexual significance.[1] The verticality, and even phallicism of boundary stones invites us, instead, to develop a more guarded hypothesis about the danger and magic involved in the horizontal passage across boundaries and the mitigating effects that verticality may somehow bring into play. This is the point of this chapter as a whole.

But to continue with this example a bit more closely, stone heaps were a common boundary marker in several cultures of the ancient world. In Greece, for instance, they were located at natural boundaries, crossroads, and even at house entrances, all places where people passed from their own domain into other's and vice versa. According to Norman O. Brown, Hermes' name is derived from the stone heaps and both the god and the marker retain the magical powers of the threshold. Hermes, of course, was the god of trade, which originally was the sanctioned license to steal.[2] Quite paradoxically, so it seems, the rod of punishment was also used as an instrument of magic and purification in Greek ritual: it was carried to crossroads in purificatory processions, placed at the entrance to the house, and was said to possess the power to transform humans from one state to another.[3]

It will not surprise us to see the concept of punishment embodied in a magical instrument such as the staff (*daṇḍa*), which is entirely vertical. The notion of retribution as a return across boundaries one had transgressed requires the magical and profoundly liminal ambiguities of such a symbol.[4] The final chapter will thus take us from the simple movement in horizontal space to the far more complex, and mythic, movement that is implied by verticality. We move into coneptual and ideological narratives in which human action is gauged in relation to cosmic processes and natural facts are thoroughly homologized. In short, we now leave the realm of images in order to take on the symbol of *daṇḍa*. But first, some words of caution are necessary in order to avoid reading such a symbol in a conceptual manner.

The total meaning of symbols that are transposed from their "natural" semantic contexts to be reconstituted in other, often theoretical ones, is seriously reduced. This is precisely what has taken place with the symbolism of the staff (*daṇḍa*) in India, which has been recorded predominantly from a juridical and political perspective.[5] The numerous lexical connotations of the term range from the simple stick to the complex concept of legal punishment.[6] The latter comprises a legitimate, even central, derivative modality of the symbolism of *daṇḍa*, as the Dharmaśāstra amply demonstrates: "For the (king's) sake the Lord formerly created his own son, Punishment (*daṇḍa*), the protector of all creatures, (an incarnation) of the law, formed of Brahman's glory"(Manu 7.14). Like the foregoing, most of the texts that employ the term *daṇḍa* seem to be referring to its meaning as punishment or government, so it stands to reason that this would serve as the primary focus of historical scholarship.[7] The problem is not the falsification of *daṇḍa*'s symbolic meaning, but its restriction to what is already a derivative and secondary intellectualization. This process is encouraged by some of the earliest dharma texts themselves: "They declare that the word *daṇḍa* is derived from the verb *damayati* ('he restrains'); therefore he shall restrain those who do not restrain themselves" (Gaut. 11.28).[8]

Two detrimental effects follow such a reduction: the secularization of Hindu polity and the allegorization of *daṇḍa* mythology. The first finds a historian of religion narrowing Manu's treatment of kingship and the royal function to a paradigm of secular power.[9] The second example shows J. D. M. Derrett's citation of Hindu legal authorities as they allegorically interpret the mythology of Daṇḍa, the god with the four tusks, many eyes, and fiery complexion in reference to justice and adjudication: "Daṇḍa comprehends within himself the dharma of both parties in a lawsuit and the four modes (tusks?) of punishment, namely rebuke, fines, mutilation and capital punishment, for the protection of the four armed society based on the castes, the eight processes of an investigation, the varied evidence (the eyes) . . . "[10]

Of course, the allegorical interpretation of a mythical figure is not ipso facto wrong, but as it translates one narrative discourse into another, it also misses the specific intentionality of the myth. Here I seek to reconsider the juridical concept of punishment by allowing the varied symbolism of the staff to emerge progressively and fully out of its numerous frames of reference. The latter consist of vegetative symbols such as sacred trees and lotus plants, sacrificial symbols such as kindling wood, ladles, and sacrificial poles, commercial symbols such as ship masts, shepard staffs, various mythological characters, such as Viṣṇu, Rudra, the Gandharvas, Devī, Kālī, Prince Daṇḍa, and a variety of mythical narratives in which these and others act. The reason for selecting such a wide variety of contexts—one can never be exhaustive—is to enable the phenomenological *Wesenschau* of *daṇḍa*.[11] The process is commonsensical and entails looking at numerous representative contexts. This results both in the enrichment of the term symbol, and in a discovery of a coherence underlying its numerous cultural applications. Only by tracing such a relatively comprehensive network can the full meaning of *daṇḍa* be construed and, in turn, can the concept of punishment be interpreted within a broader and more incisive phenomenal intentionality.[12]

Daṇḍa *in Nature*

The simplest and most immediate object to which the term *daṇḍa* refers is a stick or staff. However, the object presents itself necessarily in either vegetative or social contexts, often both. The staff is always constituted by some type of wood, and such construction material is never random or insignificant. Likewise, the staff outside of a purely natural context carries an essential social instrumentality of ritual, commercial, or political significance. Of course, the distinction between the natural and social contexts is arbitrary because, for instance, a tree becomes conspicuous only inasmuch as it is homologous with human phenomena. This observation will become clear as we begin to discuss sacred trees. Still, there is no doubt that the mapping of *daṇḍa* symbolism must begin in the natural world where it most vividly reveals the specific imagination of the Indian texts at our disposal.

The importance and sanctity of trees in India is well known but bears repeating here since the staff, in all of its configurations, embodies related properties. All twice-born males who graduate from their studies and become initiated into the householder's *āśrama* receive a staff: "That (*daṇḍa*—staff) of a Brahmin (should be made) of Palāśa wood, that of a Kṣatriya of Udumbara wood, that of a Vaiśya of Bilva wood, that of a Brahmin (should be) of length reaching the hair, that of the Kṣatriya reaching the forehead, that of the Vaiśya reaching the nostril."[13] The precise wood is a matter of some disagreement. Manu states that the Brahmin's staff is made of Palāśa or Bilva, the Kṣatriya's of Khadira or Vata, and the Vaiśya's of Pila or Udumbara.[14] The *Śāṅkhāyana Gṛhyasūtra* prescribes the Nyagrodha for a Kṣatriya. Undoubtedly all of these trees are equally important, and if I focus on a few only, it is due to considerations of space. At any rate, behind their specific qualities and uses, these various trees seem to share powerful religious characteristics that bear directly on the meaning of the staff. This may be illustrated by the Khadira, Udumbara, Nyagrodha, and Aśvattha.

The Khadira tree (*Acacia catechu*) is renowned for its great strength and hardness. According to the *Śatapatha Brāhmaṇa*, the tree emerged at the time of creation out of Prajapati's bones.[15] The hardness of the wood also accounts for its wide-ranging use in constructing pestles, seed crushers, cotton rollers, plows, bows, handles for spears, swords, and sacrificial ladles, as well as others.[16] The Khadira was also used for the construction of the axle used in the wheel of the ancient sacrificial cart.[17] Whether all these functions acquired a special valorization as a result of sharing the Khadira's qualities remains to be seen. It is clear, however, that the Khadira is far more than just a hard wood. When the gods wished to sacrifice and needed the celestial Soma, as we have seen, they created Suparṇī (mother of Garuḍa, associated with the Sun) for that purpose: "She (Suparṇī) took possession [*a-kakhada*] of Soma by means of (a stick) of Khadira wood (*Acacia catechu*) whence (the name) Khadira; and because she thereby took possession of him, therefore the sacrificial stake and the wooden sword [*sphya*] are of Khadira wood"(ŚB 3.6.2.12). The obscure myth can be related to theft or to the military, raid-oriented nature of the early Aryan sacrifices in which swiftness of vehicles and power of military implements were essential.[18]

It is clear, however, that the Khadira mediates sacrificially between the victim-sacrificer (Soma-Devas—Suparṇī) and the object of the sacrifice. Two key sacrificial implements, sword and sacrificial post, associated with the violence of the rite—as well as its efficacy—are made of Khadira. Furthermore, the Khadira is intimately linked with the potency of the Kṣatriya, with his very essence as warrior: "Just as the Peepal tree grows from Khadira, so is a hero born of a hero. May he destroy my enemies, who hate me and whom I detest."[19] From the deadly union of the two powerful trees (Peepal and Khadira) was born Arūṅdhatī, a plant used for healing sword-inflicted wounds (AV 5.5.5, 4.12). The Aśvattha possesses the characteristic of planting its roots in the shoots of other trees, particularly Khadira, thus literally growing out of them (AV 3.6). The effect was to destroy the first tree, but out of such destruction emerges the paradoxically beneficent healing qualities of the Arūṅdhatī. As we shall shortly see, the significance of this destruction-healing paradox, so important in the sacrifice, was not lost on the Hindus in other contexts as well. It is the destructive warrior-like powers of the tree that produce benefits, a symbol for the powers of the sacrificing Kṣatriya, or for the royal Kṣatriya who wields the Khadira *daṇḍa* in the court of law.

The Aśvattha (Peepal; *Ficus religiosa*) is one of India's most important trees and also possesses paradoxical qualities. According to the Gītā, the Aśvattha is Kṛṣṇa among the trees (10.26). It is the destroyer of enemies, the one who splits open the head of the enemy in a military conquest of other trees (AV 3.6.6). And yet it is also a remover of curses and protector from enemies, including the Kṣatriya's Brahmin rivals.[20] It is a tree whose roots are suspended from the sky, in fact, a tree that seems to grow upside down (AV 2.7). The renowned *Bhagavadgītā* verse (15.1) describes the Aśvattha as the indestructible tree whose roots are above, its branches below, and whose leaves are the hymns of the Veda. The *Katha Upaniṣad* also describes the tree whose branches grow downward and roots grow upward, equating it with the ultimately pure (*śukram*), with Brahman.[21]

The Aśvattha is both Kṣatriya and Brahmin (Vedic hymns), heaven and earth, destroyer and healer; it is the world (cosmos) and humanity's place in the cosmos.[22] The tree is celestial in origin (AV 5.4.3) but manifests itself in the mundane world with a downward growth that represents the immanental dynamism of the cosmic process. Significantly, just as the strength of the Aśvattha derives from the divine warrior, Indra (ŚB 12.7.1.1–9), its manifestation—the leaves—are the Vedic hymns, according to the *Gītā*.

This symbolism is further expanded by the Nyagrodha and Udumbara trees. The Nyagrodha (*Ficus indica*) with its aerial roots resembles the Aśvattha in its growth pattern . And like the Khadira, it not only symbolically represents, but actually embodies, the *kṣatra* power or essence from which its significance arises. During the Rājasūya sacrifice its fruit is prescribed as proper food for the king instead of the Soma: "The Nyagrodha is mysterously Soma the king . . . The Nyagrodha is the lordly power of the trees . . . (it) is fastened as it were by its descending growths to the ground, and supported as it were."[23] In this ritual context (to which we shall return later) the Nyagrodha represents and embodies the kṣatric power par excellence. It provides the ritual paradigm incorporated by the prospective king, and which helps transform him into a sanctified and powerful figure. The ritual context also alludes to the mythical narrative that places the ritual objects within a cosmological framework: "On the place whence by offering the sacrifice the gods went to the world of heaven they tilted over the goblets; they became the Nyagrodha trees" (AB 35.5). The Nyagrodha, therefore, not only contains the powerful juices of royalty; its descending growth forges a downward axis mundi, a ritual conduit for the transmission of divine powers, through royalty, to the vegetative world, which the king governs as well. The mythical paradigm relates directly and efficaciously to the purpose of this element in the Rājasūya: "In that the Kṣatriya as sacrificer eats the descending growths of the Nyagrodha and the fruits, verily thus he establishes in himself the lordly power of the plants and in the lordly power himself"(AB 35.5).[24] Like the Aśvattha, the Nyagrodha, with juices extracted from its fruit and implements constructed of its limbs and trunk, embodies the qualities of ideal royalty. Through the Rājasūya, as we shall see, a symbolic homology is ritually transformed into sanctification.

The same Brāhmaṇa emphasizes the identical qualities of the Udumbara tree (*Ficus glomerata*), which was "born from strength and proper food," meaning by strength the power of the Kṣatriya (AB 35.6). Like the Aśvattha, the Udumbara is also related to death and the souls of the dead.[25] It represents the death gods, primarily Yama, Kāla, Dharma, Mrityu, and others.[26] But the Udumbara's fruit is also richer and juicier than that of all the other trees and the tree itself contains the essence of the others. The Devas defeated the Asuras with fire sticks (*daṇḍa*) made of Udumbara, the only tree that remained loyal to the gods during that primordial conflict.[27] The Udumbara also has its sexual and fecund associations. Like the Nyagrodha, it is closely connected with the Gandharvas either as the residence of these fecund and sexual beings, or as the embodiment of their fertilizing powers.[28] It is not surprising, then, that the Udumbara plays a central role in the anointing of a new king. It is used for the throne the king ascends, for the goblet containing the Nyagrodha fruit, and for the branch the new king carries as *daṇḍa* (AB 37.4–5). As he approaches the Udumbara branch, the king repeats the following formula (RV 9.1.1): "I find support in the sky and the earth; I find support in expiation and inspiration; I find support in day and night; I find support in food and drink; in the holy power [*brahman*] in the lordly power (*kṣatra*), in these three worlds I find support."[29] Having ritually incorporated the qualities of the cosmic trees, the king expresses the fundamental unity of a complex universe in which he also acts as a central nexus.

We shall shortly see how these various arboreal qualities are transformed through ritual into social and commercial functions within the diverse uses to which wood is put in its form as *daṇḍa.* It bears emphasizing here that the trunk of the tree is also called *daṇḍa* (along with other terms), which appears to be a reciprocal projection of wood instruments (*daṇḍa*) back onto the tree itself. The reciprocity emphasizes the functionality and transitionality of that part which connects the roots of the tree with its branches.

If the staff is necessarily related to tree symbolism because of the emphasis placed on its constituent material, it is surprising that it should be related to the lotus plant at all. But in fact, there is a clear semantic relation. The merely formal similarity between the lotus stalk and a *daṇḍa* stick is not sufficient to explain this when we consider that few other plant categories utilize this similarity in a semantic fashion. The literary contexts in which the metaphorical identification is made are not immediately revealing either: in one case, Bhavabhūti's *Mālatīmādhava*, the narrative describes the forlorn Mādhava wandering in a charming forest, then on the banks of a lotus lake. In his separation from the beloved Mālatī, Mādhava cannot appreciate such scenes of natural beauty as the wind-shaken broad-stemmed lotuses on the lake. Possibly, they remind him of his love. Such literary associations are rather common as paradigms of perfect beauty, and none are particularly revealing.[30] But the lotus plant and the sacred tree possess important homologous qualities. Consider Kālidāsa's *Kumārasambhava* in which Śiva's wedding with Pārvatī is described in great and sympathetic detail. After the ceremony, as Śiva and Pārvatī take their seat on a ritual altar, "the Goddess Lakshmi held on them a lotus umbrella having a large lotus stick [*naladaṇḍa*] which had the splendour of strings of pearls by means of multitudes of water-drops adhering to the extremeties of leaves"(KS 7.89).[31]

Here is a clear allusion to one of the best-known symbols in Hinduism, Lakṣmī (or Śrī) and the lotus.[32] The theme hardly bears repeating, primarily the significance of the goddess and plant as manifestations of auspiciousness and fecundity.[33] Two points may be emphasized for the time being: first, the lotus, like some trees, is related to the symbolism of fertility and organic life which rests on fecund and auspicious sources: and, second, the lotus is a symbol of the generation of new life (creation), or the manifestation of reality that proceeds from the primordial matrix of unmanifest potentiality.[34] In other words, the essential feature of the lotus symbol is its dynamism and transitional function between the two fundamental ontological categories. This theme bears directly on the implicit comparison of the Goddess and the "god" Daṇḍa, which will occupy the final section of our discussion. To summarize the salient features of the lotus-stalk theme and *daṇḍa*: the symbolic relationship between the two must exist at the same level in which *daṇḍa* serves as tree trunk and relates to the vegetative-cosmological symbolism of the trees. At this level, *daṇḍa* embodies the specific transitional potency that functions between the fundamental categories of the universe, namely, its created varied manifestation and its germinal, precreated potentiality. The trunk, obviously, represents a transition between the roots and the branches. It thus contains the characteristics of both, not in a static equilibrium of qualities and quantities, but in a dynamic transition from the potentiality of roots to the manifestation of branches, and *vice versa*. The same structure applies to the lotus but in relation to a somewhat different set of symbols. Every time an author such as Kālidāsa uses similar metaphors (or even ornamentation), he draws, unconsciously perhaps, on a common stock of symbolic relations from which the metaphors and their referents derive vividness and poignancy. Note that while the tree and the lotus represent alternative or complementary visions of creation, one terrestrial, the other aquatic, *daṇḍa*, as a symbol of dynamic transition and instrumentality in relation to fundamental ontlogical categories, is shared by both.

Daṇḍa *in Society*

Aside from the staff of the initiated twice-born, which as we have seen, embodies the nature and hierarchical status of the *varṇas*, numerous implements are designated by the term *daṇḍa*. This, finally, is the basis for including them in the symbolic taxonomy of the staff, rather than the fact that they consist of this or that material. Still, there is no question that each specific tool, and the entire group as well, receives its value from the symbolic structure of *daṇḍa*'s vegetative contexts. These consist of a variety of well-known symbolic systems including the axis mundi/cosmic tree complex, generative symbols, paradoxical symbols of mediation and transition, the symbols of textures-juices-fruit as essences and powers. Any commercial or political object that is both designated by the term *daṇḍa*, and constructed of a specific sacred wood participates in this broad symbolic system and makes it immanent within the social arena.

The *daṇḍa* staff is used in a variety of ways relating to the economic life of Indians. It is the shepherd's staff that acts as the pastoral equivalent of the royal scepter. This point is utilized to great advantage by no less a scholastic text than the medieval legal digest, the *Daṇḍa-viveka*, in its opening invocation to Kṛṣṇa: "He, who, though the best person in the Universe, having highly honoured His calling in His manifestation as Kṛṣṇa, protects, as a cowherd, the cows placed under His charge, by carrying a rod [*daṇḍa*] in His hand and having been desirous of various pleasures, binds the cows with requisite strings and makes them graze again in other worlds" (DV, "Invocation," vs. 8).[35] The metaphor of the shephard is sufficiently transparent, but note that the staff functions as an instrument of control precisely in pursuit of desirable ends, including eschatological ones.

Daṇḍa is also the common designation for the handles of various implements, such as the plow (*iṣa-daṇḍa*), and is usually constructed of Khadira wood.[36] It is also used in reference to the ship's mast (*kūpa-daṇḍa*), though the compound is somewhat redundant.[37] The axle of a wheel is also *daṇḍa* (*cakra akṣadaṇḍa*) and in the case of a sacrificial car at least, should be of Khadira wood (RV 3.53.19). It is interesting to observe what the Dharmaśāstra has to say about these economic activities. Manu prohibits agriculture among the higher castes because it causes injury (*hiṁsā*) to the creatures that inhabit the earth. Despite its economic excellence, the "wooden implement [*kāṣṭa*] with the iron tip" injures earth (*bhūmī*) herself and must be restricted (MS 10.83–84). The intrinsic ambivalence of the shephard's rod is magnified in the function of the hoe, to which Manu may be alluding. The ship's mast (*kūpa-daṇḍa*) represents a far more allusive notion, one that is closely related to that of the wheel axle. Briefly, both serve as the motivating center, the hub, of a vehicle that places Hindus in relation to non-Hindus. P. V. Kane's comprehensive analysis of seafaring (*samudra saṁyāna*) paradoxically highlights both the prohibition against the practice (*Baudhāyana Dharmasūtra* 1.1.22; MS 3.158) and its economic necessity, along with its expiatory efficacy for killing a Brahmin (*Parāśara Smṛti*).[38] Obviously, the ocean is not polluting, but *mlecchas* and foreigners are. The vehicles for conveying Aryans abroad make economic profit and military conquest possible, but also threaten the integrity of dharma. While the ship's mast and wheel axle may suggest additional, more obvious, symbolic insights, most dramatic here is the mediated tension posited in a dualistic (centripetal?) geography of *āryadeśa* and everywhere else. The correlation of space and dharma is significant in India's sacred geography and plays a critical role in the relationship between the king and his land. As we shall see in the mythology of Daṇḍa, the king possesses legitimacy only in relation to his land, and the symbolism of the staff will express the tension built into that relationship.

It may be interesting to recall here the use of the *daṇḍa* in the wedding rites, though it is hardly one of direct economic significance. For three nights after the young couple's wedding, an Udumbara *daṇḍa* is placed in bed between them. Meyer indicates that the staff represents the Gandharvas who symbolically consummate, or help consummate the marriage.[39] This function brings to mind, however indirectly, the use of the Udumbara *daṇḍa* in the Rājasūya where it is placed between the Kṣatriya who will be anointed as king and the Brahmin priest who will anoint him. Though not explicitly related to the Gandharvas, the Udumbara in the consecration also embodies powerful symbols of fecundity.[40]

But *daṇḍa* finds its most frequent lexical and practical use in the sphere of political life, primarily royalty. It is the flagstaff (*ketu-daṇḍa*) of military troops and royal lineages, the pillar (*staṁbha-daṇḍa*) on which military and administrative achievements are proclaimed. These are associated both with the essential qualities of a particular royal lineage, and with the violent confrontation between legitimate kingship and its enemies in warfare.[41] Daṇḍa is also the handle of umbrellas, royal (*chatra*) or merely practical (*ātapatram*): "with great possessions, troubles gather thick; Pain grows, not lessens, with a king's position, as when one's hand must hold the sunshade's stick [*daṇḍaṁ-iva-ātapatram*]" (*Śakuntalā* 5.6).[42] The royal umbrella has been discussed in connection with the lotus plant. If the military banners proclaim the political victory of dharmic legitimacy, the chatra-*daṇḍa* defines this legitimacy in terms of the king's mediating position between earth and the cosmic canopy.[43]

Above all other usages, *daṇḍa* is first and foremost the royal scepter. This is not meant to imply that the scepter incorporates specific agricultural, commercial, and military properties. But the polyvalence and semantic richness of the symbol impregnates the scepter with themes of fecundity, prosperity, and productivity, along with power, violence, and death. The scepter is symbolically efficacious because it produces a rush of associations derived from the numerous contexts of *daṇḍa*. In the political sphere *daṇḍa* is the very embodiment of polity, including its violent and judicial aspect.[44] As Kṛṣṇa proclaims in the *Gītā*: "I am the scepter [*daṇḍa*] of the rulers of men; and I am the wise policy [*nīti*] of those who seek victory" (BG 10.38). *Daṇḍa* is the great pacifier before whom all strife ceases.[45] It is thus a symbol of peace, a beneficent and benevolent force, which contains in its fiery energy the potentiality for everything that is good in the public sphere. To be more specific yet, *daṇḍa* is the very instrument of legal punishment. This, along with numerous values we have seen it acquire through its symbolic interconnections, renders the staff as the physical and spiritual embodiment of punishment: "Varuṇa is the lord of punishment [*iśo daṇḍasya*], for he holds the sceptre [*daṇḍa*] even over kings"(Manu 9.245).

Viṣṇu later inherits these same qualities from Varuṇa: "The royal staff [*daṇḍa*] which administers punishment to even the foremost of the Daityas and Dānavas; May that sceptre of the Lord of Punishment also mete out punishment to your enemies" (*Sodasayudhastotram* of Vedāntadeśika).[46] These elements gain greater specific efficacy when we consider that *daṇḍa* is the "rod of Yama," the lord of death.[47] Perhaps death itself is the great arbitrator of right and wrong, as well as the allocator of just rewards.

At the heart of this symbolism is the paradoxical nature of the rod as an instrument of peace, and yet pain and death incarnate. Just as Yama is the ambivalent god who is the lord of death, yet when he ruled there was neither old age or death, just so the staff is essentially ambivalent and brings its central paradox to bear in mythical narratives in which it acts as a character, human or divine.[48] Interestingly, Yama was made king of the righteous departed ancestors at the same time that Viṣṇu created Daṇḍa at the request of Brahmā.[49]

What can we say, in conclusion, that the staff as commercial and political instrument or concept has acquired from its ontological and teleological status in nature, and what has it, in turn, given the juridical instrument? Or in other terms, how do the various modalities of a single symbol crossinseminate each other? The broad range of contexts in which *daṇḍa* appears encompasses significant portions of the economic and political life. Daṇḍa gives these spheres of activity a coherence and unity by placing them within the framework of cosmological values. Daṇḍin, the sixth-seventh-century C.E. author of the *Daśakumāracarita*, who must have been fascinated with the possibilities inherent in his own name, put it better than any historian of religion could:

> May the staff-like foot [*aṅghridaṇḍa*] of Trivikrama (Viṣṇu) grant you eternal bliss!—the foot which is the pole of the umbrella [*chatradaṇḍa*] in the form of the Mundane egg, which is the long stalk of the lotus [*nala- daṇḍa*], the residence of Brahmā [*śatadhṛti-bhāvanam*], which is as it were the main-mast of the ship of the earth [*kṣoniṇau kūpadaṇḍa*], which serves as the flag-staff [*ketudaṇḍa*] of the bannerlike heavenly river gliding along the sky, which is the axle of the wheel [*cakra akṣadaṇḍa*] in the form of the revolving firmament of stars, which is (as it were) the pillar [*staṁbhadaṇḍa*] that proclaims his (Viṣṇu's) victory over the three worlds, and which is the very rod of Death [*kāladaṇḍa*] to the enemies of gods.(DKC I.1)[50]

Daṇḍa *in the Sacrifice*

Thus far we have looked at a variety of contexts in which *daṇḍa* plays significant conceptual and practical roles. These contexts reveal the essential features of the staff, primarily in its bearing upon royalty. It is appropriate then, that we proceed to look at the ritual significance of *daṇḍa* in the Vedic sacrifice in general, and in the establishment of kingship itself during the royal consecration in particular.

Daṇḍa sticks are employed in a variety of miscellaneous and some important roles in the sacrifice. The handle of the sacrificial ladle is called *daṇḍa* and is usually constructed of Khadira.[51] It is also the axle of the sacrificial car, as we have noted. None of this is extremely significant when handles and axles are commonly designated *daṇḍa*. The sacrificial function does not add new connotations to *daṇḍa*'s sense of instrumentality in commercial contexts. However, a number of additional instances of greater interest may be cited.

During the Vedic sacrifice (e.g., the Soma *yajña*), the sacrificer (*yajamāna*)—in the case recorded, a Kṣatriya householder—undergoes a series of initiatory rituals called *dīkṣā*. At that time the Adhvaryu priest "hands to him a staff [*daṇḍa*] for driving away the evil spirits—the staff being a thunderbolt. It is of Udumbara wood, for him to obtain food and strength,—the Udumbara means food and strength" (ŚB 3.2.1.32–33). Similarly, during the royal consecration sacrifice (Rājasūya), after the king has had the dice cast in his hand "they (the Adhvaryu and his assistants) then silently strike him with sticks [*daṇḍa*] on the back;—by beating him with sticks they guide him safely over judicial punishment [*daṇḍabadha*]: whence the king is exempt from punishment [*adaṇḍya*], because they guide him safely over judicial punishment" (ŚB 5.4.4.7).[52]

It is not too difficult to see what these two instances have in common. The Udumbara *daṇḍa* serves a dual function in keeping with its ambivalent nature. It is a weapon, an instrument of destruction for driving away evil. At the same time it embodies the Kṣatriya's very essence or positive characteristics: nourishment and power. The idea that the staff embodies the essential characteristics of its possessor, as we have seen, lies behind the allocation of staffs to the twice-born *varṇas*. The substance of the staff and the measure of its length are said to reflect the essential features of the *varṇas* and their relative hierarchy. Here the *daṇḍa* is an instrument of expiation, but not merely in the negative sense of removing guilt. It has a positive and lasting transforming efficacy, which is actuated by the ritual contact of *daṇḍa* and king. By being struck, the king becomes *adaṇḍya*—free of punishment, despite the intrinsic violence of his office. The ritual is not just a "preemptive" symbolic punishment that renders the king unpunishable; it ritually tansforms a potential king into the manifest embodiment of divine *daṇḍa*. By the ritual contact of *daṇḍa* and Kṣatriya, kingship itself is endowed with special sacral powers. Ritual touching forges a paradigmatic identity, just as it does when the sacrificer touches the *paśu* (sacrificial animal) in order to establish a symbolic identity before offering the beast to the gods. Kingship is thus permeated by the qualities of destruction and healing, punishment and nourishment, in a coexistence of complementary oppositions that may be articulated in many social contexts only through the symbolism of *daṇḍa*. Heesterman interprets the beating as a ritual that is closely related to fertility rites, rites of passage and rejuvenation, and others. The king sits on the throne, which is the "womb of royalty." His position emulates the (temporary) death of the sun and moon, reproducing a dark liminal period between death and rebirth. It is the beating by an Udumbara *daṇḍa* that conducts the king to a safe birth and allows his natural-generative powers to emerge.[53]

As kindling stick, the Udumbara *daṇḍa* places the sacrificer of the Rājasūya in the cosmological context that plays such an important role in Daṇḍa mythology, namely the battle of the Devas and Asuras. As he places the Udumbara stick in the Āhavanīya fire, the sacrificer praises it for its power and strength. He then takes three steps in a northeasterly direction addressing the stick as the orderer of the quarters, the conqueror of the northeast where the Devas finally defeated the Asuras (AB 37.5–6). The Udumbara stick is the Devas' might embodied in Daṇḍa, as we shall see. It is also the Kṣatriya's prowess in war, and by touching his chariot and praising it as Udumbara, he guarantees conquest of the regions (AB 37.6). The Rājasūya establishes here the paradigmatic identification of king and *daṇḍa*, just as in other aspects of the ritual he is identified with Indra, Varuṇa, or other deities. The result is stated in the *Manu Smṛti* and other texts which assert that the king is the embodiment of *daṇḍa* (MS 7.17). A legal historian would regard such a claim as essentially laudatory, whereas a phenomenologist would have to place it in a broader ritual context. For it is ritual that transforms the king into an actor in the cosmic battle (process) and his instrument, as well as sign of participation, is the staff.

Daṇḍa *in Mythology*

The foregoing sections have surveyed and analyzed an arbitrarily organized sequence of contexts from which *daṇḍa* takes its meanings. "Arbitrary" because the very polyvalence of prereflective symbols implies a simultaneous presence in consciousness.[54] Since symbolic intuitions, in this sense, can never be duplicated or mirrored in the hermeneutic process, the structure of presentation is invariably dictated by an analytic hierarchy. However, the methodological transition from the primary symbolism of the staff to its mythology is a significant one. It reveals what Paul Ricoeur describes as the transitional phase between primary symbols and *gnosis*, or speculation.[55] The immediate consciousness of experience is transformed within etiological and nonetiological myths into a "thickness of narrative," which gives reflection its first locus, without yet reducing the symbols to concepts. We shall now see what the symbolism of the staff suggests to the Indian mythmaker, or how the symbol "acts" as a mythical character. Among the numerous insights that such a procedure can yield, we shall focus on those relating to punishment.

The proper name Daṇḍa and its variant Daṇḍadhara are quite common in the Epic and Purāṇic literature. Among the most frequent references is the king of the Māgadhas (Daṇḍadhara), who is described as the incarnation of the Asura Krodhahantar, and also the king's brother Daṇḍa.[56] Several Pāṇḍava warriors are named Daṇḍadhara ("wielder of *daṇḍa*"), as is one son of Dhṛtaraśtra. Like Daṇḍa, the name is included among Śiva's and Viṣṇu's one thousand names.

But among these and other figures, three mythical characters named Daṇḍa stand out in the complexity and significance of their actions.[57] The first narrative, taken from the *Rāmāyaṇa*, is less known than the others but is the most prominent one in which Daṇḍa acts as a human figure. The following is a brief summary of the myth: Prince Daṇḍa was the last-born son of Ikṣvāku. He was so named because he was stupid, ignorant, and disobedient. His father assumed that eventually *daṇḍa* (punishment) would befall the prince so he gave him that name. Daṇḍa was granted the land between Vindhya and Śaivala Mountains, which no one else desired. As the new king, he built a beautiful city called Madhumatta and chose the Brahmin Śukra Deva as priest. Daṇḍa ruled his kingdom wisely and righteously for a very long time. One Chaitra day he wandered into the Bhārgava's forest hermitage, where he saw the guru's daughter Arajā.[58] Daṇḍa became instantly and overwhelmingly infatuated. Ignoring the girl's entreaties and warnings about Śukra's wrath, he raped her. Predictably, when Śukra discovered this, he became outraged, cursing Daṇḍa and promising, strangely, among other things: "That wicked man, who placed his hand in the lit sacrificial fire [*pradīpta-hutā*], so to speak, will obtain along with his relatives a great destruction."[59] Within seven nights Daṇḍa's entire domain, including his family and his army were completly destroyed in a cataclysmic rain of dust and ashes. All of this is designed to explain, in the *Rāmāyaṇa* narrative, the condition of the land between the Vindhyas and Śaivalas, also known as the Daṇḍaka Forest notorious in the *Rāmāyaṇa* as well as the *Mahābhārata* (*Rām.*, "Uttakra Khanda," 81–83).[60]

The myth clearly contains a number of structural oppositions such as king-Brahmin, last-born son–single daughter, city-forest, and others. These figure in the much-analyzed cycle of Bhārgava myths, to which I shall return. The structural logic of binary oppositions posits the dilemmas of power and authority, violence and justice, death and life, sex and marriage. However, the structure of the myth, which is static and immutable, is not our primary interest here. The meaning of the myth and, more specifically, the phenomenological significance of the *daṇḍa* symbol, can best be discerned chronologically and by means of the character's passage in space. The narrative contains a steady progression of action and counteraction where each counteract complements its precedent in a paradoxical fashion:

1. The one hundreth son of Ikṣvāku is wild and nasty; his father gives him the name of a god who upholds dharma.
2. Daṇḍa is given the land between Vindhya and Śaivala mountains—a peripheral, wild, and undesirable location; Daṇḍa builds a beautiful city, rules wisely, and selects a great sage as *purohita*.
3. The now righteous king Daṇḍa enters the guru's hermitage, a sacred space; there he rapes Arajā, the guru's daughter.
4. Śukra is a Brahmin and a renouncer, yet he destroys not only Daṇḍa, but also his entire family and country; in effect he commits genocide.

The first curious twist in the plot is depicted by the switch between the wicked son of Ikṣvāku and Daṇḍa the righteous king. How do we account for such a change? The myth supplies two "answers": the naming of Daṇḍa and the land he was given to rule—a remote area that Ikṣvāku gave him as a last resort. These elements of the story do not explain the transition but rather depict the necessary dialectical relation of dharma and *adharma*, which renders the existence of both possible and meaningful. It is understood (as Manu explains to Ikṣvāku earlier in the myth) that a good ruler is one who applies punishment (*daṇḍa*) justly and vigorously. This is precisely what king Daṇḍa does, having, through naming, become identified with *daṇḍa* (punishment).[61] Like his naming by Ikṣvāku, Daṇḍa acquires here a social persona that determines the dharmic quality of his conduct. But he can only act so after passage to a remote "un-dharmic" land where virtue must be absent. Like the Arūṅdhatī, which emerges from the destruction of the Khadira tree, the benevolence and righteousness of Daṇḍa can only emerge in a dialectical polarity with *adharma* and, as we shall see, cannot be separated from Daṇḍa's own *adharma*.

The myth is clearly related to the Bhārgava myth cycle, the best-known characters of which are Paraśurāma, Viśvāmitra, and Śukra. Śukra himself, here Daṇḍa's *purohita*, has a notorious history within this mythical corpus. As Robert Goldman notes, Śukra was not only the priest and advisor to the Asuras in their cosmic battle against the Devas, he even betrayed his own adharmic employers.[62] Like other Bhārgava sages, Śukra was known for his explosive temper and occasional lapses into gross violations of *varṇāśrama dharma*.[63] In short, Śukra hardly represents the perfect embodiment of dharma, nor an exact counterpart to King Daṇḍa's evil. He is closer to representing a liminal, nearly antiorthodox view of Brahminhood, which is capable of great displays of power, "kṣatric," and often destructive. His punishment of Daṇḍa is a grave exaggeration of Dharmaśāstric laws of rape and shows little but a genocidal rage.[64] In the present context he manifests, like Viśvāmitra and Paraśurāma before him, the very worst and most destructive passion of "dharmic indignation," Brahminhood gone berserk, or one-sided "punishment": a ferocious, dark, and red-eyed destroyer of worlds.[65]

In conclusion, the twists and turns of the plot are quite consistent when we take into consideration the ambivalence in the nature of the fundamental symbol (*daṇḍa*). The bipolar aspect of King Daṇḍa's personality is expressed dichotomously in shifting contexts, particularly in the shift from dharma to *adharma*, from sacred to profane, and from order to chaos. Similarly, Daṇḍa as actor exhibits many of the fundamental symbolic valencies that dominate various *daṇḍa* contexts: royalty, force, destruction, death, as well as beneficence, righteousness, and prosperity. Taken as a narrrative about *daṇḍa*, the concept of punishment, the myth dynamically expands these symbolic valencies. Punishment the actor, so to speak, is a wild child of archetypal royalty. It is transformed into a dharmic force through ritual (naming) and by being given a land that requires force. Once "punishment" transgresses its confines and infringes on the Brahmin's dharma, it recoils upon itself in cataclysmic proportions.

A suggestively similar, but diametrically opposed tale is told about a thief named Daṇḍa.[66] This walking embodiment of *adharma* onced bowed before a reclining Kṛṣṇa in a Vaiṣṇava temple, which he was about to rob. Before entering the temple, he had inadvertently leveled a hole in the ground while wiping his feet. On his way out with the goods on his back, Daṇḍa was spotted and chased by the villagers, then fatally bitten by a poisonous snake. As he faced Yama for judging, Daṇḍa's little dharmic act was reckoned in his favor and he was sent to the blissful world of Viṣṇu. Brahminical didactic moralization about the tale notwithstanding, the narrative is another pendulous journey between the polarities of dharma and *adharma* in which the protagonist is guided by his ambivalent nature ("Daṇḍa"), with an emphasis here on its positive potential. Punishment acts as an eschatologically rewarding agency in a narrative that emphasizes the power of trivial acts of dharma. Both myths accentuate the fundamentally ambivalent nature of *daṇḍa* in its social and juridical contexts. The following narratives elevate punishment to cosmic proportions by placing the character, now a god, in relation to the primordial sacrifices.

Dakṣa's infamous sacrifice, from which Śiva was excluded, is depicted with reference to *daṇḍa* (staff, punishment) in the sectarian version of the *Kūrma Purāṇa*, as indicated in the following brief summary. The complacent Dakṣa commenced the sacrifice, with the god Viṣṇu, savior of the suppliants, as his protector. Finding all the sages and deities hostile toward Rudra, the venerable sage Dadhaci again warned Dakṣa that by paying homage to the unadorable and not paying the same to the adorable, a man acquires a great sin—that terrible punishments (*daṇḍa*) ordained by fate (*devakṛta*) will undoubtedly fall upon him (KP 1.14.24–27).[67]

Such a terrible punishment takes place in the shape of Rudra who emerges out of Śiva's wrath: "The lord of gods, supreme maker, created all of a sudden [*sahasā*] Rudra with the intention of breaking up the sacrifice of Dakṣa . . . He possessed one thousand heads, a thousand feet, a thousand eyes, of great arms . . . resembling the fire of the end of an Age . . . with terrible teeth, hard to look at [*duṣprekṣyam*], wielder of the conch, discus and club, holding a staff [*daṇḍa*] etc." (KP 1.14.37–39).[68]

This common characterization of Rudra resembles the *Mahābhārata*'s depiction of the "god" Daṇḍa in some of its key features: "Chastisement is a great god. In form he looks like a blazing fire. His complexion is dark like that of the petals of the blue lotus. He is equipt [*sic*] with four teeth, has four arms and eight legs, and many eyes. His ears are pointed like shafts and his hair stands upright. He has matted locks and two tongues. His face has the hue of copper, and he is clad in a lion's skin. That irresistible deity assumes such a fierce shape" (Mbh. 12.121).[69] Manu also describes a similarly ferocious creature who comes to the defense of social and sacrificial order: "But where Punishment with a black hue and red eyes [*śyāma lohitākṣa*] stalks about, destroying sinners, there the subjects are not disturbed" (Manu 7.25). Daṇḍa as a destructive god is clearly related to the darker side of Śiva's personality inasmuch as the latter is literally dark (the night), treacherous, cruel, and lord of the great destruction of the Mahākāla.[70]

The monstrous figure depicted in these passages represents the wrath of Śiva or Viṣṇu. It is literally excited into existence when dharma is violated or when a competing claim for moral and cultic legitimacy generates righteous indignation. But the creature assumes its own quasi-autonomous existence and proceeds to wreak havoc. It does not restore moral balance, but totally annihilates the world, or else it completely abolishes alternative visions, like those embodied in Dakṣa and his cosacrificers.

In another instance, Daṇḍa in the form of *bhūta* ("being") emerges from the sacrifice itself rather than spontaneously from the god's rage. When the Dānava kings violated dharma by overstepping their proper boundaries, Brahmā asked Śiva for help in restoring dharma. After one thousand years Śiva performed a sacrifice out of which the *bhūta* arose. It was similar in color to a blue lotus, but had sharp tusks, was lean-waisted, strong, of disgusting appearance, and possessed great fiery energy (Mbh. 122.60).[71]

These various narratives are not inconsistent with each other inasmuch as Daṇḍa in the form of Rudra arises in response to an "adharmic" sacrifice, whereas Daṇḍa in the form of *bhūta* emerges out of a sacrifice that is undertaken in response to the Dānava's *adharma*. The sacrifice itself is both sufficiently violent and salutary to produce a Daṇḍa-like creature such as this *bhūta*. Daṇḍa enables the proper sacrifice to proceed, and since the sacrifice is cosmogonic, it enables creation to proceed. In the Dharmaśāstras too, *daṇḍa* is important, first and foremost because it ensures the proper performance of the sacrifice.[72]

Conversely, when the anger of the god dissipates, Daṇḍa disappears and the sacrifice cannot proceed: Brahmā, the grandfather of all the worlds, wanted to perform a sacrifice but could not find a worthy priest. For a number of years he carried a fetus in his head. After one thousand years, when Brahmā sneezed, it fell out. This was Kṣupa who became a Prajāpati and Brahmā's sacrificial priest. However, due to Brahmā's happiness punishment (*daṇḍa*) disappeared, causing great confusion and violation of rules for proper conduct. The world then sank into a Kāliyuga-like chaos. Brahmā appealed to Viṣṇu for help and the latter (or Śiva?) emitted punishment (*daṇḍa*) out of his own nature. Out of his form as punishment, the god created the goddess Sarasvatī, who is the science of proper conduct (*daṇḍanīti*) (Mbh. 12.122.14–25).[73]

In all of these passages the sacrifice is not only a concrete and clearly circumscribed ritual. It involves both cosmogonic and sociogonic processes paradigmatically depicted in the intentions of Brahmā and Dakṣa. The latter narrative is particularly revealing because at the very moment when dharma seems to rule perfectly, when Brahmā's joy peaks because Kṣupa emerges as a Prajāpati priest, at the same moment Daṇḍa disappears and the sacrifice cannot be conducted. In short, social and cosmic order evaporate. The very act of creation entails chaos. The establishment of formal order, represented by the Brahminical priesthood, acts in opposition to the creative-destructive (kṣatric) energy, so Daṇḍa disappears. The restoration of Daṇḍa and progression of creation-sacrifice can only resume after the world falls into anarchy. The constant imbalance is built into the system, so to speak. It is essential to the dynamic quality of life as it is lived and experienced. This point is driven home in the following passage: "In the Kṛtayuga there was no king, kingdom, punishment [*daṇḍa*] or enforcer of punishment, but all creatures protected each other through dharma. After some time these people became lax due to delusion and no longer acted in accord with dharma. . . . The gods, becoming afraid, went to Brahmā and related all that had happened, saying that the distinction between themselves and mortals had been lost. Furthermore, no sacrifices were being performed, so they were not being fed" (Mbh. 12.59.1–15).[74]

The familiar, felicitous vision of the Kṛtayuga's perfect dharma is simply incomplete as far as the conceivers of Daṇḍa are concerned. Dharma is neither self-perpetuating nor ontologically whole outside of a dynamic and dialectical polarity with *adharma*. Order and chaos are entirely codependent as are unmanifest cosmic potentiality and the manifest plurality of existing beings. Daṇḍa functions as the condition for establishing, not so much an equilibrium between order and chaos, as the fluctuation of their dynamic interplay, in which one must always gain a temporary upper hand over the other in order for the empirical world to exist. In the absence of chaos or pure energy, Daṇḍa disappears from the world and the world's essential Form (the sacrifice) becomes petrified. In the absence of dharma, Daṇḍa acts as a ferocious, dark, drunken, and genocidal creature whose pure rage exhibits nothing less than the very antithesis of dharma, yet is the paradoxical condition for its restoration. The ambivalence of Daṇḍa, exhibited in its basic forms in the vegetative symbolism of the staff, places it at the very hub of the cosmic wheel. It is the instrumental nexus of a world process that does not proceed spontaneously through a static equilibrium of elements but requires the intervention of a specific agency—*daṇḍa*—in the form of kings, priests, or gods. At the root of this cosmic tragedy is a profound sense of the loss of an original plentitude, and a pervasive experience of the intrinsic "fallenness" of the experienced world.[75]

The fundamental sign, the staff, is a privileged indicator both of the original condition aimed at by man, and the incontrovertible knowledge of its loss as a lasting condition. As the symbol is taken from its natural context, where it indicates a dynamic transition between natural categories, it is placed in the new context of mythical time. The mythical narrative replaces the dynamism of the trunk or lotus stalk with the pendulum-like swing of events. Thus, the myth can be diagramed as the transition from original plenitude (Ikṣvāku) to crisis (his youngest son) to restoration (the Vindhya kingdom) to crisis (rape) to final "restoration" (annihilation of Daṇḍa's kingdom and the establishment of the Daṇḍaka forest). The meaning of the myth resides not in the logic of its numerous binary oppositions, but in the dramatic progression of its plot, in the dynamics of crisis and resolution played out with the symbol as personified protagonist. The drama concretizes the symbol-sign within the "fallen" state of man. Hence, it both consecrates particular social circumstances in which the sign becomes manifest and, at the same time, it places the experience of "fallenness" in relation to the wholeness to which all social relations aspire. The experience of the symbolic promise of the staff becomes fulfilled (partially and periodically) in the form of the consecrated efficacy of punishment. The staff becomes punishment and punishment becomes sanctified in myth and ritual. These cosmological observations are not merely abstract theories about the state of the universe. The Dharmaśāstras base their notion of punishment on these dynamic cosmic processes: "men who have committed crimes and have been punished by the king, go to heaven"(MS 8.318); "the gods, the Dānavas . . . the bird and snake deities give the enjoyment due from them only if they are tormented by fear of punishment" (MS 7.23). Because punishment makes Brahminical society and sacrifices possible, it bears powerful cosmic and eschatological consequences.

Daṇḍa *and the Goddess*

The key features of Daṇḍa's mythological personality and function seem to crystallize most clearly at their point of intersection with those of the ferocious goddess—Durgā or Kālī. I should state now that of the numerous shared characteristics I shall only discuss a few prominent ones.

Daṇḍa, as son of Ikṣvāku, is given a region near the Vindhya mountains for his kingdom. None of his brothers seem to merit such an undesirable location. Durgā too is known as Vindhyavāsinī, "she who resides in the Vindhya Mountains."[76] Both then reside in a remote, non-Aryan, and uncivilized region on the edge of the lands of dharma. Appropriately, both exhibit highly un-Aryan traits, beginning with their physical features, which render them, if not identical, at least compatriots. The primary common features, aside from the general ferocity and repulsiveness of demeanor, are the black complexion and red-eyes. Kālī certainly, who is Durgā's emanated passion, is essentially dark or black. Daṇḍa too, in the passages cited earlier, is described as black. The allusion to an indigenous tribal people seems rather clear, and the non-Brahminical negative connotations inescapable. In the case of both Kālī and Durgā, the red eyes are associated with either alchoholic inebriation or with the blood intoxication resulting from human blood offerings.[77] Daṇḍa's red eyes are never explained, but his fearsome tusks cannot be for any other purpose than the consumption of meat and human blood, which would account for his bloodshot eyes. And, of course, Śukra playing the role of Daṇḍa is known for his fondness for intoxicating drink.

The symbolism of the black and red colors is familiar and obviously poignant but cannot occupy much of our space.[78] Clearly, the relation of certain gods to sensory representations such as colors, fragrances, and even textures evokes an important set of phenomenological insights and ideas that extend beyond mere verticality. The lotus plant, for instance, serves as a symbol that is overflowing with sensory associations. Both Daṇḍa's and the goddess's colors are often depicted as identical with that of the lotus plant. [79] There is much more here than intellectual analogy. It is not just that the goddess (Lakṣmī) is identified with the plant when it represents this or that organic-creative principle. It is also Divinity, which is at once fragrant, tranquil, colorful, and seductive, and, at the same time, dark, foul-smelling, ferocious, and repulsive. The symbol operates at a variety of epistemological levels at once, but none are more powerful than the sensory.

At one of these levels the origins of Kālī and Daṇḍa are described in psychological terms as passion itself. Kālī springs from Durgā's forehead as the latter becomes enraged by the appearance of the demons Caṇḍa and Muṇḍa.[80] In a similar manner, Daṇḍa comes into existence as the embodied wrath of a god, be it Viṣṇu or Śiva.[81] When the god Brahmā is joyful Daṇḍa disappears.

At another, more theoretical, level of convergence between Daṇḍa and Kālī, both are depicted as important catalysts in the cyclical transition of cosmic time and dharma. Time in general is "black" because of its irrationality and mercilessness. The present age particularly, which is indicated by word play as black: the Kāliyuga ("age of darkness") is identified with the great Goddess. Kālī is not coincidentally dark and is the personification of Time itself, the sovereign of destinies and the destruction of time.[82]

Like Kālī, Daṇḍa acts as a catalyst in the transition between the cosmic ages (*yugas*). The disappearance of the sacrifice and erosion of dharma at the end of each *yuga*, including the "golden" Kṛtayuga, provoke his birth. As Daṇḍa goes on his rampage on behalf of dharma, he proceeds to destroy everything in his path in a fiery cataclysmic rage. For this reason, though both Daṇḍa and Kālī are dark, they are also described as possessing a fiery complexion.[83] The fire in Daṇḍa's complexion, as the *Kūrma Purāṇa* puts it, is the "fire of the end of the age." The destruction he brings may not be *pralaya* (end of the cosmic cycle), but it is clearly of cosmic proportions, like Kālī's rampage against the Asuras.[84] Consequently it ushers in the (temporary) reestablishment of dharma's supremacy, followed again by the disappearance of Daṇḍa, in order to recommence the cycle.

It is impossible to give a precise historical accounting of the "god" Daṇḍa. Since in many major ways he is virtually identical with Kālī (and to some extent Durgā), it is not altogether unlikely that the "mythology" and function of Daṇḍa represent a transposition of the ferocious goddess's theology into a more limited juridical context. Like the specific bogeyman calculated by parents to scare their children, Kālī serves as a perfect model for the terrors of a violated law. However, there is clearly more than mere transposition and transsexualization at work here. The symbolic network in which Daṇḍa serves as an important nexus is also related, in many important ways, to the vegetative, procreative, auspicious, and beneficent symbolism of goddesses such as Lakṣmī. Phenomenolgically, the similarities between Daṇḍa and goddesses makes sense because both play related, though not indentical, roles in the symbolic structure of Hinduism. While the Goddess, regardless of her historic origins, represents a primary ontological principle, coexistent and coequal with the principle represented by gods, Daṇḍa has no such independent existence.[85] He symbolizes a more instrumental energy, one that owes its existence to the primary cosmic principles, and plays a role only in the mediation of the dynamic interplay between the others. On the social level, it is interesting to note that punishment embodies these *pralaya*-like qualities, for it is capable of destroying the whole world (MS 7.19). In the opening verses of the *Matsya Purāṇa*, the end of the *mahāyuga* is proclaimed after a king—not a Brahmin—shows himself capable of protecting the weak from the "laws of the fish" (*matsyanyāya*), India's "laws of the jungle." This is precisely the condition that punishment is designed to prevent (MS 7.20), and yet king Manu's qualifications as protector indicate the coming destruction. Punishment is a condition for the progression of the world through destruction and reconstitution alike.

The question one may still ask about Daṇḍa, but not about Kālī, is why the ferocious and liminal physical appearance. If Daṇḍa is a mediating force between two fundamental principles, should he not be characterized in a more ambivalent physical form? The foregoing sections should have demonstrated that Daṇḍa is far more ambivalent than his revolting depiction in the *Mahābhārata* would have us believe. His monstrous appearance is only one side of a persona, chosen by the Dharmaśāstric and epic authors to demonstrate the destructive and punitive powers he embodies. But as the *Rāmāyaṇa* story and the vegetative symbols indicate, Daṇḍa can be a positive, beneficent, and even auspicious presence, as when prince Daṇḍa is given a wild land to rule, or when out of Viṣṇu's form as Daṇḍa emerged the auspicious goddess Sarasvatī who reigns over *daṇḍanīti*.[86]

In sum, Daṇḍa is the symbol for the instrumental role of chaos and violence in the world: both in the body politic and in the cosmos as a whole. Unlike Kālī's, his is not pure, independent, and primordial violence, but the instrumental force that makes farming, ruling, sacrificing, and even marriage efficacious. Life in its dynamic aspect requires various forms of mediating action in order to proceed; the same energy that acts violently and ferociously in order to actuate certain ends may be auspicious and quite sublime in pursuit of other ends. The symbol itself retains the polyvalence of such functional meanings simultaneously.

Conclusion

The phenomenological hermeneutic of *daṇḍa* symbolism offers more than a simple taxonomy of yet additional mythological material. It potentially extends the scope of religious phenomena, and the methods for their investigation, into the field of legal history. Thus, while phenomenology can never claim to demonstrate a fundamental unity of Indian culture without a serious entrapment in tautological thinking, it can expand our understanding of all interrelated aspects of culture.

It has always been easy to note our basic ambiguity in reference to punishment: it is bad because it hurts, good because it prevents us from being naughty again. But this is saying the same thing in two different ways, and we can not avoid concluding that punishment is good because it is bad. Far more interesting is the observation that legal punishment (in India) possesses positive cosmic virtues: it sends criminals to heaven, brings down the rain, and keeps Gandharvas and Rākṣasas off our backs.[87] The legal historian, as well as the Hindu jurist, may regard these as fanciful embellishments with no bearing on the law. But they are not improvised. They are serious indications, signs if you will, of the way in which juridical culture is grounded in a world view that is thoroughly and profoundly penetrated by the fundamental ambiguities of life. In such a context the staff serves as a symbol for the instrumental efficacy of political institutions in the cosmic process as a whole.

Notes

1. Van Gennep, p. 16, n. 1.

2. *Hermes the Thief* (Breat Barrington, Mass.: Lindisfarne, 1990), p. 41; cf. the Hindu god Skanda discussed in the previous chapter on thieves.

3. Ibid., p. 16; again, the Gandharva Viśvāvasu shares this ambiguity being both a guardian-protector, as well as a thief.

4. And just as important, a temporal symbol because, like stepping into a river again, one can never return to the exact place of departure before the boundary was crossed. See the section on *daṇḍa* and Kālī.

5. Throughout this chapter the italicized masculine or neuter *daṇḍa* will be used in reference to the concrete object (e.g., staff) or abstract concept (punishment). The capitalized Daṇḍa will be employed to designate the mythical character, human or divine, who bears the name.

6. See Monier-Williams, *Sanskrit-English Dictionary* (Delhi: Motilal Banarsidass, 1990).

7. To list but a few such works: John W. Spellman, *Political Theory of Ancient India* (Oxford: Oxford University, Press, 1964); Terrence Day, *The Conception of Punishment in Early Indian Literature* (Waterloo, Canada: Wilfrid Laurier University Press, 1982); J. D. M. Derrett, *Essays in Classical and Modern Hindu Law* (Leiden: E. J. Brill, 1976); Robert Lingat, *The Classical Law of India* (Berkeley: University of California Press, 1973). A more elaborate discussion of the Indian royal staff can be found in Jan Gonda's *Ancient Indian Kingship from the Religious Point of View* (Leiden: E. J. Brill, 1966), pp. 22–23. Gonda understands the scepter as the sign for the "alliance between the conception of sacredness in 'primitive' thought and that of authority."

8. Cf. Mbh. 12.15.8.

9. Thomas Coburn, "Consort of None, Śakti of All: The Vision of the Devī-māhātmya," in John Stratton Hawley and Donna Marie Wulff, eds., *The Divine Consort* (Boston: Beacon Press, 1982), p. 160.

10. Derrett, *Essays*, 1:80–85; Day, *The Conception of Punishment*, p. 61.

11. For a discussion of the method, see Douglas Allen, *Structure and Creativity in Religion* (The Hague: Mouton, 1978), p. 192.

12. The unity lent to a variety of contexts by the common use of a word like *daṇḍa* is based on the semantic predominance that the word's cumulative meaning exercises over its shifting frames of reference. For greater detail see P. Ricoeur "Structure, Word, Event," in D. Ihde, ed., *The Conflict of Inter-*

pretations: Essays in Hermeneutics (Evanston: Northwestern University Press, 1974) pp. 93–94, and, T. K. Seung, *Structuralism and Hermeneutics* (New York: Columbia University Press, 1982), p. 50.

13. *Āśvalāyana Gṛhyasūtra* 1.19.13.

14. *Manu Smṛti* 2.45.

15. ŚB 3.4.4.9.

16. J. Eggeling, *The Śatapatha Brāhmaṇa*, Sacred Books of the East, vol. 44 (Oxford: Clarendon Press, 1900), p. 374.

17. Cf. *Ṛgveda* 3.53.19.

18. Cf. J. Heesterman, *The Inner Conflict of Tradition* (Chicago: University of Chicago Press, 1985), pp. 81–94.

19. *Atharvaveda* 3.6.1; cf. also 5.5.5, 8.8.3.

20. The tree is identified with its worshipers in popular rituals that enact the "marriage" of the tree with the Banyan. Cf. Sarkar Sen Gupta, ed., *Tree Symbol Worship in India* (Calcutta: Indian Publications, 1965), pp. 30, 142. The term Pippala is closely associated also with sensual pleasure and matrimonial felicity. Cf. Wendy D. O'Flaherty, *Women, Androgynes, and Other Mythical Beasts* (Chicago: University of Chicago Press, 1980), p. 229.

21. Cf. also RV I.24.7.

22. M. Eliade, *Patterns in Comparative Religion* (New York: Meridian, 1963), p. 274.

23. AB 35.5.

24. B. Keith, trans., *Rig-veda Brahmanas* (Cambridge, Mass.: Harvard University Press, Harvard Oriental Series, vol. 25, 1920), pp. 315–16.

25. J. J. Meyer, *Trilogie altindischer Machte und Feste der Vegetation* (Zurich: Max Niehaus Verlag, 1937), 1:99.

26. Ibid., 2:40–41.

27. ŚB VI.6.3.2–3; TS V.7.2–3.

28. TS III.4.8; Meyer, *Trilogie*, 3:192.

29. Cf. Keith, *Rig-Veda Brahmanas*, p. 325.

30. Cf. Daṇḍin's *Daśakumāracarita*, I.1.

31. H. H. Wilson, trans., *Kumara Sambhavam* (Varanasi: Indological Book House, 1966), p. 92.

32. The umbrella as a symbol of royalty is equally familiar, of course. The umbrella's canopy manifests the cosmic significance of the heavens, a shield against excessive heat, and so forth. Cf. Gonda, *Ancient Indian Kingship*, chapter 8.

33. For recent works, cf. Vasudha Narayanan, "The Goddess Śrī: Blossoming Lotus and Breast Jewel of Viṣṇu," in Hawley and Wulff, *The Divine Consort*, pp. 224–37; David Kinsley, *Hindu Goddesses, Visions of the Divine Feminine in the Hindu Religious Tradition* (Berkeley: University of California Press, 1986). 34. Cf. Kinsley, *Hindu Godesses*, p. 21; Eliade, *Patterns*, pp. 190, 281.

35. Bhavatosh Bhattacharya, trans., *Dandaviveka of Vardhamana Upadhyaya* (Calcutta: Asiatic Society, 1973), p. 30.

36. *Śiśupālavadha* 18.43.

37. *Daśakumāracarita* I.1.

38. *History of Dharmaśāstra*, vol. 3 (Pune: BORI, 1973), pp. 933–38.

39. Meyer, *Tilogie*, 3:192.

40. Cf. AB 37.3; Gonda, *Ancient Indian Kingship*, pp. 84–85.

41. The *Kauṭilya Arthaśāstra* (10.6.3–22) designates the most important formation of a fighting force as the "staff array" (*vṛtti-daṇḍa*).

42. Arthur W. Ryder, trans., *Kalidasa: Translations of Shakuntala and Other Works* (London: J. M. Dent & Sons, 1928), p. 52; Monier-Williams, ed., *Śakuntalā* (Varanasi: Chowkhamba Sanskrit Series, 1961), p. 189 (5.108).

43. J. Gonda, *Ancient Indian Kinghip*, chapter 8.

44. As is well known, *daṇḍa* is one of Rudra's and Kālī's many weapons in their various battles.

45. *Śakuntalā*, 5.8.

46. W. E. Begley, *Viṣṇu's Flaming Wheel: The Iconography of the Sudarśana-Cakra* (New York: New York University Press, 1973), p. 31.

47. *Mālatīmādhava* 5.31; cf. O. von Bohtlingk, *Sanskrit Worterbuch* (Leipzig: Marker, 1923–25), "*daṇḍa*"

48. The positive side of Yama emerges in his instruction to Gautama (Mbh. 12.127), in the Naciketas episode (Mbh. 13.71), and other texts. See also Eliade, *Patterns*, p. 256.

49. Mbh. 12.92.38.

50. M. R. Kale, trans., *The Dasakumaracarita of Dandin* (Delhi: Motilal Banarsidass, 1966), p. 1.

51. AB 7.5; ŚB 7.4.1.36.

52. On the dice, cf. K. de Vreese, "The Game of Dice in Ancient India," in Oosters, *Orientalia Neerlandica: A Volume of Oriental Studies* (Leiden: Sijthoff, 1948), pp. 349–62. According to J. C. Heesterman, the game of dice symbolizes Varuṇa's establishment of cosmic order following the cardinal directions of a previously discontinuous universe. Cf. *The Ancient Indian Royal Consecration* (The Hague: Mouton, 1957), p. 151.

53. Heesterman, *The Ancient Indian*, pp. 156–157.

54. M. Eliade, *The Two and the One* (Chicago: University of Chicago Press, 1979), p. 203.

55. *The Symbolism of Evil* (Boston: Beacon Press, 1969), pp. 9, 18.

56. Mbh. 1.61.45.

57. The thief Daṇḍa from the *Padma Purāṇa* will only be briefly mentioned.

58. The name literally means maiden, the generic nature of which, as Edward W. Hopkins suggests, may indicate that the character is not altogether inconsistent with Devayanī, said to be Śukra's only daughter (Mbh. 1.76–83). Cf. *Epic Mythology* (Strassburg: Trübner, 1915), p. 179.

59. The *iva* in the text indicates a conscious metaphor likening the crime of rape to a disturbance of the sacrificial fire.

60. V. B. Shastri, ed., *Rāmāyaṇa of Vālmīki* D.A.V. Sanskrit Series, no. 20 (Lahore: D.A.V. Sanskrit Series, 1947). The Mbh. (3.197) mentions the Daṇḍaka Forest (also the Pine Forest) as the place where another Brahmin's (Kuśika) fire is still burning though his murderous rage was calmed by the intense domestic devotion and wisdom of a householder's wife. Could this pacification be due to Kuśika's Kṣatric origins?

61. The name given to any child, particularly a prince, is indicative of, and identical with, his or her essential nature. The name also unlocks the secrets of an individual's destiny, which is so closely tied to character. Cf. AV 3.13.1ff.; ŚB 7.1.2.23; 8.6.1.5ff.; Jan Gonda, *Notes on Names and the Name of God in*

Ancient India (Amsterdam: North Holand, 1970), p. 7; Ernst Cassirer, *An Essay on Man* (New Haven: Yale University Press, 1944), p. 88.

62. Robert Goldman, *Gods, Priests and Warriors: The Bhṛgus of the Mahābhārata* (New York: Columbia University Press, 1977), pp. 124–28.

63. Cf. *Matsya Purāṇa* 47.113–27; 170–213.

64. Cf. Manu 8.364.

65. Śukra is known for his fondness for liquor, a major lapse for a Brahmin and a practice related to the redness of his eyes (Mbh. 1.71.52; Goldman, *Gods*, p. 33). As we shall see, Durgā too shares the very same characteristics to similar effects (*Devī-Māhātmya* 3.33).

66. *Padma Purāṇa*, chap. 1

67. Cf. Sri Ahibhushan Bhattacharya, trans., *The Kurma Purana* (Varanasi: All Indian Kashi Raj Trust, 1972) pp. 100–101.

68. *Sahasā* means "violently," not just "suddenly"; for similar description of Asi, cf. Greg Bailey, *The Mythology of Brahmā* (New Delhi: Oxford, 1983), p. 190.

69. Pratap Chandra Roy, trans., *The* Mahabharata (Delhi: Munshiram Manoharlal, 1975), pp. 261–62.

70. Sukumari Bhattacharji, *The Indian Theogony* (Cambridge: Cambridge University Press, 1978), pp. 138–39. 71. Ibid., p. 190; cf. also *Bhāgavata Purāṇa*, 10.66.1–42.

72. Cf. Manu 7.20–21.

73. Greg Bailey, *The Mythology of Brahma*, pp. 187–88.

74. Ibid., pp. 171–72.

75. Cf. Paul Ricoeur, *The Symbolism of Evil*, pp. 161–74.

76. Kinsley, *Hindu Goddesses*, p. 99. Bhattacharji, *The Indian Theogony*, pp. 165–68.

77. *Devī-Māhātmya* 3.33; 13.8.

78. For the moral significance of the color black, to cite one source, see Wendy D. O'Flaherty, *The Origins of Evil in Hindu Mythology* (Berkeley: University of California Press, 1976), pp. 322–25.

79. Cf. Mbh. 12.121; 122.60.

80. *Devī-Māhātmya* 7.3–22.

81. Cf. Mbh. 12.122.14–25; KP 1.14.37–39.

82. Cf. Wendell C. Beane, *Myth, Cult, and Symbols in Sakta Hinduism* (Leiden: E. J. Brill, 1977), chap. 3, particularly his discussion of M. Eliade's *Images and Symbols*, trans. by Philip Mairet (London: Harvill Press, 1961), pp. 64–65.

83. Mbh. 12.121, 12.122.60; KP 1.14.38.

84. Cf. Mbh. 12.70.6–18.

85. C. Mackenzie Brown, "The Theology of Rādhā in the Purāṇas," in Hawley and Wulff, *Divine Consort*, pp. 65–69. In his Purāṇic geneology, Daṇḍa is described as the son of Dharma and Kriyā (Dakṣa's daughter), and he clearly embodies the static morality of the former along with the fiery energy of the latter. Cf. *Viṣṇu Purāṇa*, 7.5.

86. Mbh. 12.122.25.

87. Cf. *Manu Smṛti* 7.23; 8.318.

Conclusion
Back to the Body

Bruce Lincoln has had the final word on conclusions: readers who require a brief summary of the book may read the introduction again; further thoughts, ideas, and themes will be developed in the next book. In the next few pages, then, I shall neither summarize nor offer new thoughts on the numerous issues raised by the *Sense of Adharma.* Instead I will sharpen the basic question the book seeks to answer. Briefly and even crudely, I shall reask the two questions of the body: Why have we chosen the body as our focus, and how can an abstract and conceptual cultural datum like dharma (and *adharma*) be perceived, and also serve as the object of a somatic hermeneutic?

Many of the contradictions and paradoxes attributed by scholars to Hinduism, particularly in reference to dharma and *adharma*, have suggested an agenda of reconciliation, or encompassment. The apparent contradiction between the ideological norms of dharma and the contingent complexity of pragmatic action, is a prominent example. The issue rests on a longstanding methodological dualism that differentiates between ideology and economics or economic facts. Culturalists, who refuse to reduce the former to the latter, have sought emic intellectual insights for bridging this gap in order to avoid such designs as "encompassment," not to speak of functional reductions.

The phenomenological agenda, pursued as far as possible in this book, focuses on the content of perceptual experiences as the elementary "building material" of the imagination that encorporates both dharma and contingent reality in a meaningful totality. The embodied imagination, in simple terms, makes sense of dharma and *adharma* as part of an existential unity. The only method for investigating such an imagination, namely phenomenology, uses images in space and time as its raw material, but can then proceed to the loftiest conceptions of Hindu nor mative life.

In a recent review article for the *History of Religions*, Lawrence Sullivan raised an issue, which is only now beginning to occupy the minds of historians of religion, namely: "How will we come to know, in a discursive, conceptual way the knowledge of the body?"[1] Since Sullivan was addressing colleagues in the field of religion, the question clearly did not concern neurophysiological epistemology but the role of the body in transmitting cultural knowledge. This is both a profoundly important and equally daunting question. Moreover, it must not be confused with another question—that of embodiment, which still reigns supreme in the somatic agenda of culturalists. The second question, in a simplified form, runs as follows: how do cultural conceptions of the body symbolize (or "embody") knowledge of the world and of society? This question rests on the semiological assumption that the body acts as a metaphor for abstract ideas and relations: it is the body in the mind.

In the course of his review of several works on the body within diverse cultures, the boundary line between the two distinct questions became increasingly blurred. For instance, Sullivan noted that Lopez Austin has demonstrated that "ideas about the body are the surest way to understand Aztec conceptions of the universe, the state, language." The body, in other words, is a concrete semiotic tool used by the "mind" to articulate abstract intellectual conceptions. This, to repeat, is the body in the mind, not the same body whose knowledge Sullivan sought in his opening appeal. At this point of time in the fields of religion, no one would wish to claim that the physical body creates or directly (sensorily) transmits the experience of the interrelatedness of social and cosmological systems. Puruṣa's body in the famous *Ṛg-veda* hymn signifies in a homological fashion the relation of castes; it would seem absurd to take it as a paradigmatic body that perceives the *varṇa* system and the natural world by means of the mouth, arms, stomach, and so forth.

So, the original question—what is the knowledge of (more exactly by) the body?—has still not been systematically addressed in the increasingly rich literature on religion and embodiment. There is a very good reason for this lacuna because, as Sullivan noted, such an agenda would take us into the fields of neurophysiology, the sciences of cognition and communication, the phenomenology of sense perception, and others. How, short of such a scientific approach, does any given culture, and how can the researcher, articulate in nonquantitative terms the language of the body?

The very fact that the question has been posed reveals just how deeply the Cartesian dualism has penetrated our common modes of thinking, and how distorting such thinking is even of our own experiences. For it is obvious that the "body" participates in constant nonverbal communication with its environment without attendent self-reflection or cognitive awareness.[2] Examples are commonplace: the driver who suddenly snaps to attention realizing that ten minutes just went by in engrossing conversation, and that he has no recollection of anything that took place on the road. Or consider the studies discussed in chapter 2 on nonverbal rhythmic communication among families and individuals.[3] Such studies explicitly cast doubt on the practical validity of our intellectual (or ideological) commitment to the autonomous "self" freely and consciously interacting in a semiotic fashion with other selves.

As long as we frame the issue of embodiment in terms of the knowledge of the mind as opposed to the knowledge by the body, we shall remain trapped within the parameters of the problem we are trying to solve. But in a sense we are compelled to put the question in these terms. Just as life in the modern city, with its angular streets and buildings, actually shapes one's ability to perceive objects in open spaces, the ideological conditioning of Cartesian dualism limits our ability to project our awareness in certain directions. Still, it should not be too difficult to show that even in our modern urban world the mind does exist in the body as much as the body in the mind. Consider the example of the blind person who uses a cane in order to navigate a complex physical environment. Common sense tells us that this person "feels" the cane tip on different surfaces, transmitting different reverberations onto the hand. In her mind, we continue to assume, these physical behaviors of the cane are interpreted (verbally, of course): "here is a wall, now a lamp post, the curb, watch out for the steps!" But of course, this is not the case at all. Just as we are not conscious of the entire process of perception (in Merleau-Ponty's terms we do not perceive perception), neither are the blind. The cane becomes a phenomenal extension of the body-self and its physical behavior is isomorphic to the hand that holds it. The cane, in other words, is invisible or transparent, and is not a part of the "objective" world the blind person perceives.[4] Of course, the same applies to everyone in relation to various objects within their immediate environment. The glasses, even sunglasses, that you wear and at first perceive as a screen between yourself and the world gradually merge with the process of perception and disappear.

These examples can be broadened to show how a widening physical environment can become perceptually transparent to the experiencing subject. There are numerous explanations for this phenomenon, from Gibson's neurophenomenology to Merleau-Ponty's less scientific but equally valid observation that perception tends to blurr the separation between subject and world. We do learn then that the answer to Sullivan's question must begin with a reformulation of the question itself. It would now read: what are the contours of the mental-physical landscape that extends from the perceiving subject to the natural and cultural environment and back? We are now in the realm of phenomenology, where metaphysical or ontological distinctions are suspended (bracketed) in order to map out the geography of a "Mind" in its "World." Such a phenomenology leads us toward an ecological approach, because mind, in traditional societies at least, is the product of a resonant phenomenal participation in the natural processes of the world.[5]

If we take seriously the proposition that the self and the environment are two phenomenal aspects of a shared ecology—and this to be true for traditional cultures such as India—then the solution lies both in (or on) the body and its physical surrounding. These are the two directions I have taken in this book. Or rather I have attempted to explore the conditions that make such an inquiry possible in India. When Daṇḍa or when Rāma moved across different terrains in the physical landscape, each of their truly embodied imaginations communicated a knowledge of interrelatedness, of fracture, of structure and chaos. The tellers of tales listen to the language of their own body in the world to report to their listeners this knowledge. The bride's persona is transformed by passage in space due to her own experiences, and because her culture has not yet made the confusing separation between inner person and outer world.

Notes

1. Lawrence E. Sullivan, "Body Works: Knowledge of the Body in the Study of Religion," *History of Religions* 30, no. 1 (1990):86.

2. James J. Gibson calls this "sensationless perception" in *The Senses Considered as Perceptual Systems* (Boston: Houghton Mifflin, 1966), p. 2.

3. Martha Davis, ed., *Interaction Rhythms: Periodicity in Communicative Behavior* (New York: Human Sciences, 1982).

4. Cf. Michael Polanyi and Harry Prosch, *Meaning* (Chicago: University of Chicago Press, 1975), p. 33; J. M. Hull, *Touching the Rock: An Experience of Blindness* (New York: Pantheon, 1990); G. Bateson, *Steps to an Ecology of Mind*, p. 459.

5. There is a very rich literature on such an ecological approach. As a place to start, see Gregory Bateson, *Steps to an Ecology of Mind* (New York: Ballantine, 1972); For a different but related approach, see Geoffery Samuel, *Mind, Body and Culture: Anthropology and the Biological Interface* (Cambridge: Cambridge University Press, 1990); and Haywood in *Perception and Culture.*

Bibliography

Sanskrit Texts

Abhinavabhāratī. See *Nāṭyaśāstra.*

Agni Purāṇa. Ānandāśrama Sanskrit Series no. 41. Poona, 1957.

Aitareya Brāhmaṇa. With the commentary of Sāyaṇa. Bibliotheca Indica, Calcutta, 1895–86

Āpastamba Dharmasūtra. Edited by G. Bühler ed., Bombay Sanskrit Series nos. 44, 50, Bombay, 1892–94

Āpastamba Gṛhyasūtra. Mysore: Government Central Library, n.d.

Āpastamba Śrautasūtra. Gaekwad Oriental Series nos. 121, 142. Baroda: Oriental Institute, 1955, 1963.

Āśvalāyana Gṛhyasūtra. Delhi: Sri Satguru Publications, 1985.

Arthaśāstra of Kauṭilya. 5th ed. Oriental Research Institute no. 158. University of Mysore, 1986.

Atharvaveda. Varanasi: Kṛṣṇadasa Akadami, 1989.

Baudhāyana Dharmasūtra. Edited by C. Sastri ed., Kāshī Sanskrit Series no. 104. Benares, 1934.

Baudhāyana Gṛhyasūtra. Edited by S. Sastri. Mysore: Oriental Library Publications, 1920

Baudhāyana Śrautasūtra. Edited by W. Caland. 2d ed. New Delhi: Munshiram Manoharlal, 1982.

Bhagavadgītā. Edited by D. V. Gokhala. Poona Oriental Series no. 1. Poona, 1950.

Śrīmad Bhāgavata Mahāpurāṇa (Sanskrit text with English translation) Translated by C. L. Goswami. 2 vols. Gorakhpur: The Gita Press. 1971.

Bhojaprabandha of Bellala. Agara: Vinoda Pustaka Mandira, 1972.

Brahmāṇḍa Purāṇa. Edited by J. L. Shastri. Delhi, 1973.

Bṛhaddevatā of Śaunaka. Edited by A. A. Macdonell. Harvard Oriental Series no. 5. Cambridge Mass.: Harvard University Press, 1904.

Caraka Saṃhitā. Edited by R. K. Sharma and V. B. Dash. Varanasi: Chowkhamba, 1983.

Daṇḍaviveka of *Vardhamāna Upādhyāya.* Translated by B. Bhattacharya. Calcutta: Asiatic Society, 1973.

Daśakumāracarita of Daṇḍin. Edited and translated by M. R. Kale 4th ed. Delhi: Motilal Banarsidass, 1966.

Devī-Māhātmya. In *Mārkaṇḍeya Purāṇa*, translated by F. E. Pargiter. Calcutta: Asiatic Society, 1888–1904.

Dhvanyāloka of Ānandavardhana. With Locana of Abhinavagupta. Edited by Daniel H. H. Ingalls. Harvard Oriental Series no. 49. Cambridge, Mass.: Harvard University Press. 1990.

Gautama Dharmasūtra. Edited by G. Sastri. Ānandāśrama Sanskrit Series, Poona, 1931.

Gobhila Gṛhyasūtra. Translated by Hernamm Oldenberg, Sacred Books of the East, vol. 30. Delhi: Motilal Banarsidass, 1989.

Hiraṇyakeśin Gṛhyasūtra. Edited by J. Kirste. Vienna, 1889.

Hitopadeśa. Edited by Peter Peterson. Delhi: Bharatiya. 1986.

Jaiminīya Brāhmaṇa. Edited by R. Vira and L. Chandra. Sarasvati Vihara Series no. 31. Nagpur, 1954.

Jaiminīya Gṛhyasūtra. Edited by W. Caland. Lahore: Panjab Sanskrit Series, 1922.

Kāmasūtra with the *Jayamangala* commentary of Yasodhara, Bombay: Laksmivenkatesvara Steam Press, 1856.

Kāṭhaka Gṛhyasūtra. Edited by W. Caland. Lahore: Panjab Sanskrit Series, 1925.

Kathāratnakara of Hemavijaya. Munich: G. Müller, 1920.

Kathāsaritsāgara. Edited by Pandit Durgaprasad. Bombay: Nirnaya Sagara Press, 1889.

Kathāsaritsāgara of Somadeva. Delhi: Motilal Banarsidass, 1970.

Kātyāyana Smṛti. Edited and translated by P. V. Kane. Poona: BORI, 1933.

Kauśikasūtra. Edited by Maurice Bloomfield. *Journal of the American Oriental Society* 14 (1889).

Kauṭilya Arthaśāstra. Edited by R. P. Kangle. Bombay: University of Bombay, 1969.

Kṛtyakalpataru. Edited by K. V. Rangaswami Aiyangar. Baroda: Oriental Institute 1950.

Kumārasambhava. Edited by Suryakanta. New Delhi: Sahitya Akademi, 1962.

Kūrma Purāṇa. Edited and translated by A. S. Gupta. Varanasi: All India Kashi Raj Trust, 1972.

Mahābhārata. Edited by V. S. Sukthankar et. al. Poona: BORI, 1933–59.

Mālatīmādhava of Bhāvabhūti. Edited by M. Coulson. Delhi: Oxford University Press, 1989.

Mānasāra. Edited and translated by P. K. Acharya. London: Oxford University Press, 1934.

Mānava Dharmaśāstra. Edited by J. R. Gharpure. Bombay: Collection of Hindu Law Texts, 1920.

Mānava Gṛhyasūtra. Edited by R. H. Sastri. New Delhi: Panini, 1982

Mantra Patha. Edited by M. Winternitz. Delhi: Sri Satguru Publications, 1985.

Matsya Purāṇa. Ānandāśrama Sanskrit Series no. 54. Poona, 1907.

Mayamata of Mayamuni. Translated by Bruno Dagens. New Delhi: Sitaram Bharatia Institute of Scientific Research, 1985.

Mṛcchakaṭikā of Śūdraka. Varanasi: Caukhamba Surabharati Prakasana, 1985.

Naiṣadhacarita of Śrīharṣa. Edited and translated by K. K. Handiqui. Poona: Deccan College, 1965.
Nārada Smṛti. Edited by J. Jolly. Bibliotheca Indica, Calcutta, 1885–86.
Nāṭyaśāstra of Bhārata Muni with *Abhinavabhāratī.* Varanasi: Chukhamba Sanskrta Sirija Aphisa, 1972.
———. Translated by M. Ghosh. Calcutta: Manisha Granthalaya, 1966–67.
Padma Purāṇa. Ānandāśrama Sanskrit Series no. 131. Poona, 1894.
Pañcatantra. Translated by F. Edgerton. London: G. Allen & Unwin, 1965.
Pañcaviṃsa Brāhmaṇa. Translated by W. Caland. Calcutta: Asiatic Society, 1982.
Rāmāyaṇa. Edited by V. B. Shastri. D.A.V. Sanskrit Series no. 20, Lahore, 1947.
Ṛgveda with commentary of Sāyaṇacarya. Edited by V. K. Rajawade. Poona: Tilak Maharashtra Vidyapith, 1933–51.
Ṛgvidhana. See Bhat, M. S. *Vedic Tantrism.*
Śakuntalā. Chowkhamba Sanskrit Series. Varanasi, 1976.
Saṅgītaratnākara of Sarngadeva. Translated by C. K. Raja. Madras: Adyar Library, 1945.
Śaṅkhāyana Āraṇyaka. Translated by A. B. Keith. New Delhi: Oriental Books Reprint, 1975.
Śaṅkhāyana Gṛhyasūtra. Edited by S. R. Sehgal, New Delhi: Munshiram Manoharlal, 1960.
Śaṅkhāyana Śrautasūtra. Edited by Alfred Hillebrandt. New Delhi: Meharchand Lachmandas Publications, 1981.
Śatapatha Brāhmaṇa. Varanasi: Chaukhamba Sanskrta Samsthana, 1984.
Śiśupālavadha of Māgha. With commentary of Mallinātha. Edited by Pandit Durgaprasad and Pandit Sivadatta. Bombay: Pandurang Jawaji, 1940.
Skanda Purāṇa. Bombay, 1897.
Skanda Purāṇa 6.134.1–80. Translated by Cathy Benton. Ph.D. diss., Columbia University, 1991.
Sphoṭanirṇaya of Kaundabhaṭṭa. Edited by S. D. Joshi. Poona: University of Poona, 1967.
Śukranītisāra. Sonipatha—Haryana: Rshidevi Rupalala Kapura, 1983.
Suśruta Saṃhitā. Edited by S. S. Pandey. Varanasi: Krishnadas Academy, 1985.
———. Translated by K. K. Bhishagratna, Chowkhamba Sanskrit Series-. Varanasi, 1991.
Taittirīya Āraṇyaka. With Commentary of Sayaṇa. Calcutta: Bibliotheca Indica, 1872.
Taittirīya Brāhmaṇa. Delhi: Motilal Banarsidass, 1985.
Taittirīya Saṃhitā. Delhi: Motilal Banarsidass, 1986.
Upaniṣads. Edited by H. R. Bhagavan. Poona, 1927.
Vājasaneyi Saṃhitā. Edited by A. Weber. Berlin, 1851–59.
Vākyapadīya of Bhartṛhari. With commentaries by Vṛtti and Paddhati of Vṛṣabhadeva. Edited by K. A. Subramania Iyer. Poona: Deccan College, 1966.
Vākyapadīya. Translated by K. A. Subramania Iyer. Poona: Deccan College, chapter 1, 1965.
Viṣṇudharmottara. Delhi: Nag Publishers, 1985.
Viṣṇu Purāṇa. Edited by Sitararamadasonkaranatha, Calcutta, 1972.

Viṣṇu Smṛti. Edited by Jolly, J. Varanasi: Caukhamba Sanskrit Series no. 95, 1962.

Vyavahāra Mayūkha. Edited and translated by Mandlik, V. N. New Delhi: Asian Publication, 1982.

Yājñavalkya Smṛti. Edited by M. T. Ganapati Sastri. New Delhi: Munshiram Manoharlal, 1982.

Secondary Sources

Acharya, Prasanna Kumar. *An Encyclopedia of Hindu Architecture.* Delhi: Oriental Reprint, 1979.

Allen, Douglas. *Structure and Creativity in Religion.* The Hague: Mouton, 1978.

Allport, Floyd. *Theories of Perception and the Concept of Structure.* New York: John Wiley and Sons, 1955.

Antoine, L. *Rama and the Bards.* Calcutta: Writer's Workshop, 1975.

Arnhiem, Rudolf. *Art and Visual Perception: A Psychology of the Creative Eye.* Berkeley: University of California Press, 1974.

———. *Visual Thinking.* Berkeley: University of California Press, 1969.

Ardener, Edwin, Review of *Purity and Danger* by Mary Douglas. *Man,* 2 (1967):139.

Ashbery, John. *As We Know.* New York: Penguin, 1979.

Aufrecht, Theodor. *Indische Studien.* Leipzig: Brockhaus, 1878.

Augustine. *Confessions.* Translated by R. Warner. New York: American Library, 1963.

Babb, Lawrence. *The Divine Hierarchy.* New York: Columbia University Press, 1975.

Bachelard, Gaston. *The Poetics of Space.* Boston: Beacon Press, 1969.

Bailey, Greg. *The Mythology of Brahmā.* New Delhi: Oxford University Press, 1983.

Banerjee, S. "Prajāpati in the Brāhmaṇas." in *Vishveshvaranand Indological Journal,* 19 (1981):14–19.

Barthes, Roland. *Critical Essays* Evanston, Ill.: Northwestern University Press, 1972.

Basham, A. L. "Notes on Seafaring in Ancient India." In A. L. Basham. *Studies in Indian History.* Calcutta: Samadhi Publications, 1964.

Bateson, Gregory. *Steps to an Ecology of Mind.* New York: Ballantine, 1972.

Beane, Wendell C. *Myth, Cult, and Symbols in Sakta Hinduism.* Leiden: E. J. Brill, 1977.

Beck, Brenda, Peter J. Claus, Praphulladatta Goswami, and Jawaharlal Handov eds. *Folktales of India.* Chicago: University of Chicago Press, 1987.

Begley, W. E. *Viṣṇu's Flaming Wheel: The Iconography of the Sudarśana-Cakra.* New York: New York University Press, 1973.

Bergson, H. *Time and Free Will.* New York: Macmillan, 1910.

Bhat, M. S. *Vedic Tantrism: A Study of Ṛgvidhana of Śaunaka with Text and Translation.* Delhi: Motilal Banarsidass, 1987.

Bhattacharji, Sukumari. *The Indian Theogony.* Cambridge: Cambridge University Press, 1978.

Bhattacharya, A. N. ed. *One Hundred Twelve Upanisads.* Delhi: Parimal, 1987.

Bhattacharya, Bhavatosh, trans. *Dandaviveka of Vardhamana Upadhyaya.* Calcutta: Asiatic Society, 1973.

Bhattacharya, Chanchal. *The Concept of Theft in Classical Hindu Law.* New Delhi: Munshiram Manoharlal, 1990.

Bhattacharya, Deborah. *Pagalami: Ethnopsychiatric Knowledge in Bengal.* Syracuse: Maxwell School of Citizenship, 1986.

Bhattacharya, Sri Ahibhushan, trans. *The Kurma Purana.* Varanasi: All Indian Kashi Raj Trust, 1972.

Bhattacharya, T. *A Study of Vastuvidya.* Patna: Bhattacharya, 1947.

Bhishagranta, Kaviraj Kunja Lal, ed. *The Sushruta Samhita.* 3 vols. Calcutta: S. L. Bhaduri, 1907–16.

Biardeau, Madeleine. "The Childhood and Adulthood of Krishna." In Bonnefoy Yves, ed., *Mythologies,* 2:859–64. Chicago: University of Chicago, 1991.

Bloomfield, Maurice. "The Art of Stealing in Hindu Fiction." *American Journal of Philology,* 54, no. 3 (1923):193–229.

———. "The Character and Adventures of Muladeva." Proceedings of the American Philosophical Society, 52 (1913), pp. 616–650.

———. "Contributions to the Interpretation of the Veda," *JAOS* 15 (1893): 143–63.

———. *Hymns of the Atharvaveda.* Sacred Books of the East. vol. 42. New York: Greenwood Press. 1969.

———. "On Recurring Psychic Motifs in Hindu Fiction." *JAOS* 36 (1914): 68–89.

Bodewitz, H. W., trans. *Jaiminīya Brāhmaṇa.* Leiden: E. J. Brill, 1973.

Bohtlingk, Otto von. *Sanskrit Worterbuch.* Leipzig: Market & Patters, 1923.

Boner, Alice. *Vastusūtra Upaniṣad: The Essence of Form in Sacred Art.* Delhi: Motilal Banarsidass, 1982.

Bonnefoy, Yves, compiler. *Mythologies.* Translated under the direction of Wendy Doniger. Chicago: University of Chicago Press, 1992.

Brandon, S. G. F. "The Ritual Perpetuation of the Past." *Numen* 6 (1959): 112–29.

Brockington, J. *Righteous Rama.* New Delhi: Oxford University Press, 1984.

Brown, Mackenzie C. "The Theology of Rādhā in the *Purāṇas.*" In John Stratton Hawley and Donna Marie Wulff, eds., *The Divine Consort* (Boston: Beacon Press, 1982), pp. 57–71.

Brown, Norman O. *Hermes the Thief.* Great Barrington, Mass.: Lindisfarne, 1990.

Brown, Percy. *Indian Architecture.* Bombay: Taraporevala Sons, 1956.

Brown, Robert E. "New Perspectives on the History of Tala." *Journal of the Indian Musicological Society.* 16, no. 2 (1985):13–22.

Capek, Milic. "Bergson and Modern Physics." In *Boston Studies in the Philosophy of Science.* New York: Humanities Press, 1971.

Caroll, John B. *Language, Thought and Reality: Selected Writings of Benjamin Lee Whorf.* Cambridge, Mass.: MIT Press, 1956.

Cassirer, Ernst. *An Essay on Man.* New Haven: Yale University Press, 1944.

———. *The Philosophy of Symbolic Forms.* 3 vols. New Haven: Yale University Press, 1985.

Chatham, Doris Clark. "Rasa and Sculpture." In J. E. Van Lohuizen-De Leeuw, ed. *Studies in South Asian Culture.* Leiden: E. J. Brill, 1981.

Coburn, Thomas. "Consort of None, Śakti of All: The Vision of the Devī-māhātmya." In John Stratton Hawley and Donna Marie Wulff, eds., *The Divine Consort* (Boston: Beacon Press, 1982), pp. 153–65.

Coomaraswamy, A. *Early Indian Architecture.* New Delhi: Munshiram Manoharlal, 1975.

———. *Figures of Speech or Figures of Thought.* New Delhi: Munshiram Manoharlal, 1981.

———. "On the Loathly Bride." *Speculum* 20 no. 4 (1945):391–404.

Coward, Harold G. *Sphoṭa Theory of Language.* Delhi: Motilal Banarsidass, 1986.

Cowell, E. B., trans. *The Jataka, or Stories of the Buddha's Former Births.* 6 vols. London: Luzac, 1957.

Crooke, William. "The Lifting of the Bride." *Folklore,* 8 (1902):238–42.

———. *Popular Religion of Northern India.* London: Oxford University Press, 1896.

Curtis, Brian, et. al. *An Introduction to the Neurosciences.* Philadelphia: W. B. Saunders, 1972.

Dange, S. A. *Vedic Concept of the Divine Fructification.* Bombay: University of Bombay, 1971.

———. *Vedic Concept of Field.* Bombay: University of Bombay Press, 1971.

Dange, Sindhu S. *Hindu Domestic Rituals.* Delhi: Ajanta, 1985.

Daniel, E. Valentine. *Fluid Signs: Being a Person the Tamil Way.* Berkeley: University of California Press, 1984.

Daniélou, Alain. *Northern Indian Music.* New York: Frederick A. Praeger, 1969.

Daumal, Rene. *A Night of Serious Drinking,* translated by D. Coward and E. A. Lovatt. London: Routledge & Kegan Paul, 1979.

Davis, Martha, ed. *Interaction Rhythms: Periodicity in Communicative Behavior.* New York: Human Sciences, 1982.

Day, Lal B. *Folk Tales of Bengal.* London: Macmillan, 1912.

Day, Terrence. *The Conception of Punishment in Early Indian Literature.* Waterloo, Canada: Wilfrid Laurier University Press, 1982.

Delouche, Jean. *The Ancient Bridges of India.* New Delhi: Sitaram, 1984.

Deregowski, Jan. "Illusion and Culture." In R. L. Gregory and E. H. Gombrich, eds. *Illusion in Nature and Art.* (New York: Charles Scribner's Sons, 1973), pp. 161–92.

Derrett, J. D. M. "Dharmaśāstra: The Origin and Purpose of the Smṛti." In *Contributions to the Study of Indian Law and Society.* South Asia Seminar 1966–67. Philadelphia: University of Pennsylvania Press, 1967.

———. *Essays in Classical and Modern Hindu Law.* 2 vols. Leiden: E. J. Brill, 1976.

———. *Religion Law and the State in India.* London: Faber & Faber, 1968.

Derrida, Jaques. *Positions.* Translated by Alan Bass. Chicago: University of Chicago Press, 1981.

de Vreese, K. "The Game of Dice in Ancient India." In Oosters Genootschap, *Orientalia Neerlandica: A Volume of Oriental Studies.* Leiden: Sijthoff, 1948, pp. 43–58.

Didler, Anzier. *The Skin Ego.* New Haven: Yale University Press, 1989.

Dimock, Edward C. *The Place of the Hidden Moon.* Chicago: University of Chicago Press, 1966.

Dimock, Edward C. *The Thief of Love.* Chicago: University of Chicago Press, 1963.

Doniger, Wendy with Brian Smith, trans. *The Laws of Manu.* Harmondsworth: Penguin Classics, 1991.

Douglas, Mary. *Essays in the Sociology of Perception.* London: Routledge & Kegan Paul, 1982.

———. *Natural Symbols.* New York: Vintage Books, 1973.

———. *Purity and Danger.* London: Routledge & Kegan Paul, 1979.

Dreyfus, Hubert. "Sinn and Intentional Object." In Robert C. Solomon, ed., *Phenomenology and Existentialism.* Lanham, Md.: University Press of America, 1980.

du Bois, Page. *Sowing the Body: Psychoanalysis and Ancient Representations of Women.* Chicago: University of Chicago Press, 1988.

Dumézil, Georges. *L'idéologie tripartite des Indo-Europeens.* Brussells: Latomus, 1958.

Dumont, Louis. *Homo Hierarchicus.* Chicago: University of Chicago Press, 1977.

Dutt, Manmath Nath. *Dharam Shastra.* 6 vols. New Delhi: Cosmo, 1979.

Eck, Diana L. *Banaras, City of Light.* Princeton: Princeton University Press, 1982.

Eggeling, J. *The Satapatha Brahmana.* Sacred Books of the East, vol. 44. Oxford: Clarendon Press, 1900.

Eliade, M. *Images and Symbols.* New York: Search Book, 1969.

———. *Myth of the Eternal Return.* Bollingen Series 46. Princeton: Princeton University Press, 1959.

———. *Patterns in Comparative Religion.* New York: Meridian, 1963.

———. *The Sacred and the Profane.* New York: Harcourt, Brace, 1959.

———. "Le temps et l'éternité dans la pensée indienne." In *Eranos-Jahrbuch.* Zurich: Rhein-verlag, 1952.

———. *The Two and the One.* Chicago: University of Chicago Press, 1979.

Elwin, Verrier. *Folk-Tales of Mahakoshal.* New York: Arno, 1980.

———. *The Tribal Art of Middle India.* Oxford: Oxford University Press, 1951.

Erikson, E. *Gandhi's Truth: On the Origins of Militant Non-violence.* London: Faber & Faber, 1970.

Falk, Nancy. "Wilderness and Kingship in Ancient South Asia." *History of Religions,* 13, no. 1 (1973):1–15.

Fergusson, J. *History of Indian and Eastern Architecture.* Delhi: Munshiram Manoharlal, 1967.

Filliozat, Jean. *The Classical Doctrine of Indian Medicine.* Delhi: Munshiram Manoharlal, 1964.

Firth, Raymond. *Symbolism: Public and Private.* Ithaca: Cornell University Press, 1973.

Forster, E. M. *A Passage to India.* Abinger edition, New York: Holmes and Meier, 1979.

Foucault, M. *The Order of Things.* New York: Vintage Books, 1973.

Fraisse, Paul. *The Psychology of Time.* New York: Harper & Row, 1963.

Fraser, J. T. *Of Time, Passion, and Knowledge.* New York: George Braziller, 1975.

Frazer, James G. *The Golden Bough* vol. 1. New York: Macmillan, 1935.

Friedman A., and C. Donley. *Einstein as Myth and Muse*. Cambridge: Cambridge University Press, 1989.
Frutiger, A. *Signs and Symbols*. New York: Van Nostrand, 1989.
Fruzzetti, L. *The Gift of a Virgin*. New Brunswick, N. J.: Rutgers University Press, 1982.
Fruzzetti, Lina, and Akos Ostor, A. *Kinship and Ritual in Bengal*. New Delhi: South Asian Publishers, 1984.
———. "The Seed and the Earth: A Cultural Analysis of Kinship in a Bengali Town." *Contributions to Indian Sociology*, n.s., 10, no. 1 (1976):97–132.
Gajjas, Irene N. *Ancient Indian Art and the West*. Bombay: Traporevala, 1971.
Gibson, James J. The Senses Considered as Perceptual Systems. Boston: Houghton Mifflin, 1966.
———. "A Theory of Direct Visual Perception." In Joseph R. Royce and William W. Rozeboom, eds., *The Psychology of Knowing*. New York: Gordon and Breach, 1972.
Giedion, Sigfried. *The Eternal Present*. Bollingen Series 35. New York: Bollingen, 1965.
Gold, Ann Grodzins. "Sexuality, Fertility and Erotic Imagination in Rajasthani Women's Songs." In Gloria Goodwin-Tomar and Ann Grodzins Gold, *Songs, Stories, Lives: Listening to Women in Rural North India*. Unpublished manuscript, 1991.
Goldman, Robert. *Gods, Priests and Warriors: The Bhṛgus of the Mahābhārata*. New York: Columbia University Press, 1977.
———. *The Rāmāyaṇa of Vālmīki*. Princeton: Princeton University Press, 1984.
Gombrich, E. H. *Art and Illusion; a study in the psychology of pictorial representation*. New York: Pantheon Books, 1960.
Gonda, Jan. *Ancient Indian Kingship from the Religious Point of View*. Leiden: E. J. Brill, 1966.
———. "In the Beginning." In *Annals of the Bandharkar Oriental Research Institute* 63 (1982):13–62.
———. *Mantra Interpretation in the Śatapatha Brāhmaṇa*. Leiden: E. J. Brill, 1988.
———. *Notes on Names and the Name of God in Ancient India*. Amsterdam: North Holland, 1970.
———. *Prajāpati and the Year*. Amsterdam: North Holland, 1984.
———. *Vedic Literature*. Wiesbaden: Otto Harrassowitz, 1975.
———. *Vedic Ritual*. Leiden: E.J. Brill, 1980.
———. *Viṣṇuism and Śivaism*: A Comparison. London: Athlone, 1970.
Goodnow, Jaqueline. *Children Drawing*. Cambridge Mass.: Harvard University Press, 1977.
Goody, Jack. "Oral Tradition and the Reconstruction of the Past in Northern Ghana." In Jack Goody, ed. *Literacy in Traditional Societies* (Cambridge: Cambridge University Press, 1968), pp. 285–95.
Goonetilleke, William, ed. *The Orientalist*, vol 1. Bombay, 1884.
Gottlieb, Robert. "Symbolisms Underlying improvisatory Practices in Indian Music." in *Journal of the Indian Musicological Society* 16, no. 2 (1985): 23–36.

Gray, Louis H., trans., The Narrative of Bhoja. New Haven: American Oriental Society, 1950.

Gregory, Richard L. *The Intelligent Eye.* New York: McGraw-Hill, 1970.

Griffith, Ralph T. H. *The Texts of the White Yajurveda.* New Delhi: Munshiram Manoharlal, 1987.

Grimes, Ronald R. *Beginnings in Ritual Studies.* Lanham, M.: University Press of America, 1982.

Groenewegen-Frankfort, H. A. *Arrest and Movement: Space and Time in the Art of the Ancient Near East.* Cambridge, Mass.: Belknap Press of Harvard, 1987.

Grover, S. *The Architecture of India.* New Delhi: Vikas, 1980.

Gwynn, F., and J. Blotner, eds. *Faulkner in the University.* Charlottesville: University of Virginia Press, 1959.

Hand, Wayland. *Magical Healing.* Berkeley: University of California Press, 1980.

Harman, William. *The Sacred Marriage of a Hindu Goddess.* Bloomington: Indiana University Press, 1989.

Hawley, John S. *Krishna the Butter Thief.* Princeton: Princeton University Press, 1983.

Heesterman, Jan. *The Ancient Indian Royal Consecration.* The Hague: Mouton, 1957.

——— "The Conundrum of the King's Authority." In J. F. Richards, ed. *Kingship and Authority in South Asia* (Madison: University of Wisconsin Press, 1978), pp. 1–27.

———. *The Inner Conflict of Tradition.* Chicago: University of Chicago Press, 1985.

Heidegger. *Martin, Being and Time.* Translated by J. Macquarrie and E. Robinson. New York: Harper & Row, 1962.

———. *Poetry, Language, Thought.* New York: Harper & Row, 1971.

Hershman, Paul. "Hair, Sex, and Dirt." In *Man* n.s., 9, no. 2 (1974):274–99.

———. *Punjabi Kinship.* Delhi: Hindustan Publishing, 1981.

Hertzberger, R. *Bhartṛhari and the Buddhists.* Dodrecht, Holland: D. Reidel, 1986.

Hillebrandt, Alfred. *Ritualliteratur.* Strassburg: Trübner, 1897.

———. *Vedische Mythologie.* Breslau: W. Kroebner, 1927–29.

Hiltebeitel, Alf. "Draupadi's Hair." *Purusartha* 5 (1981):179–214.

———. ed. *Criminal Gods and Demon Devotees.* Albany: SUNY Press, 1989.

Hocart, A. M. "Flying through the Air." In *Indian Antiquary* 5 (1923):80–82.

Hopkins, Edward W. *Epic Mythology.* Strassburg: Trübner, 1915.

Husserl, Edmund. *Cartesian Meditations.* The Hague: M. Nijhoff, 1960.

———. *Ideas—General Introduction to Pure Phenomenology.* New York: Macmillan, 1931.

Hull, J. M. *Touching the Rock: An Experience of Blindness.* New York: Pantheon, 1990.

Huyler, Stephen. *Village India.* New York: Harry N. Abrams, 1985.

Ifeka, Caroline. "Domestic Space as Ideology in Goa, India." *Contributions to Indian Sociology*, n.s., 2, no. 2 (1987).

Inden, Ronald. *Marriage and Rank in Bengali Culture.* Berkeley: University of California Press, 1978.

Ingalls, Daniel H. H. *Sanskrit Poetry*. Cambridge, Mass.: Harvard University Press, 1979.

Jackendoff, R. *Consciousness and the Computational Mind*. Cambridge Mass.: MIT Press, 1987.

Jacobi, Hermann, ed. *Ausgewahlte Erzahlungen in Maharashtri*. Leipzig: S. Hirzel, 1886.

Jain, Jyotindra. *Painted Myths of Creation: Art and Ritual of an Indian Tribe*. New Delhi: Lalit Kala Akademi, 1984.

James, William, *A Pluralistic Universe*. London: Longmans, Gree, 1909.

Janhari, Manorama. *South India and Its Architecture*. Varanasi: Bharatiya Vidya Prakashan, 1969.

Jayakar, P. *The Earthen Drum: An Introduction to the Arts of Rural India*. New Delhi: National Museum, 1980.

Johnson, Mark. *The Body in the Mind*. Chicago: University of Chicago Press, 1986.

Jolly, Julius. *Indian Medicine*. Delhi: Munshiram Manoharlal, 1977.

Joyce, James. *A Portrait of the Artist as a Young Man*. New York: Penguin, 1976.

Kafka, Franz. "The Metamorphosis." In *The Complete Stories*. New York: Schocken Books, 1971.

Kagan, Jerome. *The Nature of the Child*. New York: Basic Books, 1984.

Kakar, Sudhir. *The Inner World: A Psycho-Analytic Study of Childhood and Society in India*. Delhi: Oxford University Press, 1978.

———. *Intimate Relations: Exploring Indian Sexuality*. Chicago: University of Chicago Press, 1990.

———. *Shamans, Mystics and Doctors*. New York: Alfred A. Knopf, 1982.

Kale, M. R., trans. *The Daśakumāracarita of Daṇḍin*. Delhi: Motilal Banarsidass, 1966.

Kane, P. V. *History of Dharmaśāstra*. 6 vols. Pune: BORI, 1974.

———. *History of Sanskrit Poetics*. Delhi: Motilal Banarsidass, 1971.

Kang, Kanwarjut Singh. *Wall Paintings of Punjab and Haryana*. Delhi: Atma Ram & Sons, 1985.

Katz Arabagian, Ruth. "Cattle Raiding and Bride Stealing." *Religion* 14 (1984):107–42.

Keith, A. B. *Religion and Philosophy of the Vedas and Upanishads*. Cambridge, Mass.: Harvard University Press, 1925.

———. Trans. *Rig-Veda Brahmanas*. Harvard Oriental Series, vol. 25. Cambridge, Mass.: Harvard University Press, 1920.

———. *The Veda of the Black Yajur School (Taittiriya Samhita)*. Cambridge, Mass.: Harvard University Press, 1914.

Kennedy, M. *The Criminal Classes in India*. Delhi: Mittal, 1985.

Kermode, Frank. *The Sense of an Ending: Studies in the Theory of Fiction*. New York: Oxford University Press, 1966.

Kinsley, David. *Hindu Goddesses: Visions of the Divine Feminine in the Hindu Religious Tradition*. Berkeley: University of California Press, 1984.

Knowels, J. *Folk Tales of Kashmir*. London: Trübner, 1893.

Koffka, K. *The Principles of Gestalt Psychology*. New York: Harcourt, Brace, 1935.

Kohler, Wolfgang. *The Task of Gestalt Psychology*. Princeton: Princeton University Press, 1969

Kohler, Wolfgang. *Gestalt Psychology.* New York: Liveright, 1929.
Kramrisch, Stella. *The Hindu Temple.* Delhi: Motilal Banarsidass, 1976.
———. *The Presence of Śiva.* Princeton: Princeton University Press, 1981.
———. Trans. *Viṣṇudharmottara*, Part III. Calcutta: Calcutta University Press, 1928.
Krois, John. *Cassirer, Symbolic Forms and History.* New Haven: Yale University Press, 1987.
Kuiper, F. B. J. *Ancient Indian Cosmogony.* New Delhi: Vikas, 1983.
Kuper, H. *An African Aristocracy.* London: Oxford University Press, 1947.
Lakoff, George. *Women, Fire, and Dangerous Things.* Chicago: University of Chicago Press, 1987.
Landy, David. *Culture, Disease and Healing.* New York: Macmillan, 1977.
Langer, Susan. *Philosophy in a New Key.* New York: New American Library, 1942.
Langer, Thomas. *The Meaning of Heidegger.* New York: Columbia University Press, 1959.
Layton, P. *The Anthropology of Art.* New York: Columbia University Press, 1981.
Leach, E. R. "Magical Hair." *Journal of the Royal Asiatic Society* 88, (1958): 147–65.
Leaf, Murray J. *Man, Mind and Science.* New York: Columbia University Press, 1979.
Leslie, Julia. *The Perfect Wife: The Orthodox Hindu Woman According to the Strīdharmapaddhati of Tryambakayajvam.* Delhi: Oxford University Press, 1989.
Lévi-Strauss, C. *The Savage Mind.* Chicago: University of Chicago Press, 1966.
Lincoln, Bruce. *Emerging from the Chrysalis.* Cambridge, Mass.: Harvard University Press, 1981.
———. *Myth, Cosmos and Society.* Cambridge, Mass.: Harvard University Press, 1986.
———. *Priests, Warriors and Cattle: A Study of the Ecology of Religions.* Berkeley: University of California Press, 1981.
Lingat, Robert. *The Classical Law of India.* Berkeley: University of California Press, 1973.
———. "Time and the Dharma." *Contributions to Indian Sociology* 6, 1 (1962):7–16.
Lipner, J. *The Face of Truth.* Albany: SUNY Press, 1986.
Lipton, E. L. "Swaddling, a Child Care Practice: Historical, Cultural, and Experimental Observations." *Pediatrics* 35 suppl. (1965).
Long, Charles. *Significations: Signs, Symbols and Images in the Interpretation of Religion.* Philadelphia: Fortress Press, 1986.
Lord, A. B. *The Singer of Tales.* Cambridge Mass.: Harvard University Press, 1960.
Luria, A. R. *Cognitive Development.* Cambridge Mass.: Harvard University Press, 1976.
———. *The Man with a Shattered World.* New York: Basic Books, 1972.
Mahapatra, Jayanta. *A Rain of Rites.* Athens: University of Georgia Press, 1982.
Malinowski, B. *Myth in Primitive Psychology.* New York: W. W. Norton, 1926.
Malraux, André. *The Voices of Silence.* New York: Doubleday, 1953.

Manser, A. R. "Image." In *Encyclopedia of Philosophy*. 4 vols. New York: Collier Macmillan, 1967.
Margalit, A. and M. Halbertal. *Idolatry: A Conceptual Analysis.* Cambridge, Mass.: Harvard University Press, forthcoming.
Marglin, Frederique. "Refining the Body, Transformative Emotion in Ritual Dance." In Owen Lynch, ed. *Divine Passions: The Social Construction of Emotion in India* (Berkeley: University of California Press, 1990), pp. 212–228.
Marriott, McKim. "Hindu Transactions: Diversity without Dualism." In B. Kapferer, ed. *Transactions and Meaning* (Philadelphia: Institute for the study of Human Issues, 1976), pp. 109–42.
———, ed. *India through Hindu Categories.* New Delhi: Sage, 1990.
Marshall, John. *Taxila: An Illustrated Account of Archeological Excavations.* Cambridge: Cambridge University Press, 1951.
McCulloch, William. *Bengali Houshold Tales.* London: Hodder and Stoughton, 1912.
Meister, Michael, ed. *Discourses on Śiva.* Philadelphia: University of Pennsylvania Press, 1981.
Merleau-Ponty, M. "The Child's Relations with Others." In James M. Edie. ed. *The Primacy of Perception.* Evanston, Ill.: Northwestern University Press.
———. *Phenomenology of Perception.* London: Routledge & Kegan Paul, 1962.
Metzger, Wolfgang. "The Phenomenal-Perceptual Field as a Central Steering Mechanism." In Joseph R. Royce and William W. Rozeboom, eds. *The Psychology of Knowing* (New York: Gordon and Breach, 1972), pp. 87–113.
Meyer, J. J. *Sexual Life in Ancient India.* New York: E. P. Dutton, 1930.
———. *Trilogie altindischer Machte und Feste der Vegetation.* 3 vols. Zurich: Max Niehaus, 1937.
Michael, Donald N. "A Cross-cultural Investigation of Closure." In David Beardslee and Michael Wertheimer, eds. *Readings in Perception* (Princeton: Van Nostrand, 1958), pp. 160–70.
Michell, George. *The Hindu Temple.* Chicago: University of Chicago Press, 1988.
Minkowski, Eugene *Vers une cosmologie.* Paris: Fernand Aubier, 1936.
———. *Lived Time: Phenomenological and Psychological Studies.* Evanston, Ill.: Northwestern University Press, 1970.
Mirashi, Vasudev Vishnu, ed., *Inscriptions of the Kalchuri-Chedi Era.* Corpus Inscriptorum Indicarum, vol. 4. Ootacamund: Government Epigraphist, 1955.
Misra, B. N. "Early Torana-Gateways as Predecessors of Temple-Doorways in Ancient Malavadesa." In Krishna Deva, Lallanji Gopal, Shri Bhagwan Singh, eds., *History and Art* (Delhi: Ramanand Vidya Bhavan, 1977), pp. 52–64.
Moffit, R. *Missionary Labors and Scenes in Southern Africa.* London: Seow, 1904.
Monier-Williams, M. *A Sanskrit-English Dictionary..* Delhi: Motilal Banarsidass, 1990.
Montagu, Ashley. *Touching: The Human Significance of the Skin.* New York: Harper & Row, 1986.

Moore, Melinda. "The Kerala House as a Hindu Cosmos." In McKim Marriott, ed., *India through Hindu Categories* (New Delhi: Sage, 1990), pp. 169–202.

Moss, David. "Bandits and Boundaries in Sardinia." *Man* 14 (1978):477–96.

Murthy. K. *Early Indian Secular Architecture.* Delhi: Sundeep Prakashan, 1987.

Nakamura, H. "Time in Indian and Japanese Thought." In J. T. Fraser, ed. *The Voices of Time* (Amherst: University of massachusetts, 1981), pp. 77–91.

Narayan, R. K. *Storytellers, Saints and Scoundrels.* Philadelphia: University of Pennsylavania Press, 1989.

Narayanan, Vasudha. "The Goddess Śrī: Blossoming Lotus and Breast Jewel of Viṣṇu." In John Stratton Hawley and Donna Marie Wulff, eds. *The Divine Consort* (Boston: Beacon Press, 1982), pp. 224–237.

Obeyesekere, Gananth. *Medusa's Hair.* Chicago: University of Chicago Press, 1984.

O'Flaherty, Wendy D. *Dreams, Illusion and Other Realities.* Chicago: University of Chicago Press, 1984.

———. *Origins of Evil in Hindu Mythology.* Berkeley: University of California Press, 1976.

———. *Other People's Myths.* New York: Macmillan, 1988.

———, trans. *The Rig Veda.* Harmondsworth: Penguin, 1984.

———. *Tales of Sex and Violence.* Chicago: University of Chicago Press, 1985

———. *Women, Androgynes, and Other Mythical Beasts.* Chicago: University of Chicago Press, 1980.

O'Flaherty, W., and J. D. M. Derrett, eds. *The Concept of Duty in South Asia.* Delhi: Vikas Publishing, 1978.

Oldenberg, H. "Akhyana Hymnen in Ṛgveda in *Zeitschrift der Deutischen Morgenslandischen Gesselschaft* 39 (1885):52–90.

———. *Aus dem alten Inden.* Berlin: Gebruder Paetel, 1910.

———. *Die Religion des Veda.* Berlin: Verlag von Wilhelm Hertz, 1894.

Pannikar, R. "Toward a Typology of Time and Temporality in the Ancient Indian Tradition." *Quarterly of Asian and Comparative Thought* 24, no. 2 (1974).

Papadakis, Andreas, et. al., eds. *Deconstruction.* New York: Rizzoli, 1989.

Parker. Henry. *Village Folk-Tales of Ceylon.* Dehiwala: Tisara Prakasakayo, 1972.

Parmentier, Richard. *The Sacred Remains.* Chicago: University of Chicago Press, 1987.

Parpola. "On the Symbol Concept." In H. Biezais, ed. *Religious Symbols and Their Functions.* Stockholm: Almquist and Wiksell, 1979.

Peirce, Charles. *Collected Papers of Charles Sanders Peirce.* Edited by Charles Hartshorne and Paul Weiss. Cambridge, Mass.: Harvard University Press 1931–35.

Pettazzoni, R. *La Confessine dei Peccati.* Bologna: Nicola Zanichelli, 1935.

Pillai, P.K.N. *Non-Ṛgvedic Mantras in the Marriage Ceremonies.* Trivandrum: Travancore Devaswam Board, 1958.

Pocock, David. "The Anthropology of Time Reckoning." *Contributions to Indian Sociology.* 7 (1964):18–29.

Polanyi, Michael, and Harry Prosch. *Meaning*. Chicago: University of Chicago Press, 1975.

Pollock, S. *The Rāmāyaṇa of Vālmīki* (Ayodhyākāṇḍa). Princeton: Princeton University Press, 1986.

Powers, Harold S. "Musical Art and Esoteric Theism: Muttusvāmi Dikṣitar's Ānandabhairavī Kīrtanams on Śiva and Śakti at Tiruvārūr." In M. Meister, ed. *Discourses on Śiva*, (Philadelphia: University of Pennsylvania Press, 1981), pp. 317–37.

Proust, M. *Swann's Way*. New York: Modern Library, 1928.

Quackenbos, George Payn, trans. *Eight Sanskrit Poems of Mayura*. New York: AMS Press, 1965.

Rajwade, A. V. "The Treatment of Time and Location in Uttararāmacarita." *Journal of the Oriental Institute* 32, no. 3 (1983).

Ralson, William R. S. *Tibetan Tales*. London: G. Routledge, 1926.

Ramanujan, A. K. *Interior Landscape*. Bloomington: Indiana University Press, 1967.

Ramanujan, A. K., David Shulman, and Velcheru Narayana Rao. *When God Is a Customer*. Berkeley: University of California Press, forthcoming.

Reed, Edward S., *James J. Gibson and the Psychology of Perception*. New Haven: Yale University Press, 1988.

Renou, Louis. "Connexion en vedique, 'cause' en bouddhique." In *Dr. C. Kunhan Raja Presentation Volume*. Madras: Adyar Library, 1946.

Ricoeur, Paul. "Structure, Word, Event." In D. Ihde, ed. *The Conflict of Interpretations: Essays in Hermeneutics*. Evanston: Northwestern University Press, 1974.

———. *The Symbolism of Evil*. Boston: Beacon Press, 1969.

———. *Time and Narrative*. 3 vols. Chicago: University of Chicago Press, 1985.

Rowell, Lewis. "Abhinavagupta, Augustine, Time and Music." *Journal of the Indian Musicological Society*. 13, no. 2 (1982):18–36.

Roy, Manisha. *Bengali Women*. Chicago: University of Chicago Press, 1975.

Ryder, Arthur W., trans. *Kalidasa: Translations of Shakuntala and Other Works*. London: J. M. Dent & Sons, 1928.

Sacks, Oliver. *The Man Who Mistook His Wife for a Hat*. London: Picador, 1985.

Samuel, Geoffery. *Mind, Body and Culture: Anthropology and the Biological Interface*. Cambridge: Cambridge University Press, 1990.

Sankalia, H. D. *Aspects of Indian History and Archeology*. Delhi: B. R. Publishing, 1977.

Sankaran, A. *Some Aspects of Literary Criticism in Sanskrit*. Madras: University of Madras Press, 1929.

Sastri, Natesa. "Story of Madana Kama Raja." In *Indian Folk Tales*. Madras: Guardian Press, 1908.

Sastri, S. N. Ghoshal. *Elements of Indian Aesthetics*. 2 vols. Varanasi Chaukambha Orientalia, 1978.

Saussure, Ferdinand de. *Course in General Linguistics*. New York: McGraw-Hill, 1959.

Sayre, Henry M. *The Object of Performance*. Chicago: University of Chicago Press, 1989.

Schmidt, Hanns-Peter. *Some Women's Rites and Rights in the Veda*. Poona: BORI, 1987.
Schneider, Marius. "Primitive Music." In G. Abraham, ed. *The New Oxford History of Music*. Oxford: Oxford University Press, 1957.
Sen Gupta, Sarkar, ed. *Tree Symbol Worship in India*. Calcutta: Indian Publications, 1965.
Sen, Nabaneeta. "Comparative Studies in Oral Epic Poetry and the Vālmīki Rāmāyaṇa." *Journal of the American Oriental Society* 86 (1966):397–409.
Seung, T. K. *Structuralism and Hermeneutics*. New York: Columbia University Press, 1982.
Sherrington, Charles. *The Integrative Action of the Nervous System*. New Haven: Yale University Press, 1947.
Shulman, David. "The Crossing of the Wilderness: Landscape and Myth in the Tamil Story of Rāma." *Acta Orientalia* 42 (1981):21–54.
———. *The King and the Clown in South Indian Myth and Poetry*. Princeton: Princeton University Press, 1985.
Singh, K. B. K. *Marriage and Family System of Rajputs*. New Delhi: Wisdom Publications, 1988.
Singh, S. D. *Land System and Feudalism in Ancient India*. Calcutta: Calcutta University Press, 1966.
Sinha, Binod Chandra. *Tree Worship in Ancient India*. New Delhi: Books Today, 1979.
Smart, Ninian. "Beyond Eliade: The Future of Theory in Religion." *Numen* 25 (1978):23–36.
Smith, Brian K. *Reflections on Resemblance, Ritual and Religion*. New York: Oxford University Press, 1989.
Smith, David. "Aspects of the Interrelationship of Divine and Human Bodies in Hinduism." *Religion*, 19 (1989):211–20.
Smith, Jonathan. *Imagining Religion*. Chicago: University of Chicago Press, 1982.
Smith, Wilfred C. *The Meaning and End of Religion*. San Francisco: Harper and Row, 1978.
Spellman, John W. *Political Theory of Ancient India*. Oxford: Oxford University Press, 1964.
Spencer, Sharon. *Space, Time and Structure in the Modern Novel*. New York: New York University Press, 1971.
Spiro, M. "Ifaluk Ghosts: An Anthropological Inquiry into Learning and Perception." In Robert Hunt, ed. *Personalities and Cultures* (Garden City New York: Natural History Press, 1967), pp. 238–50.
Staal, Fritz. "The Meaninglessness of Ritual." *Numen* 26 no. 2 (1979):2–22.
———. *Nambudiri Veda Recitation*. The Hague: Mouton, 1961.
———. "The Sound of Religion." *Numen* 33, no. 1 (1987):33–64; 185–223.
Sternbach, L. *Juridical Studies in Ancient Indian Law*. Delhi: Motilal Banarsidass, 1967.
Stokes, Maive S. *Indian Fairy Tales*. London: Ellis and White, 1880.
Strauss, Anslem. *Mirrors and Masks*. Glencoe, Il.: Free Press, 1959.
Sullivan, Lawrence E. "Body Works: Knowledge of the Body in the Study of Religion." History of Religions 30, 1 (1990):86–99.
Swynnerton, Charles. *Indian Nights' Entertainment*. New York: Arno, 1977.

Taylor, Mark C. *Erring: A Postmodern A/Theology.* Chicago: University of Chicago Press, 1981.

Thompson, William I. *Imaginary Landscape.* New York: St. Martin, 1989.

Thompson, Stith, and Jonas Balys. *The Oral Tales of India.* Bloomington: Indiana University Press, 1958.

Tillich, Paul. "The Religious Symbol." In *Symbolism in Religion and Literature.* Rollo May, ed. (New York: Braziller, 1960), pp. 75–98.

Todorov, Tzvetan. *Theories of the Symbol.* Ithaca: Cornell University Press, 1982.

Toulmin, Stephen. *Return to Cosmology.* Berkeley: University of California Press, 1981.

Trivers, Howard. *The Rhythm of Being: A Study of Temporality.* New York: Philosophy Library, 1985.

Turner, Edith. *The Spirit and the Drum.* Tucson: University of Arizona Press, 1987.

Turner, Victor. *The Forest of Symbols: Aspects of Ndembu Ritual.* Ithaca: Cornell University Press, 1967.

———. *The Ritual Process.* Ithaca: Cornell University Press, 1969.

Valéry, Paul. *Aesthetics.* Bollingen Series, 45, 13. New York: Bollingen, 1964.

van Buitenen, J. A. B. trans. *The Mahābhārata* 5 vols. Chicago: University of Chicago Press, 1973.

———. *Two Plays of Ancient India.* New York: Columbia University Press, 1968.

Van der Leeuw, G. *Religion in Essence and Manifestation.* 2 vols. Gloucester, Mass.: Peter Smith, 1967.

van Gennep, A. *Rites of Passage.* Chicago: University of Chicago Press, 1960.

Vatsyayan, Kapila. "Śiva-Naṭeśa: Cadence and Form." In M. Meister, ed., *Discourses on Śiva.* (Philadelphia: University of Pennsylvania Press, 1981), pp. 191–201.

———. *The Square and the Circle of the Indian Arts.* New Delhi: Roli Book International, 1983.

Vidyarnava, Rai Bahadur. *The Daily Practice of the Hindus.* New York: AMS Press, 1974.

von Fieandt, K. *The Perceptual World.* London: Academic Press. 1977.

Wade, Bonnie. *Music in India.* Wellsley Hills, Mass.: Riverdale, 1987.

Wagner, Roy. *Symbols That Stand for Themsleves.* Chicago: University of Chicago Press, 1986.

Warren, Scott. *The Emergence of Dialectical Theory.* Chicago: University of Chicago Press, 1984.

Weber, A. *Indische Studien.* Leipzig: Brockhaus, 1878.

Wentinck, Charles. *Modern and Primitive Art.* Oxford: Phaidon, 1979.

Whitrow, G. J. *The Natural Philosophy of Time.* London: Nelson, 1961.

Wilhelm, Friedrich. "The Concept of Dharma in Artha and Kāma Literature." In O'Flaherty and Derrett, eds. *The Concept of Duty in South Asia* (Delhi: Vikas Publishing, 1978), pp. 66–79.

Wilson, H. H., trans. *Kumara Sambhavam.* Varanasi: Indological Book House, 1966.

———. trans. *Rig-Veda Sanhita.* New Delhi: Cosmo Publications, 1977.

Witkins, H. A., ed. *Psychological Differentiations: Studies of Development.* New York: John Wiley and Sons, 1962.

Woolf, Virginia. *A Writer's Diary.* Edited by Leonard Woolf. New York: Harcourt, Brace, 1954.

Wulff, Donna. "Religion in a New Mode." *Journal of the American Academy of Religion* 54, no. 4 (1986):675–81.

Yalman, Nur. *Under the Bo Tree.* Berkeley: University of California Press, 1971.

Yatawara, T. B. *The Story of The Tunnel.* London: Luzac, 1898.

Zimmer, Heinrich R. *Artistic Form and Yoga in the Sacred Images of India.* Princeton: Princeton University Press, 1984.

———. *Hindu Medicine.* Baltimore: Johns Hopkins University Press, 1948.

———. *Myths and Symbols in Indian Art and Civilization.* Princeton: Princeton University, 1946.

Zuesse, Evan M. *Ritual Cosmos.* Athens: Ohio University Press, 1985.

Zysk, Kenneth. *Religious Healing in the Veda.* Philadelphia: American Philosophical Society, 1985.

Index

Abhinavagupta, 28–29
adharma, 8, 191
  and adultery, 173
  and dharma, 179, 187
  metaphors of, 100
  temporal force, 9–10
  See also Dharma
Aditi, 109, 152
Adultery
  in *bhakti* texts, 176–79
  as crime, 170
  in folklore, 169–70
  husband's view on, 181–86
  Kāmasūtra on, 170–76
  of Kṛṣṇa, 176–78
  lover's reasons against, 175–76
  lover's reasons for, 173–75
  Manu on, 181–86
  and theft, 179–81
  wife's reasons against, 172–73
  wife's reasons for 171–72
Agastya, 49, 160
Agni, 75, 83, 152, 168*n*102, 207
Agni Purāṇa, 141*n*61
Agnistoma, 96
Ahalyā, 176
Ajīgarta, 211*n*33
akam (poem), 155
Allport, Floyd, 76
Altamira, 116
Ambā, 167*n*82
amṛta, 208
Amulet, 103, 106, 108, 141*n*55
Ānandavardhana, 28–29
Antelope, 103–4, 108–10
Ants, 103, 106
Anu-taila oil, 96
āpaddharma
  debated, 201
  defined, 201
  and theft, 200–202
  See also Viśvāmitra
Apahāravarman, 194
Apālā, 107, 111*n*14, 155
  and bride, 94, 152, 158
  curing of, 101–2
  stories of, 91–92
  Sūkta, 97
  symbols of narrative, 93–96
Arabian Nights, 179
Arajā, 226–27
Āraṇyakāṇḍa, 44–45
Arjuna, 133, 155, 182
Arnold, Edwin, 72
Arundhatī, 217, 227
Aśoka, 127
Āśvalāyana Gṛhyasūtra, 144
Aśvattha (tree), 217–18
Atharvaveda, 91, 93, 103–4
ātman, 177
Atri, 111*n*14
Augustine, 41, 61*n*23
Austin, Lopez, 240
Axis mundi, 214, 218

Bachelard, Gaston, 13, 20

Barthes, Roland, 93
Bateson, Gregory, 138*n*5
Bathing (*snāna*), 10
  and chaos, 71
  classification of, 72
  Eliade on, 69–70
  mantras for, 73–75
  meaning of, 82–85
  phenomenology of, 76–82
  for purification, 69–70
  in rivers, 71–72, 82
Benton, Cathy, 176
Bergson, Henri, 13, 61*n*23
Bhagavadgītā, 217–18, 222
bhakti, 176, 177, 181
Bharadvāja, 211*n*33
Bhārata, 30
Bharaut, 129
Bhārgava, 227
Bhartṛhari, 12, 31
Bhattacharya, Deborah, 155
Bhaṭṭikāvyam, 133, 162
Bhils, 126–27
Bhīṣma, 167*n*82, 200, 203
Bhoja, 142*n*77, 194
Bhūmī, 129
Bialik, Chaim Nahman, 12
Biardeau, Madeleine, 140*n*53
Binary oppositions, 149, 226, 231
Birth, 94, 105
Blake, William, 138*n*13
Bodh-Gaya, 129
Body, 5, 9, 19
  of the bride, 144, 156–58
  Gestalt psychology on, 76–77
  knowledge by, 240
  metaphors of, 100–103, 155
  and mind, 77, 239–42
  and purity, 85–86
  and society, 68
  as symbol, 89–90, 240
  See also Skin; Hair; Hand; Eyes
Boundaries, 8, 19, 90, 106, 178, 182, 214
  in art, 117–18, 120–24
  crossing, 130, 134–37, 156–59
  and dharma, 116, 133
  and fences, 128–30
  and *toraṇas*, 132–33
  and trees, 31–32
  markers, 129–30
  ritual, 119–20
  in wedding, 146–48, 156–59, 163, 169
Brahmā, 136, 207–8, 229–30
brahmacārya, 159
Brahmadatta, 203
Brahman, 18
Brahmins, 9, 217, 228
  bathing rules, 73
  dharma of, 228
  as thieves, 193, 199–202
Bṛhaddevatā, 92
Bṛhaspati, 152, 170
Bride, 95, 11*n*14, 150, 151–52, 169, 207, 242
  as *kanyā*, 144
  passage of, 156–59
  during wedding, 145–46
Bridges, 6, 131, 132–33
Brown, Norman, 214
Brown, Percy, 127

Caṇḍa, 232
Caṇḍāla, 200–202
Candra, 110*n*4
Carpentry, 129
Cārudatta, 197, 200
Cassirer, Ernst, 7, 69, 75, 78
Cattle, 102, 109–10, 190
Chaos and order, 3, 8, 9, 70, 230–31. *See also* Dharma and *adharma*
Childhood, 154, 155
Chronology, 120
  calendar, 118–19
  clock time, 61*n*22
Colors, 97, 100, 102, 112*n*29, 232
Consciousness, 84–85
Coomaraswamy, A., 95, 111*n*19
Creation, 74–75, 83, 230
Criminal code, 191

Dadhaci, 228
Dakṣa, 228–29, 230
dakṣiṇā, 205
Dānava, 229, 231
Daṇḍa (character)
  a god, 220, 223
  and the goddess, 232–34

in *Mahābhārata*, 229
in Manu, 229
son of Ikṣvāku, 163, 215, 226–28, 242
thief, 228
daṇḍa (staff; scepter)
in Dharmaśāstra, 230–31
etymology, 214–15
in mythology, 225–9
in nature, 216–20
in ritual, 223–5
as staff, 109
as Viśvāvasu, 207
social contexts, 220–23
in wedding, 146–47, 159
Daṇḍadhara, 226
Daṇḍaka forest, 45, 49, 226, 231, 237*n*60
daṇḍanīti (polity), 234
Daṇḍaviveka, 221
Daṇḍin, 223
Dange, S.A., 93
Dange, S.S., 158
Daniel, Valentine, 154, 186
Daniélou, Alain, 56
Darbha grass, 145
Darśapūrṇamāsa, 109
Daśakumāracarita, 223
Daśaratha, 49
Deer, 181–82
Derrett, J.D.M., 14, 215
Derrida, Jaques, 149
Devas and Asuras, Battle of, 207, 227
acted in Mahāvrata, 24, 51–53
in *Śatapatha Brāhmaṇa*, 119
use of Udumbara, 218, 225
Devī, 215
Dharma
and *adharma*, 3, 47–48, 62*n*45, 130, 227–28, 230, 239
conflicts, 162–63, 200
defined, 7–8
metaphors of, 86, 102, 115–16, 211*n*39, 213
and order, 8–9, 143
phenomenology, 31–32
relativity of, 154, 204
and thieves, 189, 194, 209
and time, 39, 201, 203, 205, 233; *āpad*, 200–202
and Veda, 11
See also Vedas; Dharmaśāstras
Dharmaśāstras, 9, 13
on adultery, 169–70, 181–86
contingency of, 186–87, 204
and Daṇḍa, 230
and theft, 189–91
See also Manu
Dharmasūtra, 13
dhātus (elements), 97
Dhṛtarāṣtra, 168*n*104
Dice, 237*n*52
dīkṣā, 205
Dimock, Edward, 177
Disease, 98, 102, 105–7, 155
Disguise, 136–37, 193–94
Doors, 130–5, 147
Doubles, 176–77
Douglas, Mary, 19, 67–69, 89
Drum, 110
Dualism, 240–41; and monism, 4
Dumont, Louis, 8, 153
Duration, 38–40, 43, 58
Durgā, 232

Ego, 79–80, 81, 153
Eliade, Mircea, 15–16, 40, 69–70
Erikson, E., 154
Eyes, 232

Fantasy, 169–70
Fences, 132
Fergusson, J., 128–29
Fertility, 17–18, 127
Fire, 146, 152, 157
Forest, 8, 129, 130, 140, 143
Forster, E.M., 177
Fraser, J.T., 43
Frazer, James, 69, 95
Fruzzeti, Lina, 50, 186

Gāndhārī, 168
Gandharvas, 206, 212, 215, 218
Ganges (Gaṅgā), 29, 71–72, 130
Garuḍa, 135, 217
Gate, 130, 132, 140*n*53
Gavāmayana, 51
Gāyatrī, 119, 206, 208
Gehry, Frank, 6

Gestalt psychology, 7, 165
  influence of, 68–69
  on bathing, 75–82, 84–85
  on ego, 79–80
  on isomorphism, 77–78
  main ideas, 76–77
  on perception, 78–79
  on proprioception, 80–82
Ghaṭa, 195
Ghee, 104–5, 106, 113*n*48
Gibson, James, 80, 242*n*2
Gobhila, 145
Gold, 94, 96, 99, 111*n*20, 145, 151, 157
Gold, Ann, 180
Goldman, Robert, 47, 168, 227
Gonda, Jan, 34, 235*n7*
Gopal, Ram, 93
Gottlieb, Robert, 56
Gṛhyasūtras, 151
Groom, 144, 207
  actions at wedding, 146–47
  mantras for, 151–52
  possession over bride, 157–60
guṇas, 97, 100

Hair, 193
  Apālā's, 91–94
  bride's, 145, 152
  shaving, 89–90
  symbolism, 90–91
Halbertal, Moshe, 178
Hand, 145. See also *pāṇigrahaṇa*
Hand, Wayland, 95
Haradatta, 111*n*20
Hārīta, 176
Harman, William, 150
Healing, 95–7, 98, 107, 113*n*42
Heesterman, Jan, 12, 94, 143, 225
Heidegger, Martin, 6, 42, 117
Henotheism, 178
Hermes, 137, 214
Hershman, Paul, 159
Hide, 106, 108–10. *See also* Skin
Hillebrandt, A., 158
Hiraṇyagarbha, 75, 83
Hitopadeśa, 204
Hole boring, 134–5
Homology, 77, 133, 148–49; and analogy, 89
Horn, 103–4
Horse sacrifice, 181
House walls, 121, 124–27
Humphrey's Principle, 78
Husband, 162–63
Husserl, Edmund, 35*n*61
Ideology, 239
Ikṣvāku, 226–28, 231–32
Images, *n*23, 33, 59, 240
  Indian, 27–32
  naïve, 12–14
  structure of, 25–27
  and symbols, 14–23
  theory of, 8
  and time, 38, 41–43, 59, 189
Imagination, 118, 155, 239–40
Improvisation (*ālāp*), 56. *See also* Music; Time
Indra, 136, 147, 178, 218
  adultery of, 176
  and Apālā, 92–5, 113*n*41
  and Namuci, 208, 212*n*51
  in wedding formula, 152
Indraṇī, 152
Ingalls, Daniel, 28
Isomorphism, 77–78, 80, 148–49. *See also* Gestalt psychology

Jagatī (meter), 119
Jamadagni, 160
James, William, 61
Janhari, Manorama, 140*n*40
Jaratkāru, 162
Jaundice, 102–6
Jewelers, 171
jñāna (knowledge), 12. *See also* Veda
Johnson, Mark, 26
Joyce, James, 117–18
Judaism, 178

Kadra, 199
Kadrū, 205–6, 208
Kafka, Franz, 76
Kaikeyī, 49
Kaiṭabha, 207–8
Kakar, Sudhir, 155, 186
Kālī, 40, 66, 136, 215; and Daṇḍa, 232–33
Kālidāsa, 28, 219–20

kalivarjya, 39
Kaliyuga, 230
Kāma, 20, 136, 173, 176
Kāmamañjarī, 194
Kāmaśāstras, 169
Kāmasūtra, 170–76, 186
Kanasarai, 122
Kane, P.V., 52
kanyā (girl), 111*n*13, 144, 156–57. *See also* Bride
kanyādāna, 144. *See also* Marriage
karma, 48, 99
Karṇa, 162
Karpara, 195
Kaśyapa, 152, 160
Kaṭha Upaniṣad, 217
Kathāsaritsāgara, 196
  on adultery, 179–81
  and Dharmaśāstra, 186
  on thieves, 191
Kathenotheism, 178
Kāttavarāyan, 207
Kātyāyana Smṛti, 13
Kauśika Sūtra, 102, 106, 146
kāvya (poetry), 13, 27–28, 48
Kāvyaya, 203
Khadira (tree), 206, 216–17, 221, 224, 227
Kierkegaard, Soren, 42
King, 175
  initiation of, 108, 143–44, 218–19
  and land, 129, 221
  and thieves, 192–4
  See also Rājasūya; Pṛthu
Kinship, 151
Koffka, Kurt, 7
Kohler, Wolfgang, 7
kolam, 131
Kramrisch, Stella, 128
Kṛṣṇa, 17, 228
  the adulterer, 176–78
  and *daṇḍa*, 221–22
  the thief, 208
Kṛtayuga, 230
kṣatra, 218
Kṣatriya, 109, 225
Kṣetriya (disease), 102–6
Kṣupa, 230
Kumārasambhava, 219
Kuntī, 158
Kuper, H., 147
Kūrma Purāṇa, 228, 233
Kurus, 133
Kuśa grass, 73, 145, 160

Lakoff, George, 26
Lakṣmaṇa, 44–51, 120
Lakṣmī, 219, 232, 233
Langer, Susan, 55
Language, 28–29
Lankā, 49
Lascaux, 116
Latmikaik, 6
Law of the waste land, 129
Laws of the fish, 234
Leprosy, 97, 101, 103–4
Levi-Strauss, Claude, 148–49
Lincoln, Bruce, 147–49, 239
Lines, *n*10, 117, 138. *See also* Boundaries; Outlines
lokapālas (guardian deities), 139*n*32
Lomaśa, 202
Long, Charles, 16
Lotus, 219–20
Luria, A.R., 23

Mādhava, 196
Madhu, 207–8
Magic, 116, 127
  and healing in *Kauśika Sūtra*, 106, 113*n*42
  in rites of passage, 147, 214
  and skin, 89–91
  and theft, 137, 190–1, 198, 209
Mahābhārata, 182
  āpaddharma in, 201–2
  on Daṇḍa, 229
  on dharma, 205
  and theft of Veda, 207–8
Mahānagnī, 93
Mahāvrata, 63*n*51
  images of, 23–25
  interpreted, 52–55
  narrative sequence, 51–52
Maitreya, 197, 200
Malamoud, Charles, 206
Mālatīmādhava, 219
Malinowski, Branislaw, 99
Mānasāra, 141*n*61

Maṇḍiya, 192–93
Mango tree, 164*n*25
mantras, 136
  for bathing, 72–75
  Staal on, 57
  and theft of Veda, 207–8
  for wedding, 147, 151–3
Manu (a king), 234
Manu Prajāpati, 11
Manu Smṛti (Manu), 174, 180
  on boundaries, 31; in wedding, 146
  on Daṇḍa, 229
  on dharma, 11–12
  on farming, 221
  on love and sex, 170, 181–86
  on royalty, 215
  symbolism in 13, 31
  and theft, 190
Margalit, Avishai, 178
Mārīca, 44–51, 62*n*45
Marriage, 108, 185
  and Apālā, 91
  bride's perception of, 156–60
  Gandharva, 135–36
  mantras for, 151–53
  mixed, in Manu, 185
  as rite of passage, 147–49
  ritual, 144–47
Marriott, McKim, 5, 153, 155, 185–86
Matsya Purāṇa, 139*n*32, 234
Mauss, Marcel, 68
māyā, 47, 205–6, 108
Mayūra, 21
Melody, 57
Memory, 12–13
Merleau-Ponty, 3, 4, 7, 36*n*62, 69, 75, 241
Metaphor, 107, 113*n*40
Meter, 57. *See also* Gāyatrī; Jagatī; Triṣṭubh
Meyer, J.J., 144, 222
Mīmāṁsā, 28
Mīnākṣī, 150
Mind, 242
Mirror, 158
Moffit, R., 153
Mṛcchakaṭikā, 134, 197, 200
Mṛgāṅkadatta, 194
Mūladeva, 195. *See also* Vikramarāja
Muller, Max, 178
Muṇḍa, 232
Music
  and space, 58
  and time, 55–59
  and words, 57
nāda (sound), 56
Nagas, 129
Nala and Damayantī, 130, 136
Namuci, 208, 212
Nārada, 11, 45, 88*n*73
Nārāyaṇa, 207–8
nāṭya (dance, drama), 30, 58
niyoga (levirate), 183–84, 186
Nyagrodha, 218

Obeyesekere, Gananath, 70
Ocean faring, 137
O'Flaherty, Wendy, 109
Omens, 48, 155, 166*n*71
Ornamentation, 121–24
Ostor, Akos, 150, 186
Outline, 117, 119

Palita, 202
Pāṇḍu, 158
Paṇi, 207
pāṇigrahaṇa, 145, 151, 157. *See also* Marriage
Paraśurāma, 162, 227
Parmentier, Richard, 6
Pārvatī, 219
Patañjali, 28–29
Paternity, 182–84
Pech-Merle, 21–22
Perception, 24
  Gestalt on, 69, 76–77, 82
  and images, 25
  Merleau-Ponty on, 241
  of passage, 156–60
  and purity, 85
  and space, 116–18
  and theft, 190
Person, 120, 153, 155–56
Phenomenology, 3, 5, 7, 27, 67, 242
Piaget, Jean, 61*n*33
Picture frames, 120–24
Plants, 91

Plow, 104–5, 221
Pocock, David, 39, 60*n*6
Polar star, 146
Pollution
  in Dharmaśāstra, 83–84
  phenomenology of, 19–20
  Ricoeur and Douglas on, 67–71
  See also Purification
Popper, Karl, 10
Porcupine quill, 145, 152
Prabandhacintāmaṇi, 142*n*77
Prägnanz, 78
Prajāpati, 24, 58, 111*n*14, 230
  and Khadira wood, 216
  in Mahāvrata, 52–54, 58
  See also Devas and Asuras
Pregnancy, 106
Proprioception, 19, 80–82. *See also* Gestalt psychology
Pṛthu and Pṛthivī, 31, 129–30, 140*n*50
Pūjaṇī, 203
Punishment, 10, 214
  cosmological force of, 231, 234–35
  and *daṇḍa*, 222
  and spatial symbols, 213–16
Purification, 66
  of Apālā, 93, 101
  of bride, 144
  meaning of, 82–85
  and perception, 76–7
  in rivers, 71–77
Purity, 72, 83
  phenomenal, 83
  symbolic, 67–71
Pūrṇakalā, 176
Puruṣa, 89, 240
Puruṣa Sūkta, 74, 85

rāga, 55–56. *See also* Music
Rāhu, 208
Rājasūya, 94, 108, 218, 222, 224–25. *See also* King
Rajputs, 164
Rajwade, A.V., 46
Rāma, 29, 120, 130, 137, 168*n*49, 169, 213, 242
  and the abduction of Sītā, 44–51
  as dharma agent, 161–62
  See also Lakṣmaṇa; Mārīca; Rāvaṇa
Ramanujan, A.K., 179
Rāmāyaṇa, 62*n*41, 133, 169
  on Daṇḍa, 226–27
  on dharma, 161–62
  time levels in, 44–51, 120
Rape, 226–27
rasa (aesthetic pleasure), 22, 29–30, 55
ratha (vehicle), 128
Rathavas, 121, 131
Rāvaṇa, 44–51, 62*n*43, 120, 136, 161
Representation, 117, 118
Resonance (*dhvani*), 21
Ṛgveda
  on Apālā, 91–92
  bathing Hymns, 73–74
  marriage Hymns, 151–53
  See also Vedas
Rhythm, 44, 55, 57. *See also* Time
Ricoeur, Paul, 16, 18–19, 25, 67, 225
Rite of Passage, 120, 143
  marriage as, 147–49
  and perception, 156
  and "three," 159–60
  See also upanayana; *saṃskāras*
Rivers, 82, 137
Robbery, 190
Rohita and Rohiṇī, 83, 88*n*74, 102
Rudra, 104, 215, 228–29

Sacks, Oliver, 19
Sacrifice (*yajña*)
  of Dakṣa, 228–30
  and river bathing, 75
  skins used in, 108–9
  and Soma's theft, 205–6
  and time, 119
  wood used in, 224
sādhāraṇadharma, 204
Śaivala mountains, 226–27
saṁskāras, 185–86
Sanchi Stupa, 125, 127, 132
Saṅdhyā rites, 72
Saṅgīta Ratnākara, 56
Sarasvatī, 230, 234
Sarvalika, 197–98, 200
Śatapatha Brāhmaṇa

Śatapatha Brāhmaṇa (con't.)
on adultery, 181
on Viṣṇu and Asuras, 119
Sattra, 24, 53. *See also* Gavāmayana; Mahāvrata
Saussure, Ferdinand de, 15, 149
Savitṛ, 151
Sāyaṇa, 92, 93
Schelling, Friedrich, 14
Schmidt, Hanns-Peter, 94–95
Seed, 181, 183–85
Self, 4, 5, 241
Senses, 18, 155
Seven, 112*n*32, 145
Sex, 175, 179
Shakespeare, William, 177
Sherrington, Charles, 80
Shulman, David, 131
Signs, 15, 154
Śilpaśāstras, 131
Sin, 20, 67, 71, 201; and defilement, 18–19
Sītā, 29, 62*n*50, 120, 136
abandoned by Rāma, 161
abduction narrative, 44–51
as cultural ideal, 150, 169
Śītalā, 98
Śiva (a thief), 196
Śiva, 182
and Daṇḍa, 233
marriage with Mīnākṣī, 150
marriage with Pārvatī, 219
and Rudra, 229
and time, 41, 64*n*79
Skanda, 198
Skin, 82, 111, 112*nn*26, 27, 37, 131, 167*n*78
animal (hides), 24, 108–10, 114
as boundary, 89–91
of bride, 157–58
dermatology, 97–100
disease, 92, 101–5
metaphors of, 100–104, 107
theraphy, 96–97
in water, 82
Smallpox, 98
Smart, Ninian, 60*n*10, 62*n*38
Smith, Cantwell, 38
Smṛti, 11–14, 31, 204
Snānasūtra of Kātyāyana, 74
Soma, 111*n*18
and Apālā, 91–92, 101
in skin therapy, 96–97
marriage to Sūryā, 151
pressing, 94–95, 113*n*41
stolen, 167, 205–7, 217–18
Sons, 158, 183
Space, 213
perception of, 116–18
and time, 43–44, 118–20
vertical, 213–16
See also Boundaries; Time
sphoṭa, 28
Śraddha, 33*n*16
Śrī, 130, 219
śruti (revelation), 12
Staal, Frits, 24, 35*n*53
Staff, 213–35. *See also daṇḍa*
Sternbach, Ludwig, 111*n*13
Stone, 112*n*23, 127, 128, 145, 157–58
Śūdras, 72
Śukra, 226–28, 232
Sullivan, Lawrence, 240–41
Sun (Sūryā), 88*n*14, 108, 165*n*50
battle for, 53
marriage with Soma, 151
and river bathing, 73–75, 83
and skin, 100
in wedding, 147
Suparṇī, 205–6, 208, 217
Suśruta Saṃhitā, 97
svabhāva, 205
svadharma, 204
Śvetaketu Auddālaki, 170
Swing, 25
Symbols, 225
and *gnosis*, 225
and images, 7, 14–32, 38, 115–16
and religion, 5–6
sexual, 105
and thought, 154
and trace, 117
unconscious, 70–71

tāla, 56–57
tapas, 205
Taxonomy, 17, 154
Temple walls, 127–28

The Laws of Manu. See Manu
Theft (*steya*)
  and adultery, 179–81, 187*n*1
  defined, 190–91
  and dharma, 199–202
  and disguise, 195–97
  divine, 205–9
  and magic, 190, 198
  and *māyā*, 208
  social nature of, 190–91
Thieves
  Brahmin, 199–202
  Dharma of, 194, 204
  divine, 205–9
  idiot, 198–99
  and kings, 180, 191–94
  of love, 177
  and magic, 191
Three, 159–60
Three-night abstention (*trirātra-vrata*), 146
Tiger, 114*n*68
Time
  and *adharma*, 9–10
  battle for, 52–54
  conceptions in India, 39–41
  and dharma, 39–40, 202–3, 233
  and duration, 36, 42
  and images, 38, 41–43
  in Mahāvrata, 51–55
  musical, 55–59
  in *Rāmāyaṇa*, 44–51
  and space, 42–44, 117–20
Todorov, Tvetslan, 14, 15
toraṇa (gate), 121, 132–33, 141*n*64
Touch, 79–84, 107, 224
Tracy, David, 177
Trees, 127, 129, 216, 236*n*20. *See also* Aśvattha; Khadira; Nyagrodha; Udumbara
Triangles and chevrons, 121–24. *See also* Ornamentation
Triṣṭubh, 119
trivarga, 170
Trobriands, 99
Tsur, Sharaf, 211*n*17
Turner, Victor, 35*n*54, 70–71, 144, 148
Twenty-five Questions of the Vampire, 180
Uddālaka and Śvetaketu, 18
Udumbara (tree), 218–19, 224–25
upanayana, 108, 159
Upaniṣads, 177
Updike, John, 167*n*78
Urine, 104
Utanka, 163

Vāc, 206
Vaiśya, 109
Vala-taila oil, 99, 105
Valéry, Paul, 13, 20
Vālmīki, 45
Vāmadeva, 211*n*33
Van der Leeuw, 66
van Gennep, A., 144, 147–48, 157, 160, 214
Varuṇa, 73, 98, 222–23, 237*n*52; and Mitra, 88*n*74
Vastuśāstras, 131
Vāsuki, 162
Vātāpi, 49
  Veda, 8
  Bhartṛhari on, 12, 28
  on hair and skin, 90–91, 97–98
  and *jñāna*, 11–12
  and Smṛti, 31, 189, 204
  theft of, 207–8
Vena, 66
Vidyā-Sundara of Bhāratchandra, 136
Vikramarāja (Mūladeva), 192–93
Vindhya mountains, 130, 226–27
Vindhyavāsinī, 232
viraha (longing), 177
Vīraketu, 192
Vision, 80–81, 83, 107
Viṣṇu, 215, 228
  in bathing *mantras*, 73, 83
  and *daṇḍa*, 223, 229–30, 233–34
  as dwarf, 53, 119
  as Pṛthu, 130
  and Vedas, 207–8
  and the weaver, 135–36
Viṣṇu Smṛti, 74
Viṣṇudharmottara, 139*n*24
Viśvāmitra, 200–202, 227
Viśvāvasu, 159, 167*n*91, 206–7, 235*n*3

Walls, 131; and art, 126
Water, 101
  and fever, 98, 102
  effects of, 82–83
  Eliade on, 69–70
  river, 72, 74
  symbolic, 75
  in wedding, 151
Wedding, *see* Marriage
Wentinck, Charles, 118
Whorf, Benjamin, 4, 5, 118
Widow, 169
Wife
  dharma of, 161–63, 169
  reasons against adultery, 172–73
  reasons for adultery, 171–72
Wilhelm, Friedrich, 170
Womb, 112*n*32, 181
Women
  erotic classification of, 173–76
  forbidden to use *mantras*, 72
  in *Kathāsaritsāgara*, 179–80
  scorned, 174–75
  as wives, 171–73
Woolf, Virginia, 62*n*41

Yama, 98, 223, 228
yantras, 138*n*10
Yudhiṣṭhira, 113*n*48, 130, 133, 143
yugas (aeons), 39, 233–34

Zimmer, Heinrich, 113*n*426, 42